Best of
Taste of Home

VOLUME 2

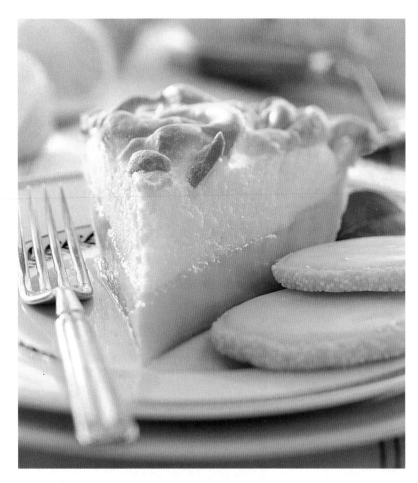

Best of Taste of Home Volume 2

Editor Krista Lanphier
Art Director Gretchen Trautman
Layout Designers Kathy Crawford, Nancy Novak
Content Production Supervisor Julie Wagner
Proofreader Linne Bruskewitz
Recipe Asset Systems Coleen Martin (Manager),
Sue A. Jurak (Specialist)
Editorial Assistant Barb Czysz

Vice President, Executive Editor/Books
Heidi Reuter Lloyd
Senior Editor/Books Mark Hagen
Creative Director Ardyth Cope
Food Director Diane Werner
Creative Director/Creative Marketing James Palmen
Vice President/Book Marketing Dan Fink
Chief Marketing Officer Lisa Karpinski

Taste of Home

Editor Ann Kaiser
Managing Editor Barbara Schuetz
Senior Art Director Sandra L. Ploy
Food Editor Patricia Schmeling
Associate Editor Cheri Mantz
Recipe Editors Mary King, Christine Rukavena
Copy Editor S.K. Enk
Layout Designer Kristen Johnson
Editorial Assistant Jane Stasik
Executive Assistant Marie Brannon
Test Kitchen Manager Karen Scales
Associate Food Editors Alicia Bozewicz RD,
Tina Johnson, Marie Parker, Annie Rundle
Test Kitchen Assistants Rita Krajcir, Sue Megonigle,
Megan Taylor
Photographers Rob Hagen (Senior), Dan Roberts,
Jim Wieland, Lori Foy
Set Stylists Jenny Bradley Vent (Senior),
Stephanie Marchese (Senior), Melissa Haberman,
Dee Dee Jacq
Food Stylists Sarah Thompson (Senior),
Kaitlyn Besasie, Tamara Kaufman
Assistant Food Stylists Alynna Malson,
Shannon Roum, Leah Rekau
Photo Studio Coordinator Kathy Swaney

Senior Vice President, Editor in Chief
Catherine Cassidy
President, Food & Entertaining Suzanne M. Grimes
President and Chief Executive Officer Mary G. Berner

Taste of Home Books
©2009 Reiman Media Group, Inc.
5400 S. 60th St., Greendale WI 53129

International Standard Book Number (10):
0-89821-714-8
International Standard Book Number (13):
978-0-89821-714-8
Library of Congress Control Number: 2008937564

All rights reserved. Printed in U.S.A.

PICTURED ON TITLE PAGE: Lemonade Meringue Pie (p. 149).

PICTURED AT RIGHT: Clockwise from upper left: Berry Cheesecake Muffins (p. 112), Next Day Turkey Primavera (p. 96), Pot Roast with Gravy (p. 77), Mac and Cheese for a Bunch (p. 190) and Russian Cream (p. 330).

Best of Taste of Home

VOLUME 2

PICTURED ON FRONT COVER. Clockwise from upper left: Danish Turkey Dumpling Soup (p. 54), Fruit and Nut Tossed Salad (p. 35), Garden-Fresh Bruschetta (p. 13), Fresh Cherry Pie (p. 145) and Fiesta Lasagna (p. 88).

PICTURED ON BACK COVER. Clockwise from upper left: Peanut Butter Cup Cheesecake (p. 162), Turkey Potpie (p. 97), Almond Berry Muffins (p. 113), Maple-Ginger Root Vegetables (p. 63), Special Mocha Cupcakes (p. 156) and Sunday Chicken Stew (p. 102).

Front cover photo by Rob Hagen. Food styled by Tamara Kaufman and Julie Herzfeldt. Set styled by Stephanie Marchese.

For other *Taste of Home* books and products, visit *www.shoptasteofhome.com*.

It Doesn't Get Any Better Than This!

Five Years and 575 of Our Best Recipes Ever Make for an Awesome Cookbook

WE'RE DOING IT again! Because you loved *The Best of Taste of Home: The First Ten Years* so much, making it one of our most successful cookbooks, we wanted to give you more of the same. So, we've created a second edition that features even *more* of *Taste of Home's* best-loved recipes!

Welcome to *The Best of Taste of Home, Volume 2*. This new edition captures 575 of the most popular recipes over a five-year period...from 2003 through 2008. In this attractive full-color cookbook, you'll find hundreds of eye-catching and delicious recipes. Need an appealing appetizer for a party? Look for yummy ideas in the Snacks & Beverages chapter on page 6. If you're bringing a culinary contribution to a church social, check out Potluck Pleasers on page 182. Regardless of whether you're looking for a dessert, main dish or even an entire meal, everything you need is within these pages.

Here are just a few of the book's special standout features:

Grand Prize Winners

As you may already know, each *Taste of Home* magazine includes the winners of a national recipe contest. We've featured those amazing hand-picked dishes from the last five years, including Grand Prize winners, runners-up and honorable mentions. Fabulous Grand Prize recipes include flavor-packed Curried Beef with Dumplings on page 84 and irresistible Rustic Nut Bars on page 126. To spot all of the Grand Prize winning dishes quickly, just look for the blue-ribbon banners!

Special Recipe Sections

It only makes sense to group together recipes that share a tasty ingredient or theme, so that's what we did! You'll find captivating sections that showcase recipes for cupcakes, lemon desserts, Christmas treats, breakfast fare, winter squash, leftover turkey and more!

Seasons of Good Taste

From holidays to the opening of farmers markets, there's always a reason to celebrate the coming of a new, bountiful season. In this chapter, you'll discover recipes for special occasions including Easter, Halloween and Christmas. Your family will love biting into main dishes such as Stuffed Ham with Raisin Sauce on page 323 or Spinach and Sausage Pork Loin on page 336. You'll also find recipes that utilize the best produce of each season and that take full advantage of the earth's bounty, such as Tomato-Cucumber Mozzarella Salad on page 327 and Cranberry Walnut Tart on page 334.

Helpful Kitchen Tips

Throughout the book, you'll discover plenty of helpful hints, fascinating culinary information and kitchen shortcuts for busy home cooks. You may find that many of these ideas help you through your already busy day!

Hundreds of Mouth-Watering Recipes

There are so many scrumptious recipes to choose from in this big, heirloom-quality book that you can make a different recipe from it every day for well over a year! From elegant entrees to whimsical desserts, the endless variety of dishes will ensure your family is satisfied. And like all *Taste of Home* recipes, rest assured, these have been approved by our Test Kitchen staff.

You'll marvel at the vibrant color photographs that accompany almost every recipe, and no doubt you'll be tempted to start cooking from this beautiful cookbook immediately. So don't waste any time getting started. From *Taste of Home* to your home, we wish you many happy cooking adventures!

A SAMPLE OF WHAT'S INSIDE. Clockwise from top left: Corn Tortilla Chicken Lasagna, (p. 197), Chunky Apple Cake (p. 184), Special Banana Nut Bread (p. 116), Vegetarian Stuffed Peppers (p. 82) and Three-Cheese Pesto Pizza (p. 23).

Snacks & Beverages

Whether you're hosting a special dinner, throwing a casual party for the big game or just looking to satisfy the kids before supper, you'll find the perfect hors d'oeuvres, snacks, thirst-quenchers and more right here!

SENSATIONAL STARTERS . Clockwise from top left: Sparkling Ginger Lemonade (p. 14), Three-Cheese Pesto Pizza (p. 23), Chicken Fingers with Lemon Sauce (p. 10), Cowboy Beef Dip (p. 19) and Garden-Fresh Bruschetta (p. 13).

teaspoons of filling in the center of wrapper. Fold bottom corner over filling; fold sides toward center over filling. Roll toward the remaining point. Moisten top corner with water; press to seal. Repeat with remaining wrappers and filling.

In an electric skillet or deep-fat fryer, heat oil to 375°. Fry spring rolls, a few at a time, for 1-2 minutes on each side or until golden brown. Drain on paper towels. Serve warm with sweet-and-sour sauce. **Yield:** about 5 dozen.

Crunchy Cucumber Rounds

(Pictured below)

PREP/TOTAL TIME: 30 min.

I found the recipe for these crisp and refreshing appetizers in an old cookbook several years ago. Make sure your cucumber slices are dry so the fruit mixture will stick to them.
—Phyllis Pollock, Erie, Pennsylvania

- **1 cup finely chopped red apple**
- **1 can (8 ounces) unsweetened crushed pineapple, drained**
- **1/4 cup finely chopped pecans, toasted**
- **1/4 cup reduced-fat sour cream**
- **1/8 teaspoon salt**
- **3 medium cucumbers**

In a small bowl, combine the apple, pineapple, pecans, sour cream and salt. Cover and refrigerate until chilled.

To score cucumbers, cut strips lengthwise through the peel. Cut each cucumber into 16 slices. Blot with paper towels to remove moisture. Spoon 1 teaspoon apple mixture on each slice. **Yield:** 4 dozen.

Pork and Shrimp Spring Rolls

(Pictured above)

PREP: 1 hour **COOK:** 5 min./batch

Give your appetizer table an Asian accent with these tasty spring rolls. The recipe makes a big batch, so guests can enjoy seconds!
—Debbie Terenzini-Wilkerson, Lusby, Maryland

- **1 pound ground pork**
- **1 can (14 ounces) bean sprouts, drained**
- **1 can (8 ounces) bamboo shoots, drained and chopped**
- **1/2 pound cooked medium shrimp, peeled, deveined and finely chopped**
- **1 can (4 ounces) mushroom stems and pieces, drained and chopped**
- **4 green onions, chopped**
- **1 tablespoon cornstarch**
- **3 tablespoons soy sauce**
- **1 tablespoon water**
- **1 teaspoon garlic powder**
- **1 teaspoon canola oil**
- **2 packages (12 ounces *each*) wonton wrappers**
Oil for frying
Sweet-and-sour sauce

In a large skillet, cook pork over medium heat until no longer pink; drain. Stir in the bean sprouts, bamboo shoots, shrimp, mushrooms and onions.

In a small bowl, whisk the cornstarch, soy sauce, water, garlic powder and oil until smooth; stir into skillet. Bring to a boil; cook and stir for 1 minute or until thickened. Remove from the heat.

Position a wonton wrapper with one point toward you. (Keep remaining wrappers covered with a damp paper towel until ready to use.) Place 2 heaping

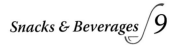

1/2 cup crumbled feta cheese
1 teaspoon dried oregano
1/4 teaspoon grated lemon peel
Pepper to taste
Assorted fresh vegetables

In a blender, combine the milk, cottage cheese, feta cheese, oregano, lemon peel and pepper; cover and process until smooth. Transfer to a small bowl. Serve with vegetables. **Yield:** 1-1/4 cups.

Party Meatballs

(Pictured below)

PREP: 30 min. **BAKE:** 1 hour

We served this scrumptious dish at our wedding. It went over so well that it's been served at other weddings and family functions, and the requests keep coming!
—Stefany Blevins, Portsmouth, Ohio

2 eggs, lightly beaten
1 can (12 ounces) evaporated milk
2 cups quick-cooking oats
1 cup finely chopped onion
2 teaspoons salt
2 teaspoons chili powder
1/2 teaspoon garlic powder
1/2 teaspoon pepper
3 pounds ground beef
SAUCE:
2 cups ketchup
1-1/2 cups packed brown sugar
1/2 cup chopped onion

In a large bowl, combine the first eight ingredients. Crumble ground beef over mixture and mix well. Shape into 1-in. balls. Place in three greased 13-in. x 9-in. x 2-in. baking dishes.

Combine the sauce ingredients; pour over meatballs. Bake, uncovered, at 325° for 1 hour or until meat is no longer pink. **Yield:** about 7 dozen.

Sensational Slush

(Pictured above)

PREP: 25 min. + freezing

Colorful and invigorating, this sweet-tart slush has become a family favorite. I freeze the mix in 2- and 4-cup containers so it can be served to individuals or the whole family. I also freeze crushed strawberries to make preparation simpler.
—Connie Friesen, Atlona, Manitoba

1/2 cup sugar
1 package (3 ounces) strawberry gelatin
2 cups boiling water
2 cups sliced fresh strawberries
1 cup unsweetened pineapple juice
1 can (12 ounces) frozen lemonade concentrate, thawed
1 can (12 ounces) frozen limeade concentrate, thawed
2 cups cold water
2 liters lemon-lime soda, chilled

In a large bowl, dissolve sugar and gelatin in boiling water. Place the strawberries and pineapple juice in a blender or food processor; cover and process until smooth. Add to the gelatin mixture. Stir in lemonade or limeade concentrates and cold water. Cover and freeze for 8 hours or overnight.

Remove from the freezer 45 minutes before serving. For each serving, combine 1/2 cup slush mixture with 1/2 cup lemon-lime soda; stir well. **Yield:** 20 servings.

A Touch of Greek Dip

PREP/TOTAL TIME: 10 min.

This pleasing dip gets its Greek-style flavor from feta cheese and lemon peel. Serve it with chips or raw vegetables when friends stop by, or try a spoonful on top of a baked potato.
—Emily Chaney, Blue Hill, Maine

1/2 cup fat-free milk
1/2 cup 1% cottage cheese

Chicken Fingers with Lemon Sauce

(Pictured below and on page 6)

PREP: 20 min. **COOK:** 5 min./batch

My husband turned up his nose when he saw me making this for the first time, but he absolutely flipped when he tasted it. I like to serve the chicken with an apple rice pilaf salad.
—*Amanda Donnelly, Fairborn, Ohio*

- 1 jar (10 ounces) lemon curd
- 1/4 cup chicken broth
- 1/2 teaspoon soy sauce
- 1/4 teaspoon ground ginger
- 1 cup buttermilk
- 1 tablespoon grated lemon peel
- 1 cup all-purpose flour
- 1/2 cup cornstarch
- 1-1/4 pounds boneless skinless chicken breasts, cut into strips
- Canola oil for frying

In a small saucepan, combine the lemon curd, broth, soy sauce and ginger. Cook and stir until combined and heated through; keep warm.

In a shallow bowl, combine buttermilk and lemon peel. In another bowl, combine flour and cornstarch. Dip the chicken strips in buttermilk mixture, then coat with flour mixture.

In an electric skillet, heat oil to 375°. Fry chicken, a few strips at a time, for 2-3 minutes on each side or until golden brown. Drain on paper towels. Serve with lemon sauce. **Yield:** 4 servings (1-1/4 cups sauce).

Savory Ham Cheesecake

(Pictured above)

PREP: 35 min. **BAKE:** 1 hour + chilling

My mom was the best cook—everything she made was special. She served this elegant cheesecake on Sunday following a Saturday ham dinner. Now my family loves it, too!
—*Shannon Soper, West Bend, Wisconsin*

- 3 cups oyster crackers, crushed
- 1 cup grated Parmesan cheese
- 1/3 cup butter, melted
- FILLING:
- 4 packages (8 ounces *each*) cream cheese, softened
- 4 eggs, lightly beaten
- 2 cups finely chopped fully cooked ham
- 2 cups (8 ounces) shredded Swiss cheese
- 1/3 cup snipped chives
- 1/4 cup minced fresh basil
- 1/4 teaspoon salt
- 1/4 teaspoon white pepper
- Assorted crackers

In a large bowl, combine the cracker crumbs, Parmesan cheese and butter. Set aside 1/4 cup for topping. Press remaining crumb mixture onto the bottom and 2 in. up the sides of a greased 9-in. springform pan. Cover and refrigerate for at least 30 minutes.

In a large bowl, beat cream cheese until smooth. Add eggs; beat on low speed just until combined (mixture will be thick). Add the ham, Swiss cheese, chives, basil, salt and pepper; beat just until combined. Pour into crust. Sprinkle with reserved crumb mixture.

Place pan on a baking sheet. Bake at 325° for 60-70 minutes or until filling is almost set. Turn oven off. Leave cheesecake in oven with door ajar for 30 minutes.

Cool on a wire rack for 10 minutes. Carefully run a knife around edge of pan to loosen; cool 1 hour longer. Refrigerate overnight. Remove sides of pan. Serve cheesecake chilled or at room temperature with crackers. **Yield:** 24-30 servings.

Cocoa for a Crowd

(Pictured below)

PREP/TOTAL TIME: 15 min.

You'll warm many hearts with this rich, satisfying cocoa. It's the perfect beverage to serve after an ice-skating outing or any winter gathering. —*Julia Livingston, Frostproof, Florida*

- **5 cups baking cocoa**
- **3 cups sugar**
- **2 teaspoons salt**
- **5 quarts water,** *divided*
- **10 quarts milk**
- **1 quart heavy whipping cream**
- **2 tablespoons vanilla extract**

Whipped cream and additional baking cocoa

In each of two large stockpots, combine 2-1/2 cups cocoa, 1-1/2 cups sugar and 1 teaspoon salt. Gradually stir 5 cups water into each pot. Bring to a boil; reduce heat. Whisk in the milk, cream and remaining water; heat through. Remove from the heat; stir in vanilla. Garnish with whipped cream and additional cocoa. **Yield:** 65 (1-cup) servings.

Roasted Carrot Dip

(Pictured above)

PREP: 15 min. **BAKE:** 45 min.

Once you start eating this delicious dip, it is difficult to stop. The smooth texture and sweet carrot flavor go great with the crisp pita wedges. —*Alana Rowley, Calgary, Alberta*

- **10 medium carrots**
- **5 garlic cloves, peeled**
- **2 tablespoons olive oil**
- **6 to 8 tablespoons water**
- **2 teaspoons white wine vinegar**
- **1/2 cup mayonnaise**
- **1/4 cup sour cream**
- **1/8 teaspoon sugar**
- **1/8 teaspoon salt**
- **1/8 teaspoon pepper**
- **4 to 6 pita breads (6 inches)**
- **2 to 3 tablespoons butter, melted**

Cut carrots in half widthwise; cut lengthwise into 1/2-in.-thick slices. In a bowl, combine the carrots, garlic and oil; toss to coat. Transfer to a greased 15-in. x 10-in. x 1-in. baking pan. Bake, uncovered, at 425° for 20 minutes. Stir; bake 15-20 minutes longer or until carrots are tender. Cool slightly.

In a blender, combine 6 tablespoons water, vinegar, mayonnaise, sour cream, sugar, salt, pepper and carrot mixture; cover and process until smooth. Add additional water if needed to achieve desired consistency. Transfer to a bowl; refrigerate until serving.

Brush both sides of pita breads with butter. Cut in half; cut each half into six wedges. Place on ungreased baking sheets. Bake at 350° for 4 minutes on each side or until lightly browned. Serve pita wedges with carrot dip. **Yield:** 8-10 servings.

Roll up jelly-roll style, starting with a short side. Thread onto metal or soaked wooden skewers.

Grill, covered, over medium heat for 5 minutes on each side or until chicken juices run clear.

Meanwhile, for the dip, in a small bowl, mash the avocados. Stir in the cilantro, onions, lime juice, mayonnaise, horseradish, garlic and salt. Serve with kabobs. **Yield:** 12 appetizers.

Pineapple Cheese Ball

PREP: 20 min. + chilling

Pineapple lends a refreshing fruity tang to this fun and tasty appetizer. Instead of one large cheese ball, you could also make two smaller ones. —Anne Halfhill, Sunbury, Ohio

- 2 **packages (8 ounces** *each***) cream cheese, softened**
- 1 **can (8 ounces) unsweetened crushed pineapple, drained**
- 1/4 **cup finely chopped green pepper**
- 2 **tablespoons finely chopped onion**
- 2 **teaspoons seasoned salt**
- 1-1/2 **cups finely chopped walnuts**
Assorted crackers

In a small bowl, beat the cream cheese, pineapple, green pepper, onion and seasoned salt until blended. Cover and refrigerate for 30 minutes. Shape into a ball; roll in walnuts. Cover and refrigerate overnight. Serve with crackers. **Yield:** 1 cheese ball (3 cups).

Spiced Orange Pecans

PREP: 10 min. **BAKE:** 30 min. + cooling

You won't be able to eat just one of these spicy–sweet nibblers. You'll want to keep them on hand for unexpected company. —Ruth Peterson, Jenison, Michigan

- 2 **egg whites, lightly beaten**
- 3 **tablespoons orange juice**
- 2 **cups pecan halves**
- 1-1/2 **cups confectioners' sugar**
- 2 **tablespoons cornstarch**
- 2 **tablespoons grated orange peel**
- 1 **teaspoon ground cinnamon**
- 3/4 **teaspoon ground cloves**
- 1/4 **teaspoon ground allspice**
- 1/8 **teaspoon salt**

In a large bowl, combine egg whites and orange juice. Add pecans and toss to coat; drain. In another large bowl, combine the remaining ingredients. Add pecans and toss to coat.

Spread in single layer in greased 15-in. x 10-in. x 1-in. baking pan. Bake at 250° for 30-35 minutes or until dry and lightly browned. Cool completely. Store in an airtight container. **Yield:** 5 cups.

Prosciutto Chicken Kabobs

(Pictured above)

PREP: 30 min. + marinating **GRILL:** 10 min.

Everyone will think you spent hours preparing these clever grilled wraps, served with a guacamole–like dip. Basil gives the chicken a lovely fresh herb flavor. —Elaine Sweet, Dallas, Texas

- 3/4 **cup five-cheese Italian salad dressing**
- 1/4 **cup lime juice**
- 2 **teaspoons white Worcestershire sauce for chicken**
- 1/2 **pound boneless skinless chicken breasts, cut into 3-inch x 1/2-inch strips**
- 12 **thin slices prosciutto**
- 24 **fresh basil leaves**
AVOCADO DIP:
- 2 **medium ripe avocados, peeled**
- 1/4 **cup minced fresh cilantro**
- 2 **green onions, chopped**
- 2 **tablespoons lime juice**
- 2 **tablespoons mayonnaise**
- 1-1/2 **teaspoons prepared horseradish**
- 1 **garlic clove, minced**
- 1/4 **teaspoon salt**

In a large resealable plastic bag, combine the salad dressing, lime juice and Worcestershire sauce; add chicken. Seal bag and turn to coat; refrigerate for 1 hour.

Drain and discard marinade. Fold prosciutto slices in half; top each with two basil leaves and a chicken strip.

Rhubarb Cheesecake Smoothies

(Pictured below)

PREP: 20 min. + cooling

We love smoothies, so there isn't much we don't use to make unusual combinations. Cream cheese adds an extra-special touch to this yummy concoction that our friends and family just love. —Kathy Specht, Cambria, California

>   2 **cups diced fresh *or* frozen rhubarb**
> 1/4 **cup water**
>   4 **tablespoons honey, *divided***
> 1-1/2 **cups vanilla ice cream**
>   1 **cup milk**
>   1 **cup frozen sweetened sliced strawberries**
>   2 **packages (3 ounces *each*) cream cheese, cubed**
> 1/2 **cup vanilla yogurt**
> 1/4 **cup confectioners' sugar**
>   5 **ice cubes**

In a large saucepan, bring the rhubarb, water and 2 tablespoons honey to a boil. Reduce heat; cover and simmer for 5-10 minutes or until rhubarb is tender. Remove from the heat; cool to room temperature.

In a blender, combine the vanilla ice cream, milk, rhubarb mixture, strawberries, cream cheese, vanilla yogurt, confectioners' sugar, ice cubes and remaining honey; cover and process for 1 minute or until smooth. Pour into chilled glasses; serve immediately. **Yield:** 6 servings.

Garden-Fresh Bruschetta

(Pictured above and on page 6)

PREP/TOTAL TIME: 30 min.

I like to serve this easy-to-fix bruschetta as either an appetizer or as a colorful side dish. —Rachel Garcia, Arlington, Virginia

>   1 **garlic clove, peeled and halved**
> 14 **slices French bread (3/4 inch thick)**
>   4 **medium tomatoes, seeded and diced**
> 1/4 **cup chopped red onion**
>   2 **tablespoons olive oil**
>   1 **tablespoon minced fresh basil**
> 1/4 **teaspoon salt**
> 1/8 **teaspoon pepper**
> 14 **fresh basil leaves**

Rub cut side of garlic over one side of each slice of bread. Place bread garlic side down on an ungreased baking sheet. Bake at 350° for 5 minutes on each side or until lightly browned.

In a bowl, combine the tomatoes, onion, oil, minced basil, salt and pepper; spoon about 2 tablespoons onto each toasted bread slice. Top each with a basil leaf. **Yield:** 14 servings.

Seeding Tomatoes

To remove the seeds from a tomato, cut it in half horizontally and remove the stem. Holding a tomato half over a bowl, scrape out the seeds with a small spoon or squeeze the tomato to force out the seeds. Then slice or diced as directed.

Mini Hot Browns

(Pictured below)

PREP/TOTAL TIME: 30 min.

My Mini Hot Browns are smaller versions of the famous sandwich. Guests quickly saddle up for juicy turkey slices and crispy bacon, piled on toasted rye bread and then topped with a rich cheese sauce. —Annette Grahl, Midway, Kentucky

- 1 teaspoon chicken bouillon granules
- 1/4 cup boiling water
- 3 tablespoons butter
- 2 tablespoons all-purpose flour
- 3/4 cup half-and-half cream
- 1 cup (4 ounces) shredded Swiss cheese
- 18 slices snack rye bread
- 6 ounces sliced deli turkey
- 1 small onion, thinly sliced and separated into rings
- 5 bacon strips, cooked and crumbled
- 2 tablespoons minced fresh parsley

In a small bowl, dissolve bouillon in water; set aside. In a small saucepan, melt butter over medium heat. Stir in flour until smooth; stir in cream and bouillon. Bring to a boil; cook and stir for 1-2 minutes or until thickened. Stir in cheese until melted. Remove from the heat.

Place bread slices on two baking sheets. Layer each with turkey, onion and cheese sauce. Sprinkle with bacon. Bake at 350° for 10-12 minutes or until heated through. Sprinkle with parsley. **Yield:** 1-1/2 dozen.

Sparkling Ginger Lemonade

(Pictured above and on page 6)

PREP: 20 min. + cooling

Chill out with this delightful cooler, perfect for springtime bridal showers or hot summer days on the deck. It's so easy to fix, you'll find yourself stirring together this refreshing lemonade time and again. —Jodi Blubaugh, Eagle Mountain, Utah

- 2 cups water
- 1 cup honey
- 2 tablespoons minced fresh gingerroot
- 2 cups club soda, chilled
- 1 cup lemon juice

In a small saucepan, bring the water, honey and ginger to a boil. Remove from the heat; cover and steep for 10 minutes. Strain, discarding ginger. Cool.

Transfer to a pitcher; stir in soda and lemon juice. Serve immediately over ice. **Yield:** 5 servings.

Caramel Fruit Dip

PREP/TOTAL TIME: 10 min.

This creamy melt-in-your-mouth dip, served with assorted fruits, makes delightful accompaniment to a cheese tray. —Trish Gehlhar, Ypsilanti, North Dakota

- 2 packages (8 ounces *each*) cream cheese, softened
- 1 cup packed brown sugar
- 1/2 cup caramel ice cream topping

Assorted fresh fruit

In a small bowl, beat cream cheese and brown sugar until smooth. Add caramel topping; beat until blended. Serve with fruit. Refrigerate leftovers. **Yield:** 3 cups.

Grilled Corn Dip

(Pictured below)

PREP: 30 min. **BAKE:** 25 min.

Great for summer, this tasty appetizer is a must-have on weekend family gatherings at our cottage. It's well worth the time it takes to grill the corn and cut it from the cob.
—*Cathy Myers, Monroeville, Ohio*

- **6 medium ears sweet corn, husks removed**
- **1 large onion, chopped**
- **1 jalapeno pepper, finely chopped**
- **2 garlic cloves, minced**
- **2 tablespoons butter**
- **1 cup mayonnaise**
- **1/2 cup sour cream**
- **1/2 teaspoon chili powder**
- **2 cups (8 ounces) shredded Monterey Jack cheese**
- **1 can (2-1/4 ounces) sliced ripe olives, drained**
- **2 tablespoons sliced green onions**

Tortilla chips

Grill corn, covered, over medium heat for 10-12 minutes or until tender, turning occasionally.

Cut corn from cobs. In a large skillet, saute the onion, jalapeno and garlic in butter for 2-3 minutes or until almost tender. Add corn; saute 1-2 minutes longer or until vegetables are tender. Remove from the heat.

In a large bowl, combine the mayonnaise, sour cream and chili powder. Stir in cheese and corn mixture. Transfer to a greased 2-qt. baking dish.

Bake, uncovered, at 400° for 25-30 minutes or until bubbly and golden brown. Sprinkle with olives and green onions; serve with chips. **Yield:** 5 cups.

Editor's Note: When cutting hot peppers, disposable gloves are recommended. Avoid touching your face.

Warm Asparagus-Crab Spread

(Pictured above)

PREP/TOTAL TIME: 30 min.

When my children entertain, I like to help them with the cooking, and this dip is always a hit. Cashew nuts give this creamy spread a nice, crunchy texture.
—*Camille Wisniewski, Jackson, New Jersey*

- **1 medium sweet red pepper, chopped**
- **3 green onions, sliced**
- **2 medium jalapeno peppers, seeded and finely chopped**
- **2 teaspoons canola oil**
- **1 can (15 ounces) asparagus spears, drained and chopped**
- **2 cans (6 ounces *each*) crabmeat, drained, flaked and cartilage removed**
- **1 cup mayonnaise**
- **1/2 cup grated *or* shredded Parmesan cheese**
- **1/2 cup chopped cashews**

Assorted crackers

In a large skillet, saute the red pepper, onions and jalapenos in oil until tender. Add the asparagus, crab, mayonnaise and Parmesan cheese; mix well.

Transfer to a greased 1-qt. baking dish. Sprinkle with cashews. Bake, uncovered, at 375° for 20-25 minutes or until bubbly. Serve with crackers. **Yield:** 3 cups.

Editor's Note: When cutting hot peppers, disposable gloves are recommended. Avoid touching your face.

longer or until very thick. Cool. Cover and refrigerate for at least 3 hours.

Stir the rice, chicken and cheese into the sauce mixture. Combine breadcrumbs and paprika in a shallow baking pan. Shape 1/4 cupfuls of chicken mixture into 2-in. balls; roll in crumb mixture. Place 3 in. apart on lightly greased baking sheets.

Bake 400° for 25-30 minutes or until heated through and golden brown. Heat the gravy; serve with pom-poms. **Yield:** 40-45 servings (2 pom-poms each).

Lemon Cream-Stuffed Grapes

(Pictured below)

PREP: 35 min. + chilling

This is a refreshing snack on a hot summer day. It's simple, plus it offers a light change from heartier party foods.
—Janis Plourde, Smooth Rock Falls, Ontario

- 4 **ounces cream cheese, softened**
- 3 **tablespoons confectioners' sugar**
- 1-1/2 **teaspoons lemon juice**
- 1/2 **teaspoon grated lemon peel**
- 1 **pound seedless globe grapes, rinsed and patted dry**

In a small bowl, beat cream cheese, confectioners' sugar, lemon juice and peel until blended. Cover and refrigerate for 1 hour.

Cut a deep "X" in the top of each grape to within 1/4 in. of bottom. Carefully spread each grape apart. Transfer cream cheese mixture to a heavy-duty resealable plastic bag; cut a small hole in a corner of bag. Pipe filling into grapes. Refrigerate until serving. **Yield:** 3 dozen.

Chicken Pom-Poms

(Pictured above)

PREP: 30 min. + chilling   **BAKE:** 25 min.

These golden baked croquettes are a fun and different way to serve chicken to a crowd. My husband and I are hosts at a mission house where we cook for groups of 30 or more each week. This recipe is a favorite with guests.
—Fran Wolfley, St. Mary, Jamaica

- 4 **celery ribs, chopped**
- 1 **large onion, finely chopped**
- 1 **cup butter, cubed**
- 2 **cups all-purpose flour**
- 3 **teaspoons poultry seasoning**
- 1 **teaspoon salt**
- 1 **teaspoon pepper**
- 2 **cartons (32 ounces *each*) chicken broth**
- 2 **cups nonfat dry milk powder**
- 1/4 **cup chicken bouillon granules**
- 16 **cups cooked long grain rice**
- 12 **cups chopped cooked chicken**
- 8 **cups (32 ounces) shredded cheddar cheese**
- 10 **cups soft bread crumbs**
- 3 **tablespoons paprika**
- 10 **jars (12 ounces *each*) chicken gravy**

In a large Dutch oven or stockpot, saute celery and onion in butter until tender. Combine the flour, poultry seasoning, salt and pepper; stir into vegetable mixture until blended. Gradually stir in broth until blended. Add the milk powder and bouillon. Cook and stir until mixture comes to a boil; cook and stir 1-2 minutes

Par-Cheesy Pizza

(Pictured above)

PREP: 45 min. **BAKE:** 15 min.

I have always received great reactions after serving my pizza at parties and get-togethers. It's easy to make and looks fantastic!
—Leslie Dumm, Cleveland Heights, Ohio

- **1 pound frozen bread dough**
- **4 thin slices salami**
- **1 to 2 medium onions**
- **1 to 2 large sweet red peppers**
- **3/4 cup pizza sauce**
- **1-1/2 cups (6 ounces) shredded part-skim mozzarella cheese**
- **4 to 6 pimiento-stuffed olives, halved**

Thaw dough according to package directions. Cut the salami into 2-1/2-in. rounds. Cut onions and red peppers into 2-in. x 1/2-in. strips.

On a lightly greased baking sheet, roll bread dough into a 12-in. square. Spread with pizza sauce. Sprinkle with cheese. Arrange the salami, onion and pepper over top to resemble a Parcheesi board.

Bake at 400° for 15-20 minutes or until the crust is lightly browned and the cheese is melted. Top the pizza with olives. **Yield:** 6 servings.

Hot Spinach Spread With Pita Chips

PREP: 30 min. **BAKE:** 20 min.

This warm, cheesy spread is absolutely scrumptious served on toasted pita wedges. Its colorful appearance makes it perfect for a holiday buffet. —Teresa Emanuel, Smithville, Missouri

- **2 cups (8 ounces) shredded Monterey Jack cheese**
- **1 package (10 ounces) frozen chopped spinach, thawed and squeezed dry**
- **1 package (8 ounces) cream cheese, cubed**

- **2 plum tomatoes, seeded and chopped**
- **3/4 cup chopped onion**
- **1/3 cup half-and-half cream**
- **1 tablespoon finely chopped seeded jalapeno pepper**
- **6 pita breads (6 inches)**
- **1/2 cup butter, melted**
- **2 teaspoons lemon-pepper seasoning**
- **2 teaspoons ground cumin**
- **1/4 teaspoon garlic salt**

In a large bowl, combine the first seven ingredients. Transfer to a greased 1-1/2-qt. baking dish. Bake, uncovered, at 375° for 20-25 minutes or until bubbly.

Meanwhile, cut each pita bread into eight wedges. Place in two 15-in. x 10-in. x 1-in. baking pans. Combine the butter, lemon-pepper, cumin and garlic salt; brush over pita wedges.

Bake for 7-9 minutes or until crisp. Serve with spinach spread. **Yield:** 16 servings (4 cups spread).

Editor's Note: When cutting hot peppers, disposable gloves are recommended. Avoid touching your face.

Very Berry-licious Smoothies

(Pictured below)

PREP/TOTAL TIME: 10 min.

Four berry flavors combine wonderfully in this cool, sweet-tart beverage. It's an ideal complement to any brunch menu, or to sip while enjoying a lazy afternoon on the patio.
—Colleen Belbey, Warwick, Rhode Island

- **2 cups cranberry juice**
- **4 cups frozen unsweetened strawberries**
- **2 cups frozen unsweetened raspberries**
- **2 cartons (6 ounces *each*) blackberry yogurt**

In a blender, combine half of each of the ingredients; cover and process until well blended. Pour into chilled glasses. Repeat with remaining ingredients. Serve smoothies immediately. **Yield:** 6 servings.

Mini Sausage Quiches

(Pictured below)

PREP: 25 min. **BAKE:** 20 min.

These bite-size quiches are loaded with sausage and cheese, plus their crescent roll bases make preparation a snap. Serve the savory "muffinettes" at any brunch or potluck gathering.
—*Jan Mead, Milford, Connecticut*

- 1/2 **pound bulk hot Italian sausage**
- 2 **tablespoons dried minced onion**
- 2 **tablespoons minced chives**
- 1 **tube (8 ounces) refrigerated crescent rolls**
- 4 **eggs, lightly beaten**
- 2 **cups (8 ounces) shredded Swiss cheese**
- 1 **cup (8 ounces) 4% cottage cheese**
- 1/3 **cup grated Parmesan cheese**

Paprika

In a large skillet, brown sausage and onion over medium heat for 4-5 minutes or until meat is no longer pink; drain. Stir in chives.

On a lightly floured surface, unroll crescent dough into one long rectangle; seal seams and perforations. Cut into 48 pieces. Press onto the bottom and up the sides of greased miniature muffin cups. Fill each with about 2 teaspoons of sausage mixture. In a large bowl, combine the eggs and cheeses. Spoon 2 teaspoonfuls over sausage mixture. Sprinkle with paprika.

Bake at 375° for 20-25 minutes or until a knife inserted in the center comes out clean. Cool for 5 minutes before removing from pans to wire racks. Serve warm. Refrigerate leftovers. **Yield:** 4 dozen.

Asparagus Brunch Pockets

(Pictured above)

PREP: 20 min. **BAKE:** 15 min.

These tasty bundles are stuffed with a flavorful asparagus–cream cheese mixture. They're wonderful for brunch or as a side dish.
—*Cynthia Linthicum, Towson, Maryland*

- 1 **pound fresh asparagus, trimmed and cut into 1-inch pieces**
- 4 **ounces cream cheese, softened**
- 1 **tablespoon milk**
- 1 **tablespoon mayonnaise**
- 1 **tablespoon diced pimientos**
- 1 **tablespoon finely chopped onion**
- 1/8 **teaspoon salt**

Pinch pepper

- 1 **tube (8 ounces) refrigerated crescent rolls**
- 2 **teaspoons butter, melted**
- 1 **tablespoon seasoned bread crumbs**

In a large saucepan, bring 1/2 in. of water to a boil. Add asparagus; cover and boil for 3 minutes. Drain and set aside.

In a small bowl, beat the cream cheese, milk and mayonnaise until smooth. Stir in the pimientos, onion, salt and pepper.

Unroll crescent dough and separate into triangles; place on an ungreased baking sheet. Spoon 1 teaspoon of cream cheese mixture into the center of each triangle; top with asparagus. Top each with another teaspoonful of cream cheese mixture. Bring three corners of dough together and twist; pinch edges to seal.

Brush dough with melted butter; sprinkle with bread crumbs. Bake at 375° for 15-18 minutes or until golden brown. **Yield:** 8 servings.

Asparagus Tips

After rinsing asparagus in cold water, snap off the ends as far down as they will easily break when bent, or cut off the tough white portion. If the stalks are large, peel the tough part from the end to just below the tip.

Cowboy Beef Dip

(Pictured below and on page 6)

PREP: 20 min. **COOK:** 25 min.

This hearty dip starring ground beef is a winner with my family. It has all kinds of yummy stuff in it, including chopped onion and bell peppers, olives, green chilies, jalapeno and cheese.
—*Jessica Klym, Killdeer, North Dakota*

- 1 **pound ground beef**
- 4 **tablespoons chopped onion,** *divided*
- 3 **tablespoons chopped sweet red pepper,** *divided*
- 2 **tablespoons chopped green pepper,** *divided*
- 1 **can (10-3/4 ounces) condensed nacho cheese soup, undiluted**
- 1/2 **cup salsa**
- 4 **tablespoons sliced ripe olives,** *divided*
- 4 **tablespoons sliced pimiento-stuffed olives,** *divided*
- 2 **tablespoons chopped green chilies**
- 1 **teaspoon chopped seeded jalapeno pepper**
- 1/4 **teaspoon dried oregano**
- 1/4 **teaspoon pepper**
- 1/4 **cup shredded cheddar cheese**
- 2 **tablespoons sour cream**
- 2 **to 3 teaspoons minced fresh parsley**

Tortilla chips

In a large skillet, cook beef, 3 tablespoons onions, 2 tablespoons red pepper and 1 tablespoon green pepper over medium heat until meat is no longer pink; drain. Stir in soup, salsa, 3 tablespoons ripe olives, 3 tablespoons pimiento-stuffed olives, chilies, jalapeno, oregano and pepper. Bring to a boil. Reduce heat; simmer, uncovered, for 5 minutes.

Transfer to a serving dish. Top with the cheese, sour cream and parsley; sprinkle top with the remaining onion, peppers and olives. Serve the dip with tortilla chips. **Yield:** 3 cups.

Editor's Note: When cutting hot peppers, disposable gloves are recommended. Avoid touching your face.

Cinnamon Mocha Coffee

(Pictured above)

PREP/TOTAL TIME: 20 min.

One snowy day, my neighbor called and invited me over to try a new beverage. It was delicious! This spiced coffee is a lovely treat any time of year. —*Bernice Morris, Marshfield, Missouri*

- 1/2 **cup ground dark roast coffee**
- 1 **tablespoon ground cinnamon**
- 1/4 **teaspoon ground nutmeg**
- 5 **cups water**
- 1 **cup milk**
- 1/3 **cup chocolate syrup**
- 1/4 **cup packed brown sugar**
- 1 **teaspoon vanilla extract**

Whipped cream, optional

In a small bowl, combine the coffee grounds, cinnamon and nutmeg; pour into a coffee filter of a drip coffeemaker. Add water; brew according to manufacturer's directions.

In a large saucepan, combine the milk, chocolate syrup and brown sugar. Cook over low heat until sugar is dissolved, stirring occasionally. Stir in the vanilla and brewed coffee.

Ladle into mugs; garnish with whipped cream if desired. **Yield:** 6 servings.

For the fritters, place onion and butter in a microwave-safe dish. Cover; microwave on high until onion is tender. Add egg, zucchini and carrot. In a bowl, combine flour, cheese, cornmeal, salt and pepper; stir in vegetable mixture just until combined.

In a skillet or deep-fat fryer, heat 2 in. of oil to 375°. Drop rounded tablespoonfuls of batter into oil. Fry for 1-2 minutes until deep golden brown, turning once. Drain on paper towels. Serve fritters with dipping sauce. **Yield:** 1-1/2 dozen fritters, 2/3 cup basil sauce and 1-1/2 cups horseradish sauce.

Sweetheart Punch

(Pictured below)

PREP: 20 min. + chilling

I received this recipe from a friend years ago and have served it at numerous special occasions. As an eye–catching option, use a heart–shaped mold to make the ice ring.
—Gretchen Montgomery, Marietta, Ohio

- **2 cups sliced fresh strawberries,** *divided*
- **6 cups water,** *divided*
- **1 can (12 ounces) frozen pink lemonade concentrate, thawed**
- **1 package (10 ounces) frozen sweetened sliced strawberries, thawed**
- **1 can (6 ounces) frozen orange juice concentrate, thawed**
- **2 liters lemon-lime soda, chilled**

Arrange 1 cup of fresh strawberries in a 4-1/2-cup ring mold; add 2 cups water. Freeze until solid. Top with the remaining fresh strawberries. Slowly pour 1 cup water into mold to almost cover berries. Freeze until solid.

In a punch bowl, combine the lemonade concentrate, thawed strawberries, orange juice concentrate and remaining water. Refrigerate until chilled.

Just before serving, stir in lemon-lime soda. Unmold ice ring by wrapping the bottom of the mold in a damp hot dishcloth; invert onto a baking sheet. Place fruit side up in punch bowl. **Yield:** 14 servings (3-1/2 quarts).

Carrot Zucchini Fritters

(Pictured above)

PREP/TOTAL TIME: 25 min.

I'm always looking for flavorful recipes that increase my veggie intake without being saturated in cheese or cream sauces. This one fills the bill. The crispy fritters are delicious and fun to eat with or without the dipping sauces.
—Laura Mize, Waco, Kentucky

- **2/3 cup sour cream plus 1/2 cup sour cream,** *divided*
- **2/3 cup lightly packed fresh basil leaves**
- **1 teaspoon lemon juice**
- **Salt and pepper to taste**
- **1/2 cup mayonnaise**
- **1/2 cup horseradish sauce**

FRITTERS:
- **2 tablespoons finely chopped onion**
- **1 tablespoon butter**
- **1 egg, lightly beaten**
- **2 medium zucchini, shredded and squeezed dry (about 1-1/2 cups)**
- **1 large carrot, shredded**
- **1/3 cup all-purpose flour**
- **1/3 cup grated Parmesan cheese**
- **1 tablespoon cornmeal**
- **1/2 teaspoon salt**
- **1/8 teaspoon pepper**
- **Oil for frying**

In a blender or food processor, place 2/3 cup sour cream, basil, lemon juice, salt and pepper; cover and process until blended. Transfer to a small bowl. In another bowl, combine the mayonnaise, horseradish and remaining sour cream. Cover and refrigerate both sauces.

Shrimp Toast Cups

(Pictured above)

PREP: 30 min. **BAKE:** 15 min./batch

These appetizers always disappear quick as a flash. The pretty toast cups lend themselves to other favorite fillings, too!
—Awynne Thurstenson, Siloam Springs, Arkansas

- 24 **slices white bread, crusts removed**
- 1 **cup butter, melted**
- 2 **packages (8 ounces *each*) cream cheese, softened**
- 1/2 **cup mayonnaise**
- 3 **tablespoons sour cream**
- 3 **tablespoons prepared horseradish**
- 3 **cans (6 ounces *each*) small shrimp, rinsed and drained**
- 16 **green onions, sliced**

Fresh dill sprigs, optional

Flatten bread with a rolling pin; cut each slice into four pieces. Place butter in a shallow dish; dip both sides of bread in butter; press into miniature muffin cups. Bake at 325° for 14 minutes or until golden brown. Remove from pans to wire racks to cool.

In a large bowl, beat the cream cheese, mayonnaise, sour cream and horseradish until blended. Just before serving, stir in shrimp and onions; spoon into cups.

Garnish cups with fresh dill sprigs if desired. Refrigerate leftovers. **Yield:** 8 dozen.

Smoky Jalapenos

(Pictured above)

PREP: 25 min. **BAKE:** 20 min.

When I make these zesty bites, there are no leftovers. They can also be made with mild banana peppers or yellow chili peppers.
—Melinda Štrable, Ankeny, Iowa

- 14 **jalapeno peppers**
- 4 **ounces cream cheese, softened**
- 14 **miniature smoked sausages**
- 7 **bacon strips**

Cut a lengthwise slit in each pepper; remove seeds and membranes. Spread a teaspoonful of cream cheese into each pepper; stuff each with a sausage.

Cut bacon strips in half widthwise; cook in microwave or skillet until partially cooked. Wrap a bacon piece around each pepper; secure the bacon with a toothpick.

Place in an ungreased 13-in. x 9-in. x 2-in. baking dish. Bake, uncovered, at 350° for 20 minutes for spicy flavor, 30 minutes for medium flavor and 40 minutes for mild flavor. **Yield:** 14 appetizers.

Editor's Note: When cutting hot peppers, disposable gloves are recommended. Avoid touching your face.

Rainbow Pepper Appetizers

PREP/TOTAL TIME: 20 min.

Company will quickly polish off this colorful pepper medley that showcases crisp–tender sweet peppers topped with chopped olives and Monterey Jack cheese.   —Marion Karlin, Waterloo, Iowa

- 1/2 **each** medium green, sweet red, yellow and orange peppers
- 1 cup (4 ounces) shredded Monterey Jack cheese
- 2 tablespoons chopped ripe olives
- 1/4 teaspoon crushed red pepper flakes, optional

Cut each pepper half into nine pieces. Place skin side down in an ungreased ovenproof skillet; sprinkle with cheese, olives and pepper flakes if desired.

Broil peppers 3-4 in. from the heat for 5-7 minutes or until the peppers are crisp-tender and the cheese is melted. **Yield:** 3 dozen.

Roasted Cumin Cashews

(Pictured below)

PREP: 15 min. **BAKE:** 50 min. + cooling

Kick up parties and get–togethers with these well–seasoned nuts. They're sweet, salty, crunchy and oh, so munchable.
—Martha Fehl, Brookville, Indiana

- 1 egg white
- 1 tablespoon water
- 2 cans (9-3/4 ounces *each*) salted whole cashews
- 1/3 cup sugar
- 3 teaspoons chili powder
- 2 teaspoons salt
- 2 teaspoons ground cumin
- 1/2 teaspoon cayenne pepper

In a large bowl, whisk egg white and water. Add cashews and toss to coat. Transfer to a colander; drain for 2 minutes. In another bowl, combine the remaining ingredients; add cashews and toss to coat.

Arrange the nut mixture in a single layer in a greased 15-in. x 10-in. x 1-in. baking pan. Bake, uncovered, at 250° for 50-55 minutes, stirring once. Cool on a wire rack. Store in an airtight container. **Yield:** 3-1/2 cups.

Zesty Snack Mix

PREP: 10 min. **BAKE:** 2-1/2 hours

Pep up a party with this crunchy, well–seasoned blend of cereal, pretzels and cheese crackers. Alter it by adding mixed nuts.
—Codie Ray, Tallulah, Louisiana

- 4 cups Corn Chex
- 4 cups Cheerios
- 4 cups pretzel sticks
- 4 cups cheese-flavored snack crackers
- 1 cup butter, melted
- 1/2 cup canola oil
- 3 tablespoons Worcestershire sauce
- 1 tablespoon garlic powder
- 1 tablespoon seasoned salt
- 1 tablespoon chili powder
- 1 teaspoon cayenne pepper

In a large bowl, combine the cereals, pretzels and crackers. Spread onto two ungreased 15-in. x 10-in. x 1-in. baking pans.

Combine the remaining ingredients; pour over the cereal mixture and toss to coat. Bake 225° for 2 to 2-1/2 hours, stirring every 30 minutes. Store in airtight containers. **Yield:** 16 cups.

Double Chocolate Fondue

PREP/TOTAL TIME: 20 min.

Thick, rich and luscious, this dip won't last long. You can also use pretzel sticks as dippers. I eat spoonfuls right out of the refrigerator!   —Cindy Stetzer, Alliance, Ohio

- 1 cup sugar
- 2 cans (5 ounces *each*) evaporated milk, *divided*
- 1/2 cup baking cocoa
- 4 squares (1 ounce *each*) unsweetened chocolate, chopped
- 2 tablespoons butter
- 1 teaspoon vanilla extract

Cubed pound cake and assorted fresh fruit

In a small saucepan, combine sugar and 1 can evaporated milk. Cook over low heat, stirring occasionally, until the sugar is dissolved.

In a small bowl, whisk the cocoa and remaining milk until smooth. Add to the sugar mixture; bring to a boil, whisking constantly.

Remove from the heat; stir in chocolate and butter until melted. Stir in vanilla. Keep warm. Serve with cake and fruit. **Yield:** 1-1/3 cups.

1 garlic clove, minced
1 teaspoon cider vinegar
1/4 teaspoon salt
Tortilla chips

Place asparagus in a large saucepan; add 1/2 in. of water. Bring to a boil. Reduce heat; cover and simmer for 2 minutes. Drain and rinse in cold water.

In a bowl, combine the asparagus, tomatoes, onion, jalapeno, cilantro, garlic, vinegar and salt. Cover and refrigerate for at least 4 hours, stirring several times. Serve with tortilla chips. **Yield:** 3 cups.

Editor's Note: When cutting hot peppers, disposable gloves are recommended. Avoid touching your face.

Three-Cheese Pesto Pizza

(Pictured above and on page 6)

PREP/TOTAL TIME: 30 min.

With a ready-made crust, this pizza can be on a serving tray in half an hour. The three-cheese blend will make slices go fast.
—Pat Stevens, Granbury, Texas

1/2 cup finely chopped red onion
1/2 cup finely chopped sweet red pepper
1 tablespoon olive oil
1 prebaked Italian bread shell crust (14 ounces)
1/2 cup prepared pesto
1 cup (4 ounces) crumbled feta cheese
1 cup (4 ounces) shredded part-skim mozzarella cheese
1 cup (4 ounces) shredded Parmesan cheese
1 can (4-1/4 ounces) chopped ripe olives
1 medium tomato, thinly sliced

In a small skillet, saute onion and red pepper in oil until tender. Remove from the heat; set aside.

Place crust on an ungreased 14-in. pizza pan. Spread pesto to within 1/2 in. of edges. Layer with the cheeses, onion mixture, olives and tomato. Bake at 400° for 15-18 minutes or until cheese is melted. **Yield:** 16 slices.

Asparagus Salsa

PREP: 20 min. + chilling

Jalapeno pepper and cilantro spice up this refreshing salsa that's made with tomatoes, onion and fresh asparagus. Serve it chilled with tortilla chips—it won't last long.
—Emma Thomas, Rome, Georgia

1 pound fresh asparagus, trimmed and cut into 1/2-inch pieces
1 cup chopped seeded tomatoes
1/2 cup finely chopped onion
1 small jalapeno pepper, seeded and finely chopped
1 tablespoon minced fresh cilantro

Hot Wings

(Pictured below)

PREP: 15 min. **BAKE:** 1 hour

These appetizers are hearty for a party—with just the right amount of "heat." My family enjoys them so much that I often serve the wings as our main course!
—Coralie Begin, Fairfield, Maine

7 to 8 pounds fresh *or* frozen chicken wingettes, thawed
4 cups ketchup
2-1/2 cups packed brown sugar
1-1/3 cups water
1 cup Louisiana-style hot sauce
1/3 cup Worcestershire sauce
2-1/2 teaspoons chili powder
2 teaspoons garlic powder
1/2 teaspoon onion powder

Place wingettes in two greased 15-in. x 10-in. x 1-in. baking pans. In a large bowl, combine the remaining ingredients. Pour over wings.

Bake, uncovered, at 350° for 1 hour or until chicken juices run clear. Spoon sauce from pans over wings if desired. **Yield:** about 6 dozen.

Salads & Dressings

Cool and crisp or warm and wonderful, these salads make a memorable meal. The homemade dressings are so good, you'll never use storebought again.

SUPER SELECTIONS. Clockwise from upper left: Apple-Brie Spinach Salad (p. 29), Hawaiian Ham Salad (p. 32), Fruit and Nut Tossed Salad (p. 35), Napa Cabbage Slaw (p. 38) and pictured center, Tomato Corn Salad (p. 29).

baking pan. Sprinkle with salt and pepper. Bake at 400° for 15-20 minutes or until tender.

In a large salad bowl, toss greens, strawberries, onion, walnuts and asparagus. In a small bowl, whisk the vinegar, sugar and remaining oil. Drizzle over salad and toss to coat. **Yield:** 6-8 servings.

Raspberry Vinaigrette

PREP/TOTAL TIME: 20 min.

When making this sweet vinaigrette, plan on 2 tablespoons of dressing for each 1-cup serving of salad greens.
—*Betty Miller, Angola, Indiana*

- 2 jars (12 ounces *each*) seedless raspberry preserves
- 1-1/4 cups sugar, *divided*
- 1/2 cup water
- 1/3 cup chopped sweet onion
- 1/4 cup balsamic vinegar
- 1 tablespoon dried tarragon
- 1 tablespoon curry powder
- 1 teaspoon white pepper
- 1 teaspoon pepper
- 1 cup olive oil
- Torn mixed salad greens

In a large saucepan, bring the preserves and 3/4 cup sugar to a boil. Remove from the heat; cool slightly. Transfer to a blender. Add the water, onion, vinegar, tarragon, curry powder, white pepper, pepper and remaining sugar; cover and process until smooth. While processing, gradually add oil in a steady stream. Serve with salad greens. **Yield:** about 4 cups.

Green Goddess Salad Dressing

PREP/TOTAL TIME: 10 min.

It's no trick to fix this time-honored dressing at home. Made with plenty of fresh ingredients, it's a real treat compared to storebought dressing. —*Page Alexander, Baldwin City, Kansas*

- 1 cup mayonnaise
- 1/2 cup sour cream
- 1/4 cup chopped green pepper
- 1/4 cup packed fresh parsley sprigs
- 3 anchovy fillets
- 2 tablespoons lemon juice
- 2 green onion tops, coarsely chopped
- 1 garlic clove, peeled
- 1/4 teaspoon pepper
- 1/8 teaspoon Worcestershire sauce

Place all ingredients in a blender; cover and process until smooth. Transfer to a bowl or jar; cover and store in the refrigerator. **Yield:** 2 cups.

Asparagus Berry Salad

(Pictured above)

PREP/TOTAL TIME: 30 min.

When strawberries and asparagus are at their peak, this salad is sensational! I like to serve it for brunch or dinner. Sometimes I add grilled chicken or salmon to create a refreshing and satisfying main dish salad. —*Trisha Kruse, Eagle, Idaho*

- 1 pound fresh asparagus, trimmed and cut into 1-inch pieces
- 3 tablespoons olive oil, *divided*
- 1/4 teaspoon salt
- 1/4 teaspoon coarsely ground pepper
- 8 cups spring mix salad greens
- 3 cups sliced fresh strawberries
- 1/2 small red onion, thinly sliced
- 1/2 cup chopped walnuts, toasted
- 2 tablespoons balsamic vinegar
- 2 teaspoons sugar

In a bowl, toss the asparagus with 1 tablespoon oil. Spread in a single layer in a greased 15-in. x 10-in. x 1-in.

1/4 teaspoon salt
1/4 teaspoon white pepper
1/4 teaspoon Worcestershire sauce
1-1/2 cups vegetable oil

Place the first eight ingredients in a blender; cover and process until smooth. While processing, gradually add oil in a steady stream. Transfer to a bowl or pitcher. Cover and refrigerate until serving. **Yield:** 2-1/2 cups.

Pecan-Pear Green Salad

(*Pictured below*)

PREP/TOTAL TIME: 15 min.

This lovely salad adds a special touch to any meal. The juicy pear slices, toasted pecans and mixed greens are coated in a tangy vinaigrette dressing that make for a pleasant sweet and crunchy combination. —*Katie Nicklas, Ridgway, Pennsylvania*

1 large ripe red pear, sliced
2 tablespoons butter, *divided*
1/2 cup coarsely chopped pecans
1/4 teaspoon salt, *divided*
2 cups mixed salad greens
2 tablespoons balsamic vinegar
2 tablespoons olive oil
Pepper to taste

In a large skillet, saute pear in 1 tablespoon butter until lightly browned, about 7 minutes. In another skillet, saute pecans in remaining butter until lightly browned, about 5 minutes; sprinkle with 1/8 teaspoon salt.

Divide salad greens between two salad plates; arrange pears over greens. Sprinkle with pecans. In a jar with a tight-fitting lid, combine the vinegar, oil, pepper and remaining salt; shake well. Drizzle over salad. **Yield:** 2 servings.

Sunny Carrot Salad

(*Pictured above*)

PREP/TOTAL TIME: 10 min.

Almonds and sunflower kernels give a pleasing crunch to this speedy yet delicious variation on traditional carrot–raisin salad. If you prefer a nuttier flavor, use 1/2 cup of sunflower kernels instead of 1/3 cup. —*Barb Hunter, Ponder, Texas*

3 cups shredded carrots
2 cups unsweetened crushed pineapple, drained
1/2 cup golden raisins
1/3 cup mayonnaise
1/2 cup sliced almonds
1/3 cup unsalted sunflower kernels

In a large serving bowl, combine the carrots, pineapple and raisins. Stir in mayonnaise. Cover and refrigerate until serving. Just before serving, add almonds and sunflower kernels; toss to coat. **Yield:** 5 servings.

Mustard-Sour Cream Salad Dressing

PREP/TOTAL TIME: 10 min.

This smooth blend with a mild mustard flavor drapes nicely over any salad or bowl of mixed greens…and it makes a big batch. —*Marian Platt, Sequim, Washington*

1/2 cup red wine vinegar
1/2 cup sour cream
1/2 cup Dijon mustard
2 teaspoons sugar
2 garlic cloves, peeled

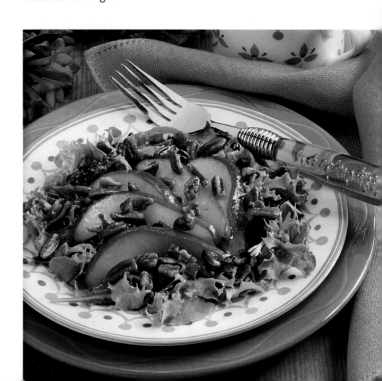

Crispy Chicken Strip Salad

(Pictured below)

PREP: 40 min. **COOK:** 10 min.

These chicken strips taste great. Combined with candied pecans, fresh raspberries and greens, and served with storebought vinaigrette, the salad is easy and delicious.
—Lillian Julow, Gainesville, Florida

- 1 tablespoon butter
- 1/2 cup pecan halves
- 2 tablespoons sugar
- 3/4 cup all-purpose flour
- 2 tablespoons minced fresh tarragon *or* 2 teaspoons dried tarragon
- 1 tablespoon grated lemon peel
- 2 eggs
- 1 pound boneless skinless chicken breast, cut into 1-inch strips
- 2 tablespoons vegetable oil
- 4 cups spring mix salad greens
- 1 cup torn Bibb *or* Boston lettuce
- 1/2 cup raspberry vinaigrette
- 2 cups fresh *or* frozen unsweetened raspberries

In a small skillet, melt butter. Add pecans and cook over medium heat until nuts are toasted, about 4 minutes. Sprinkle with sugar. Cook and stir for 2-4 minutes or until sugar is melted. Transfer to a greased foil-lined baking sheet; cool completely.

In a large resealable bag, combine the flour tarragon and lemon peel. In a shallow bowl, beat the eggs. Add chicken strips to flour mixture in batches; seal and shake to coat. Dip in eggs, then return to bag and coat again.

In a large skillet over medium heat, cook chicken in oil

for 6-8 minutes or until no longer pink, turning once.

Break the pecans apart. Toss the greens and lettuce with vinaigrette; arrange on individual plates. Top with the raspberries, chicken strips and sugared pecans.
Yield: 4 servings.

Southwestern Rice Salad

(Pictured above)

PREP/TOTAL TIME: 30 min.

The recipe for this delicious, colorful salad has been in my family for years. My mother used to bring it to many different functions, and I'm carrying on her tradition.
—Ruth Bianchi, Apple Valley, Minnesota

- 1-1/3 cups water
- 2/3 cup uncooked long grain rice
- 3/4 cup chopped green pepper
- 1/2 cup chopped red onion
- 1 medium carrot, chopped
- 3 garlic cloves, minced
- 1 tablespoon canola oil
- 1 package (16 ounces) frozen corn, thawed
- 1 can (15 ounces) black beans, rinsed and drained
- 2 medium plum tomatoes, chopped
- 1 cup salted peanuts
- 1/3 cup minced fresh cilantro
- 2/3 cup olive oil
- 1/3 cup lemon juice
- 1/2 to 1-1/2 teaspoons cayenne pepper
- 1/2 teaspoon ground cumin

In a large saucepan, bring water and rice to a boil. Reduce heat; cover and simmer for 15 minutes. Remove from the heat. Let stand for 5 minutes or until rice is tender. Rinse rice with cold water and drain. Place in a large bowl.

In a small skillet, saute the green pepper, onion, carrot and garlic in oil until crisp-tender. Add to rice. Stir in the corn, beans, tomatoes, peanuts and cilantro.

In a small bowl, combine the oil, lemon juice, cayenne and cumin. Pour over rice mixture and stir to coat. Cover and refrigerate until serving. **Yield:** 12 servings.

Grand Prize Winner

Tomato Corn Salad

(Pictured below and on page 24)

PREP/TOTAL TIME: 30 min.

Warm and colorful, this tantalizing side dish bursts with refreshing vegetable flavor. Fresh herbs and Dijon mustard add lots of pizzazz. —Carrie Skiper, Roselle Park, New Jersey

- 3 large tomatoes, chopped
- 1 small red onion, halved and thinly sliced
- 1/3 cup chopped green onions
- 1/4 cup balsamic vinegar
- 3 tablespoons minced fresh basil
- 1 tablespoon minced fresh cilantro
- 1 teaspoon salt
- 1/2 teaspoon pepper
- 4 cups fresh corn (about 9 ears of corn)
- 3 garlic cloves, peeled and thinly sliced
- 2 tablespoons olive oil
- 1 tablespoon Dijon mustard

In a large bowl, combine the first eight ingredients. In a large skillet, saute corn and garlic in oil until tender; stir in mustard. Add to vegetable mixture; toss to coat. Serve with a slotted spoon. **Yield:** 7 servings.

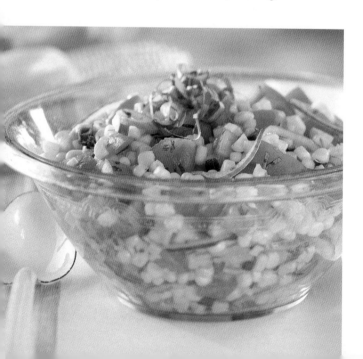

Apple-Brie Spinach Salad

(Pictured above and on page 24)

PREP/TOTAL TIME: 30 min.

In the summer, I don't like to prepare or eat large meals, so I often make salads. I'm always on the outlook for new and interesting recipes, and this one is a winner that I like to make for company. —Rhonda Crowe, Victoria, British Columbia

- 4 large apples, cut into 1/2-inch wedges
- 4 tablespoons maple syrup, *divided*
- 8 cups fresh baby spinach
- 1 round (8 ounces) Brie *or* Camembert cheese, cubed
- 1/2 cup pecan halves, toasted

DRESSING:
- 1/4 cup apple cider *or* juice
- 1/4 cup canola oil
- 3 tablespoons cider vinegar
- 1 teaspoon Dijon mustard
- 1 garlic clove, minced

Place apples on an ungreased baking sheet; brush with 2 tablespoons syrup. Broil 3-4 in. from the heat for 3 minutes. Turn; brush with remaining syrup. Broil 3-5 minutes longer or until crisp-tender.

In a large salad bowl, combine the spinach, cheese, pecans and apples. In a small saucepan, combine the dressing ingredients; bring to a boil. Pour over salad; toss to coat. **Yield:** 10 servings.

covered, over medium heat for 6-8 minutes or until golden brown, basting frequently. Turn and grill 6-8 minutes longer or until golden and tender.

In a large salad bowl, combine the greens, walnuts and blue cheese. Add apples. Drizzle with reserved dressing and toss to coat. **Yield:** 4 servings.

Balsamic Vinegar Dressing

(Pictured below)

PREP/TOTAL TIME: 25 min.

A variety of savory seasonings gives this dressing a tangy kick. It's the perfect complement to a bed of fresh greens.
—Edgar Wright, Silver Spring, Maryland

1 cup balsamic vinegar
1 cup honey
2 tablespoons minced fresh basil
3 teaspoons onion powder
2 garlic cloves, peeled
1 teaspoon white pepper
1 teaspoon dried oregano
1 teaspoon dried thyme
1 teaspoon dill weed
1 teaspoon prepared mustard
3 cups canola oil

In a blender, combine half of the first 10 ingredients; cover and process until blended. While processing, gradually add half of the oil in a steady stream. Transfer to a 1-1/2-qt. container.

Repeat with remaining ingredients. Cover and refrigerate until serving. **Yield:** 36 servings (2 tablespoons per serving).

Grilled Apple Tossed Salad

(Pictured above)

PREP: 15 min. + marinating **GRILL:** 15 min.

The grilled apples in this salad go so well with the blue cheese, walnuts and balsamic dressing. I like to serve it on pink Depression glass dessert plates from my great-grandmother.
—Paul Soska, Toledo, Ohio

6 tablespoons olive oil
1/4 cup orange juice
1/4 cup white balsamic vinegar
1/4 cup minced fresh cilantro
2 tablespoons honey
1/2 teaspoon salt
1/2 teaspoon chili sauce
1 garlic clove, minced
2 large apples, cut into wedges
1 package (5 ounces) spring mix salad greens
1 cup walnut halves
1/2 cup crumbled blue cheese

For dressing, in a bowl, combine the first eight ingredients. Pour 1/4 cup into a large resealable plastic bag; add apples. Seal bag and turn to coat; refrigerate for at least 10 minutes. Cover and refrigerate remaining dressing until serving.

Drain apples, reserving marinade for basting. Thread onto six metal or soaked wooden skewers. Grill apples,

Orange Gelatin Pretzel Salad

(Pictured above)

PREP: 30 min. + chilling

I adapted this recipe from using strawberries and strawberry gelatin. The pretzels give the refreshing layered salad a nice crunch. It's a favorite in our family.
—*Peggy Boyd, Northport, Alabama*

- **2 cups crushed pretzels**
- **3 teaspoons plus 3/4 cup sugar,** *divided*
- **3/4 cup butter, melted**
- **2 packages (3 ounces** *each***) orange gelatin**
- **2 cups boiling water**
- **2 cans (8 ounces** *each***) crushed pineapple, drained**
- **1 can (11 ounces) mandarin oranges, drained**
- **1 package (8 ounces) cream cheese, softened**
- **2 cups whipped topping**

Additional whipped topping, optional

In a small bowl, combine the pretzels and 3 teaspoons sugar; stir in the butter. Press into an ungreased 13-in. x 9-in. x 2-in. baking dish. Bake at 350° for 10 minutes. Cool on a wire rack.

In a large bowl, dissolve the gelatin in boiling water.

Add pineapple and oranges. Chill until partially set, about 30 minutes.

In a small bowl, beat the cream cheese and remaining sugar until smooth. Fold in whipped topping. Spread over crust. Gently spoon gelatin mixture over the cream cheese layer. Cover and refrigerate for 2-4 hours or until firm.

Cut into squares. Garnish with additional whipped topping if desired. **Yield:** 15 servings.

Chunky Blue Cheese Dressing

PREP/TOTAL TIME: 10 min.

This flavorful, full-bodied dressing is better than any bottled dressing I've ever tasted...and it's easy to prepare, too! I found the recipe in a church cookbook.
—*Leona Luecking, West Burlington, Iowa*

- **1/4 cup milk**
- **3 cups mayonnaise**
- **1 cup (8 ounces) sour cream**
- **4 ounces crumbled blue cheese**
- **2 teaspoons garlic salt**

Place the milk, mayonnaise, sour cream, blue cheese and garlic salt in a blender. Cover and process until smooth. Refrigerate until serving. **Yield:** about 4 cups.

Hearty Entree Salads

Colorful Turkey Salad Cups

(Pictured above)

PREP/TOTAL TIME: 30 min.

Here's a recipe that's perfect for any season. It uses cooked turkey and cranberry sauce in a light and interesting way. Guests always give this recipe two thumbs up no matter when I serve it!
—Janice Elder, Charlotte, North Carolina

- 1/2 cup jellied cranberry sauce
- 2 tablespoons orange marmalade
- 2 tablespoons hoisin sauce
- 1/2 teaspoon crushed red pepper flakes
- 3 cups cubed cooked turkey
- 1 small sweet red pepper, chopped
- 1 small sweet onion, chopped
- 1/2 cup chopped seeded peeled cucumber
- 1 medium mango, peeled and chopped
- 1 medium avocado, peeled and chopped
- 1/4 cup chopped pecans, toasted
- 2 tablespoons finely chopped candied *or* crystallized ginger
- 12 Bibb lettuce leaves
- 1/2 cup fresh mint leaves, thinly sliced
- 1/2 cup fresh basil leaves, thinly sliced

In a small saucepan, combine the cranberry sauce, orange marmalade, hoisin sauce and pepper flakes. Cook over medium heat for 2-3 minutes or until blended, stirring occasionally. Cool.

In a large bowl, combine the turkey, red pepper, onion, cucumber, mango, avocado, pecans, ginger and cranberry mixture. Spoon onto lettuce leaves; sprinkle with herbs. Refrigerate until serving. **Yield:** 6 servings.

Grilled Steak Caesar Salad

(Pictured below)

PREP/TOTAL TIME: 30 min.

This salad, with a tangy anchovy dressing, is my version of a delicious dish offered at one of our finer restaurants. My quilting group really enjoys it, served with hard rolls and a fruit dessert.
—Eleanor Froehlich
Rochester Hills, Michigan

- 4 hard-cooked egg yolks
- 4 anchovy fillets *or* 2 tablespoons anchovy paste
- 4 garlic cloves, minced
- 3 tablespoons Dijon mustard
- 2 tablespoons lemon juice
- 2 tablespoons red wine vinegar
- 1 tablespoon Worcestershire sauce
- 2 teaspoons coarsely ground pepper

- 1 teaspoon sugar
- 1 cup olive oil
- 1 boneless beef sirloin steak (about 1-1/4 pounds)
- 1 large bunch romaine, torn
- 2/3 cup shredded Parmesan cheese, *divided*
- 2 medium tomatoes, cut into wedges
- 2 cups Caesar salad croutons

In a blender or food processor, combine the first 10 ingredients; cover and process until blended. While processing, gradually add oil in a steady stream. Cover and refrigerate.

Grill steak, covered, over medium heat for 5-7 minutes on each side or until meat reaches desired doneness (for medium-rare, a meat thermometer should read 145°; medium, 160°; well-done, 170°).

In a large bowl, toss the romaine, 1/3 cup Parmesan cheese and salad dressing. Divide among salad plates. Slice the steak and arrange it and the tomatoes on salads. Top with croutons and remaining cheese. **Yield:** 6 servings.

Hawaiian Ham Salad

(Pictured above right and on page 24)

PREP: 15 min. + chilling

There's plenty of flavor and crunch in this crispy salad. I like to use both red and green apples, and sometimes I substitute celery for the water chestnuts.
—Vickie Lowrey, Fallon, Nevada

- 1 can (8 ounces) unsweetened pineapple chunks
- 3 cups cooked brown rice
- 2 cups cubed fully cooked ham
- 1 can (8 ounces) sliced water chestnuts, drained and halved
- 1/4 cup finely chopped red onion
- 1/2 cup plain yogurt
- 1/2 teaspoon salt

1 medium apple, chopped
Lettuce leaves
1/3 cup chopped macadamia
     nuts, toasted
1/4 cup flaked coconut, toasted

Drain pineapple, reserving 1 tablespoon juice. In a large bowl, combine the pineapple, rice, ham, water chestnuts and onion. Cover and refrigerate for at least 2 hours.

In a small bowl, combine the yogurt, salt and reserved pineapple juice. Pour over ham mixture and toss to coat. Stir in apple.

Serve on lettuce-lined plates; sprinkle with macadamia nuts and coconut. **Yield:** 4 servings.

Greek Seafood Salad

(Pictured below)

PREP: 25 min. + chilling

My husband and I and our six children— and now their spouses—are real seafood lovers, and this pretty combination of ingredients never fails to get "wows." It's great for summer picnics accompanied by a fresh baguette.   —Maryalice Wood Langley, British Columbia

2 medium cucumbers, peeled,
   seeded and coarsely
   chopped
1 large tomato, coarsely
   chopped
1 large onion, coarsely
   chopped
1 large green pepper,
   coarsely chopped
1 large sweet yellow pepper,
   coarsely chopped
8 ounces frozen cooked small
   shrimp, thawed
1 can (6 ounces) pitted ripe
   olives, drained and sliced
1/2 cup cubed part-skim
     mozzarella cheese
2 cans (6 ounces *each*) chunk
   tuna, drained
DRESSING:
1/4 cup white vinegar
1/4 cup crumbled feta cheese
2 tablespoons minced fresh
   parsley
2 tablespoons minced fresh
   oregano
1 garlic clove, minced
1/4 teaspoon salt
1/4 teaspoon pepper
1/2 cup olive oil

In a large bowl, combine the first eight ingredients. Gently stir in the tuna. In a small bowl, combine the vinegar, feta cheese, parsley, oregano, garlic, salt and pepper. Whisk in the oil. Pour over salad; do not toss. Cover and refrigerate for at least 1 hour. Toss just before serving. **Yield:** 10 servings.

Summer Chicken Salad

(Pictured above right)

PREP: 10 min.
COOK: 25 min. + chilling

*I found this recipe many years ago in a church cookbook. It's special enough for a fancy dinner but easy enough to fix for a light lunch. There's a nice kick to the tangy citrus dressing, which even my picky son enjoys.
—Nancy Whitford, Edwards, New York*

4 boneless skinless chicken
   breast halves (4 ounces *each*)
1 can (14-1/2 ounces) chicken
   broth

6 cups torn mixed salad
   greens
2 cups halved fresh
   strawberries
CITRUS DRESSING:
1/2 cup fresh strawberries,
     hulled
1/3 cup orange juice
2 tablespoons canola oil
1 tablespoon lemon juice
2 teaspoons grated lemon
   peel
1 teaspoon sugar
1/2 teaspoon chili powder
1/4 teaspoon salt
1/4 teaspoon pepper
1/4 cup chopped walnuts,
     toasted

Place chicken in a large skillet; add broth. Bring to a boil. Reduce heat; cover and simmer for 20-25 minutes or until juices run clear. Drain; cover and refrigerate. In a large bowl, combine the greens and sliced strawberries; refrigerate.

For the dressing, in a blender, combine the hulled strawberries, orange juice, oil, lemon juice and lemon peel, sugar, chili powder, salt and pepper. Cover and process until smooth. Pour into a small saucepan. Bring to a boil. Reduce heat; simmer for 5-6 minutes until slightly thickened. Cool slightly.

Drizzle half of the dressing over greens and berries; toss to coat. Divide among four plates. Cut chicken into 1/8-in. slices; arrange over salads. Drizzle remaining dressing over chicken; sprinkle with nuts. **Yield:** 4 servings.

Special Sesame Chicken Salad

(Pictured above)

PREP: 30 min. + chilling

With its delicious mix of crunchy peanuts, tangy dried cranberries and mandarin oranges, this colorful pasta salad is a definite crowd-pleaser. Water chestnuts and a teriyaki dressing give this main dish its Asian flare.

—*Carolee Ewell, Santaquin, Utah*

      1 package (16 ounces) bow tie pasta
      1 cup vegetable oil
    2/3 cup white wine vinegar
    2/3 cup teriyaki sauce
    1/3 cup sugar
    1/2 teaspoon pepper
      3 cans (11 ounces *each*) mandarin oranges, drained
      2 cans (8 ounces *each*) sliced water chestnuts, drained
      2 cups cubed cooked chicken
  1-1/3 cups honey roasted peanuts
      1 package (9 ounces) fresh spinach, torn
      1 package (6 ounces) dried cranberries
      6 green onions, chopped
    1/2 cup minced fresh parsley
    1/4 cup sesame seeds, toasted

Cook pasta according to package directions; drain and place in a very large bowl.

In a small bowl, combine the oil, vinegar, teriyaki sauce, sugar and pepper. Pour over pasta and toss to coat. Cover and refrigerate for 2 hours.

Immediately before serving, add the remaining ingredients; gently toss to coat. **Yield:** 22 servings (1 cup per serving).

Green Onions

It's easier and faster to cut green onions with a kitchen scissors than with a knife. If the recipe calls for quite a few, grab a bunch at one time and snip away. No need to wash a cutting board! If you cut more green onions than you need, store the leftovers in a clean glass jar with a lid and refrigerate. They'll last a couple of weeks this way.

Fruit and Nut Tossed Salad

(Pictured below and on page 24)

PREP: 20 min. **COOK:** 30 min. + cooling

With juicy strawberries, tangy mandarin oranges and crunchy pecans, this refreshing salad has plenty of appeal. It's an attractive addition to a festive menu.
—*Denise Bitner, Reedsville, Pennsylvania*

      1/4 **cup olive oil**
        2 **tablespoons plus 2 teaspoons sugar**
        2 **tablespoons white vinegar**
        1 **tablespoon minced fresh parsley**
      1/4 **teaspoon salt**
Dash hot pepper sauce
PECANS:
      1/3 **cup sugar**
        1 **cup pecan halves**
        2 **tablespoons butter**
SALAD:
        4 **cups torn fresh spinach**
        4 **cups torn romaine**
        1 **can (15 ounces) mandarin oranges, drained**
        2 **celery ribs, chopped**
        1 **cup sliced fresh strawberries**
        4 **green onions, chopped**

For the dressing, in a small bowl, whisk the oil, sugar, vinegar, parsley, salt and pepper sauce until blended. Cover and refrigerate.

For the pecans, in a large heavy skillet, melt sugar over medium-low heat without stirring until golden brown, about 30 minutes. Add pecans and butter; stir constantly until butter is melted and pecans are coated.

Remove from heat. Pour onto a foil-lined baking sheet; cool completely. Break pecans apart if necessary.

For the salad, in a bowl, combine the spinach, romaine, oranges, celery, strawberries and onions. Just before serving, drizzle with dressing; toss to coat. Top with sugared pecans. **Yield:** 8-10 servings.

Dilly Potato Salad

(Pictured above)

PREP: 40 min. + chilling

Everyone has a favorite potato salad, and this is mine. I hope you will be adventurous and give it a try. I've had lots of compliments and requests for the recipe when I make it for summertime gatherings.
—*Angela Leinenbach, Mechanicsville, Virginia*

        4 **pounds red potatoes, halved**
        5 **hard-cooked eggs**
        1 **cup chopped dill pickles**
        1 **small onion, chopped**
  1-1/2 **cups mayonnaise**
        1 **teaspoon celery seed**
      1/2 **teaspoon salt**
      1/4 **teaspoon pepper**
Paprika

Place potatoes in a large kettle; cover with water. Bring to a boil. Reduce heat; cover and cook for 20-25 minutes or until tender. Drain and cool.

Cut potatoes into 3/4-in. cubes. Chop four eggs; slice remaining egg for garnish. In a large bowl, combine the potatoes, chopped eggs, pickles and onion.

In a small bowl, combine the mayonnaise, celery seed, salt and pepper. Pour over potato mixture and stir gently to coat. Sprinkle with paprika; garnish with sliced egg. Cover and refrigerate for at least 2 hours before serving. **Yield:** 12-14 servings.

Brown Rice Lentil Salad

(Pictured below)

PREP: 10 min. **COOK:** 45 min. + chilling

My family isn't always crazy about trying new recipes. The first time I served this salad, they took tiny helpings just to appease me. But the unanimous verdict was, "It tastes great!"
—*DeAnn Howard, Lisbon, Iowa*

- 1/2 **cup uncooked brown rice**
- 1 **cup water**
- 1 **teaspoon chicken bouillon granules**
- 1 **cup cooked lentils**
- 1 **medium tomato, seeded and diced**
- 1/3 **cup thinly sliced green onion**
- 1 **tablespoon minced fresh parsley**
- 2 **tablespoons red wine vinegar**
- 1 **tablespoon olive oil**
- 2 **garlic cloves, minced**
- 2 **teaspoons lime juice**
- 2 **teaspoons Dijon mustard**
- 1/2 **teaspoon salt**
- 1/4 **teaspoon pepper**

In a small saucepan over medium heat, bring the rice, water and bouillon to a boil. Reduce heat; cover and simmer for 40 minutes or until rice is tender. Cool.

In a large bowl, combine the cooked rice, lentils, tomato, onions and parsley. In a small bowl, combine the remaining ingredients. Pour over the rice mixture; toss to coat. Cover and refrigerate for at least 1 hour.
Yield: 7 servings.

Mostaccioli Veggie Salad

(Pictured above)

PREP: 20 min. + chilling

I first sampled this salad at a church potluck several years ago. The mix of pasta, zucchini, summer squash, cucumber, sweet peppers and black olives is coated with a light vinaigrette.
—*Julie Sterchi, Harrisburg, Illinois*

- 3 **cups uncooked mostaccioli**
- 1 **medium cucumber, thinly sliced**
- 1 **small yellow summer squash, quartered and sliced**
- 1 **small zucchini, halved and sliced**
- 1/2 **cup diced sweet red pepper**
- 1/2 **cup diced green pepper**
- 1/2 **cup sliced ripe olives**
- 3 to 4 **green onions, chopped**

DRESSING:
- 1/3 **cup sugar**
- 1/3 **cup white wine vinegar**
- 1/3 **cup canola oil**
- 1-1/2 **teaspoons prepared mustard**
- 3/4 **teaspoon dried minced onion**
- 3/4 **teaspoon garlic powder**
- 1/2 **teaspoon salt**
- 1/2 **teaspoon pepper**

Cook the pasta according to package directions. Drain and rinse in cold water. Place in a large bowl; add the cucumbers, summer squash, zucchini, peppers, olives and onions.

In a jar with a tight-fitting lid, combine the dressing ingredients; shake well. Pour over pasta mixture; toss to coat. Cover and refrigerate for 8 hours or overnight. Toss again before serving. Serve with a slotted spoon.
Yield: 10 servings.

Crowd-Pleasing Taco Salad

(Pictured below)

PREP/TOTAL TIME: 30 min.

While this recipe might sound involved, it can be fixed in just 30 minutes. It's a hit at the potluck table—and I don't have to bring leftovers home after the shindig!
—Ann Cahoon, Bradenton, Florida

- 1 pound ground beef
- 1/2 cup ketchup
- 1 teaspoon dried oregano
- 1 teaspoon chili powder
- 1/2 teaspoon salt
- 1/4 teaspoon pepper
- 1 medium head iceberg lettuce, torn
- 2 medium tomatoes, diced
- 1 cup (4 ounces) shredded taco cheese
- 1 can (2-1/4 ounces) sliced ripe olives, drained
- 1/2 cup mayonnaise
- 1/4 cup taco sauce
- 1 package (10-1/2 ounces) corn chips

In a large saucepan, cook beef over medium heat until no longer pink; drain. Stir in the ketchup, oregano, chili powder, salt and pepper. Bring to a boil. Reduce heat; cover and simmer for 10 minutes.

In a large bowl, combine the lettuce, tomatoes, cheese, olives and beef mixture. Combine the mayonnaise and taco sauce; pour over salad and toss to coat. Sprinkle with corn chips. Serve immediately. **Yield:** 14-16 servings.

Fruit Salad Dressing

(Pictured above)

PREP/TOTAL TIME: 15 min.

Served with seasonal fruit, this citrusy dressing makes a refreshing side dish or dessert for your next ladies' luncheon or breakfast buffet. It's a snap to make, too!
—Shirley Haase, Madison, Wisconsin

- 2/3 cup orange juice
- 3 tablespoons lemon juice
- 1 cup sugar
- 1 egg, lightly beaten

Assorted fresh fruit

In a small saucepan, combine juices, sugar and egg. Bring to a boil; cook and stir for 1 minute or until thickened. Strain. Cover and refrigerate until serving. Serve with fresh fruit. **Yield:** about 1 cup.

A Bit About Balsamic

Balsamic vinegar is made from sweet white grapes and aged in wooden barrels for at least 10 years. You can substitute balsamic with apple cider vinegar or red wine vinegar. White wine vinegar is much stronger and sharper than balsamic and should be used sparingly.

Warm Asparagus Spinach Salad

(Pictured below)

PREP/TOTAL TIME: 30 min.

Spinach, cashews and pasta are mixed with roasted asparagus in this delightful spring salad. The mixture is topped with a light vinaigrette, seasoned with soy sauce and sprinkled with Parmesan cheese. —Kathleen Lucas, Trumbull, Connecticut

> **1-1/2 pounds fresh asparagus, trimmed and cut into 1-inch pieces**
> **2 tablespoons plus 1/2 cup olive oil,** *divided*
> **1/4 teaspoon salt**
> **1-1/2 pounds uncooked penne pasta**
> **3/4 cup chopped green onions**
> **6 tablespoons white wine vinegar**
> **2 tablespoons soy sauce**
> **1 package (6 ounces) fresh baby spinach**
> **1 cup coarsely chopped cashews**
> **1/2 cup shredded Parmesan cheese**

Place asparagus in a 13-in. x 9-in. x 2-in. baking dish. Drizzle with 2 tablespoons oil; sprinkle with salt. Bake, uncovered, at 400° for 20-25 minutes or until crisp-tender, stirring every 10 minutes. Meanwhile, cook pasta according to package directions; drain.

In a blender, combine the onions, vinegar and soy sauce; cover and process until smooth. While processing, gradually add the remaining oil in a steady steam.

In a large salad bowl, combine the pasta, spinach and asparagus. Drizzle with the dressing; toss to coat. Sprinkle with the cashews and Parmesan cheese. **Yield:** 14-16 servings.

Napa Cabbage Slaw

(Pictured above and on page 24)

PREP/TOTAL TIME: 15 min.

Chow mein noodles and snow peas give a pleasant crunch to this colorful and fresh-tasting salad. It's sure to be popular at parties and potlucks. —Genise Krause, Sturgeon Bay, Wisconsin

> **4 cups chopped napa** *or* **Chinese cabbage**
> **1 can (11 ounces) mandarin oranges, drained**
> **1 can (8 ounces) sliced water chestnuts, drained**
> **1 cup fresh snow peas, trimmed and cut into thirds**
> **1/2 cup chopped sweet red pepper**
> **1 green onion, chopped**
> **1/4 cup reduced-fat sesame ginger salad dressing**
> **1/2 cup chow mein noodles**

In a large bowl, combine the first six ingredients. Drizzle with dressing and toss to coat. Just before serving, sprinkle with chow mein noodles. **Yield:** 8 servings.

In a large bowl, combine the tuna, apple, celery, raisins, dates and walnuts. Combine yogurt and mayonnaise; add to tuna mixture and toss to coat. Serve on lettuce-lined plates; sprinkle with the cheese. **Yield:** 4 servings.

Grilled Three-Potato Salad

(Pictured below)

PREP: 25 min. **GRILL:** 10 min.

Everyone in our extended family loves to cook, so I assembled our favorite recipes in a cookbook to be handed down from generation to generation. This recipe comes from the cookbook. It's a delicious twist on traditional potato salad.
—*Suzette Jury, Keene, California*

- 3/4 **pound Yukon Gold potatoes (about 3 medium)**
- 3/4 **pound red potatoes (about 3 medium)**
- 1 **medium sweet potato, peeled**
- 1/2 **cup thinly sliced green onions**
- 1/4 **cup canola oil**
- 2 to 3 **tablespoons white wine vinegar**
- 1 **tablespoon Dijon mustard**
- 1 **teaspoon salt**
- 1/2 **teaspoon celery seed**
- 1/4 **teaspoon pepper**

Place all of the potatoes in a Dutch oven; cover with water. Bring to a boil. Reduce heat; cover and simmer for 15-20 minutes or until tender. Drain and rinse in cold water. Cut into 1-in. chunks.

Place the potatoes in a grill wok or basket. Grill, uncovered, over medium heat for 8-12 minutes or browned, stirring frequently. Transfer to a large salad bowl; add onions.

In a small bowl, whisk the oil, vinegar, mustard, salt, celery seed and pepper. Drizzle over the potato mixture and toss to coat. Serve warm or at room temperature. **Yield:** 6 servings.

Poppy Seed Fruit Salad

(Pictured above)

PREP/TOTAL TIME: 15 min.

Toasted almonds add a nice crunch to this pretty salad that's always a hit when I serve it. It's refreshing and goes with just about anything. The sweet–tart dressing can be used with any combination of fruits. —*Edie DeSpain, Logan, Utah*

- 1/4 **cup honey**
- 1/4 **cup limeade concentrate**
- 2 **teaspoons poppy seeds**
- 1 **cup halved fresh strawberries**
- 1 **cup cubed fresh pineapple**
- 1 **cup fresh blueberries**
- 1 **cup cubed seedless watermelon**
- 1/4 **cup slivered almonds, toasted**

In a small bowl, combine the honey, limeade concentrate and poppy seeds. In a serving bowl, combine the fruit. Drizzle with dressing; toss gently to coat. Sprinkle with the almonds. Serve with a slotted spoon. **Yield:** 6 servings.

Waldorf Tuna Salad

PREP/TOTAL TIME: 20 min.

I dress up tuna salad deliciously with apple, raisins, dates and walnuts...then drizzle it all with a tangy yogurt dressing.
—*Shirley Glaab, Hattiesburg, Mississippi*

- 2 **cans (6 ounces** *each***) light water-packed tuna, drained and flaked**
- 1 **large red apple, chopped**
- 1/3 **cup chopped celery**
- 1/3 **cup raisins**
- 1/3 **cup chopped dates**
- 1/4 **cup chopped walnuts**
- 1/2 **cup fat-free plain yogurt**
- 1/4 **cup reduced-fat mayonnaise**
- 4 **lettuce leaves**
- 1/4 **cup shredded reduced-fat Monterey Jack cheese**

Soups & Sandwiches

Satisfying soups and hearty sandwiches await you! They're sure to solicit plenty of smiles and compliments.

IT'S CHOW TIME. Clockwise from upper left: Minestrone with Italian Sausage (p. 43), Pizza Meatball Subs (p. 48), Danish Turkey Dumpling Soup (p. 54), Blue Cheese Clubs (p. 43) and pictured center, Firecracker Burgers (p. 55).

Turkey Muffuletta

(Pictured above)

PREP: 30 min. + chilling

You have to resist the temptation to eat this impressive, multi-layered sandwich immediately! It needs to "rest" at least 30 minutes in the refrigerator to allow the flavors to meld, but it's worth the wait. —Gilda Lester, Wilmington, North Carolina

- 1 loaf (1 pound) Italian bread
- 1/3 cup olive oil
- 3 tablespoons balsamic vinegar
- 1 tablespoon minced fresh basil *or* 1 teaspoon dried basil
- 1 garlic clove, minced
- 1/2 teaspoon salt
- 1/4 teaspoon crushed red pepper flakes
- 3/4 pound sliced deli turkey
- 6 ounces provolone cheese, thinly sliced
- 1 jar (7 ounces) roasted sweet red peppers, drained and sliced
- 1/2 cup sliced pimiento-stuffed olives
- 1 large tomato, sliced
- 3 tablespoons shredded Romano cheese
- 1 tablespoon minced fresh oregano *or* 1 teaspoon dried oregano
- 1/4 teaspoon pepper

Cut bread in half lengthwise; carefully hollow out top and bottom, leaving a 1-in. shell (discard removed bread or save for another use).

In a small bowl, combine the oil, vinegar, basil, garlic, salt and pepper flakes; brush over cut sides of bread. In the bottom bread shell, layer the turkey, provolone cheese, red peppers, olives and tomato. Sprinkle with Romano cheese, oregano and pepper. Replace bread top.

Wrap in plastic wrap; refrigerate for 30 minutes. Cut into slices. **Yield:** 6 servings.

Southwestern Turkey Soup

PREP: 20 min. **COOK:** 30 min.

This spicy soup is loaded with turkey, beans, corn and tomatoes. We like it really spicy and hot, so we tend to use all three tablespoons of jalapenos…and then some. It's so good on a wintry Midwestern day. —Brenda Kruse, Ames, Iowa

- 1 medium onion, chopped
- 1 tablespoon olive oil
- 1 can (14-1/2 ounces) chicken broth
- 2 to 3 tablespoons diced jalapeno pepper
- 3 teaspoons ground cumin
- 1-1/2 teaspoons chili powder
- 1/4 teaspoon salt
- 1/4 teaspoon cayenne pepper
- 3 cups cubed cooked turkey
- 1 can (15 ounces) black beans, rinsed and drained
- 1 can (10 ounces) diced tomatoes and green chilies, undrained
- 1-1/2 cups frozen corn

In a large saucepan, saute the onion in olive oil until tender. Stir in the chicken broth, jalapeno, cumin, chili powder, salt and cayenne. Add the turkey, beans, tomatoes and corn.

Bring to a boil. Reduce heat; cover and simmer for 20-30 minutes or until heated through. Garnish with sour cream, tortilla chips, cheese and olives if desired. **Yield:** 7 servings.

Editor's Note: When cutting hot peppers, disposable gloves are recommended. Avoid touching your face.

Spanish Gazpacho

PREP: 30 min. + chilling

There's a bounty of vegetables in this tantalizing chilled soup. Its refreshing flavor makes it an ideal addition to summer luncheons or light suppers. —Dave Schmitt, Hartland, Wisconsin

- 5 pounds tomatoes, peeled and quartered
- 3 medium carrots, quartered
- 1 large cucumber, peeled and quartered
- 1 large sweet red pepper, quartered
- 1 large green pepper, quartered
- 1 sweet onion, quartered
- 2 garlic cloves, minced
- 1/3 cup olive oil
- 3 tablespoons balsamic vinegar
- 1-1/2 teaspoons salt
- 1/2 teaspoon pepper

In batches, place all of the ingredients in a blender or food processor; cover and blend or process until the soup reaches desired consistency. Pour into a large bowl. Cover and refrigerate for 1-2 hours before serving. **Yield:** 12 servings (3 quarts).

Return to a boil. Stir in the garbanzo beans, pasta and parsley. Cook for 6-9 minutes or until the pasta is tender. Serve with Parmesan cheese. **Yield:** 11 servings (about 3 quarts).

Blue Cheese Clubs

(Pictured below and on page 40)

PREP/TOTAL TIME: 25 min.

These sandwiches look so elegant, but they're really easy to make. They're loaded with plenty of turkey, and the blue cheese spread offers a nice zip. —*Nancy Jo Leffler, DePauw, Indiana*

> 1 package (3 ounces) cream cheese, softened
> 1/2 cup crumbled blue cheese
> 4 tablespoons mayonnaise, *divided*
> 1 teaspoon dried minced onion

Dash salt and pepper
Dash Worcestershire sauce

> 8 slices white bread, toasted
> 8 slices tomato
> 8 slices deli turkey
> 4 slices Swiss cheese
> 4 slices whole wheat bread, toasted
> 8 bacon strips, cooked
> 4 lettuce leaves

In a small bowl, beat cream cheese. Add blue cheese, 1 tablespoon mayonnaise, onion, salt, pepper and Worcestershire sauce; beat until combined.

Spread over four slices of white bread; layer with tomato, turkey, Swiss cheese, wheat bread, bacon and lettuce. Spread remaining mayonnaise over remaining white bread; place over lettuce. Secure with toothpicks; cut into triangles. **Yield:** 4 servings.

Minestrone With Italian Sausage

(Pictured above and on page 40)

PREP: 25 min. **COOK:** 1 hour

I make this zippy, satisfying soup all the time, and it's my dad's favorite. The recipe makes a lot, and I have found that it freezes well and tastes just as great reheated.

—*Linda Reis, Salem, Oregon*

> 1 pound bulk Italian sausage
> 1 large onion, chopped
> 2 large carrots, chopped
> 2 celery ribs, chopped
> 1 medium leek (white portion only), chopped
> 3 garlic cloves, minced
> 1 medium zucchini, cut into 1/2-inch pieces
> 1/4 pound fresh green beans, trimmed and cut into 1/2-inch pieces
> 6 cups beef broth
> 2 cans (14-1/2 ounces *each*) diced tomatoes with basil, oregano and garlic
> 3 cups shredded cabbage
> 1 teaspoon dried basil
> 1 teaspoon dried oregano
> 1/4 teaspoon pepper
> 1 can (15 ounces) garbanzo beans *or* chickpeas, rinsed and drained
> 1/2 cup uncooked small pasta shells
> 3 tablespoons minced fresh parsley
> 1/3 cup grated Parmesan cheese

In a soup kettle, cook sausage and onion over medium heat until meat is no longer pink; drain. Stir in the carrots, celery, leek and garlic; cook for 3 minutes. Add zucchini and green beans; cook 2 minutes longer.

Stir in broth, tomatoes, cabbage, basil, oregano and pepper. Bring to a boil. Reduce heat; cover and simmer for 45 minutes.

Colony Mountain Chili

(Pictured below)

PREP: 25 min.   **COOK:** 6 hours

My husband created this chili for a local cooking contest, and it won the People's Choice award. It's loaded with beef, Italian sausage, tomatoes and beans and seasoned with chili powder, cumin and red pepper flakes for zip.
—Marjorie O'Dell, Bow, Washington

- 1 pound boneless beef sirloin steak, cut into 3/4-inch cubes
- 4 Italian sausage links, casings removed and cut into 3/4-inch slices
- 2 tablespoons olive oil, *divided*
- 1 medium onion, chopped
- 3 garlic cloves, minced
- 2 green onions, thinly sliced
- 2 teaspoons beef bouillon granules
- 1 cup boiling water
- 1 can (6 ounces) tomato paste
- 3 tablespoons chili powder
- 2 tablespoons brown sugar
- 2 tablespoons Worcestershire sauce
- 2 teaspoons ground cumin
- 1 to 2 teaspoons crushed red pepper flakes
- 1 teaspoon salt
- 1/2 teaspoon pepper
- 3 cans (14-1/2 ounces *each*) stewed tomatoes, cut up
- 2 cans (15 ounces *each*) pinto beans, rinsed and drained

Shredded cheddar cheese

In a large skillet, brown the beef and sausage in 1 tablespoon oil; drain. Transfer meat to a 5-qt. slow cooker. In the same skillet, saute the onion, garlic and green onions in remaining oil until tender. Transfer to slow cooker.

In a small bowl, dissolve bouillon in water. Stir in the tomato paste, chili powder, brown sugar, Worcestershire sauce and seasonings until blended; add to slow cooker. Stir in tomatoes and beans. Cover and cook on high for 6-8 hours or until the meat is tender. Serve with cheese if desired. **Yield:** 10 servings.

Swiss Tuna Melts

(Pictured above)

PREP/TOTAL TIME: 20 min.

We like Swiss Tuna Melts served with homemade vegetable soup. You'll love the crunch that celery gives to the creamy tuna filling.
—Karen Owen, Rising Sun, Indiana

- 1 can (6 ounces) light water-packed tuna, drained and flaked
- 3/4 cup shredded Swiss cheese
- 1/2 cup sour cream
- 1/2 cup mayonnaise
- 1/4 cup chopped onion
- 1/4 cup chopped celery

Pepper to taste

- 8 slices bread
- 2 to 3 tablespoons butter, softened

In a bowl, combine the first seven ingredients. Spread over four slices of bread, about 1/2 cup on each; top with remaining bread. Butter the outsides of sandwiches.

On a griddle or in a large skillet over medium heat, grill sandwiches for 4-5 minutes on each side or until lightly toasted. **Yield:** 4 servings.

Chunky Taco Soup

PREP: 20 min.   **COOK:** 20 min.

I've gotten great response at our church dinners and senior groups whenever I bring this easy-to-fix soup. I usually take home an empty pot and often receive requests for the recipe.
—Evelyn Buford, Belton, Missouri

- **1-1/2 pounds boneless beef sirloin *or* round steak, cut into 3/4-inch cubes**

- 1 **medium onion, chopped**
- 1 **tablespoon olive oil**
- 2 **cans (15 ounces *each*) pinto beans, rinsed and drained**
- 2 **cans (14-1/2 ounces *each*) diced tomatoes and green chilies, undrained**
- 2 **cups water**
- 1 **can (15 ounces) black beans, rinsed and drained**
- 1 **can (14-3/4 ounces) cream-style corn**
- 1 **envelope ranch salad dressing mix**
- 1 **envelope taco seasoning**
- 1/4 **cup minced fresh cilantro**

In a large kettle or Dutch oven, brown beef and onion in oil. Add the pinto beans, tomatoes, water, black beans, corn, salad dressing mix and taco seasoning. Bring to a boil. Reduce heat; cover and simmer for 20-30 minutes or until the meat is tender. Sprinkle with cilantro. **Yield:** 12 servings (about 3 quarts).

Lemony Chicken Soup

(Pictured below)

PREP: 5 min. **COOK:** 30 min.

While living in California, I enjoyed a delicious chicken–lemon soup at a local restaurant. When I returned to Texas, I longed for it but never came across a recipe. I experimented with many versions before creating this one.
—Brenda Tollett, San Antonio, Texas

- 1/3 **cup butter, cubed**
- 3/4 **cup all-purpose flour**
- 6 **cups chicken broth, *divided***
- 1 **cup milk**
- 1 **cup half-and-half cream**
- 1-1/2 **cups cubed cooked chicken**
- 1 **tablespoon lemon juice**
- 1/2 **teaspoon salt**
- 1/8 **teaspoon pepper**

Dash ground nutmeg
- 8 **lemon slices**

In a soup kettle or large saucepan, melt butter. Stir in flour until smooth; gradually add 2 cups broth, milk and cream. Bring to a boil; cook and stir for 2 minutes or until thickened.

Stir in the chicken, lemon juice, salt, pepper, nutmeg and remaining broth. Cook over medium heat until heated through, stirring occasionally. Garnish each serving with a lemon slice. **Yield:** 8 servings (2 quarts).

Apple and Prosciutto Sandwiches

(Pictured above)

PREP/TOTAL TIME: 20 min.

Prepared on an indoor grill, these Italian–style sandwiches are spread with a homemade rosemary pesto. They're wonderful on a cool day with a bowl of butternut squash soup.
—Elizabeth Bennett, Mill Creek, Washington

- 1/4 **cup olive oil**
- 1/2 **cup chopped walnuts**
- 2 **tablespoons grated Parmesan cheese**
- 2 **tablespoons minced fresh rosemary**
- 1 **loaf (12 ounces) focaccia bread**
- 8 **thin slices prosciutto**
- 1 **medium apple, sliced**
- 6 **ounces Brie cheese, rind removed and sliced**

In a blender, combine the oil, walnuts, Parmesan cheese and rosemary; cover and process until blended and nuts are finely chopped. With a bread knife, split focaccia into two horizontal layers. Spread rosemary mixture over cut sides of bread.

On bottom of bread, layer prosciutto, apple and Brie; replace bread top. Cut into quarters.

Cook on an indoor grill for 2-3 minutes or until bread is browned and cheese is melted. To serve, cut each wedge in half. **Yield:** 8 servings.

Warming Winter Squash

Grand Prize Winner

Black Bean and Pumpkin Chili

PREP: 20 min. **COOK:** 4 hours

Our family loves this slow-cooked recipe, especially on cold days. It's a wonderful variation on standard chili that freezes well and tastes even better as leftovers.
—Deborah Vliet, Holland, Michigan

- 1 medium onion, chopped
- 1 medium sweet yellow pepper, chopped
- 3 garlic cloves, minced
- 2 tablespoons olive oil
- 3 cups chicken broth
- 2 cans (15 ounces *each*) black beans, rinsed and drained
- 2-1/2 cups cubed cooked turkey
- 1 can (15 ounces) solid-pack pumpkin
- 1 can (14-1/2 ounces) diced tomatoes, undrained
- 2 teaspoons dried parsley flakes
- 2 teaspoons chili powder
- 1-1/2 teaspoons dried oregano
- 1-1/2 teaspoons ground cumin
- 1/2 teaspoon salt

In a large skillet, saute the onion, yellow pepper and garlic in oil until tender. Transfer to a 5-qt. slow cooker; stir in the remaining ingredients.

Cover and cook on low for 4-5 hours or until heated through. **Yield:** 10 servings (2-1/2 quarts).

Garlic Butternut Bisque

(Pictured above right)

PREP: 40 min. **COOK:** 30 min.

With its pleasant squash and garlic flavor and golden-orange color, this rich and creamy soup is sure to be a hit whether you serve it for an everyday meal or a holiday dinner.
—Della Clarke, Vista, California

- 2 whole garlic bulbs
- 1 teaspoon olive oil

Colorful Chicken And Squash Soup

(Pictured above)

PREP: 25 min. **COOK:** 1-1/2 hours

When I turned 40, I decided to live a healthier lifestyle, which included cooking healthier for my family. I make this nutritious soup every week, and everyone loves it.
—Trina Bigham, Fairhaven, Massachusetts

- 1 broiler/fryer chicken (4 pounds), cut up
- 13 cups water
- 5 pounds butternut squash, peeled and cubed (about 10 cups)
- 1-1/4 pounds fresh kale, chopped
- 6 medium carrots, chopped
- 2 large onions, chopped
- 3 teaspoons salt

Place chicken and water in a soup kettle. Bring to a boil. Reduce heat; cover and simmer for 1 hour or until chicken is tender.

Remove chicken from broth. Strain broth and skim fat. Return broth to the pan; add the squash, kale, carrots and onions. Bring to a boil. Reduce heat; cover and simmer for 25-30 minutes or until vegetables are tender.

When chicken is cool enough to handle, remove meat from bones and cut into bite-size pieces. Discard bones and skin. Add chicken and salt to soup; heat through. **Yield:** 14 servings (5-1/2 quarts).

3 large onions, chopped
3/4 cup chopped carrots
3/4 cup butter, *divided*
1/2 cup chopped celery
4 pounds butternut squash, peeled, seeded and cubed (about 8 cups)
6 cups chicken broth
3 tablespoons chopped fresh sage, *divided*
1/2 cup plus 1 tablespoon heavy whipping cream, *divided*
1-1/2 teaspoons salt
1/4 teaspoon pepper

Remove papery outer skin from garlic (do not peel or separate cloves). Cut tops off bulbs; brush with oil. Wrap each in heavy-duty foil. Bake at 425° for 30-35 minutes or until softened. Cool 10-15 minutes.

Meanwhile, in a Dutch oven or soup kettle, saute the onions carrots and celery in 1/2 cup butter until tender. Add the squash, broth and 2 tablespoons sage. Bring to a boil. Reduce heat; simmer, uncovered, for 25-30 minutes or until squash is tender.

Squeeze softened garlic into a small bowl; mash with a fork. Stir into squash mixture. Cool slightly. Puree squash mixture in batches in a blender; return to pan. Stir in 1/2 cup cream, salt and pepper and remaining butter; heat through.

Garnish with remaining cream and sage. **Yield:** 9 servings (3 quarts).

Gingered Butternut Squash Soup

(Pictured below)

PREP: 35 min. **COOK:** 40 min.

Roasting the squash really adds a wonderful flavor to this delightful pureed soup. If you want a true vegetarian dish, simply substitute vegetable stock for the chicken broth.
—*Kim Pettipas*
Oromocto, New Brunswick

4 **pounds butternut squash, peeled and cubed (about 8 cups)**
6 **teaspoons olive oil, *divided***
1 **large onion, chopped**
2 **tablespoons butter**
1 **tablespoon minced fresh gingerroot**
2-1/2 **teaspoons curry powder**
3/4 **teaspoon salt**
1/4 **teaspoon pepper**
3 **large potatoes, peeled and cubed**
6 **cups chicken broth**
1-1/2 **cups milk**
Sour cream, optional

Place the butternut squash in a greased 15-in. x 10-in. x 1-in. baking pan. Drizzle with 4-1/2 teaspoons oil; toss to coat. Bake, uncovered, at 450° for 30 minutes, stirring every 15 minutes. Bake 5-10 minutes longer or until tender. Set aside.

In a soup kettle, saute onion in butter and remaining oil for 5 minutes or until tender. Stir in the ginger, curry, salt and pepper; cook for 2 minutes. Stir in potatoes; cook 2 minutes longer. Stir in broth. Bring to a boil. Reduce heat; cover and simmer for 15-20 minutes or until potatoes are tender. Cool slightly.

Stir in reserved squash. In a blender, puree soup in batches until smooth. Return to the pan. Stir in milk; heat through. Garnish with sour cream if desired. **Yield:** 9 servings (about 3 quarts).

Italian Wedding Soup

(Pictured above)

PREP: 30 min. **COOK:** 45 min.

I enjoyed a similar soup for lunch at work one day and decided to re–create it at home. I love the combination of meatballs, vegetables and pasta.
—Noelle Myers, Grand Forks, North Dakota

- 2 **eggs, lightly beaten**
- 1/2 **cup seasoned bread crumbs**
- 1 **pound ground beef**
- 1 **pound bulk Italian sausage**
- 3 **medium carrots, sliced**
- 3 **celery ribs, diced**
- 1 **large onion, chopped**
- 3 **garlic cloves, minced**
- 4-1/2 **teaspoons olive oil**
- 4 **cans (14-1/2 ounces *each*) reduced-sodium chicken broth**
- 2 **cans (14-1/2 ounces *each*) beef broth**
- 1 **package (10 ounces) frozen chopped spinach, thawed and squeezed dry**
- 1/4 **cup minced fresh basil**
- 1 **envelope onion soup mix**
- 4-1/2 **teaspoons ketchup**
- 1/2 **teaspoon dried thyme**
- 3 **bay leaves**
- 1-1/2 **cups uncooked penne pasta**

In a large bowl, combine eggs and bread crumbs. Crumble beef and sausage over mixture; mix well. Shape into 3/4-in. balls.

Place the meatballs on a greased rack in a foil-lined 15-in. x 10-in. x 1-in. baking pan. Bake at 350° for 15-18 minutes or until no longer pink. Meanwhile, in a soup kettle or Dutch oven, saute carrots, celery, onion and garlic in oil until tender. Stir in the broth, spinach, basil, soup mix, ketchup, thyme and bay leaves.

Drain meatballs on paper towels. Bring soup to a boil; add meatballs. Reduce heat; simmer, uncovered, for 30 minutes. Add pasta; cook 13-15 minutes longer or until tender, stirring occasionally. Discard bay leaves before serving. **Yield:** 10 servings (2-1/2 quarts).

Pizza Meatball Subs

(Pictured below and on page 41)

PREP: 30 min. **BAKE:** 25 min.

I made these sandwiches one evening for my family, and they were a huge hit with everyone, including the picky eaters. There's plenty of sauce and cheese to complement the baked meatballs.
—Heather Begin, Athens, Maine

- 1 **egg, lightly beaten**
- 1/3 **cup steak sauce**
- 1 **cup crushed saltines**
- 1 **teaspoon onion powder**
- 1/4 **teaspoon seasoned salt**
- 1/8 **teaspoon pepper**
- 1-1/2 **pounds ground beef**
- 6 to 7 **tablespoons mayonnaise**
- 6 to 7 **submarine buns, split**
- 9 to 11 **slices process American cheese, cut into strips**
- 1 **jar (14 ounces) pizza sauce**
- 2 **cups (8 ounces) shredded part-skim mozzarella cheese**

In a large bowl, combine the egg, steak sauce, saltines, onion powder, salt and pepper. Crumble beef over mixture and mix well. Shape into 1-1/2-in. balls.

Place meatballs on a greased rack in a shallow baking pan. Bake at 375° for 20-25 minutes or until no longer pink. Drain on paper towels.

Spread mayonnaise over bun bottoms; top each with American cheese, 1 tablespoon pizza sauce, meatballs and remaining pizza sauce. Sprinkle with mozzarella cheese. Place on a baking sheet. Bake for 5-10 minutes or until cheese is melted. **Yield:** 6-7 servings.

in tomatoes, tomato sauce, vinegar, Worcestershire sauce, garlic and oregano. Bring to a boil. Reduce heat; cover and simmer for 1 hour.

Stir in the remaining ingredients. Bring to a boil. Reduce heat; cover and simmer for 1 hour or until the meat and vegetables are tender. **Yield:** 8 servings (about 2-1/2 quarts).

Roasted Yellow Pepper Soup

(Pictured below)

PREP: 25 min. **COOK:** 40 min.

We got this recipe from a good friend and Merchant Marine in New Hampshire. My husband and our two small children liked it so much that I grew my own yellow pepper plants just to prepare it. We enjoy the soup in the middle of summer as well as on cool fall days. —*Amy Spurrier, Wellsburg, West Virginia*

- 6 large sweet yellow peppers
- 1 large onion, chopped
- 1 cup chopped leeks (white portion only)
- 1/4 cup butter, cubed
- 3 small potatoes, peeled and cubed
- 5 cups chicken broth
- 1/2 teaspoon salt
- 1/2 teaspoon pepper

Shredded Parmesan cheese, optional

Halve peppers; remove and discard tops and seeds. Broil peppers 4 in. from the heat until skins blister, about 4 minutes. Immediately place peppers in a bowl; cover and let stand for 15-20 minutes.

Meanwhile, in a large saucepan, saute onion and leeks in butter until tender. Add the potatoes, broth, salt and pepper. Bring to a boil. Reduce heat; cover and simmer for 30 minutes or until potatoes are tender.

Peel off and discard charred skin from peppers. Finely chop peppers; add to potato mixture. Cool slightly.

In a blender, cover and process the soup in batches until smooth. Return to the pan; heat through (do not boil). Serve with Parmesan cheese if desired. **Yield:** 8 cups (2 quarts).

Hearty Beef Vegetable Soup

(Pictured above)

PREP: 20 min. **COOK:** 2 hours

This stew–like soup is loaded with nutritious ingredients but is easy to prepare. It gets its kick from green chilies. I like to make wonderful bread and breadsticks to serve with it. —*Sherman Snowball, Salt Lake City, Utah*

- 3 tablespoons all-purpose flour
- 1/2 teaspoon salt
- 1/4 teaspoon pepper
- 1 pound beef stew meat, cut into 1/2-inch cubes
- 2 tablespoons olive oil
- 1 can (14-1/2 ounces) Italian diced tomatoes
- 1 can (8 ounces) tomato sauce
- 2 tablespoons red wine vinegar
- 2 tablespoons Worcestershire sauce
- 3 garlic cloves, minced
- 1 teaspoon dried oregano
- 3 cups hot water
- 4 medium potatoes, peeled and cubed
- 6 medium carrots, sliced
- 2 medium turnips, peeled and cubed
- 1 medium zucchini, halved lengthwise and sliced
- 1 medium green pepper, julienned
- 1 cup sliced fresh mushrooms
- 1 medium onion, chopped
- 1 can (4 ounces) chopped green chilies
- 2 tablespoons sugar

In a large resealable plastic bag, combine the flour, salt and pepper. Add beef, a few pieces at a time, and shake to coat.

In a soup kettle or Dutch oven, brown beef in oil. Stir

Cheeseburger Paradise Soup

(Pictured above)

PREP: 30 min. **COOK:** 25 min.

I've never met a person who didn't enjoy this creamy soup, and it's hearty enough to serve as a main course with your favorite bread or rolls. —Nadina Ladimarco, Burton, Ohio

- 6 medium potatoes, peeled and cubed
- 1 small carrot, grated
- 1 small onion, chopped
- 1/2 cup chopped green pepper
- 2 tablespoons chopped seeded jalapeno pepper
- 3 cups water
- 2 tablespoons plus 2 teaspoons beef bouillon granules
- 2 garlic cloves, minced
- 1/8 teaspoon pepper
- 2 pounds ground beef
- 1/2 pound sliced fresh mushrooms
- 2 tablespoons butter
- 5 cups milk, *divided*
- 6 tablespoons all-purpose flour
- 1 package (16 ounces) process cheese (Velveeta), cubed

Crumbled cooked bacon

In a soup kettle, combine the first nine ingredients; bring to a boil. Reduce heat; cover and simmer for 15-20 minutes or until potatoes are tender.

Meanwhile, in a large skillet, cook beef and mushrooms in butter over medium heat until meat is no longer pink; drain. Add to soup. Stir in 4 cups milk; heat through.

In a small bowl, combine flour and remaining milk until smooth; gradually stir into soup. Bring to a boil; cook and stir for 2 minutes or until thickened. Reduce heat; stir in cheese until melted. Garnish with bacon.
Yield: 14 servings (about 3-1/2 quarts).

Editor's Note: When cutting hot peppers, disposable gloves are recommended. Avoid touching your face.

Asparagus Leek Chowder

PREP/TOTAL TIME: 20 min.

To us, asparagus is the taste of spring. So when this thick, creamy chowder is on the table, we know spring has arrived. —Elisabeth Harders, West Allis, Wisconsin

- 1 pound fresh asparagus, trimmed and cut into 1-inch pieces
- 3 cups sliced fresh mushrooms
- 3 large leeks (white portion only), sliced
- 6 tablespoons butter
- 1/4 cup all-purpose flour
- 1/2 teaspoon salt

Dash pepper
- 2 cups chicken broth
- 2 cups half-and-half cream
- 1 can (11 ounces) whole kernel corn, drained
- 1 tablespoon chopped pimientos

In a large saucepan, saute the asparagus, mushrooms and leeks in butter for 10 minutes or until tender. Stir in the flour, salt and pepper until blended.

Gradually stir in broth and cream. Bring to a boil. Reduce heat; cook and stir for 2 minutes or until thickened. Stir in corn and pimientos; heat through.
Yield: 7 servings.

Cheesy Corn Chowder

PREP: 30 min. **COOK:** 30 min.

I've had this chowder recipe for 30 years, and the whole family really enjoys its cheesy, corn taste. It makes a big pot—enough for seconds! —Lola Comer, Marysville, Washington

- 6 bacon strips, chopped
- 3/4 cup chopped sweet onion
- 2-1/2 cups water
- 2-1/2 cups cubed peeled potatoes
- 2 cups sliced fresh carrots
- 2 teaspoons chicken bouillon granules
- 3 cans (11 ounces *each*) gold and white corn, drained
- 1/2 teaspoon pepper
- 7 tablespoons all-purpose flour
- 5 cups milk
- 3 cups (12 ounces) shredded cheddar cheese
- 1 cup cubed process cheese (Velveeta)

In a Dutch oven, cook bacon and onion over medium heat until onion is tender. Add the water, potatoes, carrots and bouillon; bring to a boil. Reduce heat; cover and simmer for 15-20 minutes or until potatoes are tender.

Stir in corn and pepper. In a large bowl, whisk flour and milk until smooth; add to soup. Bring to a boil; cook and stir for 2 minutes or until thickened. Reduce heat. Add the cheeses; cook and stir until cheeses are melted.
Yield: 15 servings (3-3/4 quarts).

two slices of cheese; top with remaining bread. Cook sandwiches for 2-4 minutes on each side or until golden brown. **Yield:** 4 servings (2 cups relish).

Land of Enchantment Posole

(Pictured below)

PREP: 30 min. **COOK:** 1 hour

My family named this spicy soup after our state moniker, "New Mexico, Land of Enchantment." We usually make it around the Christmas holiday when we have lots of family over...and we never have leftovers. —Suzanne Caldwell, Artesia, New Mexico

- 1-1/2 **pounds pork stew meat, cut into 3/4-inch cubes**
- 1 **large onion, chopped**
- 2 **garlic cloves, minced**
- 2 **tablespoons canola oil**
- 3 **cups beef broth**
- 2 **cans (15-1/2 ounces *each*) hominy, rinsed and drained**
- 2 **cans (4 ounces *each*) chopped green chilies**
- 1 **to 2 jalapeno peppers, seeded and chopped, optional**
- 1/2 **teaspoon salt**
- 1/2 **teaspoon ground cumin**
- 1/2 **teaspoon dried oregano**
- 1/4 **teaspoon pepper**
- 1/4 **teaspoon cayenne pepper**
- 1/2 **cup minced fresh cilantro**

Tortilla strips, optional

In a soup kettle or Dutch oven, cook the pork, onion and garlic in oil over medium heat until meat is no longer pink; drain. Stir in the broth, hominy, chilies, jalapeno if desired, salt, cumin, oregano, pepper and cayenne.

Bring to a boil. Reduce heat; cover and simmer for 45-60 minutes or until meat is tender. Stir in cilantro. Serve with tortilla strips if desired. **Yield:** 5 servings.

Editor's Note: When cutting hot peppers, disposable gloves are recommended. Avoid touching your face.

Cuban Pork Sandwiches

(Pictured above)

PREP: 30 min. + marinating **BAKE:** 25 min. + standing

Seasoned pork, red and green peppers and mozzarella cheese come together in this satisfying sandwich recipe. To make it even more substantial, sometimes I add bread crumbs and Italian seasoning to the meat and vegetables. —Connie Zangla, Annadale, Minnesota

- 1 **small red onion, thinly sliced**
- 1 **cup water**
- 1 **jar (7 ounces) roasted sweet red peppers, drained and chopped**
- 1/3 **cup cider vinegar**
- 2 **garlic cloves, peeled and halved**
- 1/2 **teaspoon dried oregano**
- 1/4 **teaspoon salt**
- 1/4 **teaspoon pepper**
- 1/4 **teaspoon ground cumin**

SANDWICH:
- 1 **garlic clove, minced**
- 1 **teaspoon ground cumin**
- 1/2 **teaspoon salt**
- 1 **pork tenderloin (about 1 pound)**
- 1 **teaspoon olive oil**
- 8 **slices sourdough bread**
- 8 **slices Swiss cheese**

For the relish, in a small saucepan over medium heat, bring onion and water to a boil. Cook and stir for 1 minute; drain. Transfer to a bowl; add the roasted peppers, vinegar, garlic, oregano, salt, pepper and cumin. Let stand at room temperature for 1 hour. Discard garlic. (The relish can be made ahead and stored in the refrigerator for up to 1 week.)

For the sandwich, in a small bowl, mash the minced garlic, cumin and salt. Rub over tenderloin; place in a shallow baking pan. Bake, uncovered, at 425° for 25-30 minutes or until a meat thermometer reads 160°. Let stand for 10 minutes; thinly slice pork.

Heat oil in a large skillet over medium heat. Top four slices of bread with pork, desired amount of relish and

Chicken Soup With Potato Dumplings

(Pictured below)

PREP: 25 min.   **COOK:** 40 min.

Our family calls this comforting, old-fashioned soup our "Sunday dinner soup" because it's almost a complete dinner in a bowl. You'll love the flavor!

—*Marie McConnell, Shelbyville, Illinois*

- 1/4 cup chopped onion
- 2 garlic cloves, minced
- 1 tablespoon canola oil
- 6 cups chicken broth
- 2 cups cubed cooked chicken
- 2 celery ribs, chopped
- 2 medium carrots, sliced
- 1/4 teaspoon dried sage leaves

DUMPLINGS:
- 1-1/2 cups biscuit/baking mix
- 1 cup cold mashed potatoes (with added milk)
- 1/4 cup milk
- 1 tablespoon chopped green onion
- 1/8 teaspoon pepper

In a large saucepan, saute onion and garlic in oil for 3-4 minutes or until onion is tender. Stir in the broth, chicken, celery, carrots and sage. Bring to a boil. Reduce heat; cover and simmer for 10-15 minutes or until vegetables are tender.

In a small bowl, combine the dumpling ingredients. Drop heaping tablespoonfuls of batter onto simmering soup. Cover and simmer for 20 minutes or until a toothpick inserted in a dumpling comes out clean (do not lift cover while simmering). **Yield:** 5 servings.

Black Bean Burgers

(Pictured above)

PREP/TOTAL TIME: 25 min.

My son encouraged me to come up with a good veggie burger for him, and he gave this recipe an AAA+! Not only are they moist and flavorful, but they're very easy to freeze. Now, like my son, I prefer them over traditional burgers.

—*Clara Honeyager, North Prairie, Wisconsin*

- 1 cup frozen mixed vegetables, thawed
- 1 small onion, chopped
- 1/2 cup chopped sweet red pepper
- 1 can (15 ounces) black beans, rinsed and drained, *divided*
- 1 tablespoon cornstarch
- 2 tablespoons cold water
- 1 cup mashed potato flakes
- 1/4 cup quick-cooking oats
- 3 tablespoons whole wheat flour
- 2 tablespoons nonfat dry milk powder
- 1 egg, lightly beaten
- 1/2 teaspoon salt
- 1/4 teaspoon pepper
- 4 teaspoons canola oil
- 6 kaiser rolls, split
- 2 cups shredded lettuce
- 3/4 cup salsa

In a large microwave-safe bowl, combine the mixed vegetables, onion and red pepper. Cover and microwave on high for 2 minutes.

Coarsely mash 3/4 cup of the black beans. In a bowl, combine the cornstarch and water until smooth; stir in the mashed beans, potato flakes, oats, flour, milk powder, egg, salt and pepper. Stir in the vegetable mixture and remaining black beans. Shape into six 5/8-in.-thick patties.

In a large nonstick skillet, cook patties in oil for 4-5 minutes on each side or until lightly browned. Serve on rolls with lettuce and salsa. **Yield:** 6 servings.

Editor's Note: This recipe was tested in a 1,100-watt microwave.

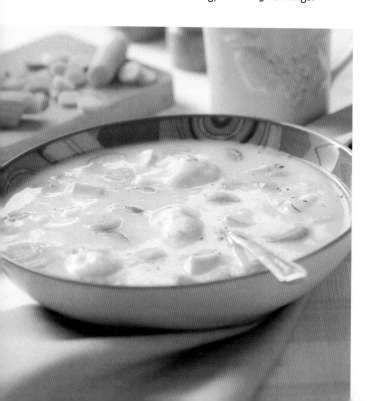

Golden Seafood Chowder

(Pictured below)

PREP: 25 min. **COOK:** 25 min.

Flavored with crab, shrimp and cheddar cheese, this chowder is so good that I make it weekly. Sometimes I substitute chicken or ham for the seafood and leave out the clam juice. Either way, this pretty soup is a winner. —Ami Paton, Waconia, Minnesota

- 1/2 cup finely chopped onion
- 1/4 cup butter, cubed
- 1 can (14-1/2 ounces) chicken broth
- 1 cup cubed peeled potato
- 2 celery ribs, chopped
- 2 medium carrots, chopped
- 1/4 cup Clamato juice
- 1/4 teaspoon lemon-pepper seasoning
- 1/4 cup all-purpose flour
- 2 cups milk
- 2 cups (8 ounces) shredded sharp cheddar cheese
- 1 can (6 ounces) crabmeat, drained, flaked and cartilage removed
- 1 cup cooked medium shrimp, peeled and deveined

In a large saucepan, saute the onion in butter until tender. Stir in the broth, potato, celery, carrots, Clamato juice and lemon-pepper seasoning. Bring to a boil. Reduce heat; cover and simmer for 15-20 minutes or until vegetables are tender.

In a small bowl, whisk the flour and milk together until smooth; add to soup. Bring to a boil; cook and stir for 2 minutes or until thickened. Reduce heat. Add the cheese, crab and shrimp; cook and stir until cheese is melted. **Yield:** 4 servings.

Buffalo Chicken Wraps

(Pictured above)

PREP/TOTAL TIME: 25 min.

Blue cheese dressing and hot pepper sauce enhance these yummy tortilla wraps. Filled with chicken, cheese, lettuce and tomatoes, they're colorful, fun to eat and easy to tote!
—Athena Russell, Florence, South Carolina

- 1 cup all-purpose flour
- 1 teaspoon salt
- 1/4 teaspoon pepper
- 1/2 cup buttermilk
- 4 boneless skinless chicken breast halves
- 1 cup canola oil
- 1/2 cup hot pepper sauce
- 1/4 cup butter, melted
- 4 spinach tortillas (10 inches)
- 1 cup shredded lettuce
- 1 cup (4 ounces) shredded cheddar cheese
- 2/3 cup chopped tomatoes
- 1/2 cup blue cheese salad dressing

In a shallow bowl, combine the flour, salt and pepper. Place buttermilk in another shallow bowl. Dip chicken in buttermilk, then roll in flour mixture.

In a large skillet, cook the chicken in oil for 8-10 minutes or until the juices run clear. Drain on paper towels; cut into strips.

In a bowl, combine the hot pepper sauce and butter. Dip chicken strips into mixture, coating both sides. Place chicken in the center of each tortilla. Layer with lettuce, cheese and tomatoes; drizzle with salad dressing. Bring up sides of tortillas; secure with toothpicks if desired. **Yield:** 4 servings.

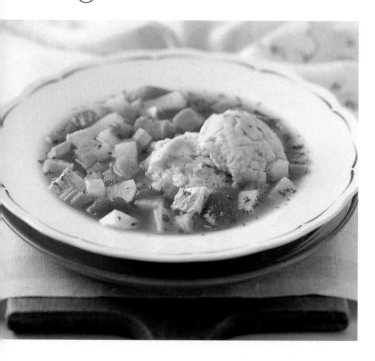

Danish Turkey Dumpling Soup

(Pictured above and on page 41)

PREP: 35 min. **COOK:** 3 hours

This recipe was handed down from my grandmother, who was a Danish caterer. My 100% Italian husband has come to expect this on chilly evenings because it not only warms the body but warms the heart as well.

—Karen Sue Garback–Pristera, Albany, New York

- 1 **leftover turkey carcass (from a 12- to 14-pound turkey)**
- 9 **cups water**
- 3 **teaspoons chicken bouillon granules**
- 1 **bay leaf**
- 1 **can (14-1/2 ounces) stewed tomatoes, cut up**
- 1 **medium turnip, peeled and diced**
- 2 **celery ribs, chopped**
- 1 **medium onion, chopped**
- 1 **medium carrot, chopped**
- 1/4 **cup minced fresh parsley**
- 1 **teaspoon salt**

DUMPLINGS:
- 1/2 **cup water**
- 1/4 **cup butter, cubed**
- 1/2 **cup all-purpose flour**
- 1 **teaspoon baking powder**
- 1/8 **teaspoon salt**
- 2 **eggs**
- 1 **tablespoon minced fresh parsley**

Place carcass, water, bouillon and bay leaf in a soup kettle. Bring to a boil. Reduce heat; cover and simmer for 1-1/2 hours.

Remove carcass. Strain broth and skim fat; discard bay leaf. Return broth to pan. Add the tomatoes, vegetables, parsley and salt. Remove turkey from bones and cut into bite-size pieces; add to soup. Discard bones. Bring to a boil. Reduce heat; cover and simmer for 25-30 minutes or until vegetables are crisp-tender.

For dumplings, in a large saucepan, bring water and butter to a boil. Combine the flour, baking powder and salt; add all at once to pan and stir until a smooth ball forms. Remove from heat; let stand for 5 minutes. Add eggs, one at a time, beating well after each addition. Continue beating until mixture is smooth and shiny. Stir in parsley.

Drop batter in 12 mounds onto simmering soup. Cover and simmer for 20 minutes or until a toothpick inserted in a dumpling comes out clean (do not lift cover while simmering). **Yield:** 6 servings (about 2 quarts).

Home Run Slugger Sub

(Pictured below)

PREP/TOTAL TIME: 15 min.

I trimmed a long loaf of French bread to make these hearty hoagies look like baseball bats. Than I stuffed them with cold cuts, veggies and cheese. —Cathy Runyon, Allendale, Michigan

- 1 **French bread baguette (1 pound and 20 inches long)**
- 1/4 **pound thinly sliced fully cooked ham**
- 1/4 **pound thinly sliced bologna**
- 1/4 **pound thinly sliced hard salami**
- 4 **romaine leaves**
- 6 **slices Swiss cheese**
- 6 **slices Colby cheese**
- 1 **medium tomato, sliced**

With a sharp knife, cut one end of the baguette into the shape of a baseball bat handle. Slice loaf in half lengthwise.

On the bottom half, layer the ham, bologna, salami, romaine, cheeses and tomato. Replace top. Secure with toothpicks if necessary. Cut into slices. **Yield:** 8 servings.

White Bean Chicken Chili

(Pictured below)

PREP: 35 min. **COOK:** 3 hours

My sister shared this chili recipe with me. I usually double it and add one extra can of beans, then serve with cheddar biscuits or warmed tortillas. The jalapeno adds just enough heat to notice but not too much for my children.
—Kristine Bowles, Albuquerque, New Mexico

- **3/4 pound boneless skinless chicken breasts, cubed**
- **1/2 teaspoon salt**
- **1/4 teaspoon pepper**
- **2 tablespoons olive oil**
- **1 medium onion, chopped**
- **4 garlic cloves, minced**
- **1 jalapeno pepper, seeded and chopped**
- **2 teaspoons dried oregano**
- **1 teaspoon ground cumin**
- **2 cans (15 ounces *each*) white kidney *or* cannellini beans, rinsed and drained, *divided***
- **3 cups chicken broth, *divided***
- **1-1/2 cups (6 ounces) shredded cheddar cheese**
- **Sour cream and minced fresh cilantro, optional**

Sprinkle chicken with salt and pepper. In a large skillet over medium heat, cook chicken in oil for 2 minutes.

Stir in the onion, garlic and jalapeno; cook 2 minutes longer. Sprinkle with oregano and cumin; cook 1 minute longer or until chicken is browned and vegetables are tender. Transfer to a 3-qt. slow cooker.

In a small bowl, mash 1 cup of beans. Add 1/2 cup broth; stir until blended. Add to the slow cooker with the remaining beans and broth.

Cover and cook on low for 3 to 3-1/2 hours or until chicken juices run clear. Stir before serving. Sprinkle with cheese. Garnish with sour cream and cilantro if desired. **Yield:** 6 servings.

Editor's Note: When cutting hot peppers, disposable gloves are recommended. Avoid touching your face.

Firecracker Burgers

(Pictured above and on page 40)

PREP: 20 min. **GRILL:** 15 min.

These tasty stuffed burgers are perfect July 4th fare. They're great with a cool, creamy macaroni salad and an icy cold beverage! —Kelly Williams, LaPorte, Indiana

- **1 pound lean ground beef**
- **1/4 cup chunky salsa**
- **4 frozen breaded cheddar cheese jalapeno peppers, thawed**
- **1/4 cup guacamole**
- **4 hamburger buns, split and toasted**
- **4 lettuce leaves**
- **1/4 cup salsa con queso dip**
- **1/4 cup sliced plum tomatoes**
- **2 tablespoons sliced ripe olives**
- **4 thin slices sweet onion**

In a bowl, combine the beef and salsa. Shape into four patties. Place a jalapeno in the center of each; wrap beef around jalapeno, forming a ball. Reshape into patties, about 3-1/2 to 4 in. in diameter and 1 in. thick.

Grill, covered, over medium-hot heat for 7-8 minutes on each side or until the meat is no longer pink. Spread the guacamole over toasted side of bun tops. On each bun bottom, layer the lettuce, a burger, con queso dip, tomatoes, olives and onion; replace tops. **Yield:** 4 servings.

Hot Pepper Prep

When handling jalapeno peppers, always wear plastic gloves. If you have to cut a large number, try this quick, safe method: First, cut off the tops of the peppers and slice them in half the long way. Then, using the small end of a melon baller, scrape out the seeds and membranes.

Side Dishes & Condiments

You'll savor this luscious lineup of recipes to go with your favorite foods.

PERFECT PARTNERS. Clockwise from upper left: Mexicorn Grits (p. 64), Pearl Onion Broccoli Bake (p. 58), Maple-Ginger Root Vegetables (p. 63), Rustic Squash Tarts (p. 64), and pictured center, Slow-Cooked Bean Medley (p. 58).

Pearl Onion Broccoli Bake

(*Pictured above and on page 57*)

PREP: 20 min. **BAKE:** 25 min.

With its creamy white cheese sauce and buttery crumb topping, this dish is great comfort food. If you're looking for a mild way to dress up broccoli, this is the recipe.
— *Charles Keating, Manchester, Maryland*

- 4 packages (8 ounces *each*) frozen broccoli cuts
- 4 cups frozen pearl onions
- 1/2 cup butter, *divided*
- 1/4 cup all-purpose flour
- 3/4 teaspoon salt
- 1/8 teaspoon pepper
- 2 cups milk
- 2 packages (3 ounces *each*) cream cheese, cubed
- 2 cups soft bread crumbs
- 1 cup (4 ounces) shredded cheddar cheese

In a large saucepan, cook broccoli in 1 in. of water until almost tender; drain. Cook pearl onions in 1 in. of water until almost tender; drain.

In a large saucepan, melt 1/4 cup butter; stir in flour, salt and pepper until smooth. Gradually add milk. Bring to a boil; cook and stir for 1-2 minutes or until thickened. Reduce heat; stir in cream cheese until smooth and blended.

Place broccoli and onions in a greased 13-in. x 9-in. x 2-in. baking dish. Add sauce and gently stir to coat. Melt the remaining butter; toss with bread crumbs. Sprinkle crumbs and cheddar cheese over vegetables.

Bake, uncovered, at 350° for 25-30 minutes or until topping is golden brown. **Yield:** 12-15 servings.

Slow-Cooked Bean Medley

(*Pictured below and on page 56*)

PREP: 25 min. **COOK:** 5 hours

I often change the variety of beans in this classic recipe, using whatever I have on hand to total five 15- to 16-ounce cans. The sauce makes any combination delicious!
— *Peggy Gwillim, Strasbourg, Saskatchewan*

- 1-1/2 cups ketchup
- 2 celery ribs, chopped
- 1 medium onion, chopped
- 1 medium green pepper, chopped
- 1 medium sweet red pepper, chopped
- 1/2 cup packed brown sugar
- 1/2 cup water
- 1/2 cup Italian salad dressing
- 2 bay leaves
- 1 tablespoon cider vinegar
- 1 teaspoon ground mustard
- 1/8 teaspoon pepper
- 1 can (16 ounces) kidney beans, rinsed and drained
- 1 can (15-1/2 ounces) black-eyed peas, rinsed and drained
- 1 can (15-1/2 ounces) great northern beans, rinsed and drained
- 1 can (15-1/4 ounces) whole kernel corn, drained
- 1 can (15-1/4 ounces) lima beans, rinsed and drained
- 1 can (15 ounces) black beans, rinsed and drained

In a 5-qt. slow cooker, combine the first 12 ingredients. Stir in the remaining ingredients. Cover and cook on low for 5-7 hours or until onion and peppers are tender. Discard bay leaves. **Yield:** 12 servings.

Editor's Note: Ingredient formulas and production facilities vary among brands. If you're concerned that your brand may contain gluten, contact the company.

cheese, salt and pepper; mix well.

Spread 2-2/3 cups russet potato mixture into each of two greased 11-in. x 7-in. x 2-in. baking dishes. Layer with 4 cups sweet potato mixture. Repeat layers. Spread with remaining russet potato mixture.

Bake, uncovered, at 350° for 15 minutes or until heated through. Combine topping ingredients; sprinkle over casseroles. Bake 2-3 minutes longer or until cheese is melted. **Yield:** 2 casseroles (10 servings each).

Springtime Barley

(*Pictured below*)

PREP/TOTAL TIME: 30 min.

While working as a sorority house mother, I occasionally filled in for the cook. The girls really liked low–fat dishes like this attractive medley. —*Sharon Helmick, Colfax, Washington*

- 1 **small onion, chopped**
- 1 **medium carrot, chopped**
- 1 **tablespoon butter**
- 1 **cup quick-cooking barley**
- 2 **cups reduced-sodium chicken broth, *divided***
- 1/2 **pound fresh asparagus, trimmed and cut into 1-inch pieces**
- 1/4 **teaspoon dried marjoram**
- 1/8 **teaspoon pepper**
- 2 **tablespoons shredded Parmesan cheese**

In a large skillet, saute the onion and carrot in butter until crisp-tender. Stir in the barley; cook and stir for 1 minute. Stir in 1 cup broth. Bring to a boil. Reduce heat; cook and stir until liquid is absorbed.

Add the asparagus. Cook for 15-20 minutes or until the barley is tender and the liquid is absorbed, stirring occasionally and adding more broth as needed. Stir in marjoram and pepper; sprinkle with Parmesan cheese. **Yield:** 4 servings.

Grand Prize Winner

Duo Tater Bake

(*Pictured above*)

PREP: 40 min. **BAKE:** 20 min. + chilling

I made this creamy and comforting potato dish for Thanksgiving and it was a winner with my family. They said to be sure to include it at every holiday dinner. It's a keeper! —*Joan McCulloch, Abbotsford, British Columbia*

- 4 **pounds russet *or* Yukon Gold potatoes, peeled and cubed**
- 3 **pounds sweet potatoes, peeled and cubed**
- 2 **cartons (8 ounces *each*) spreadable chive and onion cream cheese**
- 1 **cup (8 ounces) sour cream**
- 1/4 **cup shredded Colby-Monterey Jack cheese**
- 1/3 **cup milk**
- 1/4 **cup shredded Parmesan cheese**
- 1/2 **teaspoon salt**
- 1/2 **teaspoon pepper**

TOPPING:
- 1 **cup (4 ounces) shredded Colby-Monterey Jack cheese**
- 1/2 **cup chopped green onions**
- 1/4 **cup shredded Parmesan cheese**

Place russet potatoes in a Dutch oven and cover with water. Bring to a boil. Reduce heat; cover and cook for 15-20 minutes or until tender.

Meanwhile, place sweet potatoes in a large saucepan; cover with water. Bring to a boil. Reduce heat; cover and cook for 15-20 minutes or until tender. Drain; mash with half of the cream cheese and sour cream and all of the Colby cheese.

Drain russet potatoes; mash with the remaining cream cheese and sour cream. Add the milk, Parmesan

Asparagus on the Side

Asparagus with Mustard Sauce

(Pictured below)

PREP/TOTAL TIME: 30 min.

Here in Iowa, asparagus patches grow wild along the roads. My husband and I often go asparagus hunting on Saturday and Sunday mornings. A tangy mustard sauce complements the fresh asparagus in this easy recipe.
—*Nancy Hasbrouck, Ida Grove, Iowa*

> 2 **pounds fresh asparagus, trimmed**
> 3 **tablespoons butter, cubed**
> **Salt and pepper to taste**
> 1 **cup (8 ounces) sour cream**
> 1/4 **cup Dijon mustard**
> 2 **tablespoons red wine vinegar**
> 2 **teaspoons sugar**
> 1/8 **teaspoon crushed red pepper flakes**

Place the asparagus in a shallow baking dish; dot with the butter. Sprinkle with salt and pepper. Cover and bake at 400° for 25-30 minutes or until tender.

In a microwave-safe bowl, combine the remaining ingredients. Cover and microwave on high for 1 to 1-1/4 minutes or until heated through. Serve over asparagus. **Yield:** 6-8 servings.

Editor's Note: This recipe was tested in a 1,100-watt microwave.

Grilled Asparagus Medley

(Pictured above)

PREP/TOTAL TIME: 25 min.

This colorful veggie recipe happened by accident. One evening, I didn't have room on the grill for all the things I wanted to prepare, so I threw two of the dishes together and came up with this medley. It goes great with any grilled meat.
—*Pam Gaspers, Hastings, Nebraska*

> 1 **pound fresh asparagus, trimmed**
> 1 *each* **sweet red, yellow and green pepper, julienned**
> 1 **cup sliced fresh mushrooms**
> 1 **medium tomato, chopped**
> 1 **medium onion, sliced**
> 1 **can (2-1/4 ounces) sliced ripe olives, drained**
> 2 **garlic cloves, minced**
> 2 **tablespoons olive oil**
> 1 **teaspoon minced fresh parsley**
> 1/2 **teaspoon salt**
> 1/2 **teaspoon pepper**
> 1/4 **teaspoon lemon-pepper seasoning**
> 1/4 **teaspoon dill weed**

In a disposable foil pan, combine the vegetables, olives and garlic; drizzle with oil and toss to coat. Sprinkle with parsley, salt, pepper, lemon-pepper and dill; toss to coat.

Grill, covered, over indirect medium heat for 20-25 minutes or until the vegetables are crisp-tender, stirring occasionally. **Yield:** 8 servings.

Dilly Pickled Asparagus

(Pictured below)

PREP: 30 min.
PROCESS: 20 min. + standing

These dilled spears are really popular with my family. My granddaughter always says, "Oh, Grammy, these are soooo good!" They're easy to prepare and turn out perfect every time.
—*Annie Merrell, Fenelon Falls, Ontario*

> 6 **pounds fresh asparagus**
> 3 **large garlic cloves, halved**
> 6 **teaspoons dill seed**
> 6 **teaspoons mustard seed**
> 36 **whole peppercorns**
> 2 **quarts water**
> 2-1/2 **cups white vinegar**
> 1/2 **cup sugar**
> 3 **tablespoons canning salt**

Wash, drain and trim asparagus; cut into 4-1/2-in. spears. Discard ends or save for another use. Place asparagus in a large bowl; cover with ice water. In each of six 1-pint jars, place half of a garlic clove, 1 teaspoon dill seed, 1 teaspoon mustard seed and six peppercorns.

In a Dutch oven, bring the water, vinegar, sugar and salt to a boil. Drain asparagus; pack in jars to within 1/2 in. of top. Ladle boiling liquid over asparagus, leaving 1/4-in. headspace. Adjust caps. Process for 20 minutes in a boiling-water bath. Remove jars to wire racks to cool completely. **Yield:** 6 pints.

TOPPING:
   2 tablespoons dry bread crumbs
   1-1/2 teaspoons butter, melted

Cook noodles according to package directions; drain. In a small saucepan, melt butter. Stir in the flour, garlic salt and onion salt until smooth. Gradually stir in milk. Bring to a boil; cook and stir for 2 minutes or until thickened. Reduce heat. Add the cheese, stirring until melted. Stir in the noodles.

Transfer to a greased shallow 1-1/2-qt. baking dish. Toss bread crumbs and butter; sprinkle over top. Bake, uncovered, at 350° for 20-25 minutes or until golden brown. **Yield:** 6 servings.

German-Style Mashed Potatoes

(Pictured below)

PREP: 20 min. **COOK:** 20 min.

Comforting and filling, these tangy potatoes will warm up any meal, especially one with a German flair. They're a fitting accompaniment to sausages like bratwurst.
—Alena Horn, Austin, Texas

   3 pounds red potatoes, peeled and cubed
   2 large tart apples, peeled and chopped
   4 bacon strips, diced
   2 medium onions, sliced
   1 tablespoon sugar
   1 tablespoon cider vinegar
 3/4 teaspoon salt

Place potatoes in a large saucepan and cover with water. Bring to a boil. Reduce heat; cover and cook for 10 minutes. Add apples; cook 10 minutes longer or until potatoes and apples are tender.

Meanwhile, in a large skillet, cook bacon over medium heat until crisp. Using a slotted spoon, remove to paper towels; drain, reserving 1 tablespoon drippings. In the drippings, saute onions until lightly browned.

Drain potatoes and apples. Add sugar, vinegar and salt; mash slightly. Transfer to a serving bowl. Top with onions and bacon. **Yield:** 7 servings.

Roasted Squash Medley

(Pictured above)

PREP: 30 min. **BAKE:** 20 min.

I concocted this recipe as a way to use up some vegetables before they went bad. Everyone loved the lively blend of roasted veggies, especially the acorn and butternut squash. It goes particularly well with pork roast, pork loin or pork chops.
—Elaine Wier, Guilford, Connecticut

   1 large acorn squash, peeled and cubed
   1 small butternut squash, peeled and cubed
   2 large white potatoes, cubed
   2 large red potatoes, cubed
   1 medium green pepper, julienned
   1 medium sweet red pepper, julienned
   1 small onion, quartered
  12 whole garlic cloves, peeled
   1 teaspoon salt
   1 teaspoon garlic powder
 1/2 teaspoon pepper
 1/2 cup olive oil

In a large bowl, toss all ingredients until well coated. Arrange mixture in a single layer in two greased 15-in. x 10-in. x 1-in. baking pans.

Bake, uncovered, at 425° for 20-30 minutes or until vegetables are tender, stirring occasionally. **Yield:** 6 servings.

Cheesy Noodle Casserole

PREP: 25 min. **BAKE:** 25 min.

There's nothing like a comforting warm casserole to chase away winter chills. My simple-to-make cheese and noodle casserole is delicious and comes together in a jiffy!
—Shirley McKee, Varna, Illinois

   5 cups uncooked egg noodles
   2 tablespoons butter
   1 tablespoon all-purpose flour
 1/4 teaspoon garlic salt
 1/4 teaspoon onion salt
1-1/3 cups milk
   8 ounces process cheese (Velveeta), cubed

Fried Shoestring Carrots

(Pictured below)

PREP/TOTAL TIME: 25 min.

I came up with these fun snacks as an alternative to french fries. We like to serve them hot with ranch–style dressing as a dipping sauce. —Kim Gammill, Raymondville, Texas

- **2 cups self-rising flour**
- **1-1/2 cups water**
- **1 teaspoon salt,** *divided*
- **3/4 teaspoon cayenne pepper,** *divided*
- **1/2 teaspoon pepper,** *divided*
- **10 cups shredded carrots**
- **Oil for frying**

In a large bowl, whisk the flour, water, 1/2 teaspoon salt, 1/4 teaspoon cayenne and 1/4 teaspoon pepper until smooth. Stir in carrots. In a small bowl, combine the remaining salt, cayenne and pepper; set aside.

In an electric skillet or deep-fat fryer, heat oil to 375°. Drop spoonfuls of carrot mixture, a few at a time, into oil; cook for 3-4 minutes or until golden brown, stirring frequently. Drain on paper towels; sprinkle with reserved seasoning mixture. **Yield:** 10 servings.

Editor's Note: As a substitute for each cup of self-rising flour, place 1-1/2 teaspoons baking powder and 1/2 teaspoon salt in a measuring cup. Add all-purpose flour to measure 1 cup.

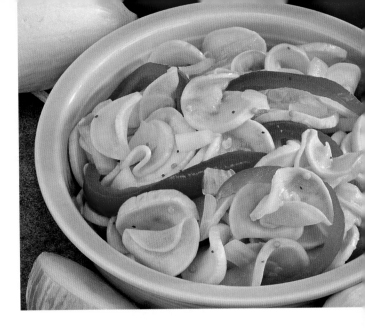

So-Sweet Squash Pickles

(Pictured above)

PREP: 30 min. + chilling

These crisp crunchy slices, seasoned with celery seed and mustard seed, have a sweet–sour taste that everyone is sure to relish! The colorful blend of yellow squash, sweet red pepper and chopped onion makes a beautiful presentation.
—Eleanor Sundman, Farmington, Connecticut

- **3 small yellow summer squash, thinly sliced**
- **1 medium onion, chopped**
- **1 large sweet red pepper, cut into 1/4-inch strips**
- **1 tablespoon salt**
- **1 cup sugar**
- **3/4 cup white vinegar**
- **3/4 teaspoon mustard seed**
- **3/4 teaspoon celery seed**
- **1/4 teaspoon ground mustard**

In a large bowl, combine the squash, onion, red pepper and salt. Cover and refrigerate for 1 hour; drain.

In a large saucepan, combine the remaining ingredients. Bring to a boil. Add squash mixture; return to a boil. Remove from the heat; cool.

Store in an airtight container in the refrigerator for at least 4 days before serving. May be stored in the refrigerator for up to 3 weeks. **Yield:** 4 cups.

Sweet Maple Syrup

There are four grades of maple syrup available to consumers. Grade A Light Amber is light and mild; Grade A Light Medium is a bit darker with more maple flavor; Grade A Dark Amber is even darker and more flavorful; and Grade B is very dark with a strong maple flavor. Deciding which one to use is simply personal preference.

Tangy Rhubarb Chutney

(Pictured below)

PREP: 25 min. **COOK:** 40 min. + chilling

My mother-in-law shared with me a great chutney recipe that I experiment with by changing the fruits. This version is a bit different, but I love the pear, onion and rhubarb combination. The longer it sets, the better it tastes!
—*Barbara Estabrook, Rhinelander, Wisconsin*

- **3 cups chopped fresh *or* frozen rhubarb**
- **1 cup packed brown sugar**
- **1 cup white balsamic vinegar**
- **1 cup finely chopped onion**
- **3/4 cup golden raisins**
- **1 tablespoon Worcestershire sauce**
- **2 teaspoons minced fresh gingerroot**
- **1 teaspoon salt**
- **3/4 teaspoon curry powder**
- **1/4 teaspoon ground nutmeg**
- **2 medium pears, peeled and diced**
- **2 tablespoons minced fresh mint**

In a large saucepan, combine the rhubarb, brown sugar, vinegar, onion, raisins, Worcestershire sauce, ginger, salt, curry and nutmeg. Cook and stir until the mixture comes to a boil. Reduce heat; simmer, uncovered, for 25-30 minutes or until the rhubarb is tender, stirring occasionally.

Add pears. Simmer, uncovered, 10-15 minutes longer or until pears are tender. Cool to room temperature. Stir in mint. Transfer to a bowl. Cover and refrigerate for at least 6 hours before serving. May be stored in the refrigerator up to 1 week. **Yield:** 4 cups.

Maple-Ginger Root Vegetables

(Pictured above and on page 57)

PREP: 35 min. **BAKE:** 45 min.

My family loves this recipe because it brings out the lovely flavors of the vegetables. It's a tasty way to introduce kids to turnips, rutabaga and parsnips—they love the drizzle of maple syrup!
—*Kelli Ritz, Innisfail, Alberta*

- **5 medium parsnips, peeled and sliced**
- **5 small carrots, sliced**
- **3 medium turnips, peeled and cubed**
- **1 large sweet potato, peeled and cubed**
- **1 small rutabaga, peeled and cubed**
- **1 large sweet onion, cut into wedges**
- **1 small red onion, cut into wedges**
- **2 tablespoons olive oil**
- **1 tablespoon minced fresh gingerroot**
- **1 teaspoon salt**
- **1/2 teaspoon pepper**
- **1 cup maple syrup**

Place the first seven ingredients in a large resealable plastic bag; add the oil, ginger, salt and pepper. Seal bag and shake to coat. Arrange vegetables in a single layer in two 15-in. x 10-in. x 1-in. baking pans coated with cooking spray.

Bake, uncovered, at 425° for 25 minutes, stirring once. Drizzle with syrup. Bake 20-25 minutes longer or until vegetables are tender, stirring once. **Yield:** 24 servings.

ungreased baking sheet. Sprinkle with pecan mixture. Arrange squash slices to within 1-1/2 in. of edges, alternating slices of butternut and acorn squash.

Fold up edges of pastry over filling, leaving centers uncovered. Brush pastry with egg. Dot squash with butter. Bake at 375° for 35-40 minutes or until golden brown. **Yield:** 2 tarts (8 servings each).

Editor's Note: This recipe was tested in a 1,100-watt microwave.

Mexicorn Grits

(*Pictured below and on page 56*)

PREP: 20 min. **BAKE:** 35 min.

I grew up on grits and have fixed them various ways. I decided to put a new twist on them with this recipe, and my husband says it's a keeper. Even the leftovers are good.
—*Barbara Moorhead, Gaffney, South Carolina*

- 4 **cups milk**
- 1/2 **cup plus 1/3 cup butter,** *divided*
- 1 **cup quick-cooking grits**
- 2 **eggs**
- 1 **can (11 ounces) Mexicorn, drained**
- 1 **can (4 ounces) chopped green chilies**
- 1 **cup (4 ounces) shredded Mexican cheese blend**
- 1 **teaspoon salt**
- 1/4 **teaspoon white pepper**
- 1 **cup shredded Parmesan cheese**

In a large saucepan, bring the milk and 1/2 cup butter to a boil. Slowly stir in the grits. Reduce heat; cook and stir for 5-7 minutes.

In a small bowl, whisk the eggs. Stir a small amount of hot grits into eggs; return all to the pan, stirring constantly. Melt remaining butter; stir into grits. Add the corn, chilies, cheese, salt and pepper.

Transfer to a greased 2-qt. baking dish. Sprinkle with Parmesan cheese. Bake, uncovered, at 350° for 35-40 minutes or until a knife inserted near the center comes out clean. **Yield:** 10 servings.

Rustic Squash Tarts

(*Pictured above and on page 56*)

PREP: 30 min. **BAKE:** 35 min.

This delicious side dish will surprise you. The rustic–looking, flaky pastry shells hold a sweet and spicy pecan layer under squash slices. —*Ann Marie Moch, Kintyre, North Dakota*

- 1 **medium butternut squash, peeled, seeded and cut into 1/8-inch slices**
- 1 **medium acorn squash, peeled, seeded and cut into 1/8-inch slices**
- 2 **tablespoons water**
- 1/4 **cup olive oil**
- 1 **tablespoon minced fresh thyme**
- 1 **tablespoon minced fresh parsley**
- 1/2 **teaspoon salt**
- 1/4 **teaspoon pepper**
- 1/2 **cup all-purpose flour**
- 1/2 **cup ground pecans**
- 6 **tablespoons sugar**
- 1/2 **teaspoon ground nutmeg**
- 1/2 **teaspoon ground cinnamon**
- 1 **package (17.3 ounces) frozen puff pastry, thawed**
- 1 **egg, lightly beaten**
- 2 **tablespoons butter**

In a large microwave-safe bowl, combine squash and water. Cover and cook on high for 5 minutes or until crisp-tender. Drain; transfer to a large resealable plastic bag. Add the oil, thyme, parsley, salt and pepper; seal bag and shake to coat. Set aside. In a small bowl, combine the flour, pecans, sugar, nutmeg and cinnamon; set aside.

Unfold pastry sheets on a lightly floured surface. Roll each pastry to 1/8-in. thickness; transfer each to an

1/4 cup butter, cubed
1 teaspoon cornstarch
1/2 cup orange juice
1 tablespoon grated orange peel

Cook broccoli according to package directions. Meanwhile, in a small saucepan, melt butter. Whisk in cornstarch until smooth. Gradually stir in orange juice; add orange peel. Bring to a boil; cook and stir for 2 minutes or until thickened. Drain broccoli; drizzle with sauce. **Yield:** 4 servings.

Curried Butternut Squash Kabobs

(Pictured below)

PREP: 30 min. + cooling **GRILL:** 10 min.

These baked squash cubes pick up a mouth–watering grilled taste along with a mild curry–butter flavor. The pretty orange side dish adds interest to summer entrees.
—Mary Relyea, Canastota, New York

1 butternut squash (2 pounds), peeled, seeded and cut into 1-inch cubes
3 tablespoons butter, melted
1 teaspoon curry powder
1/4 teaspoon salt

Place squash in a greased 13-in. x 9-in. x 2-in. baking dish. Combine the butter, curry powder and salt; drizzle over squash and toss to coat.

Bake, uncovered, at 450° for 20-25 minutes or until tender and lightly browned, stirring twice. Cool on a wire rack.

Thread the butternut squash cubes onto 12 metal or soaked wooden skewers. Grill, covered, over medium heat for 3-5 minutes on each side or until heated through. **Yield:** 12 servings.

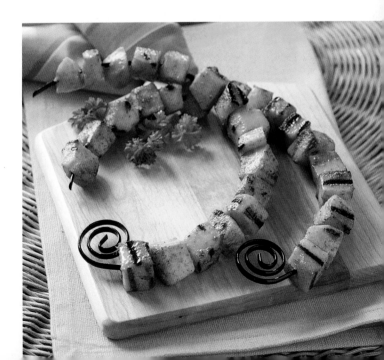

Orange Rhubarb Spread

(Pictured above)

PREP: 5 min. **COOK:** 20 min. + standing

This tangy spread is easy to make and tastes especially good on hot, buttered cinnamon toast. The recipe makes enough to have on hand well beyond the growing season.
—Betty Nyenhuis, Oostburg, Wisconsin

4 cups diced fresh *or* frozen rhubarb
2 cups water
1 can (6 ounces) frozen orange juice concentrate, thawed
1 package (1-3/4 ounces) powdered fruit pectin
4 cups sugar

In a large saucepan, bring rhubarb and water to a boil. Reduce heat; simmer, uncovered, for 7-8 minutes or until rhubarb is tender. Drain and reserve cooking liquid. Cool rhubarb and liquid to room temperature.

Place the rhubarb in a blender; cover and process until pureed. Transfer to a 4-cup measuring cup; add enough reserved cooking liquid to measure 2-1/3 cups. Return to the saucepan.

Add orange juice concentrate and pectin; bring to a full rolling boil, stirring constantly. Stir in sugar. Return to a full rolling boil; boil and stir for 1 minute. Remove from the heat; skim off foam.

Pour into jars or freezer containers; cool to room temperature, about 1 hour. Cover and let stand overnight or until set, but not longer than 24 hours. Refrigerate or freeze. **Yield:** 5 half-pints.

Broccoli with Orange Sauce

PREP/TOTAL TIME: 15 min.

As a busy working mother, I was looking for a good broccoli recipe that didn't take very long to make. This one, adapted from an old cookbook, can be whipped up in a hurry. I think you'll find it complements the rest of my favorite meal.
—Edie DeSpain, Logan, Utah

2 packages (10 ounce *each*) frozen broccoli spears

Colorful Corn

Fresh Corn Medley

(Pictured below)

PREP: 25 min. **COOK:** 20 min.

Your family will be sweet on this summery side dish that combines corn "off" the cob with green pepper, bacon, cheddar cheese and honey. It's just as delightful with frozen corn.
—Susan Paden, Mexico, Missouri

- 1 medium green pepper, chopped
- 1 small onion, chopped
- 3 tablespoons butter
- 4 cups fresh corn (about 9 ears of corn)
- 1/4 cup hot water
- 1 jar (2 ounces) diced pimientos, drained
- 1 tablespoon honey
- 1 teaspoon salt
- Dash pepper
- 1/2 cup shredded cheddar cheese
- 4 bacon strips, cooked and crumbled

In a large skillet, saute green pepper and onion in butter until tender. Add the corn, water, pimientos, honey, salt and pepper.

Bring to a boil. Reduce heat; simmer, uncovered, for 8-10 minutes or until corn is tender. Sprinkle with cheese and bacon. **Yield:** 5 servings.

Grilled Corn Salsa

(Pictured above)

PREP: 30 min.
GRILL: 30 min. + chilling

Nothing beats the flavor of grilled vegetables, and this is a super way to use your garden bounty. I grill the veggies anytime I'm grilling something else, then whip up the salsa and put it in the fridge to marinate. It's even better the next day.
—Teri Kman, Laporte, Colorado

- 8 medium ears sweet corn, husks removed
- 2 small yellow summer squash, cut into 1/2-inch slices
- 1 medium sweet red pepper, cut into four wedges
- 1 medium red onion, cut into 1/2-inch rings
- 1 medium tomato, seeded and chopped

BASIL VINAIGRETTE:

- 1/2 cup olive oil
- 1/3 cup white balsamic *or* cider vinegar
- 12 fresh basil leaves, chopped
- 1 teaspoon salt
- 1 teaspoon garlic powder
- 1 teaspoon dried oregano

Fill a soup kettle two-thirds full with water; bring to a boil. Add corn. Reduce heat; cover and simmer for 5 minutes or until crisp-tender. Remove corn; cool slightly.

Spray grill rack with cooking spray before starting the grill. Grill the corn, squash, red pepper and onion over medium heat for 8-10 minutes or until lightly browned, turning occasionally.

Cut corn from cobs; cut the squash, red pepper and onion into bite-size pieces. Transfer vegetables to a large bowl. Add tomato.

In a jar with a tight-fitting lid, combine the vinaigrette ingredients; shake well. Pour over corn mixture; toss gently to coat.

Cover and refrigerate for at least 1 hour or until chilled. Serve with a slotted spoon. **Yield:** 7-1/2 cups.

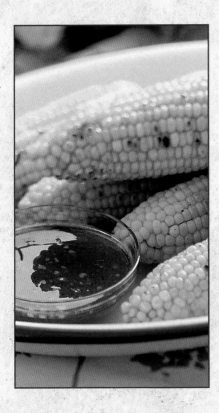

Smoky Grilled Corn

(Pictured above)

PREP: 25 min. **GRILL:** 10 min.

A friend and I cooked up this corn one evening when getting ready to grill. The buttery corn, with its sweet-spicy seasoning, won top honors over our favorite steaks.
—Linda Landers, Kalispell, Montana

      2 tablespoons plus 1-1/2 teaspoons butter
  1/2 cup honey
      2 large garlic cloves, minced
      2 tablespoons hot pepper sauce
  1/2 teaspoon salt
  1/4 teaspoon pepper
  1/4 teaspoon paprika
      6 medium ears sweet corn, husks removed

In a small saucepan, melt butter. Stir in the honey, garlic, pepper sauce and seasonings until blended; heat through. Brush over corn.

Coat grill rack with cooking spray before starting the grill. Grill, covered, over medium heat for 10-12 minutes or until the corn is tender, turning and basting occasionally. Serve corn with any remaining butter mixture. **Yield:** 6 servings.

Tomato and Corn Risotto

(Pictured below)

PREP: 15 min. **COOK:** 35 min.

This is one of my best-loved recipes because it uses items from the garden. Milk and Parmesan cheese give this side dish a creaminess everyone's sure to enjoy.
—Angela Lively, Baxter, Tennessee

  2-1/2 cups water
      2 cups milk
      3 tablespoons chicken broth
      1 large onion, finely chopped
      1 garlic clove, minced
      2 tablespoons butter
  3/4 cup uncooked arborio rice
  1-1/3 cups fresh corn (about 5 ears of corn)
      1 medium tomato, peeled, seeded and chopped
  1/2 cup grated Parmesan cheese
  1/2 cup fresh basil leaves, thinly sliced
  1/2 teaspoon salt
Pepper to taste

In a large saucepan, heat the water, milk and broth; keep warm.

In a large skillet, saute onion and garlic in butter until tender. Add rice; cook and stir for 2-3 minutes. Stir in 1 cup hot water mixture. Cook and stir until all liquid is absorbed.

Add the remaining water mixture, 1/2 cup at a time, stirring constantly. Allow the liquid to absorb between additions. Cook until the risotto is creamy and the rice is almost tender.

(Cooking time is about 20 minutes.) Stir in the remaining ingredients; heat through. **Yield:** 5 servings.

Double Corn Dressing

(Pictured above)

PREP: 25 min. **BAKE:** 40 min.

I have served this delicious dressing, made with a dry stuffing mix, to many family members and friends, and it always receives compliments. It goes great with pork or poultry.
—Berliene Grosh, Lakeland, Florida

      1 package (12 ounces) unseasoned stuffing cubes
      1 medium onion, finely chopped
  1/2 *each* medium green, sweet yellow and red pepper, chopped
      1 teaspoon garlic powder
  1/2 teaspoon salt
  1/4 teaspoon pepper
      3 eggs, lightly beaten
      1 can (15-1/4 ounces) whole kernel corn, drained
      1 can (14-3/4 ounces) cream-style corn
  1/2 cup butter, melted
  1/2 to 1 cup chicken broth

In a large bowl, combine the stuffing, onion, sweet peppers and seasonings. Add the eggs, corn and butter; toss to coat. Stir in enough broth to achieve desired moistness.

Spoon into a greased 3-qt. baking dish. Cover and bake at 350° for 25 minutes. Uncover; bake 15-20 minutes longer or until golden brown. **Yield:** 16 servings. .

Onion-Bacon Baby Carrots

(Pictured below)

PREP: 35 min. **BAKE:** 45 min.

I came up with this side dish for Thanksgiving, and it was a big hit. Now it has a place at our holiday table as well as impromptu get-togethers with family and friends.
—*Diana Morrison Poole, Rock Hill, South Carolina*

- **2 large sweet onions, sliced**
- **1 tablespoon olive oil**
- **2 pounds fresh baby carrots, halved lengthwise**
- **1 teaspoon salt**
- **1/4 teaspoon coarsely ground pepper**
- **1/4 cup maple syrup**
- **2 tablespoons butter**
- **1/2 cup french-fried onions**
- **8 bacon strips, cooked and crumbled**
- **1/4 cup chopped green onions**

In a large skillet, cook onions in oil over medium heat for 15-20 minutes or until golden brown, stirring frequently.

In a large bowl, combine the onions, carrots, salt and pepper; toss to combine. Transfer to a greased shallow 3-qt. baking dish. Cover and bake at 400° for 40-45 minutes or until tender.

Stir in the syrup and butter. Sprinkle with french-fried onions and bacon. Bake, uncovered, 5 minutes longer or until fried onions are browned. Sprinkle with green onions. Serve with a slotted spoon. **Yield:** 8 servings.

Peas in Cheese Sauce

PREP/TOTAL TIME: 20 min.

Mom dresses up convenient frozen peas with this quick-to-fix cheese sauce that our family loves.
—*June Blomquist, Eugene, Oregon*

- **4-1/2 teaspoons butter**
- **4-1/2 teaspoons all-purpose flour**
- **1/4 teaspoon salt**
- **1/8 teaspoon white pepper**
- **1-1/2 cups milk**
- **3/4 cup cubed process cheese (Velveeta)**
- **2 packages (10 ounces *each*) frozen peas, thawed**

In a large saucepan, melt the butter over low heat. Stir in the flour, salt and pepper until smooth. Gradually add the milk. Bring to a boil; cook and stir for 2 minutes or until thickened. Add the cheese; stir until melted. Stir in the peas; cook 1-2 minutes longer or until heated through. **Yield:** 8 servings.

Crumb-Coated Spaetzle

PREP/TOTAL TIME: 20 min.

Spaetzle is a cross between a curly noodle and a small dumpling. It's a traditional German accompaniment to all types of roasts, especially sauerbraten.
—*Patricia Rutherford, Winchester, Illinois*

- **2 cups all-purpose flour**
- **1 teaspoon salt**
- **2 eggs, lightly beaten**
- **3/4 cup milk**
- **1/2 cup dry bread crumbs**
- **1/2 cup butter, melted**

In a bowl, combine the flour and salt. Stir in the eggs and milk until smooth.

Fill a large kettle three-fourths full with water; bring to a boil. With a rubber spatula, press dough through a colander into boiling water. Cook and stir gently for 4-5 minutes or until spaetzle float and are tender.

Combine bread crumbs and butter. With a slotted spoon, transfer spaetzle to a large bowl; add crumb mixture and toss to coat. **Yield:** 6 servings.

Baked Cranberry Sauce

PREP/TOTAL TIME: 30 min.

We live in cranberry country and are always looking for good recipes to use them. This dish is perfect for Thanksgiving Day.
—*Kathy Olsen, Provincetown, Massachusetts*

- **1 pound fresh *or* frozen cranberries, thawed**
- **1-1/2 cups chopped pecans**
- **1 cup flaked coconut**
- **1 cup orange marmalade**

3/4 cup sugar
1/2 cup water

In a large bowl, combine all of the ingredients. Pour into a greased 11-in. x 7-in. x 2-in. baking dish. Bake, uncovered, at 350° for 25-30 minutes or until the cranberries are tender. Serve warm or cold. Refrigerate leftovers. **Yield:** 10 servings.

Orange-Glazed Acorn Squash

(Pictured below)

PREP: 15 min. **BAKE:** 55 min.

This savory side dish gets its lovely flavor from orange juice, orange zest and nutmeg. The smooth syrupy sauce is a great complement to the squash. I serve this on Christmas Eve, and everyone loves it! —Joyce Moynihan, Lakeville, Minnesota

  4 **small acorn squash**
  2 **tablespoons butter**
  1 **cup sugar**
  1 **cup orange juice**
  1/3 **cup orange juice concentrate**
  1/4 **teaspoon salt**
  1/4 **teaspoon ground nutmeg**
  1/4 **teaspoon grated orange peel**
  1/8 **teaspoon pepper**

Cut squash in half; discard seeds. Place squash cut side down in a 15-in. x 10-in. x 1-in. baking pan; add 1/2 in. of hot water. Bake, uncovered, at 350° for 30 minutes.

Meanwhile, in a saucepan, melt butter over medium heat. Stir in the remaining ingredients. Bring to a boil. Reduce heat to medium-low; cook, uncovered, for 30 minutes or until syrupy, stirring occasionally.

Drain water from baking pan; turn squash cut side up. Pour about 2 tablespoons orange glaze into each squash half. Bake 25-30 minutes longer or until squash is tender. **Yield:** 8 servings.

Herbed Tomatoes and Green Beans

(Pictured above)

PREP/TOTAL TIME: 30 min.

Looking for new ways to dress up fresh-picked green beans? With just the right amount of oregano and parsley flavor, this colorful side dish is seasoned to please.
—Maryalice Wood, Langley, British Columbia

  3 **green onions, coarsely chopped**
  2 **garlic cloves, minced**
  2 **teaspoons olive oil**
  1/2 **pound fresh green beans, trimmed**
  1/4 **cup chicken broth**
  2 **medium tomatoes, diced**
  1 **tablespoon minced fresh oregano**
  1 **tablespoon minced fresh parsley**
  1/8 **teaspoon salt**
  1/8 **teaspoon pepper**

In a small skillet, saute onions and garlic in oil until tender. Add the beans and the broth. Bring to a boil. Reduce heat; cover and simmer for 6-9 minutes or until crisp-tender.

Stir in the tomatoes and seasonings; heat through. **Yield:** 4 servings.

Storing Fresh Herbs

To keep fresh herbs in tip-top shape, snip the ends off, then wash and dry them. A salad spinner works great to remove excess water. Wrap in damp paper towels and store in a resealable plastic bag. Refrigerate, preferably in a crisper drawer.

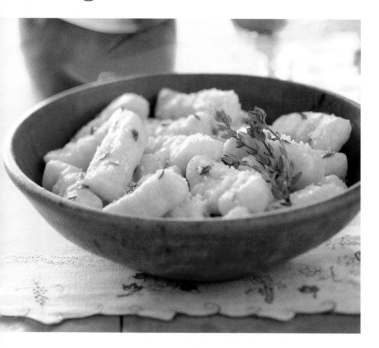

batches for 30-60 seconds or until they float. Remove with a slotted spoon; keep warm.

In a large heavy saucepan, melt butter over medium heat. Add thyme and gnocchi; stir gently to coat. Sprinkle with cheese if desired. **Yield:** 5 servings.

German Potato Salad With Sausage

(Pictured below)

PREP: 30 min. **COOK:** 6 hours

Hearty and saucy, this potato salad is an old family recipe that was updated using cream of potato soup to ease preparation. The sausage and sauerkraut give it a special zip.
—Teresa McGill, Trotwood, Ohio

- 8 **bacon strips, diced**
- 1 **large onion, chopped**
- 1 **pound smoked Polish sausage, halved and cut into 1/2-inch slices**
- 2 **pounds medium red potatoes, cut into chunks**
- 1 **can (10-3/4 ounces) condensed cream of potato soup, undiluted**
- 1 **cup sauerkraut, rinsed and well drained**
- 1/2 **cup water**
- 1/4 **cup cider vinegar**
- 1 **tablespoon sugar**
- 1/2 **teaspoon salt**
- 1/2 **teaspoon coarsely ground pepper**

In a large skillet, cook bacon over medium heat until crisp. Remove to paper towels. In the drippings, saute onion for 1 minute. Add sausage; cook until lightly browned. Add potatoes; cook 2 minutes longer.

Drain; transfer sausage mixture to a 3-qt. slow cooker. In a small bowl, combine the soup, sauerkraut, water, vinegar, sugar, salt and pepper. Pour over sausage mixture. Sprinkle with bacon.

Cover and cook on low for 6-7 hours or until potatoes are tender. **Yield:** 8 servings.

Gnocchi with Thyme Butter

(Pictured above)

PREP: 70 min. **COOK:** 10 min.

If you've never attempted homemade gnocchi, this recipe is the one to try. The gnocchi are tender with a delicate butter and thyme flavor. They're absolutely delicious as a side dish with your favorite meat or seafood.
—Annette Lear, Sanbornville, New Hampshire

- 1-1/2 **pounds russet potatoes, peeled and quartered**
- 1 **cup all-purpose flour**
- 1 **egg**
- 1 **teaspoon salt**
- 1/2 **teaspoon pepper**
- 4 **quarts water**
- 1/2 **cup butter, cubed**
- 4 **teaspoons fresh thyme leaves**

Grated Parmesan cheese, optional

Place potatoes in a large saucepan and cover with water. Bring to a boil. Reduce heat; cover and simmer for 15-20 minutes or until tender. Drain; return the potatoes to the pan.

Over very low heat, stir potatoes for 1-2 minutes or until steam has evaporated. Press through a potato ricer or strainer into a small bowl; cool slightly.

Using a fork, make a well in the potatoes; sprinkle with flour. Whisk the egg, salt and pepper; pour into well. Stir until blended. On a lightly floured surface, knead 10-12 times, forming a soft dough.

Divide the dough into four portions. On a floured surface, roll each portion into 1/2-in.-thick ropes; cut into 3/4-in. pieces. Press and roll each piece with a lightly floured fork.

In a Dutch oven, bring water to a boil. Cook gnocchi in

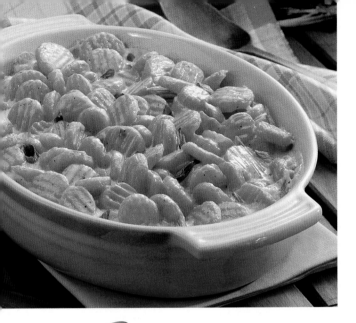

2 small yellow summer squash
1 tablespoon butter
2 teaspoons lemon juice
1 teaspoon prepared horseradish
1/2 teaspoon salt
1/8 teaspoon pepper

With a vegetable peeler or metal cheese slicer, cut very thin slices down the length of each carrot, zucchini and yellow squash, making long ribbons.

In a large skillet, saute the vegetables in the butter for 2 minutes. Stir in the remaining ingredients. Cook 2-4 minutes longer or until vegetables are crisp-tender, stirring occasionally. **Yield:** 4 servings.

Cherry Tomato Mozzarella Saute

(Pictured below)

PREP/TOTAL TIME: 25 min.

Fast to fix and full of flavor, this warm, refreshing side dish makes the most of cherry tomatoes. They're delicious combined with fresh mozzarella cubes and thyme.
—*Summer Jones, Pleasant Grove, Utah*

1/4 cup chopped shallots
1 garlic clove, minced
1 teaspoon minced fresh thyme
2 teaspoons olive oil
2-1/2 cups cherry tomatoes, halved
1/4 teaspoon salt
1/4 teaspoon pepper
4 ounces fresh mozzarella cheese, cut into 1/2-inch cubes

In a large skillet, saute the shallots, garlic and thyme in oil until tender. Add the tomatoes, salt and pepper; heat through. Remove from the heat; stir in the cheese. **Yield:** 4 servings.

Party Carrots

(Pictured above)

PREP: 15 min. **BAKE:** 20 min.

People who don't like carrots often change their minds after tasting this easy-to-fix dish. It's nice for potlucks because you can prepare it ahead of time.
—*Bertha Johnson, Indianapolis, Indiana*

2 pounds carrots, sliced
2 teaspoons chicken bouillon granules
8 ounces process cheese (Velveeta), cubed
2 tablespoons butter
1 package (8 ounces) cream cheese, cubed
4 green onions, sliced
1/4 teaspoon salt
1/4 teaspoon pepper

Place 1 in. of water in a large saucepan; add carrots and bouillon. Bring to a boil. Reduce heat. Cover and simmer for 7-9 minutes or until crisp-tender.

Meanwhile, in another large saucepan, combine process cheese and butter. Cook and stir over low heat until melted. Add the cream cheese, onions, salt and pepper. Cook and stir until cream cheese is melted.

Drain carrots; stir into cheese sauce. Transfer to a greased shallow 2-qt. baking dish. Cover and bake at 350° for 20-25 minutes or until bubbly. **Yield:** 8 servings.

Ribboned Vegetables

PREP/TOTAL TIME: 25 min.

Make the best of summer produce with this easy recipe. These colorful veggie strips, sauteed in lemon and horseradish, will add zip to any menu. —*Julie Gwinn, Hershey, Pennsylvania*

2 medium carrots
2 small zucchini

Main Dishes

The centerpiece of any home-style menu is always the main course...and you'll have the perfect one for any occasion when you turn to the mouth-watering beef, poultry, pork, seafood and meatless creations in this chapter.

EXCELLENT ENTREES. Clockwise from upper left: Cranberry Ham Loaf (p. 94), Next Day Turkey Primavera (p. 96), Bavarian Pork Loin (p. 75), Spaghetti Squash with Red Sauce (p. 98) and Turkey Potpies (p. 97).

Orange Chicken with Sweet Potatoes

(Pictured below)

PREP: 25 min. **COOK:** 3-1/2 hours

Orange peel and pineapple juice lend a fruity flavor to this super chicken and sweet potato combo. Served over rice, this appealing entree is bound to win you lots of praise.
—*Vicki Smith, Okeechobee, Florida*

- 3 medium sweet potatoes, peeled and sliced
- 2/3 cup plus 3 tablespoons all-purpose flour, *divided*
- 1 teaspoon salt
- 1 teaspoon onion powder
- 1 teaspoon ground nutmeg
- 1 teaspoon ground cinnamon
- 1 teaspoon pepper
- 4 boneless skinless chicken breast halves (5 ounces *each*)
- 2 tablespoons butter
- 1 can (10-3/4 ounces) condensed cream of chicken soup, undiluted
- 3/4 cup unsweetened pineapple juice
- 2 teaspoons brown sugar
- 1 teaspoon grated orange peel
- 1/2 pound sliced fresh mushrooms

Hot cooked rice

Layer the sweet potatoes in a 3-qt. slow cooker. In a large resealable plastic bag, combine 2/3 cup flour and seasonings; add the chicken, one piece at a time, and shake to coat.

In a large skillet over medium heat, cook chicken in butter for 3 minutes on each side or until lightly browned. Arrange chicken over sweet potatoes.

Place remaining flour in a small bowl. Stir in the soup, pineapple juice, brown sugar and orange peel until blended. Add mushrooms; pour over chicken.

Cover and cook on low for 3-1/2 to 4 hours or until a meat thermometer reads 170° and potatoes are tender. Serve with rice. **Yield:** 4 servings.

Spiral Ham with Cranberry Glaze

(Pictured above)

PREP: 15 min. **BAKE:** 3 hours

The sweet, tangy glaze that complements this ham looks so pretty, and the cranberry flavor pairs well with the meat. It's been a tradition in my home for as long as I can remember.
—*Pattie Prescott, Manchester, New Hampshire*

- 1 fully cooked spiral-sliced ham (8 pounds)
- 1 can (16 ounces) whole-berry cranberry sauce
- 1 package (12 ounces) fresh *or* frozen cranberries
- 1 jar (12 ounces) red currant jelly
- 1 cup light corn syrup
- 1/2 teaspoon ground ginger

Place ham on a rack in a shallow roasting pan. Cover and bake at 325° for 2-1/2 hours.

Meanwhile, for glaze, combine the remaining ingredients in a saucepan. Bring to a boil. Reduce heat; simmer, uncovered, until cranberries pop, stirring occasionally. Remove from the heat; set aside.

Uncover the ham; bake 30 minutes longer or until a meat thermometer reads 140°, basting twice with 1-1/2 cups glaze. Serve the remaining glaze with ham. **Yield:** 12-16 servings.

Asparagus Sausage Crepes

(Pictured below)

PREP: 20 min. **BAKE:** 20 min.

This was my favorite recipe when I was growing up in western Michigan, where asparagus is a big spring crop. With its sausage-and-cheese filling, tender asparagus and rich sour cream topping, this pretty dish will impress guests.
—Lisa Hanson, Glenview, Illinois

- 1 pound bulk pork sausage
- 1 small onion, chopped
- 1 package (3 ounces) cream cheese, cubed
- 1/2 cup shredded Monterey Jack cheese
- 1/4 teaspoon dried marjoram
- 1 cup all-purpose flour
- 1/2 teaspoon salt
- 1 cup milk
- 3 eggs
- 1 tablespoon canola oil
- 32 fresh asparagus spears (about 1 pound), trimmed

TOPPING:

- 1/4 cup butter, softened
- 1/2 cup sour cream

In a large skillet, cook the sausage and onion over medium heat until the sausage is no longer pink; drain. Stir in the cream cheese, Monterey Jack cheese and marjoram; set aside.

In a bowl, combine the flour and salt. Add milk, eggs and oil; mix well. Heat a lightly greased 8-in. nonstick skillet; pour 2 tablespoons batter into the center of skillet. Lift and tilt pan to evenly coat bottom. Cook until top appears dry; turn and cook for 15-20 seconds. Remove to a wire rack.

Repeat with remaining batter, adding oil to skillet as needed. When cool, stack crepes with waxed paper or paper towels in between.

Spoon 2 tablespoons of the sausage mixture onto the center of each crepe. Top with two asparagus spears. Roll up; place in two greased 13-in. x 9-in. x 2-in. baking dishes. Cover and bake at 375° for 15 minutes. Combine the butter and sour cream; spoon over crepes. Bake for 5 minutes longer or until heated through. **Yield:** 8 servings.

Bavarian Pork Loin

(Pictured above and on page 72)

PREP: 25 min. **COOK:** 6 hours

I received the recipe for this tender pork roast from an aunt, who made it all the time. What a delicious taste sensation with sauerkraut, carrots, onions and apples.
—Edie DeSpain, Logan, Utah

- 1 boneless whole pork loin roast (3 pounds)
- 1 can (14 ounces) Bavarian sauerkraut, rinsed and drained
- 1-3/4 cups chopped carrots
- 1 large onion, finely chopped
- 1/2 cup unsweetened apple juice
- 2 teaspoons dried parsley flakes
- 3 large tart apples, peeled and quartered

Cut roast in half; place in a 5-qt. slow cooker. In a small bowl, combine the sauerkraut, carrots, onion, apple juice and parsley; spoon over roast. Cover and cook on low for 4 hours.

Add the apples to slow cooker. Cover and cook 2 to 2-1/2 hours longer or until a meat thermometer reads 160°. Remove roast; let stand for 5 minutes before slicing. Serve with sauerkraut mixture. **Yield:** 10 servings.

Dad's Swedish Meatballs

(Pictured above)

PREP: 30 min. **COOK:** 35 min.

My father used to make these tender meatballs every year for Christmas when I was a kid. Now I carry on the tradition, and everyone still loves them.
—Michelle Lizotte, Cumberland, Rhode Island

- 1 **egg, lightly beaten**
- 1/2 **cup milk**
- 1 **cup soft bread crumbs**
- 1/2 **cup finely chopped onion**
- 1 **teaspoon salt**
- 1/4 **teaspoon ground nutmeg**
- 1/4 **teaspoon pepper**
- 1 **pound ground beef**
- 1/2 **pound ground pork**
- 1/4 **cup butter, cubed**

DILL CREAM SAUCE:
- 2 **tablespoons all-purpose flour**
- 1 **cup heavy whipping cream**
- 1 **cup beef broth**
- 1 **teaspoon salt**
- 1/2 **teaspoon dill seed**

In a large bowl, combine the first seven ingredients. Crumble beef and pork over mixture and mix well. Shape into 1-1/2-in. balls. In a large skillet, cook meatballs in butter in batches until no longer pink. Remove and keep warm.

In a small bowl, combine the sauce ingredients until blended. Stir into skillet. Bring to a boil; cook and stir for 2 minutes or until thickened. Serve with meatballs.
Yield: 6 servings.

Thai Beef Stir-Fry

(Pictured below)

PREP: 20 min. **COOK:** 20 min.

A distinctive peanut sauce complements this colorful combination of tender sirloin strips, cauliflower, carrots, broccoli and mushrooms. I like to serve it over spaghetti, but you could also use fried noodles.—Janice Fehr, Austin, Manitoba

- 1/2 **cup packed brown sugar**
- 2 **tablespoons cornstarch**
- 2 **cups beef broth**
- 1/3 **cup soy sauce**
- 1 **teaspoon onion powder**
- 1 **teaspoon garlic powder**
- 1 **teaspoon ground ginger**
- 1/4 **teaspoon hot pepper sauce**
- 2 **pounds boneless beef sirloin steak, cut into thin strips**
- 6 **tablespoons olive oil,** *divided*
- 2 **cups fresh cauliflowerets**
- 1-1/2 **cups julienned carrots**
- 4 **cups fresh broccoli florets**
- 2 **cups sliced fresh mushrooms**
- 1/4 **cup peanut butter**
Hot cooked spaghetti
- 1/2 **cup chopped peanuts**

In a bowl, combine the first eight ingredients until smooth; set aside. In a large skillet or wok, stir-fry beef in 3 tablespoons oil until meat is no longer pink. Remove and keep warm.

In the same skillet, stir-fry the cauliflower and carrots in the remaining oil for 5 minutes. Add broccoli; stir-fry for 7 minutes. Add mushrooms; stir-fry 6-8 minutes

Pot Roast with Gravy

(Pictured below)

PREP: 30 min. **COOK:** 7-1/2 hours

My family enjoys this tangy, slow-cooked beef roast with gravy. We always hope for leftovers so we can have tasty sandwiches the next day. —Deborah Dailey, Vancouver, Washington

- **1 beef bottom round roast (5 pounds)**
- **6 tablespoons balsamic vinegar, *divided***
- **1 teaspoon salt**
- **1/2 teaspoon garlic powder**
- **1/4 teaspoon pepper**
- **2 tablespoons canola oil**
- **3 garlic cloves, minced**
- **4 bay leaves**
- **1 large onion, thinly sliced**
- **3 teaspoons beef bouillon granules**
- **1/2 cup boiling water**
- **1 can (10-3/4 ounces) condensed cream of mushroom soup, undiluted**
- **4 to 5 tablespoons cornstarch**
- **1/4 cup cold water**

Cut roast in half; rub with 2 tablespoons vinegar. Combine the salt, garlic powder and pepper; rub over meat. In a large skillet, brown roast in oil on all sides. Transfer to a 5-qt. slow cooker.

Place the garlic, bay leaves and onion on the roast. In a small bowl, dissolve bouillon in boiling water; stir in soup and remaining vinegar. Slowly pour over the roast. Cover and cook on low for 7-8 hours or until meat is tender.

Remove roast; keep warm. Discard bay leaves. Whisk cornstarch and cold water until smooth; stir into cooking juices. Cover and cook on high for 30 minutes or until gravy is thickened. Slice roast; return to slow cooker and heat through. **Yield:** 10 servings.

longer or until the vegetables are crisp-tender.

Stir broth mixture and add to the pan. Bring to a boil; cook and stir for 2 minutes or until thickened. Reduce heat; add beef and peanut butter. Cook and stir over medium heat until peanut butter is blended. Serve over spaghetti. Sprinkle with peanuts. **Yield:** 6 servings.

Creamy Ham and Macaroni

(Pictured above)

PREP: 20 min. **BAKE:** 20 min.

The original comfort food, macaroni and cheese gets a makeover with the addition of cubed ham and grated Parmesan. Kids will love it! —Christy Looper, Colorado Springs, Colorado

- **2 cups uncooked elbow macaroni**
- **1/4 cup butter, cubed**
- **1/4 cup all-purpose flour**
- **2 cups milk**
- **4 teaspoons chicken bouillon granules**
- **1/4 teaspoon pepper**
- **2 cups (8 ounces) shredded cheddar cheese, *divided***
- **1-1/2 cups cubed fully cooked ham**
- **1/4 cup grated Parmesan cheese**

Cook the macaroni according to the package directions; drain and set aside. In a large saucepan, melt the butter over low heat; whisk in flour until smooth. Whisk in the milk, bouillon and pepper. Bring to a boil; cook and stir for 2 minutes or until thickened. Remove from the heat. Stir in 1 cup cheddar cheese, ham, Parmesan cheese and macaroni.

Transfer to a greased 2-qt. baking dish. Sprinkle with remaining cheddar cheese. Bake, uncovered, at 350° for 20-25 minutes or until bubbly. Let stand for 5 minutes before serving. **Yield:** 6 servings.

Breakfast Fare

Pecan Apple Pancakes

(Pictured above)

PREP: 15 min.
COOK: 10 min./batch

Weekend breakfasts are a big deal here in Texas, and these sweet, well-spiced pancakes make any breakfast special. So put on your cooking apron and invite the neighbors over!
—Sharon Richardson, Dallas, Texas

> 2 cups all-purpose flour
> 1 cup sugar
> 2 teaspoons baking powder
> 1 teaspoon baking soda
> 1 teaspoon ground cinnamon
> 1/2 teaspoon salt
> 1/2 teaspoon ground ginger
> 1/2 teaspoon ground mace
> 1/2 teaspoon ground cloves
> 2 eggs
> 1-3/4 cups buttermilk
> 3 tablespoons canola oil
> 1-3/4 cups shredded peeled apples
> 1/2 cup chopped pecans

In a large bowl, combine the first nine ingredients. In another bowl, combine the eggs, buttermilk and oil; stir into dry ingredients just until blended. Stir in apples and pecans.

Pour batter by 1/4 cupfuls onto a greased griddle over medium-low heat. Turn when bubbles form on top; cook until second side is golden brown. **Yield:** 1-1/2 dozen.

Buckwheat Brunch Crepes

(Pictured below)

PREP: 20 min. + standing
COOK: 15 min.

My husband and I enjoy these delicious crepes with sweet berry sauce and cream on Saturday mornings. We even have them for dinner with sausage and eggs. They're considered a special treat here, especially when served with maple syrup.
—Sharon Dyck, Roxton Falls, Quebec

> 5 tablespoons heavy whipping cream
> 1/2 cup sour cream
> 1/2 cup milk
> 2 eggs
> 1/3 cup all-purpose flour
> 3 tablespoons buckwheat flour *or* whole wheat flour
> 1/2 teaspoon salt
> **BERRY SAUCE:**
> 1/2 cup sugar
> 1 tablespoon cornstarch
> Dash salt
> 1/2 cup water
> 1/3 cup fresh blueberries

> 1/3 cup fresh raspberries
> 4-1/2 teaspoons butter, *divided*
> 1 teaspoon lemon juice

In a small bowl, beat the whipping cream until stiff peaks form; fold into sour cream. Cover and refrigerate.

In a small bowl, combine milk and eggs. Combine the flours and salt; add to milk mixture and mix well. Let stand for 30 minutes.

Meanwhile, for the sauce, in a small saucepan, combine the sugar, cornstarch and salt; stir in water until smooth. Bring to a boil; cook and stir for 1-2 minutes or until thickened. Add berries; cook over medium-low heat until berries burst. Add 1-1/2 teaspoons butter and lemon juice, stirring until butter is melted. Set aside and keep warm.

Melt 1 teaspoon butter in an 8-in. nonstick skillet; pour 2 tablespoons batter into the center of skillet. Lift and tilt pan to evenly coat bottom. Cook until top appears dry; turn and cook 15-20 seconds longer. Remove to a wire rack. Repeat with remaining batter, adding butter to skillet as needed. Stack crepes with waxed paper or paper towels in between and keep warm. Serve crepes with berry sauce and cream mixture. **Yield:** about 6 crepes.

Asparagus Crab Omelets

(Pictured above right)

PREP/TOTAL TIME: 30 min.

These satisfying omelets are filled with a savory blend of crabmeat, asparagus, tomatoes and provolone cheese...and they're attractive enough to serve guests. Sometimes I top the omelets with hollandaise sauce.
—Mae Jean Damron, Sandy, Utah

> 6 fresh asparagus spears, trimmed
> 4 eggs
> Dash salt
> Dash pepper

1/2 cup diced plum tomatoes

2 tablespoons butter, *divided*

1 can (6 ounces) crabmeat, drained and flaked, cartilage removed

1/2 cup (2 ounces) provolone cheese, shredded

Place asparagus in a steamer basket. Place in a saucepan over 1 in. of water; bring to a boil. Cover and steam for 4-5 minutes or until crisp-tender; set aside. In a small bowl, whisk the eggs, salt and pepper. Stir in tomatoes.

Melt 1 tablespoon butter in a small skillet over medium heat; add half of the egg mixture. As eggs set, lift edges, letting uncooked portion flow underneath. When the eggs are set, spoon half of the crab, asparagus and provolone cheese over one side; fold the omelet over filling. Cover and let stand for 1-2 minutes or until the cheese is melted. Repeat for second omelet. **Yield:** 2 servings.

Apple-Stuffed French Toast

(Pictured at right)

PREP: 20 min. + chilling
BAKE: 35 min.

This is a great breakfast dish to make ahead for the holidays or even Sunday brunch. I run a bed–and–breakfast with a tea room cafe, and this recipe is often requested by customers.
—Kay Clark, Lawrenceburg, Kentucky

1 cup packed brown sugar

1/2 cup butter, cubed

2 tablespoons light corn syrup

1 cup chopped pecans

12 slices Italian bread (1/2 inch thick)

2 large tart apples, peeled and thinly sliced

6 eggs

1-1/2 cups milk

1-1/2 teaspoons ground cinnamon

1 teaspoon vanilla extract

1/4 teaspoon salt

1/4 teaspoon ground nutmeg

CARAMEL SAUCE:

1/2 cup packed brown sugar

1/4 cup butter, cubed

1 tablespoon light corn syrup

In a small saucepan, combine the brown sugar, butter and corn syrup; cook and stir over medium heat until thickened. Pour into a greased 13-in. x 9-in. x 2-in. baking dish; top with half of the pecans, a single layer of bread and then remaining pecans. Arrange apples and remaining bread over the top.

In a large bowl, whisk the eggs, milk, cinnamon, vanilla, salt and nutmeg. Pour over bread. Cover and refrigerate overnight.

Remove from the refrigerator for 30 minutes before baking. Bake, uncovered, at 350° for 35-40 minutes or until lightly browned.

For the sauce, in a small saucepan, combine the brown sugar, butter and corn syrup. Cook and stir over medium heat until thickened. Serve with French toast. **Yield:** 6 servings.

Cornmeal Ham Cakes

(Pictured above)

PREP/TOTAL TIME: 30 min.

These cakes are hearty because of the addition of ham. My husband and I think they are great for breakfast, but we also enjoy them for supper. The tangy syrup makes them super delicious!
—Priscilla Gilbert
Indian Harbour Beach, Florida

1/2 cup all-purpose flour

1/2 cup cornmeal

2 tablespoons sugar

1/2 teaspoon baking powder

1/4 teaspoon baking soda

1/8 teaspoon salt

2 eggs, lightly beaten

1 cup buttermilk

3 tablespoons butter, melted

1 teaspoon vanilla extract

1-1/2 cups diced fully cooked ham

PINEAPPLE MAPLE SYRUP:

1 cup diced fresh pineapple

1/4 teaspoon ground cinnamon

1 tablespoon butter

1 cup maple syrup

In a large bowl, combine the first six ingredients. Combine the eggs, buttermilk, butter and vanilla; stir into dry ingredients until well blended. Fold in the ham. Pour batter by 1/4 cupfuls onto a greased hot griddle. Turn when bubbles form on top; cook until the second side is golden brown.

For syrup, in a small saucepan, saute the pineapple and cinnamon in butter for 4-6 minutes or until pineapple is browned. Stir in maple syrup. Serve with pancakes. **Yield:** 4 servings.

sauce, brown sugar, water, sesame oil, pepper flakes and ginger. Add the chicken; seal bag and turn to coat. Refrigerate for 2 hours, turning occasionally.

Drain and discard marinade. In a large bowl, toss the asparagus with olive oil and salt. On six metal or soaked wooden skewers, alternately thread one chicken piece and two asparagus pieces.

Grill, covered, over medium heat for 4-5 minutes on each side or until chicken juices run clear and asparagus is crisp-tender. Serve with dipping sauce. **Yield:** 6 servings.

Tasty Pork Ribs

(Pictured below)

PREP: 10 min. **COOK:** 6 hours

I like to serve these tender, country-style ribs over rice. The tantalizing aroma and zippy Cajun barbecue sauce are sure to make these ribs a favorite at your house.
—Michelle Rominger, Albia, Iowa

- 8 **bone-in country-style pork ribs (8 ounces *each*)**
- 1 **cup ketchup**
- 1 **cup barbecue sauce**
- 1/4 **cup packed brown sugar**
- 1/4 **cup Worcestershire sauce**
- 1 **tablespoon balsamic vinegar**
- 1 **tablespoon molasses**
- 1 **garlic clove, minced**
- 2 **tablespoons dried minced onion**
- 1 **teaspoon Cajun seasoning**
- 1 **teaspoon ground mustard**
- 1/2 **teaspoon salt**
- 1/4 **teaspoon pepper**

Place ribs in a 5-qt. slow cooker. Combine the remaining ingredients; pour over ribs.

Cover and cook on low for 6-7 hours or until meat is tender. **Yield:** 8 servings.

Grand Prize Winner

Chicken and Asparagus Kabobs

(Pictured above)

PREP: 25 min. + marinating **GRILL:** 10 min.

These Asian-inspired kabobs, served with a tasty dipping sauce, are special enough to make for guests at your next backyard get-together. Sometimes I substitute salmon for the chicken.
—Kelly Townsend, Syracuse, Nebraska

DIPPING SAUCE:
- 2 **cups mayonnaise**
- 1/4 **cup sugar**
- 1/4 **cup soy sauce**
- 2 **tablespoons sesame seeds, toasted**
- 1 **tablespoon sesame oil**
- 1/2 **teaspoon white pepper**

KABOBS:
- 1/4 **cup soy sauce**
- 2 **tablespoons brown sugar**
- 2 **tablespoons water**
- 1 **tablespoon sesame oil**
- 1 **teaspoon crushed red pepper flakes**
- 1 **teaspoon minced fresh gingerroot**
- 1-1/2 **pounds boneless skinless chicken breasts, cut into 1-1/2-inch pieces**
- 1 **pound fresh asparagus, trimmed and cut into 2-inch pieces**
- 2 **tablespoons olive oil**
- 1/2 **teaspoon salt**

Combine the sauce ingredients. Cover and refrigerate for 2-4 hours.

In a large resealable plastic bag, combine the soy

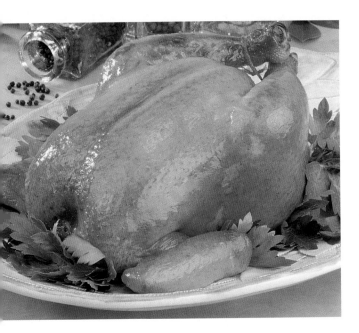

with pan drippings (cover loosely with foil if chicken browns too quickly).

Remove chicken to a serving platter and keep warm. Pour drippings and loosened browned bits into a measuring cup; skim fat and discard. Add enough broth to measure 1 cup. In a small saucepan, combine flour and broth mixture until smooth. Bring to a boil; cook and stir for 2 minutes or until thickened. Serve with the chicken. **Yield:** 4-6 servings.

Waldorf Stuffed Ham

(Pictured below)

PREP: 35 min. **BAKE:** 1-1/4 hours + standing

I wanted to try something new with my spiral ham, and this recipe just popped into my head. I served it to my husband, and he said it's a keeper. —Colleen Vrooman, Waukesha, Wisconsin

  1-1/2 **cups unsweetened apple juice**
    1/4 **cup butter, cubed**
      1 **package (6 ounces) pork stuffing mix**
      1 **medium tart apple, finely chopped**
    1/4 **cup chopped sweet onion**
    1/4 **cup chopped celery**
    1/4 **cup chopped walnuts**
      1 **fully cooked spiral-sliced ham (8 pounds)**
      1 **can (21 ounces) apple pie filling**
    1/4 **teaspoon ground cinnamon**

In a large saucepan, bring apple juice and butter to a boil. Remove from the heat; stir in the stuffing mix, apple, onion, celery and walnuts.

Place ham on a rack in a shallow roasting pan. Spoon stuffing by tablespoonfuls between ham slices. Spoon pie filling over ham; sprinkle with cinnamon.

Bake, uncovered, at 325° for 1-1/4 to 1-3/4 hours or until a meat thermometer reads 140°. Let stand for 10 minutes before serving. **Yield:** 14-16 servings.

Brined Roasting Chicken

(Pictured above)

PREP: 30 min. + marinating **BAKE:** 1 hour 20 min.

I discovered the art of brining turkey a few years ago and transferred the technique to roasting a whole chicken. I guarantee you will have a moist bird and rich flavorful gravy from the pan drippings. —Julie Noyes, Louisville, Kentucky

      8 **cups warm water**
    1/2 **cup kosher salt**
    1/4 **cup packed brown sugar**
      3 **tablespoons molasses**
      1 **tablespoon whole peppercorns, crushed**
      1 **tablespoon whole allspice, crushed**
      2 **teaspoons ground ginger**
      1 **roasting chicken**
      4 **cups cold water**
      1 **teaspoon canola oil**
  3/4 to 1 **cup chicken broth**
      1 **tablespoon all-purpose flour**

For brine, combine the first seven ingredients in a large kettle. Bring to a boil; cook and stir until salt is dissolved. Remove from the heat. Cool to room temperature.

Remove the giblets from chicken; discard. Over a large roasting pan, place cold water in a 2-gal. resealable plastic bag; add chicken. Carefully pour the cooled brine into the bag. Squeeze out as much air as possible; seal bag, turn to coat and place in pan. Refrigerate for 3-4 hours, turning several times.

Discard brine. Rinse chicken with water; pat dry. Use a skewer to close chicken openings; tie drumsticks together. Brush chicken with oil; place in a roasting pan. Bake, uncovered, at 350° for 80-90 minutes or until a meat thermometer reads 180°, basting occasionally

Tenderloin in Puff Pastry

(Pictured below)

PREP: 20 min. + chilling **BAKE:** 20 min.

I came up with this entree after combining several different recipes. I set each fillet on puff pastry, then top them with a tasty mushroom mixture. It sounds like a lot of work, but it isn't...and it's so elegant.

—*Julie Mahoney, St. Edward, Nebraska*

- 4 **beef tenderloin fillets (1-3/4 inches thick and about 5 ounces *each*)**
- 1 **tablespoon canola oil**
- 1/2 **pound sliced fresh mushrooms**
- 4 **green onions, chopped**
- 1/4 **cup butter**
- 1/2 **teaspoon salt**
- 1/4 **teaspoon pepper**
- 1 **frozen puff pastry sheet, thawed**
- 1 **egg**
- 1 **tablespoon water**

In a large skillet, brown fillets in oil on both sides. Place a wire rack on a baking sheet. Transfer fillets to wire rack; refrigerate for 1 hour. In the same skillet, saute mushrooms and onions in butter until tender; drain. Stir in the salt and pepper.

On a lightly floured surface, roll pastry into a 13-in. square. Cut into four squares. Place one fillet in the center of each square; top with mushroom mixture. Combine egg and water; brush over pastry.

Bring up corners to center and tuck in edges; press to seal. Place on a parchment paper-lined baking sheet. Cover and refrigerate for 1 hour or overnight.

Bake, uncovered, at 400° for 20-25 minutes or until the pastry is golden brown and the meat reaches desired doneness (for medium-rare, a meat thermometer should read 145°; medium, 160°; well-done, 170°).
Yield: 4 servings.

Vegetarian Stuffed Peppers

(Pictured above)

PREP: 30 min. **COOK:** 3-1/2 hours

These filling and flavorful peppers are an updated version of my mom's stuffed peppers, which were a favorite when I was growing up in upstate New York. Whenever I make them, I'm reminded of home. Try them at your house tonight.

—*Melissa McCabe, Long Beach, California*

- 6 **large sweet peppers**
- 2 **cups cooked brown rice**
- 3 **small tomatoes, diced**
- 1 **cup frozen corn, thawed**
- 1 **small sweet onion, diced**
- 1/3 **cup canned red beans, rinsed and drained**
- 1/3 **cup canned black beans, rinsed and drained**
- 3/4 **cup cubed Monterey Jack cheese**
- 1 **can (4-1/4 ounces) chopped ripe olives**
- 4 **fresh basil leaves, chopped**
- 3 **garlic cloves, minced**
- 1 **teaspoon salt**
- 1/2 **teaspoon pepper**
- 3/4 **cup meatless spaghetti sauce**
- 1/2 **cup water**
- 4 **tablespoons grated Parmesan cheese, *divided***

Cut tops off peppers and remove seeds; set aside. In a large bowl, combine the rice, tomatoes, corn, onion and beans. Stir in the Monterey Jack cheese, olives, basil, garlic, salt and pepper. Spoon into peppers.

Combine spaghetti sauce and water; pour half into an oval 5-qt. slow cooker. Add the stuffed peppers. Top with remaining sauce. Sprinkle with 2 tablespoons Parmesan cheese.

Cover and cook on low for 3-1/2 to 4 hours or until the peppers are tender and the filling is heated through. Sprinkle with remaining Parmesan cheese.
Yield: 6 servings.

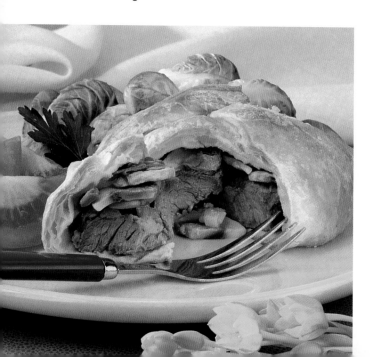

Spicy Nacho Bake

(Pictured below)

PREP: 1 hour **BAKE:** 20 min.

I made this hearty, layered Southwestern casserole for a dinner meeting once; and now, I'm asked to bring it every time we have a potluck. Everybody loves the ground beef and bean filling, and crunchy, cheesy topping. —Anita Wilson, Mansfield, Ohio

- 2 **pounds ground beef**
- 2 **large onions, chopped**
- 2 **large green peppers, chopped**
- 2 **cans (28 ounces** *each***) diced tomatoes, undrained**
- 2 **cans (15-1/2 ounces** *each***) hot chili beans**
- 2 **cans (15 ounces** *each***) black beans, rinsed and drained**
- 2 **cans (11 ounces** *each***) whole kernel corn, drained**
- 2 **cans (8 ounces** *each***) tomato sauce**
- 2 **envelopes taco seasoning**
- 2 **packages (13 ounces** *each***) spicy nacho tortilla chips**
- 4 **cups (16 ounces) shredded cheddar cheese**

In a Dutch oven or large kettle, cook the beef, onions and green peppers over medium heat until meat is no longer pink; drain. Stir in the tomatoes, beans, corn, tomato sauce and taco seasoning. Bring to a boil. Reduce heat; simmer, uncovered, for 30 minutes (mixture will be thin).

In each of two greased 13-in. x 9-in. x 2-in. baking dishes, layer 5 cups of chips and 4-2/3 cups of meat mixture. Repeat layers. Top each with 4 cups of chips and 2 cups of cheese.

Bake, uncovered, at 350° for 20-25 minutes or until golden brown. **Yield:** 2 casseroles (15 servings each).

Pretty Penne Ham Skillet

(Pictured above)

PREP/TOTAL TIME: 30 min.

I enjoy experimenting with herbs and spices to cut down on salt and sugar. This recipe takes advantage of aromatic herbs, such as parsley, basil and oregano.
—Kathy Stephan, West Seneca, New York

- 1 **package (16 ounces) penne pasta**
- 3 **cups cubed fully cooked ham**
- 1 **large sweet red pepper, diced**
- 1 **medium onion, chopped**
- 1/4 **cup minced fresh parsley**
- 2 **garlic cloves, minced**
- 1-1/2 **teaspoons minced fresh basil** *or* **1/2 teaspoon dried basil**
- 1-1/2 **teaspoons minced fresh oregano** *or* **1/2 teaspoon dried oregano**
- 1/4 **cup olive oil**
- 3 **tablespoons butter**
- 1 **can (14-1/2 ounces) chicken broth**
- 1 **tablespoon lemon juice**
- 1/2 **cup shredded Parmesan cheese**

Cook pasta according to package directions. Meanwhile, in a large skillet, saute the ham, red pepper, onion, parsley, garlic, basil and oregano in oil and butter for 4-6 minutes or until ham is browned and vegetables are tender.

Stir in the broth and lemon juice. Bring to a boil. Reduce heat; simmer, uncovered, for 10-15 minutes or until liquid is reduced by half. Drain the pasta and stir into ham mixture. Sprinkle with Parmesan cheese. **Yield:** 6 servings.

pepper. Grill asparagus, uncovered, over medium heat for 6-8 minutes or until tender, turning every 2 minutes. Cut into 1-inch pieces.

Punch the dough down. Turn onto a floured surface; divide into eight portions. Roll each portion into a 6-in. circle. Place dough directly on grill.

Grill, uncovered, over medium heat for 1-2 minutes or until bubbles form on top. Place toasted side up on two ungreased baking sheets. Top with pizza sauce, asparagus, ham and cheese. Cover and grill 2-3 minutes longer or until the bottom of the crust is golden brown. **Yield:** 8 servings.

Curried Beef with Dumplings

(Pictured below)

PREP: 30 min. **COOK:** 2-3/4 hours

I like making this robust pot roast in the winter and serve leftovers the next day. It's not only easy to prepare, but the aroma is just wonderful while it's cooking.
—Janell Schmidt, Athelstane, Wisconsin

- 1 boneless beef rump roast (3 pounds)
- 2 tablespoons olive oil
- 6 medium carrots, cut into chunks
- 1 can (14-1/2 ounces) diced tomatoes, undrained
- 1 medium onion, sliced
- 2 teaspoons curry powder
- 1 teaspoon sugar
- 2 teaspoons salt, *divided*
- 1 teaspoon Worcestershire sauce
- 1 cup hot water
- 1-2/3 cups all-purpose flour
- 3 teaspoons baking powder
- 2 tablespoons cold butter

Grilled Asparagus Pizzas

(Pictured above)

PREP: 20 min. + rising **GRILL:** 10 min.

Tired of pepperoni pizza? When we have the grill going, we like to make this recipe. The chewy, from–scratch crust is topped with pizza sauce, mozzarella cheese, asparagus and ham. Made on the grill, it's even better than delivery!
—Monica Woods, Springfield, Missouri

- 1-3/4 to 2-1/2 cups all-purpose flour
- 1 package (1/4 ounce) quick-rise yeast
- 1 tablespoon minced fresh thyme
- 1 teaspoon salt
- 1/2 teaspoon sugar
- 3/4 cup warm water (120° to 130°)
- 24 asparagus spears, trimmed
- 1 tablespoon olive oil
- 1/8 teaspoon garlic salt
- 1/8 teaspoon pepper
- 1 cup pizza sauce
- 3 ounces thinly sliced deli ham, chopped
- 2 cups (8 ounces) shredded part-skim mozzarella cheese

In large bowl, combine 1 cup flour, yeast, thyme, salt and sugar. Add water; beat until blended. Stir in enough remaining flour to form a soft dough. Turn onto a floured surface; knead until smooth and elastic, about 6-8 minutes. Place in a greased bowl, turning once to grease top. Cover and let rise in warm place until doubled, about 1 hour.

Brush asparagus with oil; sprinkle with garlic salt and

3/4 cup milk
2 tablespoons minced fresh parsley
2 tablespoons chopped pimientos

In a Dutch oven, brown roast in oil on all sides; drain. Combine the carrots, tomatoes, onion, curry powder, sugar, 1 teaspoon salt and Worcestershire sauce; pour over roast. Bring to a boil. Reduce heat to low; cover and cook for 2-1/2 hours or until meat and carrots are tender.

Remove roast and carrots; keep warm. Add hot water to pan; bring to a boil. For dumplings, combine the flour, baking powder and remaining salt in a large bowl. Cut in butter until mixture resembles fine crumbs. Stir in the milk, parsley and pimientos just until moistened.

Drop by tablespoonfuls onto simmering liquid. Cover and cook for 15 minutes or until a toothpick inserted in a dumpling comes out clean (do not lift cover while simmering). Remove the dumplings. Strain the cooking juices and serve with roast, dumplings and carrots. **Yield:** 8 servings.

Vegetarian Pasta Sauce

PREP: 35 min. **COOK:** 2 hours

Loaded with fresh vegetables and herbs, this hearty, meatless sauce is a perfect way for gardeners to make delicious use of their harvest. You can also add half a cup of red wine to the sauce during the cooking process, if you wish.
—*Jerry Tamburino, Sacramento, California*

3 medium onions, chopped
1 medium green pepper, chopped
1 medium sweet red pepper, chopped
5 garlic cloves, minced
2 tablespoons olive oil
3 medium zucchini, chopped
3 medium yellow summer squash, chopped
3 medium tomatoes, chopped
1 medium eggplant, peeled and cubed
1/2 pound sliced fresh mushrooms
2 cans (28 ounces *each*) Italian crushed tomatoes
1 can (6 ounces) tomato paste
2 cans (2-1/4 ounces *each*) sliced ripe olives, drained
1/4 cup minced fresh basil
3 tablespoons minced fresh oregano
2 tablespoons minced fresh rosemary
2 teaspoons Italian seasoning
1-1/2 teaspoons salt
1/2 teaspoon pepper

In a Dutch oven, saute the onions, peppers and garlic in olive oil until tender. Add the zucchini, summer squash, tomatoes, eggplant and mushrooms; cook and stir for 5 minutes.

Stir in the remaining ingredients. Bring to a boil. Reduce heat; simmer, uncovered, for 1-1/2 to 2 hours or until sauce is thickened. **Yield:** 14 servings (1 cup each).

Shrimp Pasta Primavera

(Pictured above)

PREP/TOTAL TIME: 15 min.

When I invite that special someone to dinner, I like to prepare something equally special. This well-seasoned pasta dish has lots of flavor...and it won't hurt your budget!
—*Shari Neff, Takoma Park, Maryland*

4 ounces uncooked angel hair pasta
8 jumbo shrimp, peeled and deveined
6 fresh asparagus spears, trimmed and cut into 2-inch pieces
2 garlic cloves, minced
1/4 cup olive oil
1/2 cup sliced fresh mushrooms
1/2 cup chicken broth
1 small plum tomato, peeled, seeded and diced
1/4 teaspoon salt
1/8 teaspoon crushed red pepper flakes
1 tablespoon *each* minced fresh basil, oregano, thyme and parsley
1/4 cup grated Parmesan cheese

Cook the angel hair pasta according to package directions. Meanwhile, in a large skillet, saute the shrimp, asparagus and garlic in oil for 3-4 minutes or until shrimp turn pink. Add the mushrooms, broth, tomato, salt and pepper flakes; simmer, uncovered, for 2 minutes.

Drain the pasta. Add the pasta and fresh herbs to the skillet; toss to coat. Sprinkle with Parmesan cheese. **Yield:** 2 servings.

Asparagus Pasta Primavera

(Pictured below)

PREP/TOTAL TIME: 25 min.

There's plenty of fresh herb flavor in this delicious pasta meal that blends asparagus, ham, mushrooms and plum tomatoes. Sometimes I like to use spinach–flavored linguine or fettuccine instead of plain pasta.

—*William Anatooskin, Burnaby, British Columbia*

- **6 tablespoons butter, cubed**
- **3 tablespoons olive oil**
- **8 garlic cloves, minced**
- **1-1/2 pounds fresh asparagus, trimmed and cut into 1-inch pieces**
- **1-1/2 cups sliced fresh mushrooms**
- **1/2 cup chopped fully cooked ham**
- **2 tablespoons *each* chopped fresh basil, oregano and rosemary**
- **4 large plum tomatoes, chopped**
- **1 teaspoon salt**
- **1/4 teaspoon pepper**
- **12 ounces uncooked linguine**
- **1/2 cup shredded Parmesan cheese**

In a large skillet, melt butter with oil over medium heat. Add garlic; cook and stir for 3 minutes. Stir in the asparagus. Cover and cook for 1 minute. Add the mushrooms, ham, basil, oregano and rosemary. Cover and cook for 5 minutes or until asparagus is crisp-tender, stirring occasionally.

Stir in the tomatoes, salt and pepper. Cook 3 minutes longer or until heated through.

Meanwhile, cook linguine according to package directions; drain and place in a large bowl. Add asparagus mixture and toss. Sprinkle with Parmesan cheese. **Yield:** 6-8 servings.

Asian Chicken Thighs

(Pictured above)

PREP: 15 min.   **COOK:** 50 min.

A thick, tangy sauce coats these golden chicken pieces in this savory skillet recipe. I like to serve them over long grain rice or with a helping of ramen noodle slaw.

—*Dave Farrington, Midwest City, Oklahoma*

- **5 bone-in chicken thighs, skin removed**
- **5 teaspoons olive oil**
- **1/3 cup warm water**
- **1/4 cup packed brown sugar**
- **2 tablespoons orange juice**
- **2 tablespoons soy sauce**
- **2 tablespoons ketchup**
- **1 tablespoon white vinegar**
- **4 garlic cloves, minced**
- **1/2 teaspoon crushed red pepper flakes**
- **1/4 teaspoon Chinese five-spice powder**
- **2 teaspoons cornstarch**
- **2 tablespoons cold water**

Hot cooked rice
Sliced green onions

In a large skillet, brown chicken over medium heat in oil for 18-20 minutes or until juices run clear. Meanwhile, in a jar with a tight-fitting lid, combine the warm water, brown sugar, orange juice, soy sauce, ketchup, vinegar, garlic, pepper flakes and five-spice powder; shake until sugar is dissolved.

Pour over the chicken. Bring to a boil. Reduce heat; simmer, uncovered, for 30-35 minutes or until chicken is tender, turning occasionally.

Combine cornstarch and cold water until smooth; gradually stir into skillet. Bring to a boil; cook and stir for 2 minutes or until thickened. Serve with rice. Garnish with green onions. **Yield:** 5 servings.

Indiana Swiss Steak

(Pictured below)

PREP: 20 min. **COOK:** 1 hour

I entered the Indiana State Beef Contest and won first place with this recipe. A mixture of picante sauce, ketchup, cider vinegar and veggies enhances the tender slices of steak that are served over pasta. I use bow tie pasta, but you could substitute rice.
—Ann Dixon, North Vernon, Indiana

- 1/4 cup all-purpose flour
- 1 teaspoon salt
- 1/2 teaspoon pepper
- 1-1/2 pounds boneless beef top round steak, cut into serving-size pieces
- 1 tablespoon canola oil
- 1 medium onion, chopped
- 3/4 cup grated carrot
- 3/4 cup water
- 1/2 cup chopped celery
- 1/2 cup chopped green pepper
- 1/2 cup ketchup
- 1/4 cup picante sauce
- 1 tablespoon cider vinegar
Hot cooked pasta

In a large resealable plastic bag, combine the flour, salt and pepper. Add beef, a few pieces at a time, and shake to coat. In a large skillet, brown beef in oil.

Combine the onion, carrot, water, celery, green pepper, ketchup, picante sauce and vinegar; pour over beef. Bring to a boil. Reduce heat; cover and simmer for 60-75 minutes or until beef is tender. Serve over the pasta. **Yield:** 6 servings.

Pecan Chicken with Chutney

(Pictured above)

PREP: 15 min. **COOK:** 20 min.

These zippy, pecan-crusted chicken breasts are so tender, and the easy-fix peach chutney adds a sweet-sour taste. I usually serve them with rice on the side.
—Carisa Bravoco, Furlong, Pennsylvania

- 3/4 cup all-purpose flour
- 1/8 teaspoon salt
- 1/8 teaspoon pepper
- 2 eggs
- 1/3 cup buttermilk
- 1/8 teaspoon hot pepper sauce
- 1 cup finely chopped pecans
- 3/4 cup dry bread crumbs
- 6 boneless skinless chicken breast halves (6 ounces *each*)
- 2 tablespoons butter
- 2 tablespoons canola oil
PEACH MANGO CHUTNEY:
- 2 cups sliced peeled fresh *or* frozen peaches, thawed
- 1 cup mango chutney

In a shallow bowl, combine the flour, salt and pepper. In another shallow bowl, whisk the eggs, buttermilk and hot pepper sauce. In a third bowl, combine the pecans and bread crumbs.

Flatten chicken to 1/4-in. thickness. Coat chicken with flour mixture, then dip in egg mixture and coat with the pecan mixture.

In a large skillet over medium heat, cook chicken in butter and oil for 8-10 minutes on each side or until juices run clear.

Meanwhile, in a small saucepan, combine peaches and chutney. Bring to a boil. Reduce heat; simmer, uncovered, for 15-20 minutes or until heated through. Serve with chicken. **Yield:** 6 servings (1-3/4 cups chutney).

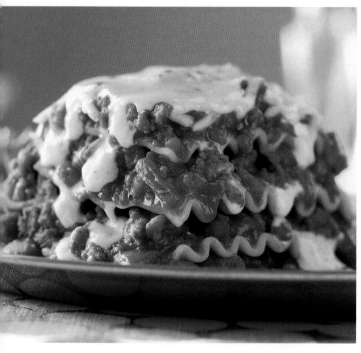

In a bowl, combine Monterey Jack and mozzarella cheeses; set aside 1 cup. Stir cottage cheese and 3/4 cup sour cream into remaining cheese mixture.

Spread 1 cup of the meat sauce into a greased 13-in. x 9-in. x 2-in. baking dish. Layer with three noodles, and a third of the cottage cheese mixture and meat sauce. Repeat layers twice (dish will be full). Cover and bake at 350° for 1 hour.

Uncover; spread with remaining sour cream. Sprinkle with reserved cheeses. Bake 10-12 minutes longer or until cheese is melted. Let stand for 20 minutes before serving. **Yield:** 12 servings.

Lime Shrimp with Asparagus

(Pictured below)

PREP/TOTAL TIME: 15 min.

For this colorful main dish, I combine shrimp, asparagus and sweet red pepper and flavor them with lime juice, lime peel, garlic and soy sauce. It may look like it takes a long time to prepare, but it goes together fast in the microwave.
—Peggy Davies, Canon City, Colorado

- 3/4 **pound fresh asparagus, trimmed and cut into 2-inch pieces**
- 1 **garlic clove, minced**
- 2 **tablespoons water**
- 3/4 **pound uncooked medium shrimp, peeled and deveined**
- 1 **medium sweet red pepper, thinly sliced**
- 1 **jalapeno pepper, seeded and finely chopped**
- 1 **teaspoon cornstarch**
- 2 **tablespoons soy sauce**
- 1 **tablespoon lime juice**
- 1/2 **teaspoon grated lime peel**

Hot cooked rice

Place the asparagus, garlic and water in a 1-1/2-qt. microwave-safe dish. Cover and microwave on high for

Fiesta Lasagna

(Pictured above)

PREP: 25 min. **BAKE:** 70 min. + standing

Loaded with Mexican–style ingredients, this filling lasagna is sure to please the whole gang, whether you make it for your family or take it to a potluck. Every bite is mmm–good!
—Karen Ann Bland, Gove, Kansas

- 1 **pound ground beef**
- 1/4 **cup chopped onion**
- 1 **can (16 ounces) refried beans**
- 1 **can (15-1/2 ounces) mild chili beans**
- 1 **can (14-1/2 ounces) Mexican stewed tomatoes, drained**
- 1 **cup salsa**
- 1 **can (4 ounces) chopped green chilies**
- 1 **envelope reduced-sodium taco seasoning**
- 1 **teaspoon dried oregano**
- 1 **teaspoon ground cumin**
- 1/4 **teaspoon garlic powder**
- 1-1/4 **cups shredded Monterey Jack cheese**
- 1-1/4 **cups shredded part-skim mozzarella cheese**
- 3/4 **cup 4% cottage cheese**
- 1-1/4 **cups sour cream,** *divided*
- 9 **lasagna noodles, cooked, rinsed and drained**

In a Dutch oven, cook beef and onion over medium heat until meat is no longer pink; drain. Stir in the beans, tomatoes, salsa, chilies and seasonings.

In a small skillet, saute red pepper and garlic in oil until tender. Remove from the heat. In another small bowl, combine the remaining ingredients; stir in red pepper mixture. Pour into crust.

Bake at 375° for 25-30 minutes or until a knife inserted near the center comes out clean. Let stand for 5 minutes before cutting. **Yield:** 8 servings.

Steaks with Cucumber Sauce

(Pictured below)

PREP: 10 min. + marinating **GRILL:** 10 min.

Tender steaks, marinated with teriyaki sauce, are accompanied by a creamy cucumber sauce in this recipe.
—*Erika Aylward, Clinton, Michigan*

- 4 **boneless beef New York strip steaks (8 to 10 ounces** *each***)**
- 3/4 **cup teriyaki sauce**
- 1/2 **cup chopped seeded peeled cucumber**
- 1/2 **cup sour cream**
- 1/2 **cup mayonnaise**
- 1 **tablespoon minced chives**
- 1/2 **to 1 teaspoon dill weed**
- 1/4 **teaspoon salt**

Place the steaks in a large resealable plastic bag; add the teriyaki sauce. Seal bag and turn to coat; refrigerate overnight. In a bowl, combine the cucumber, sour cream, mayonnaise, chives, dill and salt. Cover and refrigerate.

Drain and discard marinade. Grill steaks, uncovered, over medium-hot heat for 4-5 minutes on each side or until meat reaches desired doneness (for medium-rare, a meat thermometer should read 145°; medium, 160°; well-done, 170°). Serve with the cucumber sauce. **Yield:** 4 servings.

Grand Prize Winner

Pepperoni Spinach Quiche

(Pictured above)

PREP: 25 min. **BAKE:** 25 min.

Several years ago, I had to come up with an appetizer to serve at a party, and this colorful quiche was a hit. You can serve it as an entree, but it's great on an antipasto tray, cut into wedges.
—*Elly Townsend, Summerfield, Florida*

- 1 **tube (8 ounces) refrigerated crescent rolls**
- 1 **large sweet red pepper, chopped**
- 1 **garlic clove, minced**
- 1 **tablespoon olive oil**
- 5 **eggs, lightly beaten**
- 1/2 **cup shredded part-skim mozzarella cheese**
- 1/2 **cup frozen chopped spinach, thawed and squeezed dry**
- 1/4 **cup sliced pepperoni, cut into strips**
- 1/4 **cup half-and-half cream**
- 2 **tablespoons grated Parmesan cheese**
- 1 **tablespoon minced fresh parsley**
- 1 **tablespoon minced fresh basil** *or* **1 teaspoon dried basil**

Dash pepper

Separate the crescent dough into eight triangles; place in an ungreased 9-in. fluted tart pan with removable bottom with the points toward the center. Press onto the bottom and up the sides to form a crust; seal seams. Set aside.

Mozzarella-Stuffed Meatballs

(Pictured above)

PREP: 20 min. **COOK:** 15 min.

It's fun to watch my friends eat these meatballs for the first time. They're pleasantly surprised to find melted cheese in the middle. These meatballs are also great in a hot sub sandwich.
—Michaela Rosenthal, Woodland Hills, California

- **1 egg, lightly beaten**
- **1/4 cup prepared Italian salad dressing**
- **1-1/2 cups cubed bread**
- **2 tablespoons minced fresh parsley**
- **2 garlic cloves, minced**
- **1/2 teaspoon dried oregano**
- **1/2 teaspoon pepper**
- **1/4 teaspoon salt**
- **1/2 pound ground pork**
- **1/2 pound ground sirloin**
- **3 ounces fresh mozzarella cheese**
- **2 tablespoons canola oil**
- **1 jar (26 ounces) marinara sauce**

Hot cooked pasta

In a large bowl, combine the first eight ingredients. Crumble the pork and beef over egg mixture; mix well. Cut mozzarella into eighteen 1/2-in. cubes. Divide the meat mixture into 18 portions; shape each around a cheese cube.

In a large skillet, cook meatballs in oil in batches until no pink remains; drain. In a large saucepan, heat marinara sauce; add meatballs and heat through. Serve over pasta. **Yield:** 6 servings.

Old-Fashioned Chicken Potpie

(Pictured below)

PREP: 1 hour **BAKE:** 15 min.

I use leftover chicken broth to make this comforting family favorite. You can bake your own biscuits, like I do, or simply buy them at the store. I like to bake extra biscuits to eat with butter and jam.
—Liliane Jahnke, Cypress, Texas

- **1-1/2 cups sliced fresh mushrooms**
- **1 cup sliced fresh carrots**
- **1/2 cup chopped onion**
- **1/3 cup butter**
- **1/3 cup all-purpose flour**
- **1-1/2 cups chicken broth**
- **1-1/2 cups milk**
- **4 cups cubed cooked chicken breast**
- **1 cup frozen peas**
- **1 jar (2 ounces) diced pimientos, drained**
- **1 teaspoon salt**

BISCUIT TOPPING:
- **2 cups all-purpose flour**
- **4 teaspoons baking powder**
- **2 teaspoons sugar**
- **1/2 teaspoon salt**
- **1/2 teaspoon cream of tartar**
- **1/2 cup cold butter**
- **2/3 cup milk**

In a large saucepan, saute the mushrooms, carrots and onion in butter until tender; sprinkle with flour. Gradually stir in the broth and milk until blended. Bring to a boil; cook and stir for 2 minutes or until thickened. Add the chicken, peas, pimientos and salt ; heat through. Pour into a greased shallow 2-1/2-qt. baking dish; set aside.

For the topping, in a large bowl, combine the flour, baking powder, sugar, salt and cream of tartar. Cut in butter until mixture resembles coarse crumbs; stir in milk just until moistened. Turn on to a lightly floured surface; knead 8-10 times. Pat or roll out to 1/2-in. thickness. Cut with a floured 2-1/2-in. biscuit cutter.

Place biscuits over chicken mixture. Bake, uncovered, at 400° for 15-20 minutes or until biscuits are golden brown. **Yield:** 6-8 servings.

Grilled Raspberry Chicken

(Pictured above)

PREP: 15 min. + marinating **GRILL:** 30 min.

Raspberry vinaigrette and raspberry jam lend fruity flavor to this moist chicken dish I created. The grill gives the chicken a great taste as well. —Gloria Warczak, Cedarburg, Wisconsin

- 1 **cup plus 4-1/2 teaspoons raspberry vinaigrette,** *divided*
- 2 **tablespoons minced fresh rosemary** *or* **2 teaspoons dried rosemary, crushed,** *divided*
- 6 **bone-in chicken thighs**
- 6 **chicken drumsticks**
- 1/2 **cup seedless raspberry jam**
- 1-1/2 **teaspoons lime juice**
- 1/2 **teaspoon soy sauce**
- 1/8 **teaspoon garlic powder**

In a large resealable plastic bag, combine 1 cup vinaigrette and half of the rosemary. Add chicken. Seal bag and turn to coat; refrigerate for 1 hour.

In a bowl, combine the jam, lime juice, soy sauce, garlic powder, and remaining vinaigrette and rosemary; set aside.

Drain the chicken and discard marinade. Place the chicken skin side down on grill rack. Grill, covered, over indirect medium heat for 20 minutes. Turn; grill 10-20 minutes longer or until juices run clear, basting occasionally with the raspberry jam sauce. **Yield:** 6 servings.

Meat Loaf Wellington

(Pictured below)

PREP: 20 min. **BAKE:** 1-1/4 hours

I took what I liked from a few different recipes and came up with this cheese–stuffed loaf. I make it for neighbors and friends when they're sick. It's a pleaser! —Janine Talbot, Santaquin, Utah

- 1 **egg, lightly beaten**
- 1 **cup meatless spaghetti sauce,** *divided*
- 1/4 **cup dry bread crumbs**
- 1/2 **teaspoon salt**
- 1/4 **teaspoon pepper**
- 1-1/2 **pounds ground beef**
- 2 **cups (8 ounces) shredded part-skim mozzarella cheese,** *divided*
- 1 **tablespoon minced fresh parsley**
- 1 **tube (8 ounces) refrigerated crescent rolls**

In a large bowl, combine the egg, 1/3 cup spaghetti sauce, bread crumbs, salt and pepper. Crumble beef over mixture and mix well.

On a piece of heavy-duty foil, pat beef mixture into a 12-in. x 8-in. rectangle. Sprinkle 1 cup cheese and parsley to within 1 in. of edges. Roll up jelly-roll style, starting with a long side and peeling foil away while rolling. Seal seam and ends. Place seam side down in a greased 13-in. x 9-in. x 2-in. baking dish.

Bake, uncovered, at 350° for 1 hour; drain. Unroll crescent dough; seal seams and perforations. Drape dough over meat loaf to cover the top, sides and ends; seal ends. Bake 15-20 minutes longer or until a meat thermometer reads 160° and crust is golden brown. Let stand for 5 minutes.

Using two large spatulas, carefully transfer meat loaf to a serving platter. Sprinkle with remaining cheese. Serve with remaining spaghetti sauce. **Yield:** 8 servings.

Grand Prize Winner

Pineapple-Stuffed Cornish Hens

(Pictured below)

PREP: 20 min. **BAKE:** 55 min.

My mother brought this recipe back with her from Hawaii about 25 years ago. The tender meat, pineapple-coconut stuffing and sweet-sour sauce made it a favorite of my family and friends.
—Vicki Corners, Rock Island, Illinois

- 2 **Cornish game hens (20 ounces *each*)**
- 1/2 **teaspoon salt, *divided***
- 1 **can (8 ounces) crushed pineapple**
- 3 **cups cubed day-old bread (1/2-inch cubes), crusts removed**
- 1 **celery rib, chopped**
- 1/2 **cup flaked coconut**
- 2/3 **cup butter melted, *divided***
- 1/4 **teaspoon poultry seasoning**
- 2 **tablespoons steak sauce**
- 2 **tablespoons cornstarch**
- 2 **tablespoons brown sugar**
- 1 **cup water**
- 1 **tablespoon lemon juice**

Sprinkle inside of hens with 1/4 teaspoon salt; set aside. Drain pineapple, reserving juice. In a bowl, combine the pineapple, bread cubes, celery and coconut. Add 6 tablespoons butter; toss to coat.

Loosely stuff hens; tie legs together with kitchen string. Place on a rack in a greased shallow roasting pan. Place remaining stuffing in a greased 1-1/2-cup baking dish; cover and set aside. Add poultry seasoning and remaining salt to remaining butter. Spoon some butter mixture over hens. Bake, uncovered, at 350° for

40 minutes, basting twice with butter mixture.

Stir steak sauce and reserved pineapple juice into remaining butter mixture; baste hens. Bake reserved stuffing with hens for 30 minutes; baste hens twice.

Uncover stuffing; baste hens with remaining butter mixture. Bake 15-20 minutes longer or until a meat thermometer reads 185° for hens and 165° for stuffing in hens. Remove hens from pan; keep warm.

Pour drippings into a saucepan, skim fat. Combine cornstarch, brown sugar, water and lemon juice until smooth; add to the drippings. Bring to a boil; cook and stir for 1-2 minutes or until thickened. Serve with hens and stuffing. **Yield:** 2 servings.

Cranberry Ham Loaf

(Pictured above and on page 72)

PREP: 20 min. **BAKE:** 70 min.

A cranberry sauce topping makes this easy-to-prepare ham loaf festive enough for a holiday meal. I find it's a great way to use up leftover ham.—Ronald Heffner, Pawleys Island, South Carolina

- 1 **egg, lightly beaten**
- 1 **cup milk**
- 2 **medium onions, chopped**
- 1 **medium green pepper, chopped**
- 1 **cup soft bread crumbs**
- 1-1/2 **pounds ground fully cooked ham**
- 1 **pound bulk pork sausage**
- 1 **can (16 ounces) whole-berry cranberry sauce**
- 1/4 **cup water**
- 1 **tablespoon light corn syrup**

In a large bowl, combine the egg, milk, onions, green pepper and bread crumbs. Crumble ham and sausage over mixture; mix well.

Pat into an ungreased 9-in. x 5-in. x 3-in. loaf pan (pan will be full). Place on a baking sheet. Bake, uncovered, at 350° for 70-80 minutes or until a meat thermometer reads 160°.

In a small saucepan, combine the cranberry sauce, water and corn syrup. Bring to a boil. Reduce heat; simmer, uncovered, for 5 minutes or until thickened. Remove ham loaf to a serving platter; top with cranberry sauce. **Yield:** 8 servings.

Butterflied Pork Chop Dinner

(Pictured below)

PREP: 10 min. **COOK:** 35 min.

The sliced apple and sweet potatoes that complement these tender pork chops remind me of a crisp fall day. However, I enjoy this hearty main dish any time of year, and serve it with a salad and dinner rolls.

—Angela Leinenbach, Mechanicsville, Virginia

- 2 **butterflied pork chops (3/4 inch thick)**
- 1 **tablespoon butter**
- 1 **cup apple juice** *or* **cider,** *divided*
- 1 **teaspoon rubbed sage**
- 3/4 **teaspoon salt**
- 1/2 **teaspoon pepper**
- 2 **medium sweet potatoes, peeled and cut into 1/2-inch slices**
- 1 **green onion, thinly sliced**
- 1 **medium tart apple, peeled, cored and cut into 1/4-inch rings**
- 2 **teaspoons cornstarch**

In a skillet, brown pork chops in butter; drain. Remove from skillet and keep warm. In same skillet, combine 3/4 cup apple juice, sage, salt and pepper. Add sweet potatoes and green onion. Bring to a boil. Reduce heat.

Cover and simmer for 10 minutes; add apple rings and pork chops. Cover and simmer for 13-15 minutes or until apple rings and sweet potatoes are tender and meat juices run clear.

With a slotted spoon, remove pork chops, sweet potatoes and apple to serving plates; keep warm.

Combine the cornstarch with the remaining apple juice until smooth. Gradually stir into pan juices. Bring to a boil; cook and stir for 1-2 minutes or until thickened. Serve over pork chops, sweet potatoes and apple. **Yield:** 2 servings.

Chicken Pepper Stir-Fry

(Pictured above)

PREP/TOTAL TIME: 30 min.

With a few simple ingredients, this colorful and aromatic stir–fry comes together in half an hour. My family loves it when they're craving Chinese takeout.

—Kelly Baumgardt, Seymour, Wisconsin

- 1 *each* **small green, sweet red and sweet yellow pepper, julienned**
- 1 **medium onion, quartered**
- 2 **garlic cloves, minced**
- 4 **tablespoons olive oil,** *divided*
- 3/4 **pound boneless skinless chicken breast halves, cubed**
- 3/4 **teaspoon Cajun seasoning**
- 1/3 **cup packed brown sugar**
- 2 **teaspoons cornstarch**
- 1 **tablespoon water**
- 1 **tablespoon lemon juice**
- 1 **tablespoon honey mustard**
- 1 **teaspoon soy sauce**
- 1 **teaspoon Worcestershire sauce**

Hot cooked rice, optional

In a large skillet, stir-fry the peppers, onion and garlic in 2 tablespoons oil until crisp-tender. Remove and keep warm. In the same skillet, stir-fry chicken and Cajun seasoning in remaining oil until juices run clear.

Combine the brown sugar, cornstarch, water, lemon juice, mustard, soy sauce and Worcestershire sauce; pour over chicken. Return pepper mixture to the pan; cook and stir for 1 minutes. Serve with rice if desired. **Yield:** 3-4 servings.

After Turkey Day Suppers

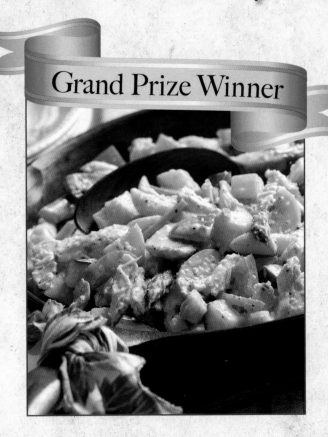

Grand Prize Winner

Next Day Turkey Primavera

(Pictured above and on page 72)

PREP/TOTAL TIME: 30 min.

I make this recipe often around the holidays. It's a wonderful way to use leftover turkey without feeling like it's a "repeat meal." I love pasta, and the creamy sauce in this primavera is so easy to make.
—Robyn Hardisty, Lakewood, California

- 1 cup uncooked penne pasta
- 8 fresh asparagus spears, trimmed and cut into 1-inch pieces
- 2/3 cup julienned carrot
- 3 tablespoons butter
- 4 large fresh mushrooms, sliced
- 1/2 cup chopped yellow summer squash
- 1/2 cup chopped zucchini
- 1-1/2 cups shredded cooked turkey
- 1 medium tomato, chopped
- 1 envelope Italian salad dressing mix
- 1 cup heavy whipping cream
- 1/4 cup grated Parmesan cheese

Cook pasta according to package directions. Meanwhile, in a large skillet, saute asparagus and carrot in butter for 3 minutes. Add the mushrooms, yellow squash and zucchini; saute until crisp-tender.

Stir in the turkey, tomato, dressing mix and cream. Bring to a boil; cook and stir for 2 minutes.

Drain pasta; add to vegetable mixture and toss to combine. Sprinkle with Parmesan cheese and toss again. **Yield:** 4 servings.

Butternut Turkey Bake

PREP: 70 min. **BAKE:** 25 min.

Butternut squash adds a little sweetness to this comforting casserole. You can use leftover turkey and even replace the salad croutons with leftover stuffing, if you wish.
—Mary Ann Dell
Phoenixville, Pennsylvania

- 1 medium butternut squash (about 2-1/2 pounds)
- 3/4 cup finely chopped onion
- 2 tablespoons butter
- 2 cups seasoned salad croutons
- 1/2 teaspoon salt
- 1/2 teaspoon poultry seasoning
- 1/2 teaspoon pepper
- 2 cups cubed cooked turkey
- 1 cup chicken broth
- 1/2 cup shredded cheddar cheese

Cut squash in half; discard seeds. Place cut side down in a 15-in. x 10-in. x 1-in. baking pan; add 1/2 in. of hot water. Bake, uncovered, at 350° for 45 minutes.

Drain water from pan; turn squash cut side up. Bake 10-15 minutes longer or until tender. Scoop out pulp; mash and set aside.

In a large skillet, saute onion in butter until tender. Stir in the croutons, salt, poultry seasoning and pepper. Cook 2-3 minutes longer or until the croutons are toasted. Stir in the squash, turkey and broth; heat through.

Transfer to a greased 1-1/2-qt. baking dish. Bake, uncovered, at 350° for 20 minutes. Sprinkle with cheese. Bake 5-10 minutes longer or until edges are bubbly and cheese is melted. **Yield:** 4 servings.

Crescent-Topped Turkey Amandine

(Pictured above right)

PREP: 20 min. **BAKE:** 30 min.

This tasty main dish is loaded with turkey flavor and a nice crunch from celery and water chestnuts. Topped with a golden crescent roll crust, almonds and cheese, it's bound to become a favorite.
—Becky Larson, Mallard, Iowa

- 3 cups cubed cooked turkey
- 1 can (10-3/4 ounces) condensed cream of mushroom soup, undiluted
- 1 can (8 ounces) sliced water chestnuts, drained

2/3 cup mayonnaise
1/2 cup chopped celery
1/2 cup chopped onion
1 tube (4 ounces) refrigerated crescent rolls
2/3 cup shredded Swiss cheese
1/2 cup sliced almonds
1/4 cup butter, melted

In a large saucepan, combine the first six ingredients; heat through. Transfer to a greased 2-qt. baking dish. Unroll crescent dough and place over turkey mixture.

Combine the Swiss cheese, sliced almonds and butter. Spoon over the dough. Bake, uncovered, at 375° for 30-35 minutes or until the crust is golden brown and the filling is bubbly. **Yield:** 4 servings.

Turkey Potpies

(Pictured at right and on page 72)

PREP: 40 min.
BAKE: 40 min. + standing

With golden brown crust and scrumptious filling, these comforting potpies will warm you down to your toes. Because it makes two large pies, you can eat one now and freeze the other for later. They bake and cut beautifully.
—Laurie Jensen, Cadillac, Michigan

2 medium potatoes, peeled and cut into 1-inch pieces
3 medium carrots, cut into 1-inch slices
1 medium onion, chopped
1 celery rib, diced
2 tablespoons butter
1 tablespoon olive oil
6 tablespoons all-purpose flour

3 cups chicken broth
4 cups cubed cooked turkey
2/3 cup frozen peas
1/2 cup plus 1 tablespoon heavy whipping cream, *divided*
1 tablespoon minced fresh parsley
1 teaspoon garlic salt
1/4 teaspoon pepper
1 package (15 ounces) refrigerated pie pastry
1 egg

In a Dutch oven, saute the potatoes, carrots, onion and celery in butter and oil until tender. Stir in flour until blended; gradually add broth. Bring to a boil; cook and stir for 2 minutes or until thickened. Stir in the turkey, peas, 1/2 cup cream, parsley, garlic salt and pepper.

Spoon into two ungreased 9-in. pie plates. Roll out the pastry to fit the top of each pie; place over filling. Trim, seal and flute edges. Cut out a decorative center or cut slits in pastry. In a small bowl, whisk the egg and remaining cream; brush over dough.

Cover and freeze one potpie for up to 3 months. Bake the remaining potpie at 375° for 40-45 minutes or until golden brown. Let stand for 10 minutes before cutting.

To use frozen potpie: Remove from the freezer 30 minutes before baking. Cover edges of crust loosely with foil; place on a baking sheet. Bake at 425° for 30 minutes. Reduce heat to 350°; remove foil. Bake 55-60 minutes longer or until golden brown. **Yield:** 2 pies (6 servings each).

Turkey Enchiladas

(Pictured above)

PREP: 40 min. **BAKE:** 40 min.

My family likes these enchiladas so much that they request a turkey dinner several times a year just so I'll make this dish with the leftovers. I usually double it because I feed three growing boys—two teenagers and my husband!
—Beverly Matthews, Pasco, Washington

3 cups cubed cooked turkey
1 cup chicken broth
1 cup cooked long grain rice
2 plum tomatoes, chopped
1 medium onion, chopped
1/2 cup canned chopped green chilies
1/2 cup sour cream
1/4 cup sliced ripe olives
1/4 cup minced fresh cilantro
1 teaspoon ground cumin
8 flour tortillas (10 inches)
1 can (28 ounces) green enchilada sauce, *divided*
2 cups (8 ounces) shredded Mexican cheese blend, *divided*

In a large saucepan, combine the first 10 ingredients. Bring to a boil. Reduce heat; simmer, uncovered, for 20 minutes. Remove from the heat.

Place 1/2 cup turkey mixture down the center of each tortilla; top each with 1 teaspoon enchilada sauce and 1 tablespoon cheese. Roll up and place seam side down in a greased 13-in. x 9-in. x 2-in. baking dish. Pour remaining enchilada sauce over top; sprinkle with remaining cheese.

Cover and bake at 350° for 30 minutes. Uncover; bake 8-10 minutes longer or until bubbly. **Yield:** 8 servings.

In a large bowl, combine the eggs, bread crumbs, Parmesan cheese, parsley, thyme and mushroom mixture. Crumble beef and sausage over mixture; mix well.

On a large piece of heavy-duty foil, pat beef mixture into a 15-in. x 10-in. rectangle. Layer the prosciutto, Havarti, basil and tomatoes to within 1 in. of edges. Roll up jelly-roll style, starting with a short side and peeling foil away while rolling. Seal seams and ends.

Place seam side down in a greased 13-in. x 9-in. x 2-in. baking dish. Bake, uncovered, at 350° for 75-85 minutes or until no pink remains and a meat thermometer reads 160°. Let stand for 5 minutes. Using two large spatulas, carefully transfer the meat loaf to a serving platter. **Yield:** 6-8 servings.

Prosciutto-Stuffed Meat Loaf

(*Pictured above*)

PREP: 45 min. **BAKE:** 1-1/4 hours

An amazing blend of flavors—including prosciutto, sun-dried tomatoes, fresh basil and two kinds of cheese—make this rolled loaf something special. —Carole Hermenau, Oviedo, Florida

- 1 cup finely chopped red onion
- 1 tablespoon olive oil
- 1 tablespoon butter
- 2 garlic cloves, minced
- 1/2 pound whole fresh mushrooms, coarsely chopped
- 3/4 teaspoon salt
- 1/2 teaspoon pepper
- 2 eggs, lightly beaten
- 1-3/4 cups soft sourdough bread crumbs
- 3/4 cup grated Parmesan cheese
- 1/3 cup minced fresh parsley
- 1 teaspoon minced fresh thyme
- 1-1/2 pounds lean ground beef
- 3/4 pound bulk Italian sausage

FILLING:
- 3 ounces thinly sliced prosciutto
- 5 ounces thinly sliced Havarti cheese
- 1-1/4 cups loosely packed basil leaves, cut into thin strips
- 1/3 cup oil-packed sun-dried tomatoes, drained and cut into strips

In a large skillet, saute onion in oil and butter for 2 minutes. Add garlic; cook 1 minute longer. Add mushrooms; cook 6-8 minutes longer or until mushrooms are tender and no liquid remains. Stir in salt and pepper.

Grand Prize Winner

Spaghetti Squash with Red Sauce

(*Pictured below and on page 72*)

PREP: 25 min. **COOK:** 15 min.

This fabulous, meatless main dish is a great way to get the kids to eat lots of vegetables...and a great way for you to use some of the fresh harvest from your garden.

—Kathryn Pehl, Prescott, Arizona

- 1 medium spaghetti squash (about 4 pounds)
- 2 cups chopped fresh tomatoes
- 1 cup sliced fresh mushrooms
- 1 cup diced green pepper
- 1/2 cup shredded carrot
- 1/4 cup diced red onion

2 **garlic cloves, minced**
2 **teaspoons Italian seasoning**
1/8 **teaspoon pepper**
1 **tablespoon olive oil**
1 **can (15 ounces) tomato sauce**
Grated Parmesan cheese, optional

Cut squash in half lengthwise; discard seeds. Place squash, cut side down, on a microwave-safe plate. Microwave, uncovered, on high for 14-16 minutes or until tender.

Meanwhile, in a large skillet, saute the tomatoes, mushrooms, green pepper, carrot, onion, garlic, Italian seasoning and pepper in oil for 6-8 minutes or until tender. Add tomato sauce; heat through.

When squash is cool enough to handle, use a fork to separate strands. Place squash on a serving platter; top with sauce. Sprinkle with Parmesan cheese if desired. **Yield:** 6 servings.

Editor's Note: This recipe was tested in a 1,100-watt microwave.

Braised Short Ribs

PREP: 25 min. **COOK:** 1-1/2 hours

I've been making these delicious ribs for at least 40 years, and they are often served when my husband and I have company for dinner. The allspice and bay leaf come through nicely, and the meat is very tender. —Mary Gill, Florence, Oregon

3 **pounds beef short ribs**
1-1/2 **teaspoons butter**
1-1/2 **teaspoons canola oil**
1 **large onion, thinly sliced**
1 **cup water**
1-1/4 **teaspoons salt**
1 **teaspoon sugar**
1/4 **teaspoon coarsely ground pepper**
2 **bay leaves**
1 **teaspoon whole allspice**
1 **tablespoon all-purpose flour**
1/4 **cup water**

In a Dutch oven, brown ribs in butter and oil for about 3 minutes on each side; drain. Remove and keep warm. In the same pan, cook and stir the onion for 2 minutes. Add water, salt, sugar and pepper, stirring to loosen browned bits from pan.

Place bay leaves and allspice on a double thickness of cheesecloth; bring up corners of cloth and tie with kitchen string to form a bag. Place in pan. Return ribs to pan. Bring to a boil. Reduce heat; cover and simmer for 1-1/2 to 1-3/4 hours or until meat is tender.

Remove ribs and keep warm. Discard spice bag. Skim fat from pan drippings. Combine flour and cold water until smooth; gradually stir into drippings. Bring to a boil; cook and stir for 2 minutes or until thickened. Serve with ribs. **Yield:** 4 servings.

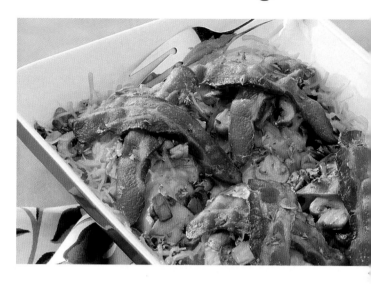

Bacon-Cheese Topped Chicken

(Pictured above)

PREP: 40 min. + marinating **BAKE:** 20 min.

Mushrooms, bacon strips and Monterey Jack cheese top these tender marinated chicken breasts. This dish gets compliments whenever I serve it. It's a family favorite.
—Melanie Kennedy, Battle Ground, Washington

1/2 **cup Dijon mustard**
1/2 **cup honey**
4-1/2 **teaspoons canola oil, *divided***
1/2 **teaspoon lemon juice**
4 **boneless skinless chicken breast halves**
1/4 **teaspoon salt**
1/8 **teaspoon pepper**
Dash paprika
2 **cups sliced fresh mushrooms**
2 **tablespoons butter**
1 **cup (4 ounces) shredded Monterey Jack cheese**
1 **cup (4 ounces) shredded cheddar cheese**
8 **bacon strips, partially cooked**
2 **teaspoons minced fresh parsley**

Combine the mustard, honey, 1-1/2 teaspoons oil and lemon juice. Pour 1/2 cup into a large resealable plastic bag; add the chicken. Seal the bag and turn to coat; refrigerate for 2 hours. Cover and refrigerate the remaining marinade.

Drain and discard marinade from chicken. In a large skillet over medium heat, brown chicken in remaining oil on all sides. Sprinkle with salt, pepper and paprika. Transfer to a greased 11-in. x 7-in. x 2-in. baking dish.

In the same skillet, saute mushrooms in butter until tender. Spoon reserved marinade over chicken. Top with cheeses and mushrooms. Place bacon strips in a crisscross pattern over chicken.

Bake, uncovered, at 375° for 20-25 minutes or until a meat thermometer reads 170°. Sprinkle with parsley. **Yield:** 4 servings.

Cube Steaks Parmigiana

(Pictured below)

PREP: 20 min. **BAKE:** 40 min.

Are you tired of chicken fried steak? This recipe dresses up cube steaks Italian-style with cheese, tomato sauce, basil and oregano. My husband and I like this main dish with a side of fettuccine Alfredo. —Sarah Befort, Hays, Kansas

- 3 tablespoons all-purpose flour
- 1/2 teaspoon salt
- 1/4 teaspoon pepper
- 2 eggs
- 3 tablespoons water
- 1/3 cup finely crushed saltines
- 1/3 cup grated Parmesan cheese
- 1/2 teaspoon dried basil
- 4 beef cube steaks (1 pound)
- 3 tablespoons canola oil
- 1-1/4 cups tomato sauce
- 2-1/4 teaspoons sugar
- 1/2 teaspoon dried oregano, *divided*
- 1/4 teaspoon garlic powder
- 4 slices part-skim mozzarella cheese
- 1/3 cup shredded Parmesan cheese

In a shallow bowl, combine the flour, salt and pepper. In another bowl, beat the eggs and water. Place the cracker crumbs, grated Parmesan cheese and basil in a third bowl.

Coat the steaks with flour mixture, then dip in egg mixture and coat with crumb mixture. In a large skillet, brown steaks in oil for 2-3 minutes on each side or until golden brown.

Arrange the steaks in a greased 13-in. x 9-in. x 2-in. baking dish. Bake, uncovered, at 375° for 25 minutes. Combine the tomato sauce, sugar, 1/4 teaspoon oregano and garlic powder; spoon over the steaks. Bake 10 minutes longer.

Top each steak with mozzarella cheese; sprinkle with shredded Parmesan cheese and the remaining oregano. Bake 2-3 minutes longer or until the cheese is melted. **Yield:** 4 servings.

Pizza Margherita

(Pictured above)

PREP: 30 min. + rising **BAKE:** 15 min.

This classic pizza starts with a chewy homemade crust topped with tomatoes, mozzarella, oregano and fresh basil. It's so scrumptious that you'll be glad the recipe makes two 13-inch pizzas! —Loretta Lawrence, Myrtle Beach, South Carolina

- 3 teaspoons active dry yeast
- 1 cup warm water (110° to 115°)
- 2 tablespoons olive oil
- 1 teaspoon sugar
- 1 teaspoon salt
- 3 cups bread flour

TOPPINGS:
- 2 cans (14-1/2 ounces *each*) diced tomatoes, drained
- 20 fresh basil leaves, thinly sliced
- 8 cups (2 pounds) shredded part-skim mozzarella cheese
- 2 teaspoons dried oregano
- 1/2 teaspoon crushed red pepper flakes
- 1/8 teaspoon salt
- 1/8 teaspoon pepper
- 2 tablespoons olive oil

In a large bowl, dissolve yeast in warm water. Add the oil, sugar, salt and 1 cup flour. Beat until smooth. Stir in enough remaining flour to form a soft dough.

Turn onto a floured surface; knead until smooth and

elastic, about 6-8 minutes. Place in a bowl coated with cooking spray, turning once to coat the top. Cover and let rise in a warm place until doubled, about 1 hour.

Punch dough down; divide in half. Roll each portion into a 13-in. circle. Transfer to two 14-in. pizza pans coated with cooking spray; build up edges slightly. Cover and let rest for 10 minutes.

For the toppings, spoon tomatoes over crusts. Top with basil, cheese, oregano, pepper flakes, salt and pepper. Drizzle with oil. Bake at 450° for 15-20 minutes or until crust and cheese are golden brown. **Yield:** 2 pizzas (8 slices each).

Brisket in a Bag

PREP: 15 min. **BAKE:** 2-1/2 hours

This tender brisket is served with a savory cranberry gravy that's made right alongside the meat. You'll want to serve the slices with mashed potatoes just so you can drizzle the delicious sauce over them. —*Peggy Stigers, Fort Worth, Texas*

- **3 tablespoons all-purpose flour, *divided***
- **1 large oven roasting bag**
- **1 fresh beef brisket (5 pounds), trimmed**
- **1 can (16 ounces) whole-berry cranberry sauce**
- **1 can (10-3/4 ounces) condensed cream of mushroom soup, undiluted**
- **1 can (8 ounces) tomato sauce**
- **1 envelope onion soup mix**

Place 1 tablespoon flour in oven bag; shake to coat. Place bag in an ungreased 13-in. x 9-in. x 2-in. baking pan; place brisket in bag.

Combine the cranberry sauce, soup, tomato sauce, soup mix and remaining flour; pour over beef. Seal bag. Cut slits in top of bag according to package directions.

Bake at 325° for 2-1/2 to 3 hours or until meat is tender. Let stand for 5 minutes. Carefully remove brisket from bag. Thinly slice meat across the grain; serve with gravy. **Yield:** 12 servings.

Editor's Note: This is a fresh beef brisket, not corned beef.

Spinach Crab Chicken

(Pictured at right)

PREP: 45 min. **COOK:** 40 min.

I altered a friend's recipe for crab–stuffed chicken to include one of my favorite vegetables, spinach. Now my husband requests this elegant entree all the time. Served over rice, it's special enough for company. —*Vicki Melies, Elkhorn, Nebraska*

- **1/2 cup finely chopped onion**
- **1/4 cup chopped fresh mushrooms**
- **1/4 cup finely chopped celery**
- **3 tablespoons butter**
- **3 tablespoons all-purpose flour**
- **1/2 teaspoon salt, *divided***
- **1 cup chicken broth**
- **1/2 cup milk**
- **4 boneless skinless chicken breast halves (6 ounces *each*)**
- **1/8 teaspoon white pepper**
- **1/2 cup dry bread crumbs**
- **1 can (6 ounces) crabmeat, drained, flaked and cartilage removed**
- **12 fresh spinach leaves, chopped**
- **1 tablespoon minced fresh parsley**
- **1 cup (4 ounces) shredded Swiss cheese**

Hot cooked rice

For sauce, in a large skillet, saute onion, mushrooms and celery in butter until tender. Stir in flour and 1/4 teaspoon salt until blended. Gradually add broth and milk. Bring to a boil; cook and stir 1-2 minutes or until thickened. Remove from the heat.

Flatten chicken to 1/4-in. thickness; sprinkle with pepper and remaining salt. In a large bowl, combine the bread crumbs, crab, spinach and parsley; stir in 1/2 cup sauce. Spoon 1/4 cup down the center of each chicken breast half. Roll up; secure with toothpicks. Place seam side down in a greased 13-in. x 9-in. x 2-in. baking dish. Top with remaining sauce.

Cover and bake at 375° for 35-45 minutes or until juices run clear. Sprinkle with cheese. Broil 4-6 in. from the heat for 5 minutes or until lightly browned. Discard toothpicks. Serve with rice. **Yield:** 4 servings.

onion; sprinkle with rosemary. Add the chicken and hot broth. Cover and cook on low for 6-7 hours or until chicken juices run clear, vegetables are tender and stew is bubbling. Stir in peas.

For dumplings, in a small bowl, combine the flour, baking powder, salt and rosemary. Combine the egg and milk; stir into dry ingredients. Drop by heaping teaspoonfuls onto simmering chicken mixture. Cover and cook on high for 25-30 minutes or until a toothpick inserted in a dumpling comes out clean (do not lift the cover while simmering). **Yield:** 6 servings.

Curried Shrimp and Apples

(Pictured below)

PREP/TOTAL TIME: 30 min.

Apples and shrimp, seasoned with curry powder, combine beautifully in this appealing main dish. Sometimes I make it with chicken instead of the shrimp.
—*Lynda Mack, Neptune Beach, Florida*

- 1 medium onion, chopped
- 2 celery ribs, chopped
- 1/4 cup butter, cubed
- 2 medium apples, sliced
- 2 teaspoons all-purpose flour
- 3/4 teaspoon curry powder
- 3/4 cup water
- 1 teaspoon chicken bouillon granules
- 3/4 pound uncooked medium shrimp, peeled and deveined

Hot cooked rice

In a large skillet, saute the onion and celery in butter for 2 minutes. Stir in apples; saute 1-2 minutes longer or until crisp-tender.

Sprinkle with flour and curry powder. Gradually whisk in water and bouillon until smooth. Add shrimp; bring to a boil. Reduce heat; simmer for 2-3 minutes or until shrimp turn pink and sauce is thickened. Serve over rice. **Yield:** 4 servings.

Sunday Chicken Stew

PREP: 30 min. **COOK:** 6-1/2 hours

I love this recipe because in the morning I can prepare and assemble everything in the slow cooker before I go to church. This leaves me plenty of time to spend with my family while Sunday dinner cooks. —*Diane Halferty, Corpus Christi, Texas*

- 1/2 cup all-purpose flour
- 1 teaspoon salt
- 1/2 teaspoon white pepper
- 1 broiler/fryer chicken (3 pounds), cut up and skin removed
- 2 tablespoons canola oil
- 3 cups chicken broth
- 6 large carrots, cut into 1-inch pieces
- 2 celery ribs, cut into 1/2-inch pieces
- 1 large sweet onion, thinly sliced
- 1 teaspoon dried rosemary, crushed
- 1-1/2 cups frozen peas

DUMPLINGS:
- 1 cup all-purpose flour
- 2 teaspoons baking powder
- 1/2 teaspoon salt
- 1/2 teaspoon dried rosemary, crushed
- 1 egg, beaten
- 1/2 cup milk

In a large resealable plastic bag, combine the flour, salt and pepper; add chicken, a few pieces at a time, and shake to coat. In a large skillet, brown chicken in oil; remove and keep warm. Gradually add broth to the skillet; bring to a boil.

In a 5-qt. slow cooker, layer the carrots, celery and

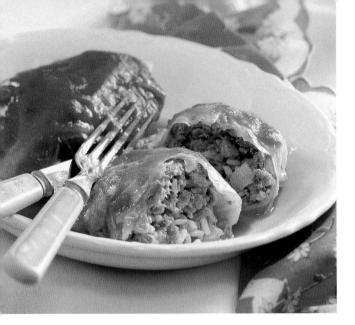

Place seven rolls, seam side down, in a 5-qt. slow cooker. Combine sauce ingredients; pour half over cabbage rolls. Top with remaining rolls and sauce. Cover and cook on low for 7-8 hours or until a meat thermometer reads 160°. **Yield:** 7 servings.

Chicken & Tomato Risotto

(Pictured below)

PREP: 25 min. **COOK:** 25 min.

If you're looking for Italian comfort food, this is it! By using store-bought spaghetti sauce, you save time when preparing this creamy dish. You'll enjoy every bite!
—*Lorraine Caland, Thunder Bay, Ontario*

> 3 cups chicken broth
> 1 pound boneless skinless chicken breasts, cut into 1-inch cubes
> 1 tablespoon olive oil
> 1-1/2 cups sliced fresh mushrooms
> 1 medium onion, chopped
> 1 garlic clove, minced
> 2 tablespoons butter
> 1 cup uncooked arborio rice
> 1 cup meatless spaghetti sauce
> 1/4 cup grated Parmesan cheese

In a small saucepan, heat broth and keep warm. In a large skillet, saute chicken in oil until no longer pink. Remove and keep warm.

In the same skillet, saute the mushrooms, onion and garlic in butter until crisp-tender. Add rice; cook and stir for 3 minutes. Carefully stir in 1 cup warm broth. Cook and stir until all of the liquid is absorbed.

Add remaining broth, 1/2 cup at a time, stirring constantly. Allow the liquid to absorb between additions. Cook until risotto is creamy and rice is almost tender. (Cooking time is about 20 minutes.)

Stir in the spaghetti sauce, cheese and reserved chicken; cook and stir until thickened. Serve immediately. **Yield:** 4 servings.

Sweet and Tender Cabbage Rolls

(Pictured above)

PREP: 40 min. **COOK:** 7 hours

I've used this recipe for more than 30 years, and the extra time it takes to assemble the rolls is well worth the effort. I always make two batches because they go so fast. You can assemble the rolls the night before and simmer them the next day.
—*Sonja Benz, Carmel, Indiana*

> 1 large head cabbage
> 2 eggs, beaten
> 1/2 cup milk
> 2 cups cooked long grain rice
> 2 jars (4-1/2 ounces *each*) sliced mushrooms, well drained
> 1 small onion, chopped
> 2 teaspoons salt
> 1 teaspoon dried parsley flakes
> 1 teaspoon dried oregano
> 1 teaspoon dried basil
> 1/2 teaspoon pepper
> 2 pounds lean ground beef
> **SAUCE:**
> 2 cans (8 ounces *each*) tomato sauce
> 1/2 cup packed brown sugar
> 2 tablespoons lemon juice
> 2 teaspoons Worcestershire sauce

Cook cabbage in boiling water just until leaves fall off head. Set aside 14 large leaves for rolls. (Refrigerate remaining cabbage for another use.) Cut out the thick vein from the bottom of each reserved leaf, making a V-shaped cut.

In a large bowl, combine the eggs, milk, rice, mushrooms, onion and seasonings. Crumble beef over mixture and mix well. Place about 1/2 cup on each cabbage leaf; overlap cut ends and fold in sides, beginning from the cut end. Roll up completely to enclose filling.

Meat Loaf Gyros

(Pictured below)

PREP: 30 min. **BAKE:** 1 hour + chilling

I always wanted to learn to make Greek gyros at home, but I was intimidated. Then I tried this recipe, and they were great. I slice leftover meat in individual portions and freeze for any time I crave a gyro. —Sharon Rawlings, Tampa, Florida

  1 egg, lightly beaten
  6 garlic cloves, minced
  3 tablespoons dried oregano
  1-1/2 teaspoons kosher salt
  1 teaspoon pepper
  1 pound ground lamb
  1 pound ground beef
TZATZIKI SAUCE:
  1 cup (8 ounces) plain yogurt
  1 medium cucumber, peeled, seeded and chopped
  2 tablespoons lemon juice
  2 garlic cloves, minced
  1/2 teaspoon salt
  1/4 teaspoon pepper
GYROS:
  8 whole gyro-style pitas (6 inches)
  3 tablespoons olive oil, *divided*
  16 slices tomato
  8 slices sweet onion, halved

In a large bowl, combine the egg, garlic, oregano, kosher salt and pepper. Crumble the lamb and beef over egg mixture; mix well.

Pat into an ungreased 9-in. x 5-in. x 3-in. loaf pan. Bake, uncovered, at 350° for 60-70 minutes or until no pink remains and a meat thermometer reads 160°. Cool completely on a wire rack. Refrigerate for 1-2 hours.

For sauce, in a small bowl, combine the yogurt, cucumber, lemon juice, garlic, salt and pepper. Cover and refrigerate until serving.

For the gyros, brush pita breads with 1 tablespoon oil; heat on a lightly greased griddle for 1 minute on each side. Keep warm. Cut the meat loaf into very thin slices. In a large skillet, fry meat loaf in remaining oil in batches until crisp.

On each pita bread, layer tomato, onion and meat loaf slices; top with some tzatziki sauce. Carefully fold pitas in half. Serve with remaining sauce. **Yield:** 8 servings.

Creamed Chicken over Biscuits

(Pictured above)

PREP/TOTAL TIME: 20 min.

A friend of mine prepared this homey dish for my husband and me after our first son was born. I've made just a few minor modifications over the years. We love all of the heartwarming comfort it offers in every bite. —Pam Kelley, Uniontown, Ohio

  1 cup cubed peeled potato
  1/2 cup diced carrot
  2 tablespoons butter
  2 tablespoons all-purpose flour
  1 cup milk
  2-1/2 teaspoons chicken bouillon granules
  1/8 teaspoon pepper
  1/2 pound boneless skinless chicken breasts, cooked and cubed
  1/2 cup frozen peas, thawed
  4 warm buttermilk biscuits

Place potato and carrot in a small saucepan. Cover with water. Bring to a boil. Reduce heat; cover and simmer for 8-10 minutes or until vegetables are tender. Drain and set aside.

In a large skillet, melt the butter. Stir in flour until smooth. Gradually whisk in milk. Add the bouillon and pepper. Bring to a boil; cook and stir for 2 minutes or until thickened. Stir in the chicken, peas and potato mixture; heat through. Serve over the biscuits. **Yield:** 2 servings.

Taco Meat Loaves

(Pictured below)

PREP: 25 min. **BAKE:** 1 hour + standing

We live in Texas and love the Southwest's spicy style of cooking. This recipe flavors plain old meat loaf so it tastes like a delicious filling for tacos. —Susan Garoutte, Georgetown, Texas

- 3 **eggs, lightly beaten**
- 2 **cups picante sauce,** *divided*
- 1 **can (16 ounces) kidney beans, rinsed and drained**
- 1 **can (11 ounces) Mexicorn, drained**
- 1 **medium onion, chopped**
- 2 **cans (2-1/4 ounces** *each***) sliced ripe olives, drained**
- 3/4 **cup dry bread crumbs**
- 1 **envelope taco seasoning**
- 1 **teaspoon ground cumin**
- 1 **teaspoon chili powder**
- 2 **pounds ground beef**
- 2 **cups (8 ounces) shredded cheddar cheese**

Additional picante sauce, optional

In a large bowl, combine the eggs, 1/2 cup picante sauce, beans, corn, onion, olives, bread crumbs, taco seasoning, cumin and chili powder. Crumble beef over mixture and mix well.

Pat into two ungreased 9-in. x 5-in. x 3-in. loaf pans. Bake, uncovered, at 350° for 50-55 minutes or until no pink remains and a meat thermometer reads 160°.

Spoon remaining picante sauce over each meat loaf; sprinkle with cheese. Bake 10-15 minutes longer or until cheese is melted. Let stand for 10 minutes before slicing. Serve with additional picante sauce if desired. **Yield:** 2 meat loaves (6 servings each).

Asian Pot Roast

(Pictured above)

PREP: 30 min. **COOK:** 2 hours 35 min.

I love Asian food, and this pot roast satisfies my cravings. The original recipe called for spinach, but I use sugar snap peas and carrots instead. Sometimes I serve the roast, vegetables and pineapple over rice or egg noodles.
  — Donna Staley, Randlemn, North Carolina

- 1 **boneless beef rump roast (3 pounds)**
- 1 **tablespoon canola oil**
- 1 **large onion, chopped**
- 1 **can (20 ounces) pineapple chunks**
- 3 **tablespoons soy sauce**
- 1 **garlic clove, minced**
- 1 **teaspoon ground ginger**
- 3 **celery ribs, sliced**
- 2 **medium carrots, sliced**
- 1 **cup fresh sugar snap peas**
- 1 **cup sliced fresh mushrooms**
- 1 to 2 **tablespoons cornstarch**
- 1/4 **cup cold water**

In a Dutch oven over medium heat, brown roast in oil on all sides; drain. Add onion. Drain pineapple, reserving juice; set pineapple aside. Combine the pineapple juice, soy sauce, garlic and ginger. Pour over roast. Bring to a boil. Reduce heat; cover and simmer for 2 hours or until meat is almost tender.

Add the celery and carrots. Cover and simmer for 20 minutes or until vegetables are crisp-tender. Add the peas, mushrooms and reserved pineapple. Cover and simmer 15 minutes longer or until the vegetables and meat are tender.

Remove the roast, vegetables and pineapple; keep warm. Skim fat from pan drippings. Combine cornstarch and cold water until smooth; gradually stir into the drippings. Bring to a boil; cook and stir for 2 minutes or until thickened. Slice roast across the grain. Serve meat, vegetables and pineapple with gravy. **Yield:** 6 servings.

Breads, Rolls & Muffins

Tempting fresh-baked goods are the perfect accompaniment to any meal. They're also great as a snack or even as special gifts during the holidays.

HOME-BAKED GOODIES. Clockwise from upper left: Parker House Dinner Rolls (p. 111), Special Banana Nut Bread (p. 116), Tomato Focaccia (p. 115), Vanilla Cinnamon Rolls (p. 118) and pictured center, Berry Cheesecake Muffins (p. 112).

Maple Walnut Rolls

(Pictured below)

PREP: 45 min. + rising **BAKE:** 20 min. + cooling

For old-fashioned flavor, you can't beat this attractive nut roll. The recipe makes four loaves, so you'll have enough to serve family and friends during the holiday season.
—Elleen Oberreuter, Danbury, Iowa

- 6 to 7 cups all-purpose flour
- 3 tablespoons sugar
- 2 packages (1/4 ounce *each*) active dry yeast
- 1 teaspoon salt
- 1 cup (8 ounces) sour cream
- 1 cup butter, softened
- 1/2 cup water
- 3 eggs, lightly beaten

FILLING:
- 3/4 cup butter, melted
- 1/2 cup sugar
- 3 tablespoons maple syrup
- 5 cups ground walnuts

ICING:
- 2 cups confectioners' sugar
- 2 to 3 tablespoons milk

In a large bowl, combine 2 cups flour, sugar, yeast and salt. In a small saucepan, heat sour cream, butter and water to 120°-130°; add to dry ingredients. Beat on medium speed for 2 minutes. Add eggs and 1/2 cup flour; beat 2 minutes longer. Stir in enough remaining flour to form a soft dough.

Turn onto a floured surface; knead until smooth and elastic, 6-8 minutes. Place in a greased bowl; turn once to grease top. Cover and let rise in a warm place until doubled, about 1-1/4 hours. Punch the dough down; divide into four portions. Roll each portion into a 14-in. x 12-in. rectangle.

For the filling, in a large bowl, combine butter, sugar and syrup; stir in walnuts. Sprinkle 1 cup over each rectangle. Roll up jelly-roll style, starting with a long side; pinch seam to seal. Place seam side down on greased baking sheets. Cover and let rise in a warm place until doubled, about 45 minutes.

Bake at 350° for 20-25 minutes or until lightly browned. Remove from pans to wire racks to cool. Combine icing ingredients; drizzle over rolls. **Yield:** 4 loaves.

Vermont Honey-Wheat Bread

PREP: 30 min. + rising **BAKE:** 30 min. + cooling

You don't have to be a health nut to enjoy this hearty loaf. Made with whole wheat flour, oats and wheat germ, this bread gets its pleasant sweetness from honey and maple syrup.
—Roderick Crandall, Hartland, Vermont

- 2 packages (1/4 ounce *each*) active dry yeast
- 3/4 cup warm water (110° to 115°)
- 1 cup old-fashioned oats
- 1 cup warm buttermilk (110° to 115°)
- 1/3 cup butter, softened
- 1-1/2 cups whole wheat flour
- 1/2 cup maple syrup
- 1/2 cup honey
- 1/3 cup toasted wheat germ
- 2 eggs, beaten
- 1 teaspoon salt
- 3 to 4 cups all-purpose flour

TOPPING:
- 1 egg white
- 1 tablespoon water
- 1/4 cup old-fashioned oats

In a small bowl, dissolve yeast in warm water. In a large bowl, combine the oats, buttermilk and butter; add yeast mixture. Add the whole wheat flour, syrup, honey, wheat germ, eggs and salt; beat on low speed for 30 seconds. Beat on high for 3 minutes. Stir in enough all-purpose flour to form a firm dough.

Turn onto a floured surface; knead until smooth and elastic, 6-8 minutes. Place in a bowl coated with cooking spray, turning once to coat top. Cover and let rise in a warm place until doubled, about 1 hour.

Punch the dough down. Shape into two loaves; place each in a 9-in. x 5-in. x 3-in. loaf pan coated with cooking spray. Cover and let rise in a warm place until doubled, about 45 minutes.

Beat egg white and water; brush over loaves. Sprinkle with oats. Bake at 375° for 30-35 minutes or until golden brown. Cool for 10 minutes before removing from pans to wire racks to cool completely. **Yield:** 2 loaves.

long side; pinch seam to seal.

Cut each into six rolls. Place cut side up in two greased 9-in. square baking pans. Cover and let rise in a warm place until doubled, about 30 minutes. Bake at 350° for 25-30 minutes or until golden brown. Cool on wire racks for 5 minutes. Combine glaze ingredients; drizzle over warm rolls. **Yield:** 1 dozen.

Editor's Note: This recipe was tested in a 1,100-watt microwave.

Sunshine Sweet Rolls

(Pictured above)

PREP: 30 min. + rising **BAKE:** 25 min.

This bread–machine recipe is my new favorite. The cream cheese filling and drizzled icing make these golden brown rolls a special treat for breakfast or snacking.

—*Alice Vivian Shepherd, Maryville, Tennessee*

- 1-1/2 **cups warm water (110° to 115°)**
- 1/4 **cup canola oil**
- 1/4 **cup shredded carrot**
- 4-1/2 **cups all-purpose flour**
- 1/4 **cup sugar**
- 1-1/2 **teaspoons salt**
- 2 **teaspoons active dry yeast**

FILLING:
- 1 **package (8 ounces) cream cheese, softened**
- 1/4 **cup sugar**
- 1 **teaspoon vanilla extract**
- 1 **package (3 ounces) cook-and-serve vanilla pudding mix**
- 1 **jar (6 ounces) carrot baby food**
- 1 **teaspoon ground cinnamon**

GLAZE:
- 1/2 **cup confectioners' sugar**
- 2 to 3 **teaspoons orange juice**
- 1/2 **teaspoon grated orange peel**
- 1/4 **teaspoon vanilla extract**

In bread machine pan, place the first seven ingredients in order suggested by manufacturer. Select dough setting (check dough after 5 minutes of mixing; add 1 to 2 tablespoons of water or flour if needed).

Meanwhile, for the filling, combine cream cheese, sugar and vanilla; set aside. In a microwave-safe bowl, combine pudding mix, baby food and cinnamon. Cover and microwave on high for 2 minutes; stir.

When cycle is completed, turn dough onto a lightly floured surface. Divide in half; shape each portion into a ball. Roll each into a 9-in. x 8-in. rectangle. Spread cream cheese mixture to within 1/2 in. of edges; top with carrot mixture. Roll up jelly-roll style, starting with a

Cheddar Skillet Corn Bread

(Pictured below)

PREP/TOTAL TIME: 30 min.

With their crispy edges, wedges of this corn bread go well with just about any meal. I like to pair it with a hearty bowl of chili or a Southwestern chicken casserole.

—*Terri Adrian, Lake City, Florida*

- 2 **tablespoons butter**
- 2 **packages (8-1/2 ounces *each*) corn bread/muffin mix**
- 2 **eggs, beaten**
- 1/2 **cup milk**
- 1/2 **cup plain yogurt**
- 1 **can (14-3/4 ounces) cream-style corn**
- 1/2 **cup shredded cheddar cheese**

HONEY BUTTER:
- 1/2 **cup butter, softened**
- 2 **tablespoons honey**

Place butter into a deep 10-in. ovenproof skillet. Place in a 400° oven for 4-6 minutes or until melted.

Meanwhile, in a large bowl, combine the corn bread mix, eggs, milk and yogurt until blended. Stir in corn and cheese. Pour into hot skillet. Bake at 400° for 20-25 minutes or until a toothpick inserted near the center comes out clean. Cut into wedges.

In a small bowl, mix butter and honey together. Serve with warm corn bread. **Yield:** 12 servings.

For the pumpernickel dough, add cocoa and molasses to third bowl; mix well. Gradually add enough rye flour to make a stiff dough. Turn onto a floured surface; knead until smooth and elastic, 6-8 minutes. Place in a greased bowl, turning once to grease top. Cover and set aside. Let all three bowls rise in a warm place until doubled, about 1 hour.

Punch doughs down; divide each in half. Shape each portion into a 15-in. rope. Place a rope of each dough on a greased baking sheet and braid; seal ends. Repeat with remaining ropes. Cover and let rise until doubled, about 45 minutes. Beat egg white and water together; brush over braids. Bake at 350° for 25-30 minutes or until golden brown. Remove to wire racks to cool.
Yield: 2 loaves (12 slices each).

Tricolor Braid

(Pictured above)

PREP: I hour + rising **BAKE:** 25 min. + cooling

This impressive loaf is wonderfully dense and chewy. It takes some time to prepare, but the results are worth the extra effort.
—Cindi Paulson, Anchorage, Alaska

- 2 **packages (1/4 ounce** *each***) active dry yeast**
- 2-1/3 **cups warm water (110° to 115°)**
- 1/4 **cup butter, softened**
- 2 **tablespoons honey**
- 3 **teaspoons salt**
- 3-1/3 **to 3-2/3 cups all-purpose flour**
WHEAT DOUGH:
- 2 **tablespoons toasted wheat germ**
- 2 **tablespoons molasses**
- 1 **cup plus 2 to 5 tablespoons whole wheat flour**
PUMPERNICKEL DOUGH:
- 2 **tablespoons baking cocoa**
- 2 **tablespoons molasses**
- 1 **cup plus 2 to 5 tablespoons rye flour**
TOPPING:
- 1 **egg white**
- 1 **tablespoon water**

In a large bowl, dissolve yeast in warm water. Add butter, honey, salt and 2-1/3 cups all-purpose flour; beat for 2 minutes. Divide evenly among three bowls.

To the first bowl, add enough remaining all-purpose flour to make a stiff dough; mix well. Turn onto a floured surface; knead until smooth and elastic, 6-8 minutes. Place in a greased bowl, turning once to grease top. Cover and set aside.

For the wheat dough, add wheat germ and molasses to the second bowl; mix well. Gradually add enough wheat flour to make a stiff dough. Turn onto a floured surface; knead until smooth and elastic, 6-8 minutes. Place in a greased bowl, turning once to grease top. Cover and set aside.

Orange-Rhubarb Breakfast Bread

(Pictured below)

PREP: 20 min. **BAKE:** 55 min. + cooling

I love starting my day with a slice of this fabulous sweet bread alongside eggs, sausage and orange juice. It's full of tangy flavor and crunchy slivered almonds.
—Sonya Goergen, Moorhead, Minnesota

- 1/3 **cup butter, softened**
- 1 **cup sugar**
- 2 **eggs**
- 1 **teaspoon vanilla extract**
- 2 **cups all-purpose flour**
- 1-1/2 **teaspoons baking powder**
- 1/2 **teaspoon baking soda**
- 1/2 **teaspoon salt**
- 1/4 **teaspoon ground ginger**
- 1/4 **teaspoon ground nutmeg**
- 1/2 **cup orange juice**
- 1 **cup chopped fresh** *or* **frozen rhubarb**
- 1/2 **cup slivered almonds**
- 2 **teaspoons grated orange peel**

In a large bowl, cream butter and sugar. Add eggs, one at a time, beating well after each addition. Beat in vanilla.

Combine the flour, baking powder, baking soda, salt, ginger and nutmeg; add to creamed mixture alternately with orange juice. Fold in the rhubarb, almonds and orange peel.

Transfer to a greased 9-in. x 5-in. x 3-in. loaf pan. Bake at 350° for 55-65 minutes or until a toothpick inserted near the center comes out clean. Cool for 10 minutes before removing from pan to a wire rack. **Yield:** 1 loaf.

Editor's Note: If using frozen rhubarb, measure rhubarb while still frozen, then thaw completely. Drain in a colander, but do not press liquid out.

Black Raspberry Bubble Ring

PREP: 35 min. + rising **BAKE:** 25 min.

I first made this pretty bread years ago for a 4–H project. It helped me win Grand Champion for my county. It takes a little prep work, but never fails to really impress.
—Kila Frank, Reedsville, Ohio

> 1 **package (1/4 ounce) active dry yeast**
> 1/4 **cup warm water (110° to 115°)**
> 1 **cup warm milk (110° to 115°)**
> 1/4 **cup plus 2 tablespoons sugar**, *divided*
> 1/2 **cup butter, melted**, *divided*
> 1 **egg**
> 1 **teaspoon salt**
> 4 **cups all-purpose flour**
> 1 **jar (10 ounces) seedless black raspberry preserves**

SYRUP:
> 1/3 **cup corn syrup**
> 2 **tablespoons butter, melted**
> 1/2 **teaspoon vanilla extract**

In a large bowl, dissolve yeast in warm water. Add the milk, 1/4 cup sugar, 1/4 cup butter, egg, salt and 3-1/2 cups flour. Beat until smooth. Stir in enough remaining flour to form a soft dough.

Turn onto a floured surface; knead until smooth and elastic, 6-8 minutes. Place in a greased bowl, turning once to grease top. Cover and let rise in a warm place until doubled, about 1-1/4 hours.

Punch the dough down. Turn onto a lightly floured surface; divide into 32 pieces. Flatten each into a 3-in. disk. Place about 1 teaspoon of preserves on the center of each piece; bring edges together and seal. Place 16 of the filled dough balls in a greased 10-in. fluted tube pan. Brush with half of the remaining butter; sprinkle with 1 tablespoon sugar. Top with the remaining balls, butter and sugar. Cover and let rise until doubled, about 35 minutes.

Bake at 350° for 25-30 minutes or until golden brown. Combine syrup ingredients; pour over warm bread. Cool for 5 minutes before inverting onto a serving plate. **Yield:** 1 loaf.

Parker House Dinner Rolls

(Pictured above and on page 106)

PREP: 1 hour + rising **BAKE:** 10 min.

You won't be able to eat just one of my mom's famous yeast rolls. They're light and fluffy with a wonderful flavor…and even more delicious served warm with a little butter.
—Susan Hansen, Auburn, Alabama

> 1/2 **cup shortening**
> 1/4 **cup sugar**
> 2 **teaspoons salt**
> 1-1/2 **cups boiling water**
> 2 **tablespoons active dry yeast**
> 1/2 **cup warm water (110° to 115°)**
> 3 **eggs**
> 6-3/4 to 7-1/4 **cups all-purpose flour**
> 1/4 **cup butter, melted**

In a large bowl, combine the shortening, sugar and salt. Stir in boiling water. Cool to 110°-115°. Dissolve yeast in warm water. Add yeast mixture, eggs and 3 cups flour to shortening mixture; mix well. Stir in enough remaining flour to form a soft dough.

Turn onto a floured surface; knead until smooth and elastic, 6-8 minutes. Place in a greased bowl, turning once to grease top. Cover and let rise in a warm place until doubled, about 45 minutes.

Punch the dough down; turn onto a lightly floured surface. Roll the dough to 1/2-in. thickness. Cut with a 2-1/2-in. biscuit cutter. Fold circles in half; press edges to seal. Place 2 in. apart on baking sheets coated with cooking spray. Cover and let rise until doubled, about 30 minutes.

Bake at 400° for 10-12 minutes or until golden brown. Remove to wire racks. Brush with butter. Serve warm. **Yield:** 3 dozen.

Magnificent Muffins

Berry Cheesecake Muffins

(Pictured above and on page 106)

PREP: 30 min. **BAKE:** 25 min./batch

I adapted this recipe over the years for my family, and they think it's wonderful. Not only are the muffins delicious, but they're bursting with fantastic color, too.
—*Jeanne Bilhimer, Midland, Michigan*

- 1/3 **cup butter, softened**
- 3/4 **cup sugar**
-   2 **eggs**
- 1-1/2 **cups all-purpose flour**
- 1-1/2 **teaspoons baking powder**
-   1 **teaspoon ground cinnamon**
- 1/3 **cup milk**
- **CREAM CHEESE FILLING:**
-   2 **packages (3 ounces *each*) cream cheese, softened**
- 1/3 **cup sugar**
-   1 **egg**
- 3/4 **cup fresh raspberries**
- 3/4 **cup fresh blueberries**
- **STREUSEL TOPPING:**
- 1/4 **cup all-purpose flour**
-   2 **tablespoons brown sugar**
- 1/2 **teaspoon ground cinnamon**
-   1 **tablespoon cold butter**

In a large bowl, cream butter and sugar until light and fluffy. Add eggs, one at a time, beating well after each addition. Combine the flour, baking powder and cinnamon; add to creamed mixture alternately with milk. Fill greased or paper-lined muffin cups one-third full.

For the filling, beat the cream cheese, sugar and egg together until smooth. Fold in the berries. Drop one rounded tablespoonful into the center of the batter for each muffin. (Muffin cups will be full.)

For the topping, combine the flour, brown sugar and cinnamon; cut in the butter until mixture is crumbly. Sprinkle over the batter.

Bake at 375° for 25-30 minutes or until a toothpick comes out clean. Cool for 5 minutes. Remove the muffins and transfer to wire racks. Serve warm. Refrigerate leftovers. **Yield:** 21 muffins.

Walnut Raspberry Muffins

(Pictured below)

PREP: 25 min. **BAKE:** 20 min./batch

Raspberries are my favorite berry, so this recipe is tops with me. The walnuts give the muffins a nice crunch. You can dress them up by using foil liners instead of paper.
—*Elisa Lochridge, Tigard, Oregon*

- 2/3 **cup cream cheese, softened**
- 1/3 **cup butter, softened**
- 1-1/2 **cups sugar**
-   2 **egg whites**
-   1 **egg**
- 1-1/2 **teaspoons vanilla extract**
-   2 **cups all-purpose flour**
-   1 **teaspoon baking powder**
- 1/4 **teaspoon baking soda**
- 1/2 **cup buttermilk**
-   2 **cups fresh *or* frozen raspberries**
- 1/4 **cup chopped walnuts**

In a large bowl, beat the cream cheese, butter and sugar until light and fluffy. Add the egg whites, egg and vanilla; beat well. Combine the flour, baking powder and baking soda; add to creamed mixture alternately with buttermilk. Fold in the raspberries and walnuts.

Fill paper-lined muffin cups three-fourths full. Bake at 350° for 20-24 minutes or until a toothpick comes out clean. Cool for 5 minutes before removing from pans to wire racks. Serve warm. **Yield:** 1-1/2 dozen.

Editor's Note: If using frozen raspberries, do not thaw before adding to batter.

Almond Berry Muffins

(Pictured above)

PREP: 20 min. **BAKE:** 20 min.

I brought these moist muffins to the office and they were a hit. If strawberries aren't in season, just substitute with frozen cut strawberries directly from the freezer.
—Deborah Feinberg
East Setauket, New York

- 1-1/4 **cups sliced almonds,** *divided*
- 1 **egg white, lightly beaten**
- 1-1/2 **cups sugar,** *divided*
- 1/4 **cup shortening**
- 1/4 **cup butter, softened**
- 2 **eggs**
- 1 **teaspoon vanilla extract**
- 1/2 **teaspoon almond extract**
- 2 **cups all-purpose flour**
- 1 **teaspoon baking powder**
- 1/2 **teaspoon salt**
- 1/4 **teaspoon baking soda**
- 3/4 **cup buttermilk**
- 1-1/4 **cups fresh strawberries,** **chopped**

In a bowl, combine 1 cup almonds and egg white. Add 1/2 cup sugar; toss to coat. Spoon into a greased 15-in. x 10-in. x 1-in. baking pan. Bake at 350° for 9-11 minutes or until golden brown, stirring occasionally.

In a large bowl, cream shortening, butter and remaining sugar until light and fluffy. Add eggs, one at a time, beating well after each addition. Beat in extracts. Combine the flour, baking powder, salt and baking soda; add to the creamed mixture alternately with buttermilk. Fold in the strawberries and remaining almonds.

Fill greased or paper-lined muffin cups two-thirds full. Sprinkle with sugared almonds. Bake at 350° for 20-25 minutes or until a toothpick comes out clean. Cool for 5 minutes before removing from pans to wire racks. **Yield:** 1-1/2 dozen.

Lemon Pound Cake Muffins

(Pictured below)

PREP: 15 min. **BAKE:** 20 min.

I make these lemony muffins for all kinds of occasions. My family asks for them often because they're so good!
—Lola Baxter, Winnebago, Minnesota

- 1/2 **cup butter, softened**
- 1 **cup sugar**
- 2 **eggs**
- 1 **teaspoon vanilla extract**
- 1/2 **teaspoon lemon extract**
- 1-3/4 **cups all-purpose flour**
- 1/2 **teaspoon salt**
- 1/4 **teaspoon baking soda**
- 1/2 **cup sour cream**

GLAZE:
- 2 **cups confectioners' sugar**
- 3 **tablespoons lemon juice**

In a large bowl, cream the butter and sugar until light and fluffy. Beat in the eggs and extracts. Combine the flour, salt and baking soda; add to creamed mixture alternately with sour cream.

Fill greased or paper-lined muffin cups three-fourths full. Bake at 400° for 18-20 minutes or until a toothpick comes out clean. Cool for 5 minutes before removing from pan to a wire rack.

Combine the glaze ingredients; drizzle over muffins. Serve warm. **Yield:** 1 dozen.

White Chocolate Macadamia Muffins

(Pictured above)

PREP: 20 min. **BAKE:** 15 min.

I love making muffins because they're so versatile and everyone loves them. These remind me of my favorite cookies. They're real kid-pleasers.
—Lorie Roach, Buckatunna, Mississippi

- 1-3/4 **cups all-purpose flour**
- 3/4 **cup sugar**
- 2-1/2 **teaspoons baking powder**
- 1/2 **teaspoon salt**
- 1 **egg**
- 1/2 **cup milk**
- 1/4 **cup butter, melted**
- 3/4 **cup vanilla** *or* **white chips**
- 3/4 **cup chopped macadamia** **nuts**

GLAZE:
- 1/2 **cup vanilla** *or* **white chips**
- 2 **tablespoons heavy** **whipping cream**

In a bowl, combine the flour, sugar, baking powder and salt. In another bowl, whisk the egg, milk and butter; stir into dry ingredients just until moistened. Fold in the chips and nuts.

Fill paper-lined muffin cups two-thirds full. Bake at 400° for 15-18 minutes or until a toothpick comes out clean. Cool for 5 minutes before removing from pan to a wire rack.

For glaze, in a small microwave-safe bowl, melt chips with cream; stir until smooth. Drizzle over warm muffins. **Yield:** 1 dozen.

Fruit and Nut Stollen

(Pictured below)

PREP: 40 min. + rising **BAKE:** 15 min.

Making this stollen has become a tradition for our family. Everyone looks forward to it at Christmas.
—*Rebekah Radewahn, Wauwatosa, Wisconsin*

- **4 to 4-1/2 cups all-purpose flour**
- **1/4 cup sugar**
- **3 teaspoons active dry yeast**
- **1 teaspoon ground cardamom**
- **1/2 teaspoon salt**
- **1-1/4 cups milk**
- **1/2 cup plus 3 tablespoons butter, softened, divided**
- **1 egg**
- **1/4 cup *each* raisins and dried cranberries**
- **1/4 cup *each* chopped dried pineapple and apricots**
- **1/4 cup *each* chopped pecans, almonds, Brazil nuts and walnuts**
- **1/2 teaspoon lemon extract**

LEMON GLAZE:
- **1 cup confectioners' sugar**
- **4-1/2 teaspoons lemon juice**

In a large bowl, combine 2 cups flour, sugar, yeast, cardamom and salt. In a small saucepan, heat milk and 1/2 cup butter to 120°-130°. Add to dry ingredients; beat just until moistened. Add egg; beat until smooth. Stir in enough remaining flour to form a soft dough (dough will be sticky).

Turn onto a floured surface; knead until smooth and elastic, 6-8 minutes. Place in a bowl coated with cooking spray, turning once to coat top. Cover and let rise in a warm place until doubled, about 1 hour. Combine the dried fruits, nuts and extract; set aside.

Punch dough down. Turn onto a lightly floured surface; knead fruit mixture into dough. Divide into thirds. Roll each portion into a 10-in. x 8-in. oval. Melt

remaining butter; brush over dough. Fold a long side over to within 1 in. of opposite side; press edges lightly to seal. Place on baking sheets coated with cooking spray. Cover and let rise until doubled, about 45 minutes.

Bake at 375° for 14-16 minutes or until golden brown. Remove to wire racks. Combine glaze ingredients; drizzle over loaves. **Yield:** 3 loaves.

Pretty Pumpkin Cinnamon Buns

PREP: 45 min. + rising **BAKE:** 25 min.

I make sticky buns and cinnamon rolls quite often because my husband truly enjoys them. One day I had some fresh pumpkin on hand and decided to try pumpkin cinnamon buns. We loved the results! —*Glenda Joseph, Chambersburg, Pennsylvania*

- **2 tablespoons active dry yeast**
- **1/2 cup warm water (110° to 115°)**
- **4 eggs**
- **1 cup shortening**
- **1 cup canned pumpkin**
- **1 cup warm milk (110° to 115°)**
- **1/2 cup sugar**
- **1/2 cup packed brown sugar**
- **1/3 cup instant vanilla pudding mix**
- **1/3 cup instant butterscotch pudding mix**
- **1 teaspoon salt**
- **7 to 8 cups all-purpose flour**

FILLING:
- **1/4 cup butter, melted**
- **1 cup packed brown sugar**
- **2 teaspoons ground cinnamon**

ICING:
- **3 tablespoons water**
- **2 tablespoons butter, softened**
- **1 teaspoon ground cinnamon**
- **2 cups confectioners' sugar**
- **1-1/2 teaspoons vanilla extract**

In a large bowl, dissolve the yeast in warm water. Add the eggs, shortening, pumpkin, warm milk, sugars, pudding mixes, salt and 6 cups flour. Beat until smooth. Stir in enough remaining flour to form a soft dough (dough will be sticky).

Turn onto a floured surface; knead until smooth and elastic, 6-8 minutes. Place in a greased bowl, turning once to grease top. Cover and let rise in a warm place until doubled, about 1 hour.

Punch dough down; divide in half. Roll each portion into a 12-in. x 8-in. rectangle; brush with butter. Combine brown sugar and cinnamon; sprinkle over dough to within 1/2 in. of edges.

Roll up jelly-roll style, starting with a long side; pinch seams to seal. Cut each into 12 slices. Place cut side down in two greased 13-in. x 9-in. x 2-in. baking pans. Cover and let rise until doubled, about 30 minutes.

remaining flour to form a soft dough.

Turn onto a floured surface; knead until smooth and elastic, 6-8 minutes. Place in a greased bowl, turning once to grease top. Cover; let rise in a warm place until doubled, about 30 minutes.

Punch the dough down. On a lightly floured surface, roll dough into a 12-in. circle. Place on a greased 12-in. pizza pan. Brush with oil. Combine the Parmesan cheese, rosemary, garlic and salt; sprinkle over dough. Arrange onion rings and tomatoes over top, pressing down lightly.

Bake at 400° for 15-20 minutes or until crust is golden brown. Cut into wedges. **Yield:** 10 servings.

Poppy Seed Onion Bread

(Pictured below)

PREP: 10 min. **BAKE:** 3-4 hours + cooling

For ease and convenience, I use a bread machine for this golden-crusted savory loaf. It has great onion flavor that tastes wonderful when used to make sandwiches.
—Sue Ashford, Blountville, Tennessee

  1-1/4 **cups water (70° to 80°)**
     2 **tablespoons butter, softened**
     2 **tablespoons brown sugar**
   1/4 **cup dried minced onion**
  1-1/2 **teaspoons salt**
     1 **teaspoon poppy seeds**
   1/2 **teaspoon onion powder**
   1/2 **teaspoon pepper**
     3 **cups bread flour**
     2 **tablespoons nonfat dry milk powder**
     3 **teaspoons active dry yeast**

In bread machine pan, place all ingredients in order suggested by manufacturer. Select basic bread setting. Choose crust color and loaf size if available.

Bake according to bread machine directions (check dough after 5 minutes of mixing; add 1 to 2 tablespoons of water or flour if needed). **Yield:** 1 loaf (1-1/2 pounds).

Bake at 350° for 22-28 minutes or until golden brown. For the icing, in a small bowl, combine the water, butter and cinnamon. Add confectioners' sugar and vanilla; beat until smooth. Spread over buns. Serve warm. **Yield:** 2 dozen.

Tomato Focaccia

(Pictured above and on page 107)

PREP: 30 min. + rising **BAKE:** 15 min.

What makes this focaccia bread so delicious is the topping. The combination of Parmesan cheese, garlic, rosemary, tomato and onion can't be beat.—Mary Lou Wayman, Salt Lake City, Utah

 2-1/2 **to 3 cups all-purpose flour**
    1 **teaspoon salt**
    1 **teaspoon sugar**
    3 **teaspoons active dry yeast**
    1 **cup warm water (110° to 115°)**
    1 **tablespoon olive oil**
TOPPING:
    1 **tablespoon olive oil**
    2 **tablespoons grated Parmesan cheese**
    1 **tablespoon minced fresh rosemary**
    2 **garlic cloves, minced**
  1/4 **teaspoon salt**
    1 **small red onion, thinly sliced and separated into rings**
    3 **to 4 medium plum tomatoes, thinly sliced**

In a large bowl, combine 2-1/2 cups flour, salt and sugar. Dissolve the yeast in warm water; stir in olive oil. Add to the dry ingredients; beat until smooth. Stir in enough

Special Banana Nut Bread

(Pictured above and on page 107)

PREP: 25 min. **BAKE:** 1 hour + cooling

This extra-special banana bread makes a wonderful gift for friends and neighbors. The recipe makes two loaves, so I can serve one and keep the other one in the freezer. I always have a last-minute gift on hand.
—Beverly Sprague, Catonsville, Maryland

       3/4 **cup butter, softened**
         1 **package (8 ounces) cream cheese, softened**
         2 **cups sugar**
         2 **eggs**
    1-1/2 **cups mashed ripe bananas (about 4 medium)**
       1/2 **teaspoon vanilla extract**
         3 **cups all-purpose flour**
       1/2 **teaspoon baking powder**
       1/2 **teaspoon baking soda**
       1/2 **teaspoon salt**
         2 **cups chopped pecans,** *divided*
ORANGE GLAZE:
         1 **cup confectioners' sugar**
         3 **tablespoons orange juice**
         1 **teaspoon grated orange peel**

In a large bowl, cream the butter, cream cheese and sugar until light and fluffy. Add eggs, one at a time, beating well after each addition. Beat in bananas and vanilla. Combine the flour, baking powder, baking soda and salt; add to creamed mixture. Fold in 1 cup pecans.

   Transfer to two greased 8-in. x 4-in. x 2-in. loaf pans. Sprinkle with remaining pecans. Bake at 350° for 1 to 1-1/4 hours or until a toothpick inserted near the center comes out clean.

   Whisk the glaze ingredients together; drizzle over loaves. Cool for 10 minutes before removing from pans to wire racks. **Yield:** 2 loaves.

Fruit-Nut Pumpkin Bread

PREP: 30 min. **BAKE:** 1 hour + cooling

My family says our Thanksgiving and Christmas dinner wouldn't be complete without this easy bread. I bake a variety to suit everybody—one plain, one with just nuts, one with raisins and dried cranberries, and one with everything.
—Priscilla Gilbert, Indian Harbour Beach, Florida

    2-2/3 **cups sugar**
         1 **can (15 ounces) solid-pack pumpkin**
         1 **cup canola oil**
         4 **eggs**
         1 **teaspoon vanilla extract**
    3-1/2 **cups all-purpose flour**
    1-1/2 **teaspoons ground cinnamon**
         1 **teaspoon salt**
         1 **teaspoon baking soda**
       1/4 **teaspoon ground cloves**
    1-1/2 **cups coarsely chopped walnuts**
       2/3 **cup golden raisins**
       2/3 **cup raisins**
       2/3 **cup dried cranberries**
CRANBERRY CREAM CHEESE SPREAD:
       1/2 **cup dried cranberries**
    1-1/2 **cups boiling water**
         1 **package (8 ounces) cream cheese, softened**
       1/3 **cup chopped walnuts**

In a large bowl, beat the sugar, pumpkin, oil, eggs and vanilla until well blended. Combine the flour, cinnamon, salt, baking soda and cloves; gradually beat into pumpkin mixture until blended. Fold in the walnuts, raisins and cranberries.

   Transfer to two greased 9-in. x 5-in. x 3-in. loaf pans. Bake at 350° for 60-70 minutes or until a toothpick inserted near the center comes out clean. Cool for 10 minutes before removing from pans to wire racks.

   For spread, place cranberries in a small bowl; add boiling water. Let stand for 5 minutes; drain. In a small mixing bowl, beat cream cheese until smooth. Beat in cranberries and walnuts until blended. Serve with bread. **Yield:** 2 loaves and 1 cup spread.

Honey-Oat Pan Rolls

PREP: 45 min. + rising **BAKE:** 20 min.

Since these tender rolls require only one rising, they are relatively quick to make. Whole wheat flour and hearty oats make them nutritious, too. —Arlene Kay Butler, Ogden, Utah

2-1/2 **to 2-3/4 cups all-purpose flour**
   3/4 **cup whole wheat flour**
   1/2 **cup old-fashioned oats**
     2 **packages (1/4 ounce** *each***) active dry yeast**
     1 **teaspoon salt**
     1 **cup water**

1/4 **cup honey**
5 **tablespoons butter,** *divided*
1 **egg**

In a large bowl, combine 1 cup all-purpose flour, whole wheat flour, oats, yeast and salt. In a small saucepan, heat the water, honey and 4 tablespoons butter to 120°-130°. Add to dry ingredients; beat just until moistened. Add egg; beat until combined. Stir in enough remaining all-purpose flour to form a soft dough.

Turn onto a floured surface; knead until smooth and elastic, 6-8 minutes. Place in a greased bowl, turning once to grease top. Cover and let rise in a warm place until doubled, about 1 hour.

Punch dough down. Turn onto a lightly floured surface; divide into 24 pieces. Shape each into a ball. Place in a greased 13-in. x 9-in. x 2-in. baking pan. Cover and let rise until doubled, about 30 minutes.

Bake at 375° for 20-22 minutes or until golden brown. Melt remaining butter; brush over rolls. Remove from pan to a wire rack. **Yield:** 2 dozen.

Pull-Apart Bacon Bread

(Pictured below)

PREP: 15 min. **BAKE:** 25 min.

I baked this tender and tasty bread for my husband, and he just raved about it! When I'm out of bacon, I substitute bacon bits.
—*Terri Christensen, Montague, Michigan*

12 **bacon strips, diced**
2 **tubes (12 ounces** *each***) refrigerated buttermilk biscuits**
2 **cups (8 ounces) shredded part-skim mozzarella cheese**
1 **tablespoon Italian salad dressing mix**
2 **teaspoons olive oil**

In a large skillet, cook bacon over medium heat until cooked but not crisp. Using a slotted spoon, remove to paper towels to drain. Separate biscuits; cut each biscuit into quarters.

In a large bowl, combine the mozzarella cheese, dressing mix, olive oil and bacon. Place half of the biscuit pieces in a greased 10-in. fluted tube pan; sprinkle with half of the cheese mixture. Top with remaining biscuit pieces and cheese mixture.

Bake at 375° for 25-30 minutes or until golden brown. Cool for 5 minutes before inverting onto a serving plate. Serve immediately. **Yield:** 12 servings.

Pecan Lemon Loaf

(Pictured above)

PREP: 20 min. **BAKE:** 50 min. + cooling

A pretty glaze gives this tender, nutty bread an extra boost of lemony flavor. For variety, substitute grated orange peel and orange juice for the lemons.
—*Laura Comitz, Enola, Pennsylvania*

1/2 **cup butter, softened**
1-1/2 **cups sugar,** *divided*
2 **eggs**
2 **cups all-purpose flour**
1 **teaspoon baking powder**
1/2 **teaspoon salt**
3/4 **cup sour cream**
1 **cup chopped pecans, toasted**
1 **tablespoon grated lemon peel**
1/4 **cup lemon juice**

In a large bowl, cream butter and 1 cup sugar until light and fluffy. Add eggs; mix well. Combine the flour, baking powder and salt; add to creamed mixture alternately with sour cream. Fold in pecans and lemon peel.

Transfer to a greased 9-in. x 5-in. x 3-in. loaf pan. Bake at 350° for 50-60 minutes or until a toothpick inserted near the center comes out clean.

In a small saucepan, combine lemon juice and remaining sugar. Cook and stir over medium heat until sugar is dissolved. Pour over warm bread. Cool completely on a wire rack before removing from pan. **Yield:** 1 loaf.

Vanilla Cinnamon Rolls

(Pictured below and on page 106)

PREP: 30 min. + rising **BAKE:** 20 min.

This is the best recipe I have found for cinnamon rolls. They're so tender with a delightful vanilla flavor and yummy frosting. When I serve them to my family, they disappear in no time.
—Linda Martin, Warsaw, Indiana

- 2 cups cold milk
- 1 package (3.4 ounces) instant vanilla pudding mix
- 2 packages (1/4 ounce *each*) active dry yeast
- 1/2 cup warm water (110° to 115°)
- 1/2 cup plus 2 tablespoons butter, melted, *divided*
- 2 eggs
- 2 tablespoons sugar
- 1 teaspoon salt
- 6 cups all-purpose flour

FILLING:
- 1/2 cup packed brown sugar
- 1 teaspoon ground cinnamon

FROSTING:
- 1 cup packed brown sugar
- 1/2 cup heavy whipping cream
- 1/2 cup butter, cubed
- 2 cups confectioners' sugar

Whisk milk and pudding mix together for 2 minutes; set aside. In a large bowl, dissolve yeast in warm water. Add 1/2 cup butter, eggs, sugar, salt and 2 cups flour. Beat on medium speed for 3 minutes. Add pudding; beat until smooth. Stir in enough remaining flour to form a soft dough (dough will be sticky).

Turn onto a floured surface; knead until smooth and elastic, 6-8 minutes. Place in a greased bowl, turning once to grease top. Cover and let rise in a warm place until doubled, about 1 hour.

Punch dough down. Turn onto a floured surface;

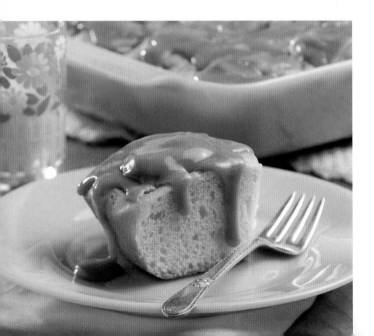

divide in half. Roll each portion into an 18-in. x 11-in. rectangle; brush with remaining butter. Combine brown sugar and cinnamon; sprinkle over dough to within 1/2 in. of edges.

Roll up jelly-roll style, starting with a long side; pinch seams to seal. Cut each into 16 slices. Place cut side down in two greased 13-in. x 9-in. x 2-in. baking dishes. Cover and let rise until doubled, about 30 minutes. Bake at 350° for 20-25 minutes or until golden brown.

Meanwhile, in a large saucepan, combine the brown sugar, cream and butter. Bring to a boil; cook and stir for 2 minutes. Remove from the heat. Beat in confectioners' sugar with a hand mixer until creamy. Frost rolls. Serve warm. **Yield:** 32 rolls.

Grand Prize Winner

Pumpkin Scones With Berry Butter

PREP: 25 min. + chilling **BAKE:** 15 min.

These delightful scones are perfect on a cold winter day with a steaming hot cup of coffee. They also make a wonderful hostess gift arranged in a basket.—Judy Wilson, Sun City West, Arizona

- 2 tablespoons dried cranberries
- 1/2 cup boiling water
- 1/2 cup butter, softened
- 3 tablespoons confectioners' sugar

DOUGH:
- 2-1/4 cups all-purpose flour
- 1/4 cup packed brown sugar
- 2 teaspoons baking powder
- 1-1/2 teaspoons pumpkin pie spice
- 1/4 teaspoon salt
- 1/4 teaspoon baking soda
- 1/2 cup cold butter
- 1 egg
- 1/2 cup canned pumpkin
- 1/3 cup milk
- 2 tablespoons chopped pecans, optional

Place cranberries in a small bowl; add boiling water. Let stand for 5 minutes; drain and chop. In a small bowl, beat butter until light and fluffy. Add confectioners' sugar and cranberries; mix well. Cover and refrigerate for at least 1 hour.

In a large bowl, combine the flour, brown sugar, baking powder, pie spice, salt and baking soda. Cut in butter until mixture resembles coarse crumbs. In a small bowl, whisk the egg, pumpkin and milk; add to crumb mixture just until moistened. Stir in pecans if desired.

Turn dough onto a floured surface; knead 10 times.

Cheddar Loaves

(Pictured below)

PREP: 25 min. + rising **BAKE:** 35 min. + cooling

Swirls of cheddar cheese give these loaves an exquisite flavor. Try a slice or two for sandwiches, toasted for breakfast or served on the side with a Caesar salad. —Agnes Ward, Stratford, Ontario

- **3 teaspoons active dry yeast**
- **1/2 cup warm water (110° to 115°)**
- **2 cups warm milk (110° to 115°)**
- **2 tablespoons butter, melted**
- **2 eggs**
- **3 teaspoons sugar**
- **2 teaspoons salt**
- **6 to 6-1/2 cups all-purpose flour**
- **2 cups (8 ounces) shredded sharp cheddar cheese**

In a large bowl, dissolve yeast in warm water. Add the milk, butter, eggs, sugar, salt and 6 cups flour. Beat on medium speed for 3 minutes. Stir in enough remaining flour to form a soft dough.

Turn onto a lightly floured surface; knead until smooth and elastic, 6-8 minutes. Place in a greased bowl, turning once to grease top. Cover and let rise in a warm place until doubled, about 1 hour.

Punch dough down. Turn onto a lightly floured surface; knead cheese into the dough. Divide in half; shape each portion into a 6-in. round loaf. Place on greased baking sheets. Cover and let rise until doubled, about 45 minutes.

Bake at 350° for 35-40 minutes or until golden brown. Remove from pans to wire racks to cool. Refrigerate leftovers. **Yield:** 2 loaves.

Pat into an 8-in. circle. Cut into eight wedges; separate wedges and place on a greased baking sheet.

Bake at 400° for 12-15 minutes or until golden brown. Serve warm with berry butter. **Yield:** 8 scones and about 1/2 cup butter.

Feta and Chive Muffins

(Pictured above)

PREP: 15 min. **BAKE:** 20 min.

This is a springtime variation on a savory muffin my husband has made for years. It has a light texture, almost like a popover, and tastes best eaten hot from the oven.
—Angela Buchanan, Boulder, Colorado

- **1-1/2 cups all-purpose flour**
- **3 teaspoons baking powder**
- **1/4 teaspoon salt**
- **2 eggs**
- **1 cup milk**
- **2 tablespoons butter, melted**
- **1/2 cup crumbled feta cheese**
- **3 tablespoons snipped chives**

In a bowl, combine the flour, baking powder and salt. In another bowl, whisk the eggs, milk and butter together; stir into dry ingredients just until moistened. Fold in the feta cheese and the chives.

Fill greased or paper-lined muffin cups two-thirds full. Bake at 400° for 18-22 minutes or until a toothpick comes out clean. Cool for 5 minutes before removing from pan to a wire rack. Serve warm. Refrigerate leftovers. **Yield:** 1 dozen.

Strawberry Popovers

(Pictured above)

PREP: 20 min. **BAKE:** 30 min.

These tender popovers "pop up" nicely in the oven and hold a delicate cream filling dotted with fresh chopped strawberries. If you don't have a popover pan on hand, you can try muffin cups.
—*Sandy Holton-Vanthoff, San Diego, California*

- **1 cup heavy whipping cream**
- **1/3 cup sugar**
- **1 teaspoon vanilla extract**
- **2 cups chopped fresh strawberries**

POPOVERS:
- **4-1/2 teaspoons shortening**
- **4 eggs**
- **2 cups milk**
- **2 cups all-purpose flour**
- **1 tablespoon sugar**
- **1 teaspoon salt**

In a medium bowl, beat the cream until it begins to thicken. Add the sugar and vanilla; beat until stiff peaks form. Fold in the chopped strawberries. Cover and refrigerate until serving.

For the popovers, using 1/2 teaspoon shortening for each cup, grease the bottom and sides of nine popover cups. In a small bowl, beat eggs; beat in milk. Add the flour, sugar and salt; beat until smooth (do not overmix). Fill prepared cups half full.

Bake at 450° for 15 minutes. Reduce heat to 350°; bake 15 minutes longer or until very firm. Immediately cut a slit in the top of each popover to allow steam to escape. Spoon strawberry filling into popovers. Serve immediately. **Yield:** 9 servings.

Parmesan Breadsticks

(Pictured below)

PREP: 40 min. + rising **BAKE:** 10 min.

These tender breadsticks fill the kitchen with a tempting aroma when they are baking, and they're wonderful served warm. My family tells me I can't make them too often.
—*Gaylene Anderson, Sandy, Utah*

- **2 packages (1/4 ounce *each*) active dry yeast**
- **1-1/2 cups warm water (110° to 115°)**
- **1/2 cup warm milk (110° to 115°)**
- **3 tablespoons sugar**
- **3 tablespoons plus 1/4 cup butter, softened, *divided***
- **1 teaspoon salt**
- **4-1/2 to 5-1/2 cups all-purpose flour**
- **1/4 cup grated Parmesan cheese**
- **1/2 teaspoon garlic salt**

In a large bowl, dissolve yeast in warm water. Add the milk, sugar, 3 tablespoons butter, salt and 2 cups flour. Beat until smooth. Stir in enough remaining flour to form a soft dough.

Turn onto a floured surface; knead until smooth and elastic, 6-8 minutes. Place in a greased bowl, turning once to grease top. Cover and let rise in a warm place until doubled, about 45 minutes.

Punch the dough down. Turn onto a floured surface; divide into 36 pieces. Shape each piece into a 6-in. rope. Place 2 in. apart on greased baking sheets. Cover and let rise until doubled, about 25 minutes.

Melt remaining butter; brush over dough. Sprinkle with cheese and garlic salt. Bake at 400° for 8-10 minutes or until golden brown. Remove from pans to wire racks. **Yield:** 3 dozen.

Five-Topping Bread

PREP: 30 min. + rising **BAKE:** 20 min.

You can't go wrong with this recipe. The tender, golden brown loaves have a great combination of seasonings. They go well with any meal and are even great for sandwiches.
—*Traci Wynne, Falls Church, Virginia*

- 1 package (1/4 ounce) active dry yeast
- 3/4 cup warm water (110° to 115°)
- 1 cup warm milk (110° to 115°)
- 1/4 cup sugar
- 1/4 cup butter, softened
- 1 egg, *separated*
- 2 teaspoons salt, *divided*
- 4 to 4-1/2 cups all-purpose flour
- 1 tablespoon water
- 1 teaspoon *each* poppy seeds, sesame seeds and caraway seeds
- 1 teaspoon dried minced onion

In a large bowl, dissolve yeast in warm water. Add the milk, sugar, butter, egg yolk, 1-1/2 teaspoons salt and 2 cups flour. Beat on medium speed for 3 minutes. Beat until smooth. Stir in enough remaining flour to form a soft dough (dough will be sticky).

Turn onto a floured surface; knead until smooth and elastic, 6-8 minutes. Place in a bowl coated with cooking spray, turning once to coat top. Cover and let rise in a warm place until doubled, about 1 hour.

Punch dough down. Turn onto a lightly floured surface; divide in half. Shape into two round loaves. Place each on a baking sheet coated with cooking spray. Beat egg white and water; brush over loaves.

Combine the poppy seeds, sesame seeds, caraway seeds, dried onion and remaining salt; sprinkle over the loaves. Cover and let rise in a warm place until doubled, about 30 minutes.

Bake at 375° for 20-25 minutes or until golden brown. Cut the bread into wedges; serve warm. **Yield:** 2 loaves (10 servings each).

Christmas Morning Croissants

(Pictured above right)

PREP: 50 min. + chilling **BAKE:** 20 min.

Growing up in France I often enjoyed buttery croissants with a cup of hot chocolate for breakfast. I re-created this experience for my family with this recipe. Now, it's a Christmas tradition!
—*Tish Stevenson, Grand Rapids, Michigan*

- 2 packages (1/4 ounce *each*) active dry yeast
- 1 cup warm water (110° to 115°)
- 1-1/4 cups cold butter, *divided*
- 5 cups all-purpose flour
- 1/3 cup sugar
- 1-1/2 teaspoons salt

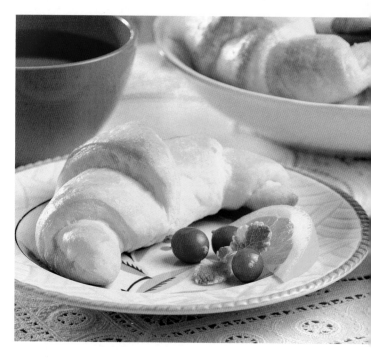

- 3/4 cup evaporated milk
- 2 eggs
- 1 tablespoon water

In a large bowl, dissolve yeast in warm water; let stand for 5 minutes. Melt 1/4 cup butter; set aside. Combine 1 cup flour, sugar and salt; add to yeast mixture. Add the milk, 1 egg and melted butter; beat until smooth.

Place remaining flour in a large bowl; cut in remaining cold butter until crumbly. Add yeast mixture; mix well. Do not knead. Cover and refrigerate overnight.

Punch dough down. Turn onto a lightly floured surface; knead about six times. Divide dough into four pieces. Roll each piece into a 16-in. circle; cut each circle into eight wedges.

Roll up wedges from the wide ends and place croissants point side down and 3 in. apart onto ungreased baking sheets. Curve ends to form crescents. Cover and let rise in a warm place for 1 hour.

Beat water and remaining egg; brush over rolls. Bake at 325° for 20-25 minutes or until lightly browned. Serve warm. **Yield:** 32 rolls.

Yeast Know-How

To make sure active dry yeast (not quick-rise yeast) is alive and active, you may want to proof it first. Dissolve one package of yeast and 1 teaspoon sugar in 1/4 cup warm water (110° to 115°). Let stand for 5 to 10 minutes. If the mixture foams up, the yeast mixture can be used because the yeast is active. If it does not foam, the yeast is dead and should be discarded.

Cookies, Bars & Candies

Stacking your goodie tray high is a cinch with oodles of decadent recipes at your fingertips.

SCRUMPTIOUS TREATS. Clockwise from upper left: Elegant Dipped Cherries (p. 131), Glazed Peanut Butter Bars (p. 133), Berry-Cream Cookie Snaps (p. 129), Delicate Mint Thins (p. 125) and pictured center, Hazelnut-Espresso Sandwich Cookies (p. 136).

squares; cut in half if desired.

Place on dessert plates with a scoop of ice cream. Top with sauce; sprinkle with pecans. **Yield:** 20 servings.

Iced Pumpkin Cookies

PREP: 45 min. **BAKE:** 15 min./batch + cooling

My young son, Joshua, likes testing, or should I say consuming, these chunky cookies! The combination of dried fruit, nuts, spices and vanilla chips is fantastic. —Johna Nilson, Vista, California

  1 cup butter, softened
1/2 cup sugar
1/2 cup packed brown sugar
  1 egg
  1 cup canned pumpkin
  1 cup all-purpose flour
  1 cup whole wheat flour
1-1/2 teaspoons ground cinnamon
  1 teaspoon baking powder
  1 teaspoon ground ginger
1/2 teaspoon salt
1/2 teaspoon baking soda
1/2 teaspoon ground nutmeg
1/4 teaspoon ground cloves
  1 cup granola without raisins
  1 cup chopped walnuts
  1 cup vanilla *or* white chips
  1 cup dried cranberries
ICING:
1/4 cup butter, softened
  2 cups confectioners' sugar
  3 tablespoons milk

In a large bowl, cream butter and sugars until light and fluffy. Beat in egg and pumpkin. Combine the flours, cinnamon, baking powder, ginger, salt, baking soda, nutmeg and cloves; gradually add to creamed mixture. Stir in the granola, walnuts, chips and cranberries.

Drop by tablespoonfuls 2 in. apart onto greased baking sheets. Bake at 350° for 15-18 minutes or until lightly browned. Remove to wire racks to cool.

In a small bowl, combine icing ingredients until smooth. Frost cookies. Store in the refrigerator. **Yield:** 3 dozen.

Blond Brownies a la Mode

(Pictured above)

PREP: 25 min. **BAKE:** 25 min. + cooling

We have a lot of church socials and I'm always looking for something new and different to prepare. These brownies, drizzled with a sweet maple sauce, are a sure hit.
—Pat Parker, Chester, South Carolina

3/4 cup butter, softened
  2 cups packed brown sugar
  4 eggs
  2 teaspoons vanilla extract
  2 cups all-purpose flour
  2 teaspoons baking powder
  1 teaspoon salt
1-1/2 cups chopped pecans
MAPLE CREAM SAUCE:
  1 cup maple syrup
  2 tablespoons butter
1/4 cup evaporated milk
Vanilla ice cream and chopped pecans

In a large bowl, cream butter and brown sugar until light and fluffy. Add eggs, one at a time, beating well after each addition. Beat in vanilla. Combine the flour, baking powder and salt; gradually add to creamed mixture. Stir in pecans.

Spread into a greased 13-in. x 9-in. x 2-in. baking pan. Bake at 350° for 25-30 minutes or until a toothpick inserted near the center comes out clean. Cool on a wire rack.

For the sauce, combine syrup and butter in a saucepan. Bring to a boil; cook and stir for 3 minutes. Remove from the heat; stir in milk. Cut brownies into

Light vs. Dark Brown Sugar

Both light and dark brown sugar are a mixture of granulated sugar and molasses. Light brown sugar has a delicate flavor. Dark brown sugar, which has more molasses, has a stronger more intense flavor. They can be used interchangeably depending on your personal preference.

Lemon Tea Cookies

(Pictured below)

PREP: 25 min. + chilling **BAKE:** 10 min.

These sandwich cookies have a lovely lemon filling and a rich, buttery flavor. My mother got the recipe from a friend in the 1950s. Mom always made them at Christmas, and now my sister and I do the same. —Phyllis Dietz, Westland, Michigan

- 3/4 cup butter, softened
- 1/2 cup sugar
- 1 egg yolk
- 1/2 teaspoon vanilla extract
- 2 cups all-purpose flour
- 1/4 cup finely chopped walnuts

FILLING:

- 3 tablespoons butter, softened
- 4-1/2 teaspoons lemon juice
- 3/4 teaspoon grated orange peel
- 1-1/2 cups confectioners' sugar
- 2 drops yellow food coloring, optional

In a large bowl, cream butter and sugar until light and fluffy. Beat in the egg yolk and vanilla. Gradually add flour. Shape into two 14-in. rolls; reshape each roll into a 14-in. x 1-1/8-in. x 1-1/8-in. block. Wrap each in plastic wrap. Refrigerate overnight.

Unwrap and cut into 1/4-in. slices. Place 2 in. apart on ungreased baking sheets. Sprinkle half of the cookies with nuts, gently pressing into dough. Bake at 400° for 8-10 minutes or until golden brown around the edges. Remove to wire racks to cool.

For the filling, in a small bowl, cream butter, lemon juice and orange peel until fluffy. Gradually add confectioners' sugar until smooth. Tint yellow if desired. Spread about 1 teaspoon on bottom of the plain cookies; place nut-topped cookies over filling. **Yield:** about 4-1/2 dozen.

Delicate Mint Thins

(Pictured above and on page 122)

PREP: 20 min. + chilling **BAKE:** 20 min. + cooling

When I was newly married, I needed something fancy to impress my relatives at a reunion and came up with these cookies. I received many compliments on their subtle flavor.
—Kristine McDaniel, Kettering, Ohio

- 1/2 cup butter, softened
- 1/2 cup sugar
- 1 egg yolk
- 1/2 teaspoon vanilla extract
- 1-1/2 cups all-purpose flour
- 1-1/2 teaspoons baking powder
- 1/8 teaspoon salt
- 3 tablespoons milk
- 1 cup fresh mint, finely chopped
- 1-2/3 cups semisweet chocolate chips
- 1 tablespoon shortening

In a large bowl, cream butter and sugar until light and fluffy. Beat in egg yolk and vanilla. Combine the flour, baking powder and salt; add to creamed mixture alternately with milk, mixing well after each addition. Stir in mint. Shape into two 8-in. rolls; wrap each in plastic wrap. Refrigerate for 2 hours or until firm.

Unwrap and cut into 1/4-in. slices. Place 1 in. apart on greased baking sheets. Bake at 350° for 8-12 minutes or until edges are golden. Remove to wire racks to cool.

In a microwave-safe bowl, melt chocolate chips and shortening; stir until smooth. Dip each cookie halfway; allowing excess to drip off. Place on waxed paper; let stand until set. **Yield:** about 4-1/2 dozen.

Chocolate Mint Dreams

(Pictured below)

PREP/TOTAL TIME: 30 min.

Since chocolate and mint create my favorite flavor combination, I can eat these dainty shortbread–like treats by the dozen. But I manage to save some for guests because they make my cookie trays look so elegant. —Anne Revers, Omaha, Nebraska

> 3/4 cup butter, softened
> 1 cup confectioners' sugar
> 2 squares (1 ounce *each*) unsweetened chocolate, melted and cooled
> 1/4 teaspoon peppermint extract
> 1-1/2 cups all-purpose flour
> 1 cup miniature semisweet chocolate chips

ICING:

> 2 tablespoons butter, softened
> 1 cup confectioners' sugar
> 1 to 2 tablespoons milk
> 1/4 teaspoon peppermint extract
> 1 to 2 drops green food coloring

DRIZZLE:

> 1/2 cup semisweet chocolate chips
> 1/2 teaspoon shortening

In a large bowl, cream butter and confectioners' sugar. Beat in chocolate and mint extract. Gradually add flour. Stir in chocolate chips. (Dough will be soft.)

Drop by tablespoonfuls 2 in. apart on ungreased baking sheets. Bake at 375° for 6-8 minutes or until firm. Cool for 2 minutes before removing to wire racks to cool completely.

Meanwhile, combine icing ingredients; spread over cooled cookies. Let set. In a microwave, melt chocolate chips and shortening; stir until smooth. Drizzle over cookies. **Yield:** 4 dozen.

Grand Prize Winner

Rustic Nut Bars

(Pictured above)

PREP: 20 min. **BAKE:** 35 min. + cooling

Everyone will jump with joy when they bite into these chewy, gooey bars. They'll love the cookie crust and the nutty topping. —Barbara Driscoll, West Allis, Wisconsin

> 1 tablespoon plus 3/4 cup cold butter, *divided*
> 2-1/3 cups all-purpose flour
> 1/2 cup sugar
> 1/2 teaspoon baking powder
> 1/2 teaspoon salt
> 1 egg, lightly beaten

TOPPING:

> 2/3 cup honey
> 1/2 cup packed brown sugar
> 1/4 teaspoon salt
> 6 tablespoons butter, cubed
> 2 tablespoons heavy whipping cream
> 1 cup chopped hazelnuts, toasted
> 1 cup roasted salted almonds
> 1 cup salted cashews, toasted
> 1 cup pistachios, toasted

Line a 13-in. x 9-in. x 2-in. baking pan with foil; grease the foil with 1 tablespoon butter. Set aside.

In a large bowl, combine the flour, sugar, baking powder and salt; cut in remaining butter until mixture resembles coarse crumbs. Stir in egg until blended (mixture will be dry).

Press firmly onto the bottom of prepared pan. Bake at 375° for 18-20 minutes or until edges are golden brown. Cool on a wire rack.

For the topping, in a large heavy saucepan, bring the honey, brown sugar and salt to a boil over medium heat until sugar is smooth; stirring often. Boil without stirring for 2 minutes. Add butter and cream. Bring to a boil; cook and stir for 1 minute or until smooth. Remove from the heat; stir in the hazelnuts, almonds, cashews and pistachios. Spread over crust.

Bake at 375° for 15-20 minutes or until topping is bubbly. Cool completely on a wire rack. Using foil, lift bars out of pan. Discard foil; cut into squares. **Yield:** about 3 dozen.

Lavender Cookies

(Pictured below)

PREP: 30 min. **BAKE:** 10 min./batch

I am a wedding and event planner and one of my brides who had a lavender-themed wedding served these unusual cookies at her reception. They were so good, I asked her for the recipe.
—Glenna Tooman, Boise, Idaho

- **1/2 cup shortening**
- **1/2 cup butter, softened**
- **1-1/4 cups sugar**
- **2 eggs**
- **1 teaspoon vanilla extract**
- **1/2 teaspoon almond extract**
- **2-1/4 cups all-purpose flour**
- **4 teaspoons dried lavender flowers**
- **1 teaspoon baking powder**
- **1/2 teaspoon salt**

In a large bowl, cream the shortening, butter and sugar. Add eggs, one at a time, beating well after each addition. Beat in extracts. Combine the flour, lavender, baking powder and salt; gradually add to creamed mixture and mix well.

Drop by rounded teaspoonfuls 2 in. apart onto baking sheets lightly coated with cooking spray.

Bake at 375° for 8-10 minutes or until golden brown. Cool for 2 minutes before removing to wire racks. Store in an airtight container. **Yield:** about 7 dozen.

Creamy Cashew Brownies

(Pictured above)

PREP: 15 min. **BAKE:** 25 min. + chilling

My sister-in-law dubbed me the "dessert queen" because of treats like this that I take to our family get-togethers. The brownies have a fudge-like texture and a rich cream cheese topping.
—Karen Wagner, Danville, Illinois

- **1 package fudge brownie mix (13-inch x 9-inch pan size)**
- **1/3 cup water**
- **1/4 cup canola oil**
- **1 egg**
- **1 cup (6 ounces) semisweet chocolate chips**

TOPPING:
- **2 packages (8 ounces *each*) cream cheese, softened**
- **1-1/2 cups confectioners' sugar**
- **1 teaspoon vanilla extract**
- **1 cup salted cashews, coarsely chopped**
- **1/2 cup hot fudge ice cream topping, warmed**

In a large bowl, combine the brownie mix, water, oil and egg. Stir in chips. Spread into a greased 13-in. x 9-in. x 2-in. baking pan.

Bake at 350° for 25-27 minutes or until a toothpick inserted near the center comes out clean (do not overbake). Cool on a wire rack.

For topping, in a large bowl, beat the cream cheese, confectioners' sugar and vanilla until smooth. Spread over brownies. Sprinkle with cashews; drizzle with hot fudge topping. Refrigerate before cutting. Store in the refrigerator. **Yield:** 2 dozen.

to creamed mixture. Stir in 2 cups chips and coconut.

Drop by tablespoonfuls 2 in. apart onto ungreased baking sheets. Bake at 350° for 8-10 minutes or until lightly browned. Cool for 10 minutes before removing to wire racks to cool completely.

In a microwave, melt the remaining chocolate chips; stir until smooth. First frost cooled cookies, then drizzle with melted chocolate. **Yield:** 6-1/2 dozen.

Chocolate Heart Cookies

(Pictured below)

PREP: 30 min. **BAKE:** 10 min. + cooling

For an elegant look, I dust dessert plates with cocoa powder, drizzle them with melted raspberry fruit spread and place two of these melt–in–your–mouth cookies in the center.
—T. Moore, Oaklyn, New Jersey

  1 **cup butter, softened**
1/2 **cup sugar**
  1 **teaspoon vanilla extract**
  2 **cups all-purpose flour**
1/4 **cup baking cocoa**
  1 **cup vanilla *or* white chips**
  2 **tablespoons shortening, *divided***
1/2 **cup semisweet chocolate chips**

In a small bowl, cream butter and sugar until light and fluffy. Beat in vanilla. Combine the flour and cocoa; gradually add to creamed mixture.

On a lightly floured surface, roll out the dough to 1/4-in. thickness. Cut with a 3-in. heart-shaped cookie cutter. Place 2 in. apart on ungreased baking sheets. Bake at 375° for 8-10 minutes or until firm. Remove to wire racks to cool.

In a microwave-safe bowl, heat vanilla chips and 1 tablespoon shortening until melted, stirring frequently. Dip both sides of cookies into melted mixture.

In another microwave-safe bowl, heat the chocolate chips and remaining shortening until melted, stirring frequently. Drizzle over the cookies. Place on wire racks to dry. **Yield:** about 2 dozen.

Coconut Pecan Cookies

(Pictured above)

PREP: 30 min. **BAKE:** 10 min. + cooling

With chocolate chips and coconut in the batter and a yummy pecan–coconut frosting, these cookies will remind you of German chocolate cake. A drizzle of chocolate tops them off in a festive way. —*Diane Selich, Vassar, Michigan*

  1 **egg, lightly beaten**
  1 **can (5 ounces) evaporated milk**
2/3 **cup sugar**
1/4 **cup butter, cubed**
1-1/4 **cups flaked coconut**
1/2 **cup chopped pecans**
COOKIE DOUGH:
  1 **cup butter, softened**
3/4 **cup sugar**
3/4 **cup packed brown sugar**
  2 **eggs**
  1 **teaspoon vanilla extract**
2-1/4 **cups all-purpose flour**
  1 **teaspoon baking soda**
  1 **teaspoon salt**
  4 **cups (24 ounces) semisweet chocolate chips, *divided***
1/4 **cup flaked coconut**

For the frosting, in a large saucepan, combine the egg, evaporated milk, sugar and butter. Cook and stir over medium-low heat for 10-12 minutes or until slightly thickened and mixture reaches 160°. Stir in the coconut and pecans. Set aside.

For the cookie dough, in a large bowl, cream butter and sugars until light and fluffy. Add eggs, one at a time, beating well after each addition. Beat in vanilla. Combine the flour, baking soda and salt; gradually add shape, return to oven for 1 minute to soften. Repeat with remaining batter.

Just before serving, pipe or spoon filling into cookie shells. Dip end of cookie into strawberries and additional sugar. Refrigerate leftovers. **Yield:** about 2 dozen.

Chocolate Pecan Bars

(Pictured below)

PREP: 25 min. **BAKE:** 25 min. + cooling

The chewy, chocolaty bars are great for Thanksgiving or Christmas...and always a big hit with everyone. They're easy to prepare and make a big batch. We find them simply irresistible.
—Carole Fraser, North York, Ontario

> 2/3 cup butter, softened
> 1/3 cup sugar
> 2 cups all-purpose flour
> **FILLING:**
> 6 squares (1 ounce *each*) semisweet chocolate
> 1-1/4 cups light corn syrup
> 1-1/4 cups sugar
> 4 eggs, lightly beaten
> 1-1/4 teaspoons vanilla extract
> 2-1/4 cups chopped pecans
> **DRIZZLE:**
> 4 squares (1 ounce *each*) semisweet chocolate
> 1-1/4 teaspoons shortening

In a small bowl, cream butter and sugar until light and fluffy. Beat in flour. Press into a greased 15-in. x 10-in. x 1-in. baking pan. Bake at 350° for 12-15 minutes or until golden brown.

Meanwhile, for the filling, in a large saucepan, melt chocolate with corn syrup over low heat; stir until smooth. Remove from the heat. Stir in the sugar, eggs and vanilla. Add pecans.

Spread evenly over hot crust. Bake for 25-30 minutes or until firm around the edges. Cool on a wire rack. Melt chocolate and shortening; stir until smooth. Drizzle over bars. **Yield:** 4 dozen.

Berry-Cream Cookie Snaps

(Pictured above and on page 123)

PREP: 40 min. + chilling **BAKE:** 30 min. + cooling

My mom and I created this recipe by combining two others. These cute cookies are crispy on the outside and light and fluffy inside. You could also bake the cookies flat and serve the filling as a cookie dip if you like. *—Crystal Briddick, Colfax, Illinois*

> 4 ounces cream cheese, softened
> 1/4 cup sugar
> 2 tablespoons seedless strawberry jam
> 1/4 cup heavy whipping cream, whipped
> 1 to 3 drops red food coloring, optional
> **BATTER:**
> 1/2 cup sugar
> 1/3 cup all-purpose flour
> 2 egg whites
> 1/4 teaspoon vanilla extract
> 1/8 teaspoon salt
> 1/4 cup butter, melted and cooled
> 1/2 cup chopped fresh strawberries
> Additional sugar

Combine the cream cheese, sugar and jam until blended. Fold in the whipped cream and food coloring if desired. Chill.

For the batter, whisk together the sugar, flour, egg whites, vanilla and salt until smooth. Whisk in butter until blended. Line baking sheets with parchment paper. Preparing four cookies at a time, drop batter by 1-1/2 teaspoonfuls 4 in. apart onto prepared pan. Bake at 400° for 5-8 minutes or until edges are lightly browned.

Immediately remove one cookie at a time from parchment and form into a tube around a greased clean round wooden clothespin. Press lightly to seal; hold until set, about 20 seconds. Remove cookie from clothespin; place on waxed paper to cool. Continue with remaining cookies. If cookies become too cool to

Festive Holiday Bites

Grand Prize Winner

Cookie Dough Truffles

(Pictured above)

PREP: 1 hour + chilling

The flavorful filling at the center of these yummy candies tastes like genuine chocolate chip cookie dough...without the worry of uncooked eggs. That's what makes them so appealing. Plus, they're easy to make.
 —*Lanita Dedon, Slaughter, Louisiana*

- **1/2 cup butter, softened**
- **3/4 cup packed brown sugar**
- **1 teaspoon vanilla extract**
- **2 cups all-purpose flour**
- **1 can (14 ounces) sweetened condensed milk**
- **1/2 cup miniature semisweet chocolate chips**
- **1/2 cup chopped walnuts**
- **1-1/2 pounds semisweet candy coating, chopped**

In a large bowl, cream the butter and brown sugar until light and fluffy. Beat in vanilla. Gradually add flour, alternately with milk, beating well after each addition. Stir in the chocolate chips and walnuts. Shape into 1-in. balls; place on waxed paper-lined baking sheets. Loosely cover and refrigerate for 1-2 hours or until firm.

In a microwave-safe bowl, melt candy coating; stir until smooth. Dip balls in coating, allowing excess to drip off; place on waxed paper-lined baking sheets. Refrigerate until firm, about 15 minutes. If desired, melt remaining candy coating again and drizzle over candies. Store in the refrigerator. **Yield:** 5-1/2 dozen.

Butterscotch Eggnog Stars

(Pictured at right)

PREP: 25 min. + chilling
BAKE: 10 min.

These yellow star–shaped cookies with a "stained–glass" center are almost too pretty to eat! The icing isn't mandatory, but does add a special touch.
 —*Cheryl Hemmer, Swansea, Illinois*

- **2/3 cup butter, softened**
- **1 cup sugar**
- **1/4 cup eggnog**
- **1 egg**
- **2 cups all-purpose flour**
- **3/4 teaspoon baking powder**
- **1/4 teaspoon salt**
- **1/4 teaspoon ground nutmeg**
- **1/2 cup crushed hard butterscotch candies**
- **OPTIONAL ICING:**
- **1-1/2 cups confectioners' sugar**
- **1/4 teaspoon rum extract**
- **2 to 3 tablespoons eggnog**
- **Yellow colored sugar, optional**

In a large bowl, cream butter and sugar until light and fluffy. Beat in eggnog and egg. Combine the flour, baking powder, salt and nutmeg; gradually add to creamed mixture and mix well. Divide dough in half.

On a lightly floured surface, roll out one piece of dough at a time to 1/4-in. thickness. Cut with a floured 3-1/2-in. star cutter. Cut out centers with a 1-1/2-in. star cutter. Line baking sheets with foil; grease foil.

Place large star cutouts on prepared baking sheets. Sprinkle 1 teaspoon candy in center of each. Repeat with remaining dough; reroll small cutouts if desired. Bake at 375° for 6-8 minutes or until edges are golden. Cool on baking sheets for 5 minutes. Carefully slide foil and cookies from baking sheets onto wire racks to cool.

For icing, beat confectioners' sugar, rum extract and enough eggnog to achieve drizzling consistency. Drizzle over cooled cookies. Sprinkle with colored sugar if desired. Let stand until hardened. **Yield:** about 3 dozen.

Editor's Note: This recipe was tested with commercially prepared eggnog.

Elegant Dipped Cherries

(Pictured above and on page 122)

PREP: 1-1/4 hours + freezing

Here's a sure way to impress holiday guests. These sweet maraschino cherries are wrapped in chocolate, then dipped in melted vanilla chips. A chocolate drizzle dresses them up for serving on a festive plate of sweets.
—Sedora Brown, Waynesboro, Virginia

- 1 jar (10 ounces) maraschino cherries with stems, well drained
- 3 tablespoons butter, melted
- 2 tablespoons light corn syrup
- 1 square (1 ounce) unsweetened chocolate
- 2 teaspoons half-and-half cream
- 2 cups confectioners' sugar
- 1 cup vanilla *or* white chips
- 2-1/2 teaspoons shortening, *divided*
- 1/2 cup semisweet chocolate chips

Pat cherries dry with paper towels and set aside. In a large bowl, combine the butter, corn syrup, unsweetened chocolate and cream. Stir in the confectioners' sugar.

Knead until smooth. Roll into 18 balls; flatten each into a 2-in. circle. Wrap each circle around a cherry and lightly roll in hands. Place cherries, stem side up, in a shallow paper-lined container. Cover and freeze for at least 2 hours.

The day before serving, remove the cherries from freezer. In a microwave-safe bowl, melt vanilla chips and 1-1/2 teaspoons shortening; stir until smooth.

Holding onto the stem, dip each cherry into vanilla mixture; set on waxed paper to set. Melt chocolate chips and remaining shortening; stir until smooth. Drizzle over the candies. Refrigerate until firm. Store candies in an airtight container.
Yield: 1-1/2 dozen.

Pinwheels and Checkerboards

(Pictured below right)

PREP: 30 min. + chilling
BAKE: 10 min.

My mom used to make these cookies every Christmas, and I still love them. They are so colorful...and you can get two kinds of cookies from one dough!
—Jill Heatwole, Pittsville, Maryland

- 1-1/4 cups butter, softened
- 1 cup packed brown sugar
- 1/2 cup sugar
- 2 eggs
- 1/4 teaspoon vanilla extract
- 4 cups all-purpose flour
- 1 teaspoon baking powder
- 1 teaspoon salt
- 1/4 teaspoon baking soda
- Red and green gel food coloring
- 1 square (1 ounce) unsweetened chocolate, melted and cooled

In a large bowl, cream butter and sugars. Beat in eggs and vanilla. Combine flour, baking powder, salt and baking soda; gradually add to creamed mixture. Divide dough into fourths. Tint one portion red and one portion green. Stir chocolate into another portion. Wrap chocolate and plain portions in plastic wrap; chill for 1 hour or until easy to handle.

For pinwheel cookies, divide red and green portions in half. Roll out each portion between waxed paper into a 9-in. x 6-in. rectangle. Refrigerate for 30 minutes. Remove waxed paper. Place one green rectangle over a red rectangle. Roll up tightly jelly-roll style, starting with a long side; wrap in plastic wrap. Repeat. Chill for 2 hours or until firm.

For checkerboard cookies, divide plain and chocolate portions in half. Roll out each portion between waxed paper into a 6-in. x 4-in. rectangle. Cut each rectangle lengthwise into eight 1/2-in. strips. Stack the strips in groups of four, alternating plain and chocolate strips and forming eight separate stacks. Form a four-stack block by alternating chocolate-topped and plain-topped stacks. Repeat. Press together gently. Wrap in plastic. Chill for at least 2 hours.

Unwrap and cut pinwheel and checkerboard dough into 1/4-in. slices. Place 1 in. apart on ungreased baking sheets. Bake at 375° for 9-11 minutes or until set. Remove to wire racks to cool. **Yield:** 6 dozen pinwheel and 4 dozen checkerboard cookies.

Coffee and Cream Brownies

(Pictured above)

PREP: 25 min. **BAKE:** 25 min. + cooling

A friend gave me the recipe for these rich cake-like brownies. Topped with a creamy coffee-enhanced filling and a chocolate glaze, I like to garnish each square with a coffee bean.
—Michelle Tiemstra, Lacombe, Alberta

- 1/2 cup butter, cubed
- 3 squares (1 ounce *each*) unsweetened chocolate, chopped
- 2 eggs
- 1 cup sugar
- 1 teaspoon vanilla extract
- 2/3 cup all-purpose flour
- 1/4 teaspoon baking soda
FILLING:
- 1 tablespoon heavy whipping cream
- 1 teaspoon instant coffee granules
- 2 tablespoons butter, softened
- 1 cup confectioners' sugar
GLAZE:
- 1 cup (6 ounces) semisweet chocolate chips
- 1/3 cup heavy whipping cream

In a saucepan over low heat, melt butter and chocolate; cool slightly. In a small bowl, beat eggs, sugar and vanilla; stir in the chocolate mixture. Combine flour and baking soda; add to the chocolate mixture. Spread into a greased 8-in. square baking pan. Bake at 350° for 25-30 minutes or until a toothpick inserted near the center comes out clean (do not overbake). Cool on a wire rack.

For the filling, combine cream and coffee granules in a small bowl; stir until coffee is dissolved. In a small bowl, beat butter and confectioners' sugar. Add coffee mixture; beat until creamy. Spread over brownies.

For the glaze, in a small saucepan, combine chips and cream. Cook and stir over low heat until chocolate is melted and mixture is thickened. Cool slightly. Carefully spread over filling. Let stand for 30 minutes or until glaze is set. Cut into squares. Store in the refrigerator. **Yield:** 16 servings.

Slice and Bake Lemon Gems

(Pictured below)

PREP: 25 min. + chilling **BAKE:** 10 min./batch + cooling

Rolled in colorful sprinkles, these melt-in-your-mouth cookies are pretty enough for a party. I make a lot of them for holiday cookie trays.   —Delores Edgecomb, Atlanta, New York

- 3/4 cup butter, softened
- 1/2 cup confectioners' sugar
- 1 tablespoon grated lemon peel
- 1 cup all-purpose flour
- 1/2 cup cornstarch
- 1/4 cup colored nonpareils
LEMON ICING:
- 1 cup confectioners' sugar
- 2 tablespoons lemon juice
- 1/2 teaspoon grated lemon peel

In a small bowl, cream the butter and confectioners' sugar until light and fluffy. Beat in the lemon peel. Combine the flour and cornstarch; gradually add to creamed mixture and mix well. Cover and refrigerate for 1 hour or until easy to handle.

Shape into a 1-3/4-in.-diameter roll; roll in the nonpareils. Wrap in plastic wrap. Refrigerate for 2-3 hours or until firm.

Unwrap and cut into 1/4-in. slices. Place 1 in. apart on ungreased baking sheets. Bake at 375° for 9-11 minutes or until set and edges are lightly browned. Cool for 1 minute before removing to wire racks to cool completely.

In a small bowl, combine icing ingredients. Spread over cookies. **Yield:** 28 cookies.

Glazed Peanut Butter Bars

(Pictured below and on page 122)

PREP: 15 min. **BAKE:** 20 min. + cooling

Memories of lunchtime at school and my aunt Shelly's kitchen come to mind when I bite into these sweet, chewy bars. My husband is the biggest fan of these peanut butter and chocolate treats. —Janis Luedtke, Thornton, Colorado

   3/4 **cup butter, softened**
   3/4 **cup creamy peanut butter**
   3/4 **cup sugar**
   3/4 **cup packed brown sugar**
    2 **teaspoons water**
    2 **eggs**
1-1/2 **teaspoons vanilla extract**
1-1/2 **cups all-purpose flour**
1-1/2 **cups quick-cooking oats**
   3/4 **teaspoon baking soda**
   1/2 **teaspoon salt**
GLAZE:
1-1/4 **cups milk chocolate chips**
   1/2 **cup butterscotch chips**
   1/2 **cup creamy peanut butter**

In a large bowl, cream the butter, peanut butter, sugars and water. Beat in eggs and vanilla. Combine the flour, oats, baking soda and salt; gradually add to creamed mixture.

Spread into a greased 15-in. x 10-in. x 1-in. baking pan. Bake at 325° for 18-22 minutes or until lightly browned.

For glaze, in a microwave-safe bowl, melt both kinds of chips with peanut butter; pour over warm bars and spread evenly. Cool completely on a wire rack before cutting. **Yield:** 4 dozen.

Almond Sugar Cookies

(Pictured above)

PREP/TOTAL TIME: 30 min.

It's a tradition in our house to start baking Christmas cookies early in the season. This nutty, glazed melt–in–your–mouth cookie is one of my favorites.
—Lisa Hummell, Phillipsburg, New Jersey

    1 **cup butter, softened**
   3/4 **cup sugar**
    1 **teaspoon almond extract**
    2 **cups all-purpose flour**
   1/2 **teaspoon baking powder**
   1/4 **teaspoon salt**
Additional sugar
GLAZE:
    1 **cup confectioners' sugar**
1-1/2 **teaspoons almond extract**
   2 to 3 **teaspoons water**
Green food coloring, optional
Sliced almonds, toasted

In a large bowl, cream butter and sugar until light and fluffy. Beat in almond extract. Combine the flour, baking powder and salt; gradually add to creamed mixture. Roll into 1-in. balls.

Place 2 in. apart on ungreased baking sheets. Coat bottom of a glass with cooking spray; dip in sugar. Flatten cookies with prepared glass, dipping glass in sugar again as needed.

Bake at 400° for 7-9 minutes or until the edges are lightly browned. Cool for 1 minute before removing to wire racks.

For the glaze, whisk together the confectioners' sugar, almond extract and enough water to achieve glaze consistency. Tint with food coloring if desired; drizzle over cookies. Sprinkle with almonds. **Yield:** about 4-1/2 dozen.

Nice and Soft Sugar Cookies

(Pictured below)

PREP: 1-1/2 hours + chilling
BAKE: 5 min./batch + cooling

The holidays just wouldn't be the same without cutout cookies. This easy recipe yields cookies so soft, they'll melt in your mouth. Have fun baking them in your favorite holiday shapes.
—*Cathy Hall, Phoenix, Arizona*

    1 cup butter, softened
1-1/2 cups confectioners' sugar
    1 egg
1-1/2 teaspoons vanilla extract
2-1/2 cups self-rising flour
FROSTING:
2-1/2 cups confectioners' sugar
    1/4 cup water
    4 teaspoons meringue powder
    1/4 cup light corn syrup
Green, red and yellow food coloring

In a large bowl, cream butter and confectioners' sugar until light and fluffy. Beat in egg and vanilla. Gradually add flour. Divide dough in half. Cover and refrigerate for 2 hours or until easy to handle.

On a lightly floured surface, roll out one portion of dough to 3/16-in. thickness. Cut with floured cookie cutters. Place 2 in. apart on ungreased baking sheets.

Bake at 375° for 5-7 minutes or until set. Cool for 2 minutes before removing from pans to wire racks to cool completely. Repeat with remaining dough.

For frosting, in a small bowl, beat the confectioners' sugar, water and meringue powder on low speed just until combined. Beat on high for 4 minutes or until soft peaks form. Add corn syrup; beat 1 minute longer.

Tint with food coloring of your choice. Cover frosting with damp paper towels or plastic wrap between uses. Spread and/or pipe frosting on cookies. Let stand until set. **Yield:** 3-1/2 dozen.

Irish Mint Brownies

(Pictured above)

PREP: 45 min. **BAKE:** 30 min. + chilling

I wanted something special to take to a church potluck, so I invented these layered, chocolate–mint treats. They are great for St. Patrick's Day. —*Lori Risdal, Sioux City, Iowa*

    1 cup butter, cubed
    4 squares (1 ounce *each*) bittersweet chocolate, chopped
    4 eggs
    2 cups sugar
    2 teaspoons vanilla extract
1-1/2 cups all-purpose flour
    1 cup (6 ounces) double dark chocolate chips *or* semisweet chocolate chips
    1/2 cup chopped walnuts
FILLING:
    4 squares (1 ounce *each*) white baking chocolate, chopped
    1/4 cup refrigerated Irish cream-flavored nondairy creamer
    1 cup heavy whipping cream
    15 Andes Crème de Menthe candies, chopped
ICING:
    12 squares (1 ounce *each*) bittersweet chocolate, chopped
    1 cup heavy whipping cream
    2 tablespoons butter
Andes Crème de Menthe candies, halved, optional

In a saucepan over low heat, melt butter and bittersweet chocolate; cool slightly. In a large bowl, beat eggs, sugar and vanilla. Stir in chocolate mixture. Gradually add flour until blended. Stir in chips and walnuts. Spread into a greased 13-in. x 9-in. x 2-in. baking pan. Bake at 350° for 30-35 minutes or until a toothpick inserted near the center comes out clean (do not overbake). Cool on a wire rack.

For the filling, in a small saucepan, combine the white chocolate and creamer. Cook and stir over low heat until smooth; remove from the heat. Refrigerate for 30-40 minutes or until chilled. Beat heavy cream until soft peaks form; fold into white chocolate mixture. Beat on medium speed until stiff peaks form, about 4 minutes. Fold in chopped candies. Spread over brownies. Cover and refrigerate.

For the icing, in a small saucepan, combine bittersweet chocolate and cream. Cook and stir over low heat until chocolate is melted and smooth; remove from the heat. Stir in butter until melted. Cool to room temperature. Carefully spread over filling. Cover and refrigerate for 1 hour or until icing is set. Cut into bars. Garnish with additional candy halves if desired. Store in the refrigerator. **Yield:** 2-1/2 dozen.

Meringue Fudge Drops

PREP: 30 min. **BAKE:** 30 min. + cooling

An almond-flavored meringue, fudgy filling and a sprinkling of pistachio nuts make these bite-size morsels a special addition to holiday dessert trays. —Charlotte Elliott, Neenah, Wisconsin

- 2 **egg whites**
- 1/4 **teaspoon almond extract**
- 1/8 **teaspoon cream of tartar**
- 1/8 **teaspoon salt**
- 1/2 **cup sugar**

TOPPING:
- 1/2 **cup semisweet chocolate chips**
- 3 **tablespoons butter**
- 2 **egg yolks, lightly beaten**
- 2 **tablespoons confectioners' sugar**
- 2 **tablespoons chopped pistachio nuts**

Place egg whites in a small bowl and let stand at room temperature for 30 minutes. Line baking sheets with parchment paper; set aside. Beat egg whites with almond extract, cream of tartar and salt on medium speed until soft peaks form. Add sugar, 1 tablespoon at a time, beating on high until stiff peaks form and sugar is dissolved.

Drop the meringue mixture by teaspoonfuls onto prepared sheets. With a small spoon, make a small indentation in the center of each. Bake at 250° for 30-35 minutes or until dry to the touch.

For topping, combine chocolate chips and butter in a small saucepan. Cook and stir over medium-low heat until chips are melted and mixture is smooth. Combine egg yolks and confectioners' sugar. Reduce heat to low. Gradually whisk into chocolate mixture. Cook and stir for 1 minute longer or until mixture reaches 160°. Cool to room temperature, whisking several times. Spoon into center of meringue. Sprinkle with chopped pistachio nuts. **Yield:** 4-1/2 dozen.

Frosted Rhubarb Cookies

(Pictured below)

PREP: 30 min. **BAKE:** 10 min./batch + cooling

We have two prolific rhubarb plants, so I'm always looking for new ways to use the harvest. The recipe for these soft, delicious cookies, flavored with coconut, was given to me by a friend.
—Shauna Schneyder, Idaho Falls, Idaho

- 1 **cup shortening**
- 1-1/2 **cups packed brown sugar**
- 2 **eggs**
- 3 **cups all-purpose flour**
- 1 **teaspoon baking soda**
- 1/2 **teaspoon salt**
- 1-1/2 **cups diced fresh *or* frozen rhubarb**
- 3/4 **cup flaked coconut**

FROSTING:
- 1 **package (3 ounces) cream cheese, softened**
- 1 **tablespoon butter, softened**
- 1-1/2 **cups confectioners' sugar**
- 3 **teaspoons vanilla extract**

In a large bowl, cream shortening and brown sugar. Beat in eggs. Combine the flour, baking soda and salt; gradually add to creamed mixture and mix well. Fold in the rhubarb and coconut.

Drop by rounded tablespoonfuls 2 in. apart onto greased baking sheets. Bake at 350° for 10-14 minutes or until golden brown. Cool for 1 minute before removing to wire racks to cool completely.

For frosting, in a small bowl, beat cream cheese and butter until fluffy. Beat in confectioners' sugar and vanilla. Spread over cookies. **Yield:** 4 dozen.

Editor's Note: If using frozen rhubarb, measure rhubarb while still frozen, then thaw completely. Drain in a colander, but do not press liquid out.

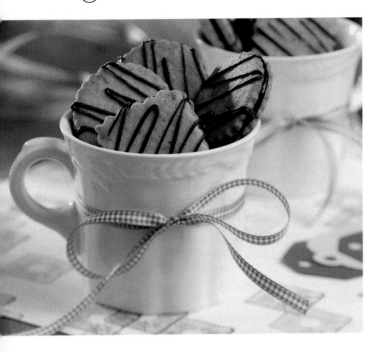

Hazelnut-Espresso Sandwich Cookies

(Pictured above and on page 122)

PREP: 45 min. + chilling **BAKE:** 10 min./batch + cooling

The inspiration for this cute cookie came from my sister's description of a hazelnut cookie she tried in Italy. She declared my version to be a wonderful approximation. My family likes to help fill them. —Cindy Beberman, Orland Park, Illinois

- 1 cup butter, softened
- 1-1/4 cups sugar
- 1 egg
- 1 egg yolk
- 4 teaspoons instant espresso granules
- 2 teaspoons vanilla extract
- 2-1/2 cups all-purpose flour
- 1/2 teaspoon salt
- 1/2 teaspoon baking powder
- 1 cup finely ground hazelnuts

FILLING:
- 1 cup heavy whipping cream
- 1-1/4 cups milk chocolate chips
- 1-3/4 cups semisweet chocolate chips, *divided*

In a large bowl, cream the butter and sugar until light and fluffy. Beat in the egg, yolk, espresso granules and vanilla. Combine the flour, salt and baking powder; gradually add to the creamed mixture and mix well. Stir in the hazelnuts.

Divide dough into thirds; flatten each portion into a circle. Wrap each in plastic wrap; refrigerate for 1 hour or until easy to handle.

On a lightly floured surface, roll out one portion of the dough to 1/8-in. thickness. Cut with a floured 1-1/2-in. cookie cutter; place 1/2 in. apart on ungreased baking sheets. Repeat with the remaining dough; chill and reroll scraps.

Bake at 375° for 6-8 minutes or until edges begin to brown. Remove to wire racks to cool.

For filling, in a small saucepan, bring cream to a boil. Remove from the heat; stir in milk chocolate chips and 3/4 cup semisweet chocolate chips until melted. Transfer to a bowl; refrigerate for 1-1/2 hours or until filling reaches spreading consistency, stirring occasionally.

Spread filling over the bottom of half of the cookies; top with remaining cookies. Melt remaining semisweet chips; drizzle over cookies. Let stand until set. Store in an airtight container in the refrigerator. **Yield:** 3 dozen.

Frosted Cookie Brownies

PREP: 30 min. **BAKE:** 40 min. + cooling

Years ago, my children and I came up with these bars by combining two of their favorite brownie recipes. With a crisp cookie crust and a fluffy frosting, these brownies are the most requested treats at our house.

—Alicia French, Crestline, California

- 1 tube (18 ounces) refrigerated chocolate chip cookie dough
- 3 cups miniature marshmallows
- 2 cups (12 ounces) semisweet chocolate chips
- 1 cup butter, cubed
- 4 eggs
- 2 teaspoons vanilla extract
- 1 cup all-purpose flour
- 1/2 teaspoon baking powder
- 1/4 teaspoon salt
- 1 cup chopped walnuts

FROSTING:
- 2 cups miniature marshmallows
- 6 tablespoons milk
- 1/4 cup butter, softened
- 2 squares (1 ounce *each*) unsweetened chocolate
- 3 cups confectioners' sugar

Press cookie dough into a greased 13-in. x 9-in. x 2-in. baking pan. Bake at 350° for 10 minutes.

Meanwhile, in a large saucepan, combine marshmallows, chips and butter; cook and stir over low heat until melted and smooth. Transfer to a large bowl; cool. Beat in eggs and vanilla. Combine the flour, baking powder and salt; stir into marshmallow mixture. Stir in nuts.

Spread over cookie crust. Bake for 30-35 minutes or until a toothpick inserted near the center comes out clean. Cool on a wire rack.

For frosting, in a small saucepan, combine the marshmallows, milk, butter and chocolate. Cook and stir over low heat until smooth. Remove from the heat; beat in confectioners' sugar until smooth. Frost brownies. Cut into bars. **Yield:** 15 servings.

Chocolate Pretzels

(Pictured above)

PREP: 30 min. **BAKE:** 10 min./batch + cooling

A rich chocolate coating accented with crushed peppermint makes these pretzels hard to resist. My grandkids and I love making them together! —Karen Nemeth, Calgary, Alberta

- 1/2 **cup butter, softened**
- 1/2 **cup shortening**
- 1 **cup confectioners' sugar**
- 1 **egg**
- 1-1/2 **teaspoons vanilla extract**
- 2-1/4 **cups all-purpose flour**
- 1/2 **cup baking cocoa**
- 1 **teaspoon salt**

GLAZE:
- 3 **squares (1 ounce *each*) semisweet chocolate**
- 3 **tablespoons butter**
- 3 **cups confectioners' sugar**
- 5 **tablespoons water**
- 1/2 **cup vanilla *or* white chips**

In a large bowl, cream the butter, shortening and confectioners' sugar until light and fluffy. Beat in egg and vanilla. Combine the flour, cocoa and salt; gradually add to creamed mixture.

Shape into 1-in. balls. Roll each into a 7-in. rope. On greased baking sheets, form each rope into a pretzel shape, placing 2 in. apart. Bake at 375° for 8-9 minutes or until firm. Cool for 1 minute before removing to wire racks to cool completely.

For the glaze, in a microwave-safe bowl, melt the chocolate and butter; stir until smooth. Stir in the confectioners' sugar and water until smooth. Dip the pretzels in glaze; place on waxed paper. Melt the vanilla chips; drizzle over half of the pretzels. Let stand until completely set. Store in an airtight container. **Yield:** 4 dozen.

Dipped Pecan Spritz

(Pictured below)

PREP: 25 min. **BAKE:** 5 min. + cooling

This is my husband's favorite Christmas cookie. They look lovely at the center of festive holiday cookie plates...and they are always the first to disappear.
—Sylvia Neudorf, Abbotsford, British Columbia

- 1-1/2 **cups butter, softened**
- 1 **cup sugar**
- 1 **egg**
- 1 **teaspoon vanilla extract**
- 1/2 **teaspoon almond extract**
- 3 **cups all-purpose flour**
- 1 **cup finely ground pecans**
- 1 **teaspoon baking powder**
- 3/4 **cup semisweet chocolate chips**
- 1-1/2 **teaspoons shortening, *divided***
- 3/4 **cup vanilla *or* white chips**

Colored sprinkles

In a large bowl, cream the butter and sugar until light and fluffy; beat in egg and extracts. Combine the flour, pecans and baking powder; gradually add to the creamed mixture.

Using a cookie press fitted with disk of your choice, press dough 2 in. apart onto ungreased baking sheets. Bake at 375° for 5-7 minutes or until set (do not brown). Remove to wire racks to cool.

In a microwave, melt the chocolate chips and 3/4 teaspoon shortening; stir until smooth. Melt the vanilla chips and remaining shortening at 70% power; stir until smooth.

Dip half the amount of cookies halfway in semisweet chocolate mixture; allow excess to drip off. Place on waxed paper to harden. Dip remaining cookies halfway in vanilla mixture; allow excess to drip off. Place on waxed paper and sprinkle coated area with colored sprinkles. Let harden. **Yield:** 12-1/2 dozen.

each rectangle diagonally into 18 slices. Place cut side down on greased baking sheets. Bake for 20-25 minutes or until firm and crisp, turning once. Remove to wire racks to cool.

In a microwave-safe bowl, melt chocolate chips and 1 tablespoon shortening; stir until smooth. Drizzle over both sides of cookies. Place on waxed paper; let stand until set.

Melt white chocolate and remaining shortening; stir until smooth. Drizzle over both sides of cookies. Place on waxed paper; let stand until set. Store in an airtight container. **Yield:** 3 dozen.

Peanut Butter Blondies

(Pictured below)

PREP: 30 min. **BAKE:** 35 min. + cooling

The kids I babysit for just love these moist chewy bars. There's plenty of peanut butter flavor and a yummy chocolate frosting.
—Karla Johnson, Tyler, Minnesota

- 3/4 cup creamy peanut butter
- 2/3 cup butter, softened
- 1 cup packed brown sugar
- 1/2 cup sugar
- 2 eggs
- 1 teaspoon vanilla extract
- 1-3/4 cups all-purpose flour
- 1 teaspoon baking powder
- 1/3 cup milk
- 1 cup peanut butter chips
FROSTING:
- 1/4 cup butter, softened
- 1/4 cup baking cocoa

Door County Cherry Biscotti

(Pictured above)

PREP: 40 min. **BAKE:** 50 min. + cooling

With a subtle flavor, these biscotti are just sweet enough, with a hint of almond and good level of cinnamon. Roger, my husband, especially likes to eat them with ice cream.
—Joanne Surfus, Sturgeon Bay, Wisconsin

- 3 eggs
- 1/2 cup butter, softened
- 1 cup plus 3 tablespoons sugar, *divided*
- 1 teaspoon almond extract
- 3-2/3 cups all-purpose flour
- 1/2 teaspoon baking powder
- 1/4 teaspoon baking soda
- 1 cup dried cherries
- 1 cup slivered almonds, toasted
- 1 cup (6 ounces) semisweet chocolate chips
- 1 tablespoon plus 2 teaspoons shortening, *divided*
- 4 squares (1 ounce *each*) white baking chocolate

Separate one egg; set aside. In a large bowl, cream butter and 1 cup plus 2 tablespoons sugar until light and fluffy. Beat in 2 eggs and reserved egg yolk. Beat in extract. Combine the flour, baking powder and baking soda; gradually add to creamed mixture.

Turn onto a floured surface. Knead in cherries and almonds. Divide dough in half; shape each portion into a 12-in. x 3-in. rectangle. Transfer to a greased baking sheet. Beat reserved egg white; brush over dough. Sprinkle with remaining sugar. Bake at 350° for 28-30 minutes or until lightly browned. Cool for 10 minutes.

Transfer to a cutting board; with a serrated knife, cut

2 tablespoons milk
1 tablespoon light corn syrup
1 teaspoon vanilla extract
1-1/2 cups confectioners' sugar
1/3 cup peanut butter chips

In a large bowl, cream the peanut butter, butter and sugars. Beat in eggs and vanilla. Combine the flour and baking powder; add to creamed mixture alternately with milk. Stir in chips.

Spread into a greased 13-in. x 9-in. x 2-in. baking pan. Bake at 325° for 35-40 minutes or until a toothpick inserted near the center comes out clean (do not overbake). Cool on a wire rack.

For frosting, in a small bowl, combine the butter, cocoa, milk, corn syrup and vanilla. Gradually add confectioners' sugar; beat until smooth. Frost brownies. Sprinkle with chips. Cut into bars. **Yield:** 2 dozen.

Almond Truffle Brownies

PREP: 15 min. **BAKE:** 25 min. + chilling

This wonderful recipe is one my mom shared with me. These fudgy almond delights take several steps to make, but the extra effort is well worth it! —Lynn Snow, Taylors, South Carolina

1 package fudge brownie mix (13-inch x 9-inch pan size)
1/2 cup water
1/2 cup canola oil
1 egg
3/4 cup chopped almonds
1 teaspoon almond extract
FILLING:
1 cup (6 ounces) semisweet chocolate chips
1 package (8 ounces) cream cheese, softened
1/4 cup confectioners' sugar
2 tablespoons milk
1/2 teaspoon almond extract
TOPPING:
1/2 cup semisweet chocolate chips
1/4 cup heavy whipping cream
1/2 cup sliced almonds, toasted

In a large bowl, combine the first six ingredients. Pour into a greased 13-in. x 9-in. x 2-in. baking pan. Bake at 350° for 23-25 minutes or until a toothpick inserted near the center comes out clean (do not overbake). Cool on a wire rack.

For the filling, in a microwave, melt the chocolate chips; stir until smooth. In a large bowl, beat cream cheese and confectioners' sugar. Add milk, extract and melted chips; mix well. Spread over brownies. Refrigerate for 1 hour or until firm.

For topping, in a small saucepan, melt chips and cream over low heat, stirring occasionally. Spread over filling. Sprinkle with almonds. Refrigerate at least 1 hour longer before cutting. **Yield:** 1-1/2 dozen.

Chewy Apple Oatmeal Cookies

(Pictured above)

PREP: 20 min. **BAKE:** 10 min./batch

My family has always loved oatmeal raisin cookies, but I wanted to try a new twist on the classic recipe. We enjoy apples, so I thought the dried fruit would make a good addition.
—Jan Marshall, Fenton, Missouri

1 cup butter, softened
1 cup packed brown sugar
1/2 cup sugar
2 eggs
1 teaspoon vanilla extract
1-1/2 cups all-purpose flour
2 teaspoons ground cinnamon
1 teaspoon baking soda
1/4 teaspoon salt
3 cups old-fashioned oats
1/2 cup chopped dried apples

In a large bowl, cream butter and sugars until light and fluffy. Beat in eggs and vanilla. Combine the flour, cinnamon, baking soda and salt; gradually add to creamed mixture, beating well after each addition. Stir in oats and apples.

Drop by rounded tablespoonfuls 2 in. apart onto ungreased baking sheets. Bake at 350° for 10-12 minutes or until golden brown. Let stand for 1 minute before removing to wire racks. **Yield:** 4 dozen.

♪ About Baking Powder

Taste of Home recipes that call for baking powder use double-acting, which contains two types of acid that react differently. The first acid releases gases when mixed with liquid, and the second releases gases when exposed to heat. They work together to give plenty of lift to baked goods.

Cakes & Pies

Scrumptious cakes, palate-pleasing pies, cheesecakes and tasty cupcakes
make a fabulous finale for everyday suppers or special occasions.
Any way you slice it, these sweet treats won't disappoint.

TRIED-AND-TRUE TREATS. Clockwise from upper left: Lemonade Meringue Pie (p. 149), Elegant Chocolate Torte
(p. 146), Summer Celebration Ice Cream Cake (p. 153), Special Mocha Cupcakes (p. 156) and Peanut Butter Cup
Cheesecake (p. 162).

Carefully run a knife around edge of pan to loosen; remove sides of pan. Top with remaining pecan halves; drizzle with 2 tablespoons chocolate sauce. Serve with remaining sauce. **Yield:** 16-20 servings.

Editor's Note: This recipe was tested in a 1,100-watt microwave.

Layered Carrot Cake

PREP: 50 min. **BAKE:** 30 min. + cooling

I never liked carrot cake until I tried this one. The rich, moist cake with orange–flavored frosting is now a family tradition for special occasions. Sometimes I add cranberries with the raisins.
—Anna Morgan, Eatonville, Washington

- 1 package (18-1/4 ounces) yellow cake mix
- 1 package (3.4 ounces) instant vanilla pudding mix
- 2 teaspoons ground cinnamon
- 4 eggs
- 2/3 cup orange juice
- 1/2 cup canola oil
- 3 cups grated carrots
- 1/2 cup raisins
- 1/2 cup chopped walnuts
ORANGE CREAM CHEESE FROSTING:
- 1 package (8 ounces) cream cheese, softened
- 1/2 cup butter, softened
- 3 cups confectioners' sugar
- 1 to 2 tablespoons orange juice
- 1 tablespoon grated orange peel

In a large bowl, combine the cake mix, pudding mix and cinnamon. Whisk the eggs, orange juice and oil together; add to dry ingredients. Beat until well blended. Stir in the carrots, raisins and nuts (the batter will be thick).

Pour into two greased and floured 9-in. round baking pans. Bake at 350° for 30-35 minutes or until a toothpick inserted near the center comes out clean. Cool for 10 minutes before removing from pans to wire racks to cool completely.

For frosting, in a large bowl, beat cream cheese and butter until fluffy. Add the confectioners' sugar, orange juice and peel; beat until smooth. Spread frosting between layers and over top and sides of cake. Store in the refrigerator. **Yield:** 12-14 servings.

Chocolate Pecan Ice Cream Torte

(Pictured above)

PREP: 20 min. + freezing

This delectable dessert layers two of our favorite ice cream flavors, chocolate and butter pecan, on a shortbread crust, along with chocolate candy pieces, toasted pecans and caramel topping. It never fails to impress our guests.
—Kelly Arvay, Barberton, Ohio

- 1 jar (12-1/4 ounces) caramel ice cream topping
- 2 milk chocolate candy bars (1.55 ounces *each*), chopped
- 12 pecan shortbread cookies, crushed
- 3 tablespoons butter, melted
- 1 cup pecan halves, toasted, *divided*
- 1/2 gallon butter pecan ice cream, slightly softened
- 1/2 gallon chocolate ice cream, slightly softened

In a microwave-safe bowl, combine the caramel topping and candy bars. Microwave, uncovered, on high for 1-1/2 minutes or until candy bars are melted, stirring every 30 seconds. Cool.

Combine the cookie crumbs and butter. Press onto the bottom of a greased 10-in. springform pan. Chop 1/2 cup pecans; set aside. Spoon half of the butter pecan ice cream over crust. Drizzle with 2 tablespoons chocolate sauce; sprinkle with 1/4 cup chopped pecans.

Spread half of the chocolate ice cream over top. Drizzle with 2 tablespoons chocolate sauce; sprinkle with remaining chopped pecans.

Spoon remaining butter pecan ice cream around the edge of pan; spread remaining chocolate ice cream in center of pan. Cover and freeze overnight.

Zest for Life

Zest (called grated orange peel above) is the outer rind of citrus fruits. To make zest, use a knife to remove thin strips of the peel, being careful not to include the white membrane, and mince finely. Or rub the whole fruit over a hand grater.

Add remaining salt to egg whites; beat on medium speed until soft peaks form. Gradually beat in remaining sugar, about 2 tablespoons at a time, on high until stiff glossy peaks form and sugar is dissolved. Gradually fold into batter just until blended. Divide among prepared pans.

Bake at 375° for 20-25 minutes or until tops spring back when lightly touched. Invert pans; cool for 20 minutes. Remove from pans to wire racks; cool completely. Remove waxed paper.

For the filling, beat the cream until it begins to thicken. Add confectioners' sugar and vanilla; beat until stiff peaks form. Cover and refrigerate until assembling.

For the frosting, in a large saucepan, melt butter and chocolate over low heat. Remove from the heat. Stir in coffee, vanilla and enough confectioners' sugar to achieve frosting consistency. Spread filling between layers. Frost top and sides of cake. Garnish with pecans if desired. **Yield:** 12 servings.

Mocha Nut Torte

(Pictured above)

PREP: 40 min. + chilling **BAKE:** 20 min. + cooling

My husband doesn't like chocolate cake, but this spectacular three-layer torte is a favorite of his. I've been using this recipe for special occasions, such as birthdays, for many years.
—Megan Shepherdson, Winnipeg, Manitoba

- 7 **eggs,** *separated*
- 1 **cup sugar,** *divided*
- 1 **teaspoon vanilla extract**
- 1-1/4 **cups ground walnuts**
- 1-1/4 **cups ground pecans**
- 1/4 **cup dry bread crumbs**
- 1 **teaspoon baking powder**
- 3/4 **teaspoon salt,** *divided*

FILLING:
- 1 **cup heavy whipping cream**
- 1/2 **cup confectioners' sugar**
- 1 **teaspoon vanilla extract**

MOCHA FROSTING:
- 1/4 **cup butter, cubed**
- 4 **squares (1 ounce** *each***) unsweetened chocolate**
- 1/2 **cup brewed coffee**
- 2 **teaspoons vanilla extract**
- 3 to 3-1/4 **cups confectioners' sugar**

Pecan halves, optional

Line three 9-in. round baking pans with waxed paper; set aside. Place egg whites in a large bowl; let stand at room temperature for 30 minutes.

Meanwhile, in another bowl, beat egg yolks until slightly thickened. Gradually add 1/2 cup sugar, beating until thick and lemon-colored. Beat in vanilla. Combine nuts, crumbs, baking powder and 1/2 teaspoon salt; stir into yolk mixture until combined.

Strawberry Shortbread Pie

(Pictured below)

PREP: 15 min. + chilling

My husband enjoys this pie so much that I always make an extra one just for him! To save time, use a purchased shortbread crust.
—Sherry Maurer, Manheim, Pennsylvania

- 3/4 **cup sugar**
- 3 **tablespoons cornstarch**
- 1-1/2 **cups water**
- 1 **package (3 ounces) strawberry gelatin**
- 4 **cups sliced fresh strawberries**
- 1 **shortbread crust (9 inches)**

In a small saucepan, combine the sugar, cornstarch and water until smooth. Bring to a boil; cook and stir for 2 minutes or until thickened. Remove from the heat; stir in gelatin powder until dissolved. Transfer to a small bowl. Chill until partially set.

Place sliced strawberries in the crust; pour gelatin mixture over the berries. Cover and refrigerate until set. **Yield:** 6-8 servings.

Grand Prize Winner

Rhubarb Swirl Cheesecake

(Pictured below)

PREP: 40 min. **BAKE:** 1 hour + chilling

I love cheesecake and my husband loves white chocolate, so this is a special dessert for us. The rhubarb adds a tartness that complements the sweet flavors well.
—*Carol Witczak, Tinley Park, Illinois*

- 2-1/2 cups thinly sliced fresh *or* frozen rhubarb
- 1/3 cup plus 1/2 cup sugar, *divided*
- 2 tablespoons orange juice
- 1-1/4 cups graham cracker crumbs
- 1/4 cup butter, melted
- 3 packages (8 ounces *each*) cream cheese, softened
- 2 cups (16 ounces) sour cream
- 1 tablespoon cornstarch
- 2 teaspoons vanilla extract
- 1/2 teaspoon salt
- 3 eggs, lightly beaten
- 8 squares (1 ounce *each*) white baking chocolate, melted

In a large saucepan, bring rhubarb, 1/3 cup sugar and orange juice to a boil. Reduce heat; cook and stir until thickened and rhubarb is tender. Set aside.

Combine cracker crumbs and butter. Press onto the bottom of a greased 9-in. springform pan. Place on a baking sheet. Bake at 350° for 7-9 minutes or until lightly browned. Cool on a wire rack.

In a large bowl, beat cream cheese, sour cream, cornstarch, vanilla, salt and remaining sugar until smooth. Add eggs; beat just until combined. Fold in white chocolate. Pour half of the filling into crust. Top with half of the rhubarb sauce; cut through batter with a knife to gently swirl rhubarb. Layer with remaining filling and rhubarb sauce; cut through top layers with a knife to gently swirl rhubarb.

Place pan on a double thickness of heavy-duty foil (about 16 in. square). Securely wrap foil around pan. Place in a large baking pan; add 1 in. of hot water to larger pan. Bake at 350° for 60-70 minutes or until center is almost set.

Cool on a wire rack for 10 minutes. Carefully run a knife around edge of pan to loosen; cool 1 hour longer. Cover and chill overnight. Remove sides of pan. Refrigerate leftovers. **Yield:** 12-14 servings.

Editor's Note: If using frozen rhubarb, measure rhubarb while still frozen, then thaw completely. Drain in a colander, but do not press liquid out.

Butternut Squash Cake Roll

PREP: 15 min. **BAKE:** 15 min. + chilling

I love the flavor of winter squash, especially in sweet desserts. This pretty cake roll is perfect for an autumn special occasion.
—*Elizabeth Nelson, Manning, North Dakota*

- 3 eggs
- 1 cup sugar
- 2/3 cup mashed cooked butternut squash
- 3/4 cup all-purpose flour
- 1 teaspoon baking soda
- 1/2 teaspoon ground cinnamon
- 1 cup finely chopped walnuts, optional

Confectioners' sugar

FILLING:
- 1 package (8 ounces) cream cheese, softened
- 2 tablespoons butter, softened
- 1 cup confectioners' sugar
- 3/4 teaspoon vanilla extract

Additional confectioners' sugar, optional

In a large bowl, beat eggs; gradually beat in sugar. Add squash and mix well. Combine the flour, baking soda and cinnamon; add to squash mixture and mix well.

Line a 15-in. x 10-in. x 1-in. baking pan with waxed paper; grease and flour the paper. Spread batter evenly into pan. Sprinkle with walnuts if desired. Bake at 375° for 13-15 minutes or until a toothpick inserted near the center comes out clean. Cool on a wire rack for 10 minutes.

Turn cake onto a kitchen towel dusted with confectioners' sugar. Gently peel off waxed paper. Roll up cake in the towel, jelly-roll style, starting with a short side. Cool completely on a wire rack.

For the filling beat the cream cheese, butter, confectioners' sugar and vanilla until smooth. Unroll

9-in. pie plate. Transfer pastry to pie plate; trim even with edge of plate. Add filling. Roll out remaining pastry; make a lattice crust. Trim, seal and flute edges.

Bake at 425° for 10 minutes. Reduce heat to 375°; bake 45-50 minutes longer or until crust is golden brown. Cool on a wire rack. **Yield:** 8 servings.

Frosty Mocha Pie

(Pictured below)

PREP: 20 min. + freezing

This pie is so creamy and rich-tasting that no one would guess it's light. The added bonus is that you can make it a day or two ahead and keep it in the freezer until needed.
—Lisa Varner, Greenville, South Carolina

    4 ounces reduced-fat cream cheese
  1/4 cup sugar
  1/4 cup baking cocoa
    1 tablespoon instant coffee granules
  1/3 cup fat-free milk
    1 teaspoon vanilla extract
    1 carton (12 ounces) frozen reduced-fat
      whipped topping, thawed
    1 extra-servings-size graham cracker crust
      (9 inches)
Reduced-calorie chocolate syrup, optional

In a large bowl, beat the cream cheese, sugar and cocoa until smooth. Dissolve coffee granules in milk. Stir coffee mixture and vanilla into cream cheese mixture; fold in whipped topping.

Pour into crust. Cover and freeze for at least 4 hours. Remove from the freezer 10 minutes before serving. Drizzle with chocolate syrup if desired. **Yield:** 10 servings.

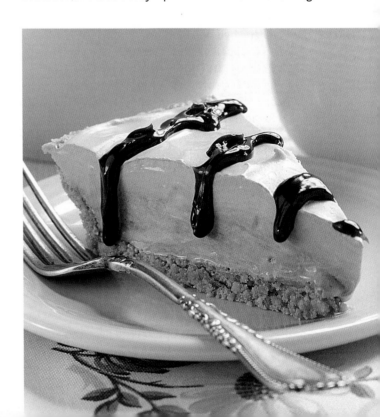

cake; spread filling evenly over cake to within 1 in. of edges. Roll up again. Cover and refrigerate for 1 hour. Just before serving, dust with confectioners' sugar if desired. **Yield:** 10 servings.

Fresh Cherry Pie

(Pictured above)

PREP: 25 min. **BAKE:** 55 min. + cooling

This ruby-red treat, with a hint of almond and a good level of cinnamon, has just the right amount of sweetness. The cherries peeking out of the lattice crust make it pretty, too.
—Josie Bochek, Sturgeon Bay, Wisconsin

  1-1/4 cups sugar
    1/3 cup cornstarch
      1 cup cherry juice
      4 cups fresh tart cherries, pitted *or* frozen pitted
        tart cherries, thawed
    1/2 teaspoon ground cinnamon
    1/4 teaspoon ground nutmeg
    1/4 teaspoon almond extract
PASTRY:
      2 cups all-purpose flour
    1/2 teaspoon salt
    2/3 cup shortening
      3 to 4 tablespoons cold water

In a large saucepan, combine sugar and cornstarch; gradually stir in cherry juice until smooth. Bring to a boil; cook and stir for 2 minutes or until thickened. Remove from the heat. Add the cherries, cinnamon, nutmeg and extract; set aside.

For the pastry, in a large bowl, combine flour and salt; cut in shortening until crumbly. Gradually add cold water, tossing with a fork until a ball forms. Divide pastry in half so that one ball is slightly larger than the other.

On a lightly floured surface, roll out larger ball to fit a

Banana Nut Cake

(Pictured above)

PREP: 20 min. **BAKE:** 30 min. + cooling

Sweet, buttery frosting and a sprinkling of chopped nuts top this yummy cake that's loaded with banana and pecan flavor. Serve it with a hot cup of coffee or a cold glass of milk.
—Marlene Saunders, Lincoln, Nebraska

- 1/2 **cup butter, softened**
- 1 **cup sugar**
- 2 **eggs**
- 1/2 **teaspoon vanilla extract**
- 1-1/4 **cups all-purpose flour**
- 3/4 **teaspoon baking soda**
- 1/2 **teaspoon salt**
- 3/4 **cup mashed ripe banana**
- 1/2 **cup chopped pecans, toasted**

BUTTER PECAN FROSTING:
- 1/2 **cup butter, softened**
- 1/4 **cup milk**
- 1 **teaspoon vanilla extract**

Dash salt
- 2 to 2-1/2 **cups confectioners' sugar**
- 1 **cup finely chopped pecans, toasted**

Additional chopped pecans, optional

In a large bowl, cream butter and sugar together. Add eggs, one at a time, beating well after each addition. Stir in vanilla. Combine the flour, baking soda and salt; add to creamed mixture, beating just until combined. Fold in banana and pecans.

Pour into a greased 8-in. square baking dish. Bake at 350° for 30-35 minutes or until a toothpick inserted near the center comes out clean. Cool on a wire rack.

For the frosting, beat the butter until light and fluffy. Beat in the milk, vanilla, salt and enough confectioners'

sugar to achieve spreading consistency. Stir in toasted pecans. Frost cake. Garnish with additional pecans if desired. **Yield:** 9 servings.

Grand Prize Winner

Elegant Chocolate Torte

(Pictured below and on page 140)

PREP: 50 min. **BAKE:** 30 min. + cooling

When I want to serve a really special dessert, I turn to this recipe time and again. The tender, four-layer chocolate cake has a yummy pudding-like filling.
—Lois Gallup Edwards, Woodland, California

- 1/3 **cup all-purpose flour**
- 3 **tablespoons sugar**
- 1 **teaspoon salt**
- 1-3/4 **cups milk**
- 1 **cup chocolate syrup**
- 1 **egg, lightly beaten**
- 1 **tablespoon butter**
- 1 **teaspoon vanilla extract**

BATTER:
- 1/2 **cup butter, softened**
- 1-1/4 **cups sugar**
- 4 **eggs**
- 1 **teaspoon vanilla extract**
- 1-1/4 **cups all-purpose flour**
- 1/3 **cup baking cocoa**
- 3/4 **teaspoon baking soda**
- 1/4 **teaspoon salt**
- 1-1/2 **cups chocolate syrup**

1/2 cup water
FROSTING:
    2 cups heavy whipping cream
  1/4 cup chocolate syrup
  1/4 teaspoon vanilla extract

In a small saucepan, combine flour, sugar and salt. Stir in milk and syrup until smooth. Bring to a boil over medium heat, stirring constantly; cook and stir for 1-2 minutes or until thickened.

Remove from heat. Stir a small amount of hot mixture into egg; return all to the pan, stirring constantly. Bring to a gentle boil; cook and stir for 2 minutes. Remove from heat; stir in butter and vanilla. Cool to room temperature, stirring often.

For the batter, in a large bowl, cream butter and sugar until light and fluffy. Add eggs, one at a time, beating well after each. Stir in vanilla. Combine dry ingredients; add to creamed mixture alternately with syrup and water. Beat just until combined.

Pour into two greased and floured 9-in. round baking pans. Bake at 350° for 30-35 minutes or until a toothpick comes out clean. Cool for 10 minutes; remove from pans to wire racks to cool.

Cut each cake in half horizontally. Place one bottom layer on a serving plate; spread with a third of the filling. Repeat layers twice. Top with remaining cake layer. Beat the frosting ingredients together until stiff peaks form; spread or pipe over top and sides of cake. **Yield:** 16 servings.

Raspberry Cherry Pie

PREP: 20 min. **BAKE:** 1 hour + cooling

No one can resist a slice (or two!) of this tart "cherry–berry" pie. Growing up, my sister and I requested this treat for our birthdays instead of cake. Now it's a favorite of my own family.
—Mari Anne Warren, Milton, Wisconsin

1-1/2 cups sugar
    3 tablespoons quick-cooking tapioca
    2 cups fresh *or* frozen unsweetened raspberries
    1 cup fresh, frozen *or* canned tart cherries
    1 teaspoon lemon juice
PASTRY:
    3 cups all-purpose flour
    2 teaspoons sugar
1-1/2 teaspoons salt
  1/2 teaspoon baking powder
    1 cup shortening
    1 egg
    5 to 6 tablespoons cold water
    1 teaspoon white vinegar
    1 tablespoon butter

In a bowl, combine sugar and tapioca. Add the raspberries, cherries and lemon juice; toss to coat. Let stand for 15 minutes. Meanwhile, for the pastry, in a large bowl, combine the flour, sugar, salt and baking powder; cut in shortening until crumbly. Combine the egg, water and vinegar. Gradually add to flour mixture, tossing with a fork until dough forms a ball.

Divide the dough in half. On a lightly floured surface, roll out one portion to fit a 9-in. pie plate. Place pastry in plate; trim even with edge.

Spoon filling into pastry. Dot with butter. Roll out remaining pastry to fit top of pie; make decorative cutouts with water; place on top of pie. Cover edges loosely with foil. Bake at 350° for 60-70 minutes or until golden brown. Cool on a wire rack. Store in the refrigerator. **Yield:** 8 servings.

Cream Cheese Blueberry Pie

(Pictured above)

PREP: 20 min. + cooling

Fresh blueberries and a rich cream cheese layer are combined in this fruity and refreshing pie.
—Lisieux Bauman, Cheektowaga, New York

    4 ounces cream cheese, softened
  1/2 cup confectioners' sugar
  1/2 cup heavy whipping cream, whipped
    1 pastry shell (9 inches), baked
  2/3 cup sugar
  1/4 cup cornstarch
  1/2 cup water
  1/4 cup lemon juice
    3 cups fresh *or* frozen blueberries

In a bowl, beat the cream cheese and confectioners' sugar until smooth. Fold in the whipped cream. Spread into pastry shell.

In a large saucepan, combine the sugar, cornstarch, water and lemon juice until smooth; stir in the blueberries. Bring to a boil over medium heat; cook and stir for 2 minutes or until thickened. Cool. Spread over the cream cheese layer. Refrigerate until serving. **Yield:** 6-8 servings.

Luscious Lemon Desserts

Lemon Chiffon Cake

(Pictured above)

PREP: 25 min.
BAKE: 50 min. + cooling

This moist, airy cake was my dad's favorite. My mom revamped the original recipe to include lemons. I'm not much of a baker, so I don't make it very often—but it's well worth the effort.
—*Trisha Kammers Clarkston, Washington*

- **7 eggs, *separated***
- **2 cups all-purpose flour**
- **1-1/2 cups sugar**
- **3 teaspoons baking powder**
- **1 teaspoon salt**
- **3/4 cup water**
- **1/2 cup canola oil**
- **4 teaspoons grated lemon peel**
- **2 teaspoons vanilla extract**
- **1/2 teaspoon cream of tartar**

LEMON FROSTING:
- **1/3 cup butter, softened**
- **3 cups confectioners' sugar**
- **4-1/2 teaspoons grated lemon peel**
- **Dash salt**
- **1/4 cup lemon juice**

Let eggs stand at room temperature for 30 minutes. In a large bowl, combine the flour, sugar, baking powder and salt. In another bowl, whisk the egg yolks, water, oil, lemon peel and vanilla; add to dry ingredients. Beat until well blended.

In another large bowl, beat egg whites and cream of tartar on medium speed until soft peaks form; fold into batter. Gently spoon into an ungreased 10-in. tube pan. Cut through batter with a knife to remove air pockets.

Bake on the lowest oven rack at 325° for 50-55 minutes or until top springs back when lightly touched. Immediately invert the pan; cool completely, about 1 hour.

Run a knife around the side and center tube of pan. Remove cake to a serving plate. Combine the frosting ingredients; beat until smooth. Spread over top of cake. **Yield:** 12-16 servings.

Lemonade Icebox Pie

(Pictured below)

PREP: 15 min. + chilling

This dessert comes to mind immediately when I put together my favorite summer meal. High and fluffy, it has a creamy, smooth consistency and a refreshing lemonade flavor.
—*Cheryl Maczko, Eglon, West Virginia*

- **1 package (8 ounces) cream cheese, softened**
- **1 can (14 ounces) sweetened condensed milk**
- **3/4 cup lemonade concentrate**
- **1 carton (8 ounces) frozen whipped topping, thawed**
- **Yellow food coloring, optional**
- **1 graham cracker crust (9 inches)**

In a large bowl, beat the cream cheese until smooth. Gradually beat in the milk until blended. Beat in the lemonade concentrate. Fold in the whipped topping and food coloring if desired. Pour into the crust. Cover and refrigerate until set. **Yield:** 8 servings.

Lemonade Meringue Pie

(Pictured above and on page 140)

PREP: 30 min.
BAKE: 15 min. + chilling

Lemonade concentrate and lemon juice give this special pie an excellent citrus flavor. I also like to add some lemon zest on top of the meringue.
—Kay Seiler, Greenville, Ohio

- 3 **eggs, *separated***
- 1 **package (4.6 ounces) cook-and-serve vanilla pudding mix**
- 1-1/4 **cups milk**
- 1 **cup (8 ounces) sour cream**
- 1/3 **cup lemonade concentrate**
- 1 **teaspoon lemon juice**
- 1/4 **teaspoon cream of tartar**
- 6 **tablespoons sugar**
- 1 **pastry shell (9 inches), baked**

Place egg whites in a small bowl; let stand at room temperature for 30 minutes. Meanwhile, in a large saucepan, combine the pudding mix, milk and sour cream until smooth. Cook and stir over medium heat until thickened and bubbly, about 5 minutes. Reduce heat; cook and stir 2 minutes longer.

Remove from the heat. Gradually whisk 1 cup hot filling into egg yolks; return all to the pan. Bring to a gentle boil; cook and stir for 2 minutes. Remove from the heat. Gently stir in lemonade concentrate; keep warm.

Add lemon juice and cream of tartar to egg whites; beat on medium speed until soft peaks form. Gradually beat in the sugar, 1 tablespoon at a time, on high until stiff glossy peaks form and the sugar is dissolved.

Pour warm filling into pastry shell. Spread meringue over filling, sealing edges to pastry.

Bake at 350° for 15-20 minutes or until meringue is golden brown. Cool on a wire rack for 1 hour. Refrigerate for at least 3 hours before serving. **Yield:** 6-8 servings.

Lemony White Chocolate Cheesecake

(Pictured below)

PREP: 30 min.
BAKE: 65 min. + chilling

Although it takes some time to prepare this eye–catching cheesecake, the combination of tangy lemon and rich white chocolate is hard to beat. It's always a huge hit!
—Marlene Schollenberge Bloomington, Illinois

- 1-1/4 **cups all-purpose flour**
- 2 **tablespoons confectioners' sugar**
- 1 **teaspoon grated lemon peel**
- 1/2 **cup cold butter, cubed**

FILLING:

- 4 **packages (8 ounces *each*) cream cheese, softened**
- 1-1/4 **cups sugar**
- 2 **tablespoons all-purpose flour**
- 2 **tablespoons lemon juice**
- 2 **tablespoons heavy whipping cream**
- 2 **teaspoons vanilla extract**
- 4 **eggs, lightly beaten**
- 10 **squares (1 ounce *each*) white baking chocolate, melted and cooled**
- 2 **teaspoons grated lemon peel**

Place a 9-in. springform pan on a double thickness of heavy-duty foil (about 18 in. square). Securely wrap foil around pan; set aside.

In a small bowl, combine the flour, confectioners' sugar and lemon peel; cut in butter until crumbly. Press onto the bottom and 1 in. up the sides of prepared pan. Place on a baking sheet. Bake at 325° for 25-30 minutes or until golden brown. Cool on a wire rack.

For the filling, in a large bowl, beat cream cheese, sugar, flour, lemon juice, cream and vanilla until well blended. Add eggs; beat on low speed just until combined. Stir in white chocolate and lemon peel. Pour into crust.

Place pan in a large baking pan; add 1 in. of hot water to larger pan. Bake at 325° for 65-85 minutes or until center is just set and top appears dull.

Remove pan from the water bath. Cool on a wire rack for 10 minutes. Carefully run a knife around the edge of pan to loosen; cool 1 hour longer. Refrigerate overnight. Remove sides of pan before slicing. **Yield:** 12 servings.

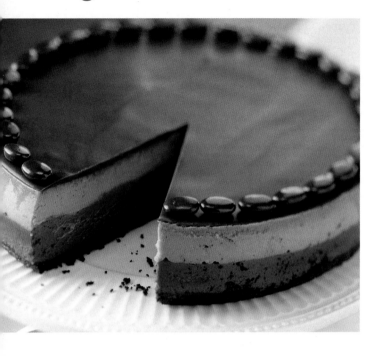

until combined. Stir in vanilla. Divide batter in half. Stir melted chocolate into one portion; pour over crust. Stir coffee mixture into the remaining batter; gently spoon over chocolate layer.

Place pan on a double thickness of heavy-duty foil (about 16 in. square). Securely wrap the foil around pan. Place in a large baking pan; add 1 in. of hot water to larger pan.

Bake at 325° for 45-50 minutes or until center is just set and top appears dull. Remove springform pan from water bath. Cool on a wire rack for 10 minutes. Carefully run a knife around edge of pan to loosen; cool 1 hour longer. Refrigerate overnight.

In a microwave-safe bowl, melt chocolate chips and butter; stir until smooth. Spread over cheesecake. Remove sides of pan. Garnish with coffee beans if desired. Refrigerate leftovers. **Yield:** 16 servings.

Layered Mocha Cheesecake

(Pictured above)

PREP: 30 min. **BAKE:** 45 min. + chilling

In my search for the perfect mocha cheesecake, I ended up combining a few of my favorite recipes to create this delicious version. It's as much a feast for the eyes as for the palate!
—Sue Gronholz, Beaver Dam, Wisconsin

- 1-1/2 cups cream-filled chocolate sandwich cookie crumbs
- 1/4 cup butter, melted

FILLING:
- 2 tablespoons plus 1-1/2 teaspoons instant coffee granules
- 1 tablespoon boiling water
- 1/4 teaspoon ground cinnamon
- 4 packages (8 ounces *each*) cream cheese, softened
- 1-1/2 cups sugar
- 1/4 cup all-purpose flour
- 4 eggs, lightly beaten
- 2 teaspoons vanilla extract
- 2 cups (12 ounces) semisweet chocolate chips, melted and cooled

GLAZE:
- 1/2 cup semisweet chocolate chips
- 3 tablespoons butter

Chocolate-covered coffee beans, optional

Combine cookie crumbs and butter; press onto the bottom of a greased 9-in. springform pan. In a small bowl, combine the coffee granules, water and cinnamon; set aside.

In a large bowl, beat the cream cheese, sugar and flour until smooth. Add eggs; beat on low speed just

Raspberry Patch Cream Pie

(Pictured below)

PREP: 35 min. + chilling

Our family loves raspberries, and this pie keeps the flavor and firmness of the berries intact. The delicious combination of the berry–gelatin and cream cheese layers has everyone coming back for seconds. —Allison Anderson, Raymond, Washington

- 1 cup graham cracker crumbs
- 1/2 cup sugar
- 5 tablespoons butter, melted

FILLING:
- 1 package (8 ounces) cream cheese, softened
- 1/4 cup confectioners' sugar
- 2 teaspoons milk
- 1 teaspoon vanilla extract

TOPPING:
- 3/4 cup sugar
- 3 tablespoons cornstarch

1-1/3 cups cold water
1/4 cup raspberry gelatin powder
3 cups fresh raspberries

Combine the cracker crumbs, sugar and butter. Press onto the bottom and up the sides of an ungreased 9-in. pie plate. Bake at 350° for 9-11 minutes or until set. Cool on a wire rack.

For filling, combine the cream cheese, confectioners' sugar, milk and vanilla. Carefully spread over crust.

For topping, in a small saucepan, combine the sugar, cornstarch and water until smooth. Bring to a boil; cook and stir for 2 minutes or until thickened. Remove from the heat; stir in gelatin until dissolved. Cool to room temperature. Refrigerate until slightly thickened.

Arrange the raspberries over filling. Spoon the gelatin mixture over the berries. Refrigerate until set. **Yield:** 6-8 servings.

Berry Pinwheel Cake

PREP: 30 min. **BAKE:** 10 min. + chilling

Perfect for special meals, this lovely chiffon cake is a nice change from strawberry pie or shortcake. It's easier to make than you think. Plus, the waxed paper–lined pan makes cleanup a breeze!
—*Becky Ruff, Monona, Iowa*

4 egg yolks
2 eggs
1/2 cup sugar
4-1/2 teaspoons water
2 teaspoons canola oil
1 teaspoon vanilla extract
1 cup cake flour
1 teaspoon baking powder
1/2 teaspoon salt
Confectioners' sugar
FILLING:
1 cup heavy whipping cream
1 tablespoon sugar
3 tablespoons lemon curd
2 cups chopped fresh strawberries

In a large bowl, beat the egg yolks, eggs and sugar until thick and lemon-colored. Beat in the water, oil and vanilla. Combine the flour, baking powder and salt; gradually add to the egg mixture. Grease a 15-in. x 10-in. x 1-in. baking pan and line with waxed paper; grease and flour the paper. Spread batter into pan.

Bake at 375° for 10-12 minutes or until cake springs back when lightly touched. Cool for 5 minutes. Turn cake onto a kitchen towel dusted with confectioners' sugar. Peel off waxed paper. Roll up cake in towel jelly-roll style, starting with a short side. Cool on a wire rack.

For the filling beat the cream until soft peaks form; add sugar, beating until stiff. Fold in lemon curd; gradually fold in strawberries. Unroll cake; spread filling evenly to within 1/2 in. of edges. Roll up again; dust

with confectioners' sugar. Cover and chill for 1 hour before serving. Refrigerate leftovers. **Yield:** 8 servings.

Honey Pecan Pie

(Pictured above)

PREP: 25 min. **BAKE:** 45 min. + cooling

Looking for a sweet ending to a holiday meal? This attractive pecan pie is bound to please with its traditional filling and honey–glazed pecans. —*Cathy Hudak, Wadsworth, Ohio*

4 eggs
1 cup chopped pecans
1 cup light corn syrup
1/4 cup sugar
1/4 cup packed brown sugar
2 tablespoons butter, melted
1 teaspoon vanilla extract
1/2 teaspoon salt
1 unbaked pastry shell (9 inches)
TOPPING:
3 tablespoons butter
1/3 cup packed brown sugar
3 tablespoons honey
1-1/2 cups pecan halves

In a large bowl, combine the eggs, pecans, corn syrup, sugars, butter, vanilla and salt. Pour into pastry shell. Bake at 350° for 30 minutes.

In a small saucepan, melt butter over medium heat. Stir in brown sugar and honey until combined. Stir in pecan halves until coated. Spoon over pie.

Bake 15-20 minutes longer or until bubbly and golden brown. Cool completely on a wire rack. Refrigerate leftovers. **Yield:** 8 servings.

Mascarpone Cheesecake

(Pictured below)

PREP: 30 min. **BAKE:** 50 min. + chilling

This rich dessert is sure to delight with its creamy filling, whipped topping and sweet caramel drizzle. It is a perfect dessert for a weekend dinner or potluck contribution.
—Deanna Polito-Laughinghouse
Raleigh, North Carolina

  3/4 **cup graham cracker crumbs**
    3 **tablespoons sugar**
    3 **tablespoons butter, melted**
FILLING:
    2 **packages (8 ounces *each*) cream cheese, softened**
    2 **cartons (8 ounces *each*) Mascarpone cheese**
    1 **cup sugar**
    1 **tablespoon lemon juice**
    1 **tablespoon vanilla extract**
    4 **eggs, lightly beaten**
TOPPING:
    1 **envelope whipped topping mix**
    1 **tablespoon caramel ice cream topping**

Place a greased 9-in. springform pan on a double thickness of heavy-duty foil (about 18 in. square). Securely wrap foil around pan.

Combine cracker crumbs and sugar; stir in butter. Press onto the bottom of prepared pan. Place pan on a baking sheet. Bake at 325° for 10 minutes. Cool on a wire rack.

For filling, in a large bowl, beat the cheeses, sugar, lemon juice and vanilla until smooth. Add eggs; beat on low speed just until combined. Pour over crust. Place springform pan in a large baking pan; add 1 in. of hot water to larger pan.

Bake at 325° for 50-60 minutes or until center is just set and top appears dull. Remove springform pan from water bath. Cool on a wire rack for 10 minutes. Carefully run a knife around the edge of pan to loosen; cool 1 hour longer.

Refrigerate overnight. Remove sides of pan. Before serving, prepare the topping mix according to package directions. Garnish the cheesecake with whipped topping; drizzle with caramel. Refrigerate leftovers.
Yield: 12 servings.

Grand Prize Winner

Butternut Cream Pie

(Pictured above)

PREP: 35 min. + chilling

Last fall, my garden was loaded with squash. I enjoy experimenting with recipes, so I came up with this creamy pie. It really went over well at Thanksgiving dinner.
—Sandra Kreuter, Burney, California

    1 **medium butternut squash (about 2 pounds)**
  1/4 **cup hot water**
    1 **package (8 ounces) cream cheese, softened**
  1/4 **cup sugar**
    2 **tablespoons caramel ice cream topping**
    1 **teaspoon ground cinnamon**
  1/2 **teaspoon salt**
  1/2 **teaspoon ground ginger**
  1/4 **teaspoon ground cloves**
    1 **package (5.1 ounces) instant vanilla pudding mix**
  3/4 **cup milk plus 2 tablespoons milk**
    1 **pastry shell (9 inches), baked**
Whipped cream and toasted flaked coconut

Cut squash in half; discard seeds. Place squash cut side down in a microwave-safe dish; add hot water. Cover and microwave for 13-15 minutes or until tender. When cool enough to handle, scoop out pulp and mash. Set aside 1-1/2 cups squash (save remaining squash for another use).

In a bowl, beat the cream cheese until smooth. Stir in the squash until blended. Add the sugar, caramel topping, cinnamon, salt, ginger and cloves; beat until blended. Add the pudding mix and milk; beat on low speed for 2 minutes.

Spoon into the pastry shell. Refrigerate for at least 3 hours. Garnish with whipped cream and coconut. **Yield:** 6-8 servings.

Rhubarb Upside-Down Cake

(Pictured below)

PREP: 30 min. **BAKE:** 40 min. + cooling

This light and airy yellow cake is moist but not too sweet, and the caramelized rhubarb topping adds tangy flavor and eye appeal. We like it served with strawberry ice cream.
—*Joyce Rowe, Stratham, New Hampshire*

2/3 cup packed brown sugar
3 tablespoons butter, melted
2-1/4 cups diced fresh *or* frozen rhubarb
4-1/2 teaspoons sugar
BATTER:
6 tablespoons butter, softened
3/4 cup sugar
2 eggs, *separated*
1 teaspoon vanilla extract
1 cup plus 2 tablespoons all-purpose flour
1-1/2 teaspoons baking powder
1/2 teaspoon salt
1/4 cup milk
1/4 teaspoon cream of tartar
Whipped cream, optional

Combine brown sugar and butter. Spread into a greased 9-in. round baking pan. Layer with rhubarb; sprinkle with sugar. Set aside.

In a large bowl, cream butter and sugar. Beat in egg yolks and vanilla. Combine the flour, baking powder and salt; add to creamed mixture alternately with milk.

Beat egg whites and cream of tartar on medium speed until stiff peaks form. Gradually fold into creamed mixture, about 1/2 cup at a time. Gently spoon over rhubarb (pan will be full, about 1/4 in. from top of pan).

Bake at 325° for 50-60 minutes or until cake springs back when lightly touched. Cool for 10 minutes before inverting onto a serving plate. Serve warm with whipped cream if desired. **Yield:** 10-12 servings.

Editor's Note: If using frozen rhubarb, measure rhubarb while still frozen, then thaw completely. Drain in a colander, but do not press liquid out.

Summer Celebration Ice Cream Cake

(Pictured above and on page 140)

PREP: 15 min. **BAKE:** 20 min. + freezing

I wanted to make my youngest son an ice cream cake one year for his summer birthday. He picked the flavors and I decided to try my favorite brownie recipe as a crust. It worked!
—*Krista Frank, Rhododendron, Oregon*

1 cup sugar
3 tablespoons butter, melted
3 tablespoons orange yogurt
1 egg
1 teaspoon grated orange peel
1 teaspoon vanilla extract
3/4 cup all-purpose flour
1/3 cup baking cocoa
1 cup (6 ounces) semisweet chocolate chips
1-3/4 quarts vanilla ice cream, softened
4 to 6 squares (1 ounce *each*) semisweet chocolate
1 tablespoon shortening
Mixed fresh berries

Line an 8-in. square baking dish with foil and grease the foil; set aside. In a large bowl, combine the sugar, butter, yogurt, egg, orange peel and vanilla until blended. Combine the flour and cocoa; stir into sugar mixture. Add chocolate chips.

Spread into prepared dish. Bake at 325° for 20-25 minutes or until a toothpick inserted near the center comes out with moist crumbs. Cool on a wire rack.

Spread ice cream over cake. Cover and freeze for 3 hours or until firm.

Remove from the freezer 10 minutes before serving. In a microwave-safe bowl, melt chocolate and shortening; stir until smooth. Using foil, lift dessert out of dish; gently peel off foil. Cut into squares. Garnish with berries and drizzle with chocolate. **Yield:** 9 servings.

Strawberry Swirl Cheesecake

(Pictured above)

PREP: 1 hour **BAKE:** 1-1/4 hours + chilling

This dessert is doubly delicious, with two creamy layers...one strawberry, one vanilla. To avoid cracking, run the knife just through the very top when swirling the strawberry puree.
—Mary Ellen Friend, Ravenswood, West Virginia

- 1-1/4 cups all-purpose flour
- 1 tablespoon sugar
- 1 teaspoon grated lemon peel
- 1/2 cup cold butter

FILLING:
- 4 packages (8 ounces *each*) cream cheese, softened
- 1-1/3 cups sugar
- 2 tablespoons all-purpose flour
- 2 tablespoons heavy whipping cream
- 4 eggs, lightly beaten
- 1 tablespoon lemon juice
- 2 teaspoons vanilla extract
- 1 cup pureed fresh strawberries, *divided*
- 8 to 10 drops red food coloring, optional

In a small bowl, combine the flour, sugar and lemon peel; cut in butter until crumbly. Pat dough onto the bottom and 1 in. up the sides of a greased 9-in. springform pan. Place on a baking sheet. Bake at 325° for 15-20 minutes or until lightly browned. Cool on a wire rack.

For the filling, in a large bowl, beat the cream cheese, sugar, flour and cream until smooth. Add the eggs; beat on low speed just until combined. Beat in lemon juice and vanilla just until blended. Pour 2-1/2 cups of the batter into a bowl; set aside.

Stir 3/4 cup pureed strawberries and food coloring if desired into remaining batter. Pour into crust. Place pan on a double thickness of heavy-duty foil (about 16 in. square). Securely wrap foil around pan. Place in a large baking pan. Add 1 in. of hot water to larger pan. Bake for 35 minutes.

Carefully pour reserved batter over bottom layer. Spoon remaining pureed berries over batter in three concentric circles. Carefully cut through top layer only with a knife to swirl. Bake 40-50 minutes longer or until center is almost set. Remove pan from water bath. Cool on a wire rack for 10 minutes. Carefully run a knife around edge of pan to loosen; cool 1 hour longer. Refrigerate overnight. **Yield:** 12 servings.

Lemon Coconut Cake

PREP: 1 hour + cooling **BAKE:** 20 min. + cooling

If you're pressed for time, use a white cake mix and dress it up with the filling and frosting from this recipe. This is a lovely dessert for spring and summer.
—LaDonna Reed, Ponca City, Oklahoma

- 5 egg whites
- 3/4 cup shortening
- 1-1/2 cups sugar
- 1-1/2 teaspoons vanilla extract
- 2 cups all-purpose flour
- 2 teaspoons baking powder
- 1 teaspoon salt
- 1 cup milk

FILLING:
- 3/4 cup sugar
- 2 tablespoons cornstarch
- Dash salt
- 3/4 cup cold water
- 2 egg yolks
- 3 tablespoons lemon juice
- 1 tablespoon butter

FROSTING:
- 3/4 cup shortening
- 3-3/4 cups confectioners' sugar
- 1 teaspoon vanilla extract
- 1/3 cup water
- 1-1/4 cups flaked coconut

Place egg whites in a bowl; let stand at room temperature for 30 minutes. In a large bowl, cream shortening and sugar until light and fluffy. Beat in vanilla. Combine flour, baking powder and salt; add to creamed mixture alternately with milk. Beat egg whites until stiff peaks form; fold into creamed mixture.

Pour into three greased and floured 9-in. round baking pans. Bake at 350° for 18-20 minutes or until a toothpick comes out clean. Cool for 10 minutes; remove from pans to wire racks to cool completely.

For filling, in a heavy saucepan, combine sugar, cornstarch and salt. Stir in water until smooth. Cook and stir over medium-high heat until thickened. Reduce heat; cook and stir 2 minutes longer. Remove from heat. Stir a small amount of filling into egg yolks; return all to pan, stirring constantly. Bring to a boil; cook and stir 2 minutes longer. Remove from heat. Stir in lemon juice and butter. Cool, without stirring, to room temperature.

For frosting, in a large bowl, cream shortening and confectioners' sugar until light and fluffy; beat in vanilla. Gradually add water, beating until smooth. Spread filling between cake layers. Frost top and sides of cake; sprinkle with coconut. **Yield:** 12-14 servings.

Frozen Peanut Parfait Pies

(Pictured below)

PREP: 20 min. + freezing

This crowd–pleasing dessert will be the hit of any potluck or party. And although it seems like a lot of trouble to make these luscious pies, with only six ingredients, they're actually very easy.
—Anne Powers, Munford, Alabama

- 1 package (8 ounces) cream cheese, softened
- 1 can (14 ounces) sweetened condensed milk
- 1 carton (16 ounces) frozen whipped topping, thawed
- 1 jar (11-3/4 ounces) hot fudge ice cream topping, warmed
- 2 cups dry roasted peanuts
- 2 pastry shells (9 inches), baked

In a large bowl, beat cream cheese and condensed milk until smooth; fold in whipped topping. Spread a fourth of the mixture into each pie shell. Drizzle each with a fourth of the fudge topping; sprinkle each with 1/2 cup peanuts. Repeat layers.

Cover and freeze for 4 hours or overnight. Remove from the freezer 5 minutes before cutting. **Yield:** 2 pies (6-8 servings each).

Fresh Fruit Tarts

(Pictured above)

PREP: 20 min. + chilling **BAKE:** 15 min. + cooling

These luscious tarts are the jewels of the party whenever I serve them. You can bake the shells ahead and freeze them, then fill and decorate the tarts the day of the gathering.
—Dona Erhart, Stockbridge, Michigan

- 1-1/2 cups all-purpose flour
- 1/4 cup sugar
- 1/4 teaspoon salt
- 1/2 cup cold butter, cubed
- 1 egg, lightly beaten

FILLING:
- 4 ounces cream cheese, softened
- 1/4 cup sweetened condensed milk
- 2 tablespoons lemon juice

Assorted fresh berries
- 2 tablespoons apricot preserves

In a large bowl, combine the flour, sugar and salt. Cut in butter until mixture resembles coarse crumbs. Add egg; mix with a fork until blended. Shape dough into a ball. Cover and refrigerate for 1 hour or until easy to handle.

Divide dough into six portions. Press each portion into a greased 4-1/2-in. tart pan. Bake at 350° for 15-20 minutes or until edges are lightly browned. Cool for 10 minutes before removing from pans to wire racks to cool completely.

For the filling, beat cream cheese until smooth. Beat in sweetened condensed milk and lemon juice. Spoon 2 rounded tablespoonfuls into each cooled tart shell. Arrange berries over filling.

In a small saucepan, melt preserves over medium heat; stir until smooth. Brush over berries. **Yield:** 6 servings.

Cupcakes Galore

Special Mocha Cupcakes

(Pictured above and on page 140)

PREP: 25 min.
BAKE: 20 min. + cooling

Topped with a fluffy frosting and chocolate sprinkles, these extra-rich, extra-delicious cupcakes smell wonderful while baking and taste even better!
—Mary Bilyeu, Ann Arbor, Michigan

- 1-1/2 cups all-purpose flour
- 1 cup sugar
- 1/3 cup baking cocoa
- 1 teaspoon baking soda
- 1/2 teaspoon salt
- 2 eggs
- 1/2 cup cold brewed coffee
- 1/2 cup canola oil
- 3 teaspoons cider vinegar
- 3 teaspoons vanilla extract

MOCHA FROSTING:
- 3 tablespoons milk chocolate chips
- 3 tablespoons semisweet chocolate chips
- 1/3 cup butter, softened
- 2 cups confectioners' sugar
- 1 to 2 tablespoons brewed coffee
- 1/2 cup chocolate sprinkles

In a small bowl, combine the flour, sugar, cocoa, baking soda and salt. In a small bowl, whisk the eggs, coffee, oil, vinegar and vanilla. Add to dry ingredients; mix well.

Fill paper-lined muffin cups three-fourths full. Bake at 350° for 20-25 minutes or until a toothpick inserted in centers comes out clean. Cool for 10 minutes before removing from pan to a wire rack to cool.

For the frosting, in a small microwave-safe bowl, melt the chips; stir until smooth. Add butter; beat until blended. Gradually beat in the confectioners' sugar and coffee. Pipe frosting onto cupcakes. Top with sprinkles; gently press down.
Yield: 1 dozen.

Raspberry Peach Cupcakes

(Pictured below)

PREP: 25 min.
BAKE: 15 min. + cooling

These easy cupcakes, which start with a cake mix, have an appealing combination of fresh fruit and white chocolate. The luscious lemon buttercream frosting adds a citrus tang to the sweet treats.
—Arlene Kay Butler, Ogden, Utah

- 1 cup vanilla *or* white chips
- 6 tablespoons butter, cubed
- 1 package (18-1/4 ounces) white cake mix
- 1 cup milk
- 3 eggs
- 1 teaspoon vanilla extract
- 1 cup fresh raspberries
- 1/2 cup chopped peeled fresh peaches *or* frozen unsweetened peach slices, thawed and chopped

LEMON FROSTING:
- 1/2 cup butter, softened
- 3 cups confectioners' sugar
- 2 tablespoons lemon juice
- Fresh raspberries and peach pieces, optional

1/2 teaspoon baking soda
1/4 cup baking cocoa
1 cup water
1 cup canola oil
1/2 cup butter, cubed
2 eggs
1/3 cup buttermilk
1 teaspoon vanilla extract

CARAMEL ICING:
1 cup packed brown sugar
1/2 cup butter, cubed
1/4 cup milk
2 to 2-1/4 cups confectioners' sugar

1/2 cup mashed ripe banana
1 teaspoon vanilla extract
1 cup all-purpose flour
1/2 teaspoon baking soda
1/2 teaspoon ground nutmeg
1/4 teaspoon salt
1/4 cup sour cream

CREAM CHEESE FROSTING:
4 ounces cream cheese, softened
1/2 teaspoon vanilla extract
1-3/4 cups confectioners' sugar
3 tablespoons chopped walnuts

In a microwave-safe bowl, combine the chips and butter. Microwave at 70% power until melted; stir until smooth. In a large bowl, combine the cake mix, milk, eggs, vanilla and melted chips; beat on low speed for 30 seconds. Beat on medium for 2 minutes. Fold in the raspberries and peaches.

Fill paper-lined muffin cups three-fourths full. Bake at 350° for 15-20 minutes or until a toothpick comes out clean. Cool for 10 minutes before removing from pans to wire racks to cool completely.

For the frosting, in a small bowl, beat the butter, confectioners' sugar and lemon juice until smooth. Frost cupcakes. Top with fruit if desired. **Yield:** 2 dozen.

In a large bowl, combine the flour, sugar, salt and baking soda. In a large saucepan over medium heat, bring cocoa, water, oil and butter to a boil. Gradually add to dry ingredients; mix well. Combine eggs, buttermilk and vanilla; gradually add to batter and mix well (batter will be very thin).

Fill paper-lined muffin cups three-fourths full. Bake at 350° for 15-20 minutes or until a toothpick comes out clean. Cool for 10 minutes before removing from pans to wire racks to cool completely.

For the icing, in a heavy saucepan, combine brown sugar, butter and milk. Cook and stir over low heat until sugar is dissolved. Increase heat to medium. Do not stir. Cook for 3-6 minutes or until bubbles form in center of mixture and syrup turns amber. Remove from the heat; transfer to a small bowl. Cool to room temperature. Gradually beat in confectioners' sugar. Spread over cupcakes. **Yield:** 2 dozen.

In a small bowl, cream butter and sugar. Add eggs, one at a time, beating well after each addition. Add banana and vanilla; mix well. Combine the flour, baking soda, nutmeg and salt; add to creamed mixture alternately with sour cream.

Fill paper-lined muffin cups half full. Bake at 350° for 18-22 minutes or until a toothpick comes out clean. Cool for 10 minutes before removing from pan to a wire rack to cool completely.

For the frosting, in a small bowl, combine cream cheese and vanilla. Gradually beat in confectioners' sugar. Frost cupcakes; sprinkle with walnuts. Store in the refrigerator. **Yield:** 1 dozen.

Texas Chocolate Cupcakes

(Pictured above)

PREP: 30 min.
BAKE: 15 min. + cooling

My husband remembers his mother making "little black cupcakes with caramel icing." I never thought about putting caramel icing on chocolate cupcakes, but boy, was I wrong. It's to die for!
—Cathy Bodkins, Dayton, Virginia

2 cups all-purpose flour
2 cups sugar
1 teaspoon salt

Walnut Banana Cupcakes

(Pictured at right)

PREP: 25 min.
BAKE: 20 min. + cooling

What makes these tender banana cupcakes extra special is the nutmeg, but make sure it's fresh. They're amazingly good; I get requests for them all the time.
—Rachel Krupp
Perkiomenville, Pennsylvania

1/4 cup butter, softened
3/4 cup sugar
2 eggs

Chocolate Carrot Cake

(Pictured above)

PREP: 35 min. **BAKE:** 25 min. + cooling

Finely shredding the carrots gives this cake nice texture. The walnuts sprinkled on top add crunch, but you can leave them off if you prefer. —Pamela Brown, Williamsburg, Michigan

- 2 cups all-purpose flour
- 2 cups sugar
- 1/2 cup baking cocoa
- 1 teaspoon baking soda
- 1/2 teaspoon salt
- 4 eggs
- 1-1/4 cups canola oil
- 3 cups finely shredded carrots

FROSTING:
- 1 package (8 ounces) cream cheese, softened
- 1/2 cup butter, softened
- 3-3/4 cups confectioners' sugar
- 1/4 cup baking cocoa
- 3 teaspoons vanilla extract
- 1/4 cup chopped walnuts
- 1/4 cup semisweet chocolate chips

Line two 9-in. round baking pans with waxed paper; grease the paper and set aside. In a large bowl, combine the flour, sugar, cocoa, baking soda and salt. Add the eggs, oil and carrots; beat until combined. Pour into prepared pans.

Bake at 350° for 25-30 minutes or until a toothpick inserted near the center comes out clean. Cool for 10 minutes before removing from pans to wire racks to cool completely.

For the frosting, in a large bowl, beat cream cheese and butter until smooth. Beat in confectioners' sugar, cocoa and vanilla until smooth. Place one cake layer on a serving plate; spread with half of the frosting. Repeat layers. Sprinkle with walnuts and chocolate chips. **Yield:** 12-16 servings.

Crumbleberry Pie

(Pictured below)

PREP: 15 min. **BAKE:** 50 min.

Pear slices and blueberries add wonderful flavor to this simple-to-make pie. The almonds in the filling add just the right touch of nutty goodness. —Maria Regakis, Somerville, Massachusetts

Pastry for single-crust pie (9 inches)
- 6 tablespoons butter, softened
- 1/2 cup sugar
- 2 eggs
- 1 cup finely ground almonds
- 1/4 cup all-purpose flour
- 1 large pear, peeled and thinly sliced

TOPPING:
- 3/4 cup all-purpose flour
- 1/3 cup packed brown sugar
- 1/4 teaspoon almond extract
- 1/3 cup cold butter
- 1 cup fresh *or* frozen blueberries

Line a 9-in. pie plate with pastry; set aside. In a small bowl, cream butter and sugar until light and fluffy. Add eggs, one at a time, beating well after each addition. Stir in almonds and flour.

Spread into pastry shell. Arrange pear slices over filling. Bake at 350° for 25-30 minutes or until light golden brown.

For the topping, combine the flour, brown sugar and extract; cut in butter until crumbly. Sprinkle blueberries over pears; sprinkle with crumb topping.

Bake 25-30 minutes longer or until golden brown. Serve warm. Refrigerate leftovers. **Yield:** 6-8 servings.

Editor's Note: If using frozen blueberries, do not thaw before adding to filling.

Cherry Gingerbread Cupcakes

PREP: 30 min. **BAKE:** 20 min. + cooling

A maraschino cherry in the center and frosting with a hint of lemon complements these little spice cakes. Making them is a surefire way to get my dad to come over for a cup of coffee.
—Laura McAllister, Morganton, North Carolina

- 1/2 cup shortening
- 1 cup sugar
- 2 eggs
- 1 cup molasses
- 3 cups all-purpose flour
- 1 teaspoon baking soda
- 1 teaspoon ground ginger
- 1 teaspoon ground cinnamon
- 1 cup buttermilk
- 1/2 cup chopped walnuts
- 24 maraschino cherries, well drained

LEMON CREAM CHEESE FROSTING:
- 4 ounces cream cheese, softened
- 1/4 cup butter, softened
- 1 teaspoon vanilla extract
- 1 teaspoon grated lemon peel
- 1-3/4 to 2 cups confectioners' sugar

In a large bowl, cream the shortening and sugar until light and fluffy. Add the eggs and molasses; mix well. Combine the flour, baking soda, ginger and cinnamon; add to creamed mixture alternately with buttermilk. Stir in the walnuts.

Fill paper-lined muffin cups two-thirds full; place a maraschino cherry in the center of each. Bake at 375° for 20-24 minutes or until a toothpick inserted in the centers comes out clean. Cool for 10 minutes before removing from pans to wire racks to cool completely.

For the frosting, in a small bowl, beat cream cheese and butter until smooth; add vanilla and lemon peel. Gradually beat in the confectioners' sugar. Frost cupcakes. **Yield:** 2 dozen.

Cinnamon Apple Cheesecake

(Pictured above right)

PREP: 40 min. **BAKE:** 40 min. + chilling

An attractive topping of cinnamon-spiced apples slices and a homemade oat-and-walnut crust make this creamy dessert a definite showstopper. —Emily Ann Young, Edmond, Oklahoma

- 1/2 cup butter, softened
- 1/4 cup packed brown sugar
- 1 cup all-purpose flour
- 1/4 cup quick-cooking oats
- 1/4 cup finely chopped walnuts
- 1/2 teaspoon ground cinnamon
- 2 packages (8 ounces *each*) cream cheese, softened

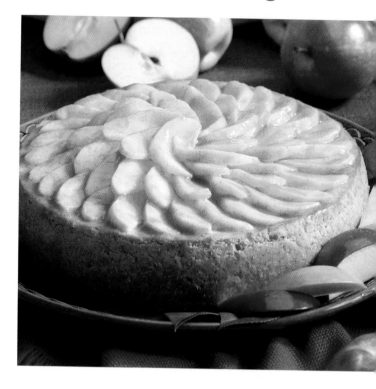

- 1 can (14 ounces) sweetened condensed milk
- 1/2 cup apple juice concentrate
- 3 eggs, lightly beaten

TOPPING:
- 2 medium apples, peeled and sliced
- 1 tablespoon butter
- 1 teaspoon cornstarch
- 1/4 teaspoon ground cinnamon
- 1/4 cup apple juice concentrate

In a small bowl, cream butter and brown sugar until light and fluffy. Gradually add flour, oats, walnuts and cinnamon until well blended. Press onto the bottom and 1-1/2 in. up the sides of a greased 9-in. springform pan.

Place on a baking sheet. Bake at 325° for 10 minutes or until set. Cool on a wire rack.

In a large bowl, beat cream cheese until fluffy. Beat in milk and apple juice concentrate until smooth. Add eggs; beat on low speed just until combined (batter will be thin). Pour into crust.

Return pan to baking sheet. Bake at 325° for 40-45 minutes or until center is almost set. Cool on a wire rack for 10 minutes. Carefully run a knife around edge of pan to loosen; cool 1 hour longer. Refrigerate overnight.

For the topping, in a large skillet, cook and stir the apples in butter over medium heat until crisp-tender, about 5 minutes. Cool to room temperature. Arrange over the cheesecake.

In a small saucepan, combine the cornstarch, cinnamon and apple juice concentrate until smooth. Bring to a boil. Reduce heat; cook and stir for 1 minute or until thickened. Immediately brush over apples. Refrigerate for 1 hour or until chilled. Remove sides of pan. Refrigerate leftovers. **Yield:** 12 servings.

Carrot Cheesecake

(Pictured below)

PREP: 25 min. **BAKE:** 65 min. + chilling

My family can't wait to dig into this creamy make-ahead dessert. Unlike traditional cheesecake, a streusel topping is sprinkled over the filling. —Misty Wellman, Scottsdale, Arizona

    2 cups graham cracker crumbs
1/4 cup sugar
1/3 cup butter, melted
FILLING:
    3 packages (8 ounces *each*) cream cheese, softened
1-1/4 cups sugar
    2 tablespoons brown sugar
    3 eggs, lightly beaten
1/4 cup heavy whipping cream
    2 tablespoons cornstarch
    1 tablespoon sour cream
1-1/2 teaspoons vanilla extract
    1 teaspoon lemon juice
1/2 teaspoon ground cinnamon
1-1/3 cups chopped carrots, cooked and pureed
TOPPING:
    1 cup graham cracker crumbs
    2 tablespoons brown sugar
1-1/2 teaspoons ground cinnamon
1/4 cup butter, melted

Combine crumbs and sugar; stir in butter. Press onto the bottom and 2 in. up the sides of a greased 9-in. springform pan. Place on a baking sheet. Bake at 350° for 6-8 minutes. Cool on a wire rack.

For the filling, in a large bowl, beat cream cheese and sugars until smooth. Add eggs; beat on low speed just until combined. Stir in the cream, cornstarch, sour cream, vanilla, lemon juice and cinnamon. Fold in carrots.

Pour into crust. Place pan on a double thickness of heavy-duty foil (about 16 in. square). Securely wrap foil around pan. Place in a larger baking pan. Add 1 in. of hot water to larger pan. Bake at 350° for 55-60 minutes until center is just set.

Combine the topping ingredients; sprinkle over the filling. Bake 7-10 minutes longer. Remove the pan from water bath. Cool on a wire rack for 10 minutes. Carefully run a knife around the edge of pan to loosen; cool 1 hour longer. Refrigerate overnight. Remove sides of pan. **Yield:** 10-12 servings.

Peaches & Cream Pie

PREP: 20 min. **BAKE:** 1 hour + cooling

This eye-catching pie packed with juicy peaches is irresistible. Its creamy, fruity filling is a refreshing change of pace from traditional peach pie. —Emma Rea, Columbia, South Carolina

    3 cups all-purpose flour
    1 teaspoon salt
    1 cup plus 2 tablespoons cold butter
    1 egg
    1 teaspoon cider vinegar
    5 to 7 tablespoons ice water
FILLING:
    5 cups sliced peeled peaches
    1 teaspoon lemon juice
3/4 cup plus 1 tablespoon sugar, *divided*
    3 tablespoons all-purpose flour
3/4 teaspoon ground cinnamon
1/4 teaspoon salt
1/2 cup heavy whipping cream
    1 tablespoon butter

In a bowl, combine the flour and salt; cut in butter until mixture resembles coarse crumbs. Combine egg and vinegar; add to flour mixture. Add water, 1 tablespoon at a time, until dough forms a ball.

Divide dough in half. Roll out one portion to fit a 9-in. pie plate; transfer to pie plate. Trim pastry even with edge; set aside.

For the filling, in a large bowl, combine the peaches and lemon juice. In another bowl, combine 3/4 cup sugar, flour, cinnamon and salt; stir in cream. Pour over the peaches; gently toss to coat. Spoon into the crust. Dot with butter.

Roll out remaining pastry; make a lattice crust. Seal and flute edges. Sprinkle with remaining sugar. Cover edges loosely with foil.

Bake at 425° for 15 minutes. Reduce heat to 350°; bake for 45-50 minutes or until peaches are tender and crust is golden brown. Cool on a wire rack. **Yield:** 6-8 servings.

Pineapple Upside-Down Cupcakes

(Pictured above)

PREP: 30 min. **BAKE:** 30 min. + cooling

I have baked cupcakes for years since I served as a room mother for my three children. These easy-to-prepare, jumbo treats make an attractive dessert for special occasions or everyday.
—Barbara Hahn, Park Hills, Missouri

- 6 tablespoons butter, cubed
- 1 cup packed light brown sugar
- 2 tablespoons light corn syrup
- 1 small pineapple, peeled, cored and cut into 1/2-inch slices
- 12 maraschino cherries, well drained
- 3 eggs
- 2 cups sugar
- 1 cup canola oil
- 1 cup (8 ounces) sour cream
- 2 teaspoons vanilla extract
- 2-1/2 cups all-purpose flour
- 1/2 teaspoon baking powder
- 1/2 teaspoon baking soda
- 1/2 teaspoon salt

Whipped topping, optional

Line greased jumbo muffin cups with waxed paper; grease the paper and set aside. In a small saucepan, melt butter over low heat; stir in brown sugar and corn syrup. Cook and stir over medium heat until sugar is dissolved. Remove from the heat. Spoon 1 tablespoonful into each muffin cup; top each with a pineapple slice and a cherry.

In a large bowl, beat eggs and sugar until thickened and lemon-colored. Beat in the oil, sour cream and vanilla until smooth. Combine the flour, baking powder, baking soda and salt. Add to egg mixture; mix well.

Fill muffin cups two-thirds full. Bake at 350° for 28-32 minutes or until a toothpick comes out clean. Cool for 5 minutes before inverting onto wire racks to cool completely. Garnish with whipped topping if desired. **Yield:** 1 dozen jumbo cupcakes.

Fudgy Nut Coffee Pie

(Pictured below)

PREP: 15 min. + freezing

My mother served this pretty pie for my birthday dinner one year, and now it's one of my favorites. Sometimes I garnish the pie with dollops of whipped cream.—Amy Theis, Billings, Montana

- 1-1/2 cups confectioners' sugar
- 1/2 cup heavy whipping cream
- 6 tablespoons butter, cubed
- 3 squares (1 ounce *each*) unsweetened chocolate
- 3 tablespoons light corn syrup

Dash salt

- 1 teaspoon vanilla extract
- 1 chocolate crumb crust (9 inches)
- 3/4 cup coarsely chopped pecans, *divided*
- 3 pints coffee ice cream, softened

In a small saucepan, combine the confectioners' sugar, cream, butter, chocolate, corn syrup and salt. Cook and stir over low heat until smooth. Remove from the heat. Stir in vanilla. Cool completely.

Spread 1/2 cup cooled fudge sauce over the crust. Sprinkle with 1/4 cup pecans. Freeze for 20 minutes or until set. Spread with half of the ice cream. Freeze for 1 hour or until firm. Repeat layers. Cover and freeze for 4 hours or until firm.

Just before serving, drizzle the remaining fudge sauce over the pie and sprinkle with remaining chopped pecans. **Yield:** 8 servings.

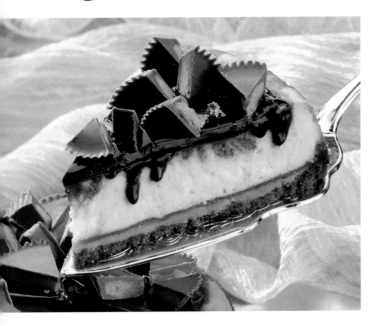

In a microwave-safe bowl, heat 1/4 cup fudge topping on high for 30 seconds or until thin; fold into reserved cream cheese mixture. Carefully pour over filling; cut through with a knife to swirl.

Place pan on a baking sheet. Bake at 350° for 55-65 minutes or until center is almost set. Cool on a wire rack for 10 minutes. Carefully run a knife around edge of pan to loosen; cool 1 hour longer.

Microwave remaining fudge topping for 30 seconds or until warmed; spread over cheesecake. Garnish with peanut butter cups. Refrigerate overnight. Remove sides of pan. Refrigerate leftovers. **Yield:** 12-14 servings.

Editor's Note: Reduced-fat or generic brands of peanut butter are not recommended for this recipe.

Peanut Butter Cup Cheesecake

(Pictured above and on page 140)

PREP: 20 min. **BAKE:** 55 min. + chilling

After I volunteered to bring dessert to a holiday party, I made this pie and brought it. It not only tastes luscious, but it looks great, too! —Dawn Lowenstein, Hatboro, Pennsylvania

- 1-1/4 **cups graham cracker crumbs**
- 1/4 **cup crushed cream-filled chocolate sandwich cookies**
- 1/4 **cup sugar**
- 6 **tablespoons butter, melted**
- 3/4 **cup creamy peanut butter**

FILLING:
- 3 **packages (8 ounces *each*) cream cheese, softened**
- 1 **cup sugar**
- 1 **cup (8 ounces) sour cream**
- 3 **eggs, lightly beaten**
- 1-1/2 **teaspoons vanilla extract**
- 1 **cup hot fudge ice cream topping, *divided***
- 6 **peanut butter cups, cut into small wedges**

In a bowl, combine cracker crumbs, cookie crumbs, sugar and butter. Press onto the bottom and 1 in. up the sides of a greased 9-in. springform pan. Place on a baking sheet.

Bake at 350° for 7-9 minutes or until set. Cool on a wire rack. In a microwave-safe bowl, heat peanut butter on high for 30 seconds or until softened. Spread over crust to within 1 in. of edges.

For the filling, in a large bowl, beat the cream cheese, sugar and sour cream until smooth. Add eggs; beat on low speed just until combined. Stir in vanilla. Pour 1 cup into a bowl; set aside. Pour remaining filling over peanut butter layer.

Frozen Strawberry Pie

(Pictured below)

PREP: 25 min. + freezing

I work full-time, so I like the fact that these yummy, attractive pies can be made ahead. I serve each slice with a dollop of whipped cream, a strawberry and chocolate curls.
—Awynne Thurstenson, Siloam Springs, Arkansas

- 1 **package (8 ounces) cream cheese, softened**
- 1 **cup sugar**
- 1 **teaspoon vanilla extract**
- 4 **cups chopped fresh strawberries**
- 1 **carton (12 ounces) frozen whipped topping, thawed**
- 1/2 **cup chopped pecans, toasted**
- 2 **chocolate crumb crusts (9 inches)**

In a large bowl, beat the cream cheese, sugar and vanilla extract until smooth. Beat in the strawberries. Fold in the whipped topping and pecans. Pour into crusts. Cover and freeze for 3-4 hours or until firm. Remove from the freezer 15-20 minutes before serving. **Yield:** 2 pies (6 servings each).

Cranberry Zucchini Wedges

(Pictured above)

PREP: 15 min. **BAKE:** 30 min. + cooling

These cake wedges have wonderful flavor and a tender texture. They're great for brunch, and pretty, too—with bits of pineapple, cranberries and zucchini.
—Redawna Kalynchuk, Waskatenau, Alberta

- 1 can (20 ounces) pineapple chunks
- 3 cups all-purpose flour
- 1-3/4 cups sugar
- 1 teaspoon baking powder
- 1 teaspoon baking soda
- 1 teaspoon salt
- 3 eggs
- 1 cup canola oil
- 2 teaspoons vanilla extract
- 1 cup tightly packed shredded zucchini
- 1 cup fresh *or* frozen cranberries, halved
- 1/2 cup chopped walnuts
Confectioners' sugar

Drain the pineapple, reserving 1/3 cup juice (save the remaining juice for another use). Place the pineapple and reserved juice in a blender; cover and process until smooth. Set aside.

In a bowl, combine the flour, sugar, baking powder, baking soda and salt. In a bowl, whisk the eggs, oil, vanilla and pineapple mixture; beat into the dry ingredients until blended. Fold in the zucchini, cranberries and nuts.

Pour into two greased and floured 9-in. round baking pans. Bake at 350° for 30-35 minutes or until a toothpick inserted near the center comes out clean. Cool for 10 minutes before removing from pans to wire racks to cool completely. Just before serving, dust with confectioners' sugar. **Yield:** 2 cakes (8 wedges each).

Caramel-Pecan Apple Pie

(Pictured below)

PREP: 45 min. **BAKE:** 55 min. + cooling

The wonderful smell of this pie takes me back to my Granny's table in Virginia. Its scrumptious taste will put smiles on everybody's faces. —Gloria Castro, Santa Rosa, California

- 7 cups sliced peeled tart apples
- 1 teaspoon lemon juice
- 1 teaspoon vanilla extract
- 3/4 cup chopped pecans
- 1/3 cup packed brown sugar
- 3 tablespoons sugar
- 4-1/2 teaspoons ground cinnamon
- 1 tablespoon cornstarch
- 1/4 cup caramel ice cream topping, room temperature
- 1 unbaked pastry shell (9 inches)
- 3 tablespoons butter, melted
STREUSEL TOPPING:
- 3/4 cup all-purpose flour
- 2/3 cup chopped pecans
- 1/4 cup sugar
- 6 tablespoons cold butter
- 1/4 cup caramel ice cream topping, room temperature

In a large bowl, toss apples with lemon juice and vanilla. Combine the pecans, sugars, cinnamon and cornstarch; add to apple mixture and toss to coat. Pour caramel topping over bottom of pastry shell; top with apple mixture (shell will be full). Drizzle with butter.

For the streusel topping, combine the flour, pecans and sugar. Cut in butter until mixture resembles coarse crumbs. Sprinkle over filling.

Bake at 350° for 55-65 minutes or until filling is bubbly and topping is browned. Immediately drizzle with caramel topping. Cool on a wire rack. **Yield:** 8 servings.

Just Desserts

For some folks, dessert is the best part of the meal! With these favorite recipes for crisps, cobblers, candies, puddings, ice cream and more, no sweet tooth will ever have to do without.

HAPPY ENDINGS. Clockwise from upper left: Peach Rhubarb Crisp (p. 177), White Chocolate Berry Dessert (p. 174), Gingerbread Pudding Cake (p. 179), Fluffy Lemon Squares (p. 181) and Banana Split Brownie Pie (p. 180).

beat until smooth. Cover and refrigerate for 1 hour.

Heat a lightly greased 8-in. nonstick skillet. Stir batter; pour 2 tablespoons into center of skillet. Lift and tilt pan to evenly coat bottom. Cook until top appears dry; turn and cook 15-20 seconds longer. Remove to a wire rack. Repeat with remaining batter, greasing skillet as needed. When cool, stack crepes with waxed paper or paper towels in between.

For the topping, in a small saucepan, combine sugar and cornstarch; stir in water and lemon juice until smooth. Bring to a boil over medium heat; cook and stir for 1 minute or until thickened. Stir in extract and food coloring if desired. Cool. Add strawberries.

For the filling, in a small bowl, beat the cream until stiff peaks form; set aside. In a large bowl, beat the cream cheese, confectioners' sugar and vanilla until smooth; fold in whipped cream. Spoon 2 rounded tablespoons of filling down the center of each crepe; roll up. Top with strawberry topping. **Yield:** 22 crepes.

Strawberry Crepes

(Pictured above)

PREP: 25 min. + chilling **COOK:** 1 hour

I always feel like a French chef when I serve these pretty crepes. Although they take a little time to prepare, they're well worth the effort. My guests are always impressed.
—*Debra Latta, Port Matilda, Pennsylvania*

  1-1/2 cups milk
    3 eggs
    2 tablespoons butter, melted
  1/2 teaspoon lemon extract
  1-1/4 cups all-purpose flour
    2 tablespoons sugar
Dash salt
TOPPING:
  1/2 cup sugar
    2 tablespoons cornstarch
    3/4 cup water
    1 tablespoon lemon juice
    1 teaspoon strawberry extract
  1/4 teaspoon red food coloring, optional
    4 cups sliced fresh strawberries
FILLING:
    1 cup heavy whipping cream
    1 package (8 ounces) cream cheese, softened
    2 cups confectioners' sugar
    1 teaspoon vanilla extract

In a large bowl, combine milk, eggs, butter and extract. Combine flour, sugar and salt; add to milk mixture and

Chocolate Chip Mousse

(Pictured below)

PREP/TOTAL TIME: 15 min. + cooling

Chocolate always makes for a wonderful dessert. For your special occasion, reach for this recipe for a rich and creamy chocolate mousse.
—*Taste of Home Test Kitchen, Greendale, Wisconsin*

  1 cup (6 ounces) semisweet chocolate chips
  1 package (8 ounces) cream cheese, softened
  1 teaspoon vanilla extract
  1 carton (8 ounces) frozen whipped topping, thawed

In a microwave or heavy saucepan, melt chocolate chips; stir until smooth. Cool for 20 minutes.

Meanwhile, in a small bowl, beat cream cheese and vanilla until smooth; beat in melted chocolate. Fold in whipped topping. Spoon into dessert dishes. Refrigerate until serving. **Yield:** 4 servings.

For ganache, in a microwave-safe bowl, melt chocolate chips with cream; stir until smooth. Cool slightly; spread over filling. Refrigerate for 1-2 hours or until set. Carefully run a knife around edge of pan to loosen; remove sides of pan. Garnish with pecan halves. Refrigerate leftovers. **Yield:** 14-16 servings.

Pumpkin Rice Pudding

(Pictured below)

PREP: 15 min. **BAKE:** 25 min.

This pudding is the queen of comfort foods! It's creamy, spicy and smells incredible while baking. What a great way to use up leftover rice. —Dee Falk, Stromsburg, Nebraska

- **4 cups milk**
- **1 can (15 ounces) solid-pack pumpkin**
- **3/4 cup sugar**
- **1 teaspoon ground cinnamon**
- **1/2 teaspoon salt**
- **1/2 teaspoon ground ginger**
- **1/4 teaspoon ground cloves**
- **2 eggs, beaten**
- **3 cups cooked rice**
- **1/2 teaspoon vanilla extract**
- **Vanilla ice cream, optional**

In a large saucepan, combine the first seven ingredients. Bring to a boil over medium heat, stirring constantly. Gradually stir a small amount of milk mixture into the eggs; return all to the pan. Bring to a gentle boil, stirring constantly. Remove from the heat. Stir in rice and vanilla.

Pour into a greased 13-in. x 9-in. x 2-in. baking dish. Bake, uncovered, at 375° for 25-30 minutes or until a knife inserted near the center comes out clean. Serve warm with ice cream if desired. Refrigerate leftovers. **Yield:** 8 servings.

Praline Chocolate Dessert

(Pictured above)

PREP: 25 min. + chilling **BAKE:** 10 min. + cooling

A cookie crumb crust, luscious layers of praline and cream cheese, and a chocolate glaze make this rich dessert a true showstopper. It's worth the extra effort and freezes well, too. —Korrie Bastian, Clearfield, Utah

- **2 cups cream-filled chocolate sandwich cookie crumbs**
- **1/2 cup butter, melted**
- **1 cup chopped pecans**
- **PRALINE:**
- **1-1/2 cups butter, cubed**
- **1 cup packed brown sugar**
- **1 teaspoon vanilla extract**
- **FILLING:**
- **2 packages (8 ounces *each*) cream cheese, softened**
- **1/2 cup confectioners' sugar**
- **1/3 cup packed brown sugar**
- **GANACHE:**
- **1 cup (6 ounces) semisweet chocolate chips**
- **1/2 cup heavy whipping cream**
- **Pecan halves**

In a small bowl, combine cookie crumbs and butter. Press onto the bottom of a greased 9-in. springform pan. Place on a baking sheet. Bake at 350° for 10 minutes. Cool on a wire rack. Sprinkle with pecans.

For the praline, in a large saucepan over medium heat, bring the butter and brown sugar to a boil, stirring constantly. Reduce heat; simmer, uncovered, for 10 minutes. Remove from the heat; stir in vanilla. Pour over pecans. Refrigerate for 1-2 hours or until set.

In a large bowl, beat the filling ingredients until smooth. Spread over praline layer. Refrigerate for 1-2 hours or until set.

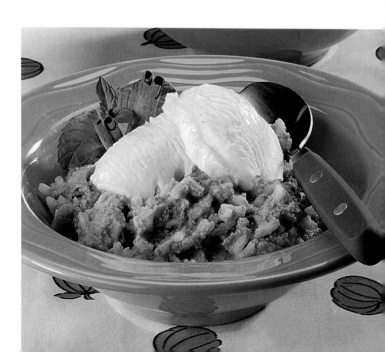

Cappuccino Cherry Trifle

(Pictured below)

PREP: 20 min. **COOK:** 15 min. + chilling

This is a rich dessert that's as pretty to look at as it is good to eat. The combination of dark sweet cherries, chocolate and homemade coffee custard is a real winner.
—Katie Sloan, Charlotte, North Carolina

- 3/4 cup sugar
- 1/4 cup cornstarch
- 2 tablespoons instant coffee granules
- 1 tablespoon baking cocoa
- 1-1/2 cups milk
- 2 tablespoons water
- 4 egg yolks, beaten
- 2 teaspoons vanilla extract
- 2-3/4 cups heavy whipping cream
- 2 loaves (10-3/4 ounces *each*) frozen pound cake, thawed and cut into 1-inch cubes
- 1 can (15 ounces) pitted dark sweet cherries
- 1 cup (6 ounces) semisweet chocolate chips

For the custard, combine the sugar, cornstarch, coffee granules and cocoa in a large saucepan. Stir in milk and water until smooth. Bring to a boil over medium heat; cook and stir for 1-2 minutes or until thick and bubbly.

Remove from the heat. Stir a small amount of hot mixture into yolks; return all to the pan, stirring constantly. Bring to a gentle boil; cook and stir 2 minutes longer. Remove from the heat; gently stir in vanilla. Refrigerate until cool.

In a large bowl, beat cream until stiff peaks form. Fold 2-1/2 cups whipped cream into cooled custard. Set aside the remaining whipped cream for garnish.

Place half of the cake cubes in a 3-qt. trifle bowl. Drain cherries, reserving juice; sprinkle cake with 3-4 tablespoons cherry juice. Top with half of the cherries, 1/3 cup chocolate chips and half of the custard mixture. Repeat layers. Garnish with reserved whipped cream and remaining chocolate chips. **Yield:** 12-14 servings.

Grandmother's Bread Pudding

(Pictured above)

PREP: 10 min. **BAKE:** 45 min.

Comforting is the best way to describe this lovely, flavorful bread pudding. And the drizzle of tangy lemon sauce offers a little zing!
—Edna Butler, Los Fresnos, Texas

- 5 eggs
- 3 cups milk
- 1-1/4 cups sugar
- 1 cup half-and-half cream
- 1/4 cup butter, melted and cooled
- 2 teaspoons vanilla extract
- 1 teaspoon almond extract
- 1/2 teaspoon ground nutmeg
- 4 cups cubed day-old white bread
- 4 cups cubed day-old wheat bread
- 1/3 cup raisins
- **SAUCE:**
- 1-1/2 cups sugar
- 1/3 cup cornstarch
- 1/4 teaspoon salt
- 2-1/4 cups cold water
- 3 egg yolks, beaten
- 1/3 cup lemon juice
- 2 tablespoons butter

In a large bowl, combine the first eight ingredients. Stir in the bread cubes and raisins. Transfer to a greased 13-in. x 9-in. x 2-in. baking dish. Bake, uncovered, at 350° for 45-55 minutes or until a knife inserted near the center comes out clean.

For the lemon sauce, combine the sugar, cornstarch, salt and water in a large saucepan until smooth. Bring to a boil over medium heat, stirring constantly. Remove from the heat.

...

Stir a small amount of hot filling into egg yolks; return all to the pan, stirring constantly. Bring to a gentle boil; cook and stir for 2 minutes.

Remove from the heat; gently stir in lemon juice and butter. Serve with bread pudding. Refrigerate leftovers. **Yield:** 12-15 servings.

Ladyfinger Lemon Torte

(Pictured below)

PREP: 30 min. + chilling + freezing

Golden ladyfingers frame the luscious custard filling of this lovely frozen dessert. Everyone enjoys the yummy combination of sweetness and lemony zest.

—Mrs. J. H. Carroll, Ottawa, Ontario

  5 **egg yolks, lightly beaten**
1-1/2 **cups sugar,** *divided*
  3/4 **cup lemon juice**
  2 **egg whites**
  1 **tablespoon grated lemon peel**
  2 **cups heavy whipping cream**
  2 **packages (3 ounces** *each***) ladyfingers, split**
Lemon peel and fresh mint leaves

In a heavy saucepan, combine egg yolks, 1-1/4 cups sugar, lemon juice and egg whites. Bring to a boil over medium heat; cook and stir for 8-10 minutes or until mixture reaches 160° or is thick enough to coat a metal spoon. Remove from heat. Cool quickly by placing pan in a bowl of ice water; stir for 2 minutes. Stir in lemon peel. Transfer to a bowl, press plastic wrap onto surface of custard. Chill for 2-3 hours or until partially set.

In a large bowl, beat the cream on medium speed until soft peaks form. Gradually beat in the remaining sugar, 1 tablespoon at a time, on high until stiff peaks form. Gradually fold whipped cream into the cooled lemon mixture.

Arrange 24 ladyfingers around edge of an ungreased

9-in. springform pan. Arrange 16 ladyfingers on bottom of pan. Spread with half of lemon mixture. Arrange remaining ladyfingers over lemon mixture; top with remaining lemon mixture.

Cover and freeze overnight. Remove from the freezer 5 minutes before cutting. Remove sides of the pan. Garnish with lemon peel and mint. **Yield:** 12 servings.

Caramel Chocolate Trifle

(Pictured above)

PREP: 20 min. **BAKE:** 20 min. + cooling

Every year at our family reunion we have a dessert competition, as well as dishes that have been passed down from generation to generation. This recipe is a family favorite.

—Barb Hausey, Independence, Missouri

  1 **package (9 ounces) devil's food cake mix**
  2 **packages (3.9 ounces** *each***) instant chocolate pudding mix**
  1 **carton (12 ounces) frozen whipped topping, thawed**
  1 **jar (12-1/4 ounces) caramel ice cream topping**
  1 **package (7-1/2 or 8 ounces) English toffee bits** *or* **almond brickle chips**

Prepare and bake cake according to package directions for an 8-in. square baking pan. Cool on a wire rack. Prepare pudding according to package directions.

Cut cake into 1-1/2-in. cubes; place half of the cubes in a 3-qt. trifle bowl or large glass serving bowl; lightly press down to fill in gaps. Top with half *each* of the whipped topping, pudding, caramel topping and toffee bits; repeat layers. Cover and refrigerate until serving. **Yield:** 16 servings.

Cool & Creamy Sensations

Grand Prize Winner

Strawberry Cheesecake Ice Cream

(Pictured above)

PREP: 20 min. + cooling
FREEZE: 2 hours

This custard–like ice cream is so rich and creamy that it tastes like you fussed for hours. But it's easy to make…and pretty, too. I like to serve it with chocolate fudge sauce.—Irene Yoder, Fillmore, New York

- 3 **cups sugar**
- 3 **tablespoons all-purpose flour**

Pinch salt

- 8 **cups milk**
- 4 **eggs, lightly beaten**
- 1 **package (8 ounces) cream cheese, cubed**
- 1 **teaspoon vanilla extract**
- 3 **cups fresh *or* frozen unsweetened strawberries, thawed**
- 2 **cups heavy whipping cream**

In a heavy saucepan, combine the sugar, flour and salt. Gradually add milk until smooth. Bring to a boil over medium heat; cook and stir for 2 minutes or until thickened. Remove from the heat; cool slightly. Whisk a small amount of hot milk mixture into the eggs; return all to the pan, whisking constantly. Cook and stir over low heat until mixture reaches at least 160° and coats the back of a metal spoon. Stir in the cream cheese until melted.

Remove from the heat. Cool quickly by placing pan in a bowl of ice water; stir for 2 minutes. Stir in vanilla. Press plastic wrap onto surface of custard. Refrigerate for several hours or overnight.

Stir the strawberries and cream into the custard. Fill cylinder of ice cream freezer two-thirds full; freeze according to the manufacturer's directions. Refrigerate the remaining mixture until ready to freeze. When ice cream is frozen, transfer to a freezer container; freeze for 2-4 hours before serving. **Yield:** 1 gallon.

Peach Ice Cream

PREP: 15 min. + chilling
FREEZE: 30 min.

When peaches are in season, this recipe is at the top of my list. The pureed fruit lends a fresh flavor to the silky–smooth ice cream. You'll have to make it more than once, though, because the first batch never lasts long!
—Toni Box, Weaver, Alabama

- 2 **cups half-and-half cream**
- 3-1/2 **cups sugar**
- 3/4 **teaspoon salt**
- 6 **eggs, beaten**
- 4 **cups heavy whipping cream**
- 2 **teaspoons vanilla extract**
- 6 **to 8 medium peach, peeled and sliced *or* 4 cups frozen unsweetened peach slices**

In a saucepan, heat half-and-half to 175°; stir in the sugar and salt until dissolved. Whisk a small amount of hot cream mixture into the eggs. Return all to the pan, whisking constantly. Cook and stir over low heat until the mixture reaches at least 160° and coats the back of a metal spoon.

Remove from the heat. Cool quickly by placing pan in a bowl of ice water; stir for 2 minutes. Stir in whipping cream and vanilla. Press plastic wrap onto surface of custard. Refrigerate for several hours or overnight.

In a blender or food processor, puree peaches. Stir into the custard. Fill cylinder of ice cream freezer two-thirds full; freeze according to manufacturer's directions.

Refrigerate the remaining mixture until ready to freeze, stirring before freezing each batch. Allow to ripen in an ice cream freezer or firm up in the refrigerator freezer for 2-4 hours before serving. **Yield:** about 3 quarts.

Butter Pecan Ice Cream

(Pictured above right)

PREP: 15 min. + chilling
FREEZE: 30 min.

This thick buttery ice cream sure beats store–bought versions. And with its pretty color and plentiful pecan crunch, it's nice enough to serve guests at a summer party.
—Jenny White, Glen, Mississippi

- 1/2 **cup chopped pecans**
- 1 **tablespoon butter**
- 1-1/2 **cups half-and-half cream**
- 1 **cup packed brown sugar**
- 2 **eggs, lightly beaten**

3 cups milk
3 cups half-and-half cream
9 squares (1 ounce *each*) semisweet chocolate
2-3/4 cups sugar
3/4 teaspoon salt
6 cups heavy whipping cream
3 cups miniature marshmallows
2-1/4 cups miniature semisweet chocolate chips
1-1/2 cups chopped pecans
6 teaspoons vanilla extract

In a large saucepan, combine the milk and half-and-half; heat to 175°. Add the chocolate, sugar and salt; stir until chocolate is melted and sugar is dissolved.

Remove from the heat. Cool quickly by placing pan in a bowl of ice water; stir for 2 minutes. Cool completely. Transfer to a large bowl; stir in the remaining ingredients. Cover and refrigerate for at least 30 minutes.

Fill cylinder of ice cream freezer two-thirds full; freeze according to the manufacturer's directions. Refrigerate the remaining mixture until ready to freeze. When the ice cream is frozen, transfer to a freezer container; freeze for 2-4 hours before serving. **Yield:** about 4-1/2 quarts.

Chocolate Ice Cream Sandwiches

(Pictured above)

PREP: 20 min.
BAKE: 10 min. + cooling

These cute, chewy cookies made with two kinds of chocolate form a perfect sandwich for vanilla ice cream...or any flavor you prefer. I really enjoy making desserts for my family, and this one hits the spot on hot Texas days.
—Michelle Wolford, San Antonio, Texas

1/3 cup butter, softened
1/3 cup sugar
1/3 cup packed brown sugar
1 egg
1/2 teaspoon vanilla extract
3/4 cup plus 2 tablespoons all-purpose flour
1/4 cup baking cocoa
1/2 teaspoon baking powder
1/4 teaspoon baking soda
1/4 teaspoon salt
1/2 cup semisweet chocolate chips
1 pint vanilla ice cream

In a bowl, cream the butter and sugars. Beat in the egg and vanilla. Combine the flour, cocoa, baking powder, baking soda and salt; add to creamed mixture and mix well.

Drop by rounded tablespoonfuls 2 in. apart onto greased baking sheets, forming 16 cookies. Flatten slightly with a glass. Sprinkle with chocolate chips. Bake at 375° for 8-10 minutes or until set. Remove to wire racks to cool.

To assemble the sandwiches, place 1/4 cup ice cream on the bottom of half the cookies. Top with remaining cookies. Wrap each in plastic wrap. Freeze overnight. **Yield:** 8 ice cream sandwiches.

1/2 cup heavy whipping cream
1 teaspoon vanilla extract

In a small skillet, toast pecans in butter for 5-6 minutes or until lightly browned. Cool.

In a heavy saucepan, heat half-and-half to 175°; stir in the brown sugar until dissolved. Whisk a small amount of hot cream mixture into the eggs; return all to the pan, whisking constantly. Cook and stir over low heat until mixture reaches at least 160° and coats the back of a metal spoon.

Remove from the heat. Cool quickly by placing pan in a bowl of ice water; stir for 2 minutes. Stir in whipping cream and vanilla. Press plastic wrap onto the surface of custard. Refrigerate for several hours or overnight. Stir in toasted pecans.

Fill cylinder of ice cream freezer two-thirds full; freeze according to the manufacturer's directions. Refrigerate remaining mixture until ready to freeze. Allow to ripen in ice cream freezer or firm up in the refrigerator freezer for 2-4 hours before serving. **Yield:** 1 quart.

Rocky Road Ice Cream

(Pictured at right)

PREP: 15 min. + cooling
FREEZE: 30 min.

My daughters like it when I put this ice cream in cones. We especially like the marshmallows, chocolate chips and chopped pecans. Sometimes we even add extra chips on top...and dollops of whipped cream, too!
—Dale Langford, Atwater, California

Cranberry-Topped Lemon Tarts

(Pictured above)

PREP: 45 min. + chilling **BAKE:** 20 min. + cooling

The delicious combination of colors and tangy-sweet flavors makes this a very pretty, very special dessert. You'll receive a ton of compliments on your culinary expertise.
—Ruth Lee, Troy, Ontario

      2 cups all-purpose flour
      3 tablespoons sugar
    3/4 teaspoon salt
      1 cup cold butter
TOPPING:
      3 cups fresh *or* frozen cranberries
  1-1/4 cups sugar
    1/4 cup water
FILLING:
      5 eggs
  1-1/2 cups sugar
    3/4 cup lemon juice
    1/3 cup butter, softened
      4 teaspoons grated lemon peel
GARNISH:
      1 medium lemon, cut into 1/4-inch slices
    1/2 cup sugar
    1/4 cup water

In a bowl, combine the flour, sugar and salt; cut in butter until mixture resembles coarse crumbs. Stir until dough forms a ball. Divide into eight portions; press each onto the bottom and up the sides of eight 4-in. tart pans.

Cover and refrigerate for 20 minutes. Bake at 350° for 20-25 minutes or until golden brown. Cool on wire racks.

For the topping, in a large saucepan, combine the cranberries, sugar and water. Cook over medium heat until berries have popped, about 20 minutes.

Meanwhile, for the filling, in a small saucepan, whisk eggs. Stir in the sugar, lemon juice, butter and lemon peel. Cook and stir over medium heat for 20-25 minutes or until filling is thickened and reaches 160°. Transfer to a small bowl; cover and refrigerate for 1 hour. Transfer berry topping to another bowl; refrigerate until serving.

Spoon filling into tart shells. Chill, uncovered, until set. For garnish, in a small saucepan, bring lemon slices, sugar and water to a boil. Reduce heat; simmer, uncovered, for 20-25 minutes or until lemon is tender. Cut slices in half; chill.

Just before serving, spoon cranberry topping over tarts. Garnish with lemon slices. **Yield:** 8 servings.

Chocolate-Covered Cheesecake Squares

PREP: 1 hour **BAKE:** 35 min. + freezing

Satisfy your cheesecake craving with these bite-sized treats. Dipped in chocolate, these sweet, creamy delights are party favorites. But be warned...you won't be able to eat just one!
—Esther Neustaeter, La Crete, Alberta

      1 cup graham cracker crumbs
    1/4 cup finely chopped pecans
    1/4 cup butter, melted
FILLING:
      2 packages (8 ounces *each*) cream cheese, softened
    1/2 cup sugar
    1/4 cup sour cream
      2 eggs, lightly beaten
    1/2 teaspoon vanilla extract
COATING:
     24 squares (1 ounce *each*) semisweet chocolate
      3 tablespoons shortening

Line a 9-in. square baking pan with foil and grease the foil. In a small bowl, combine the graham cracker crumbs, pecans and butter. Press into prepared pan; set aside.

For the filling, in a large bowl, beat cream cheese, sugar and sour cream until smooth. Add eggs; beat on low just until combined. Stir in vanilla. Pour over crust.

Bake at 325° for 35-40 minutes or until the center is almost set. Cool on a wire rack. Refrigerate until chilled. Freeze overnight.

In a microwave-safe bowl, melt the chocolate and shortening, stirring occasionally until smooth. Cool slightly. Using foil, lift cheesecake out of pan. Gently peel off foil; cut into 49 squares. Remove a few pieces at a time for dipping; keep remaining squares refrigerated until ready to dip.

Using a toothpick, completely dip the squares, one at a time, in melted chocolate. Place on waxed paper-lined baking sheets; spoon about 1 teaspoon of the chocolate over each. (Reheat chocolate if needed to finish dipping.) Let stand for 20 minutes or until set. Store in an airtight container in the refrigerator or freezer. **Yield:** 49 servings.

Rich Hot Fudge Sauce

(Pictured below)

PREP/TOTAL TIME: 30 min.

I've made this scrumptious topping ever since the early 1980s. It always turns out smooth and yummy. The dark chocolate flavor, with a hint of rum extract, is not overly sweet but still satisfies a chocoholic's cravings. —Carol Hunihan, Ann Arbor, Michigan

- 1 cup heavy whipping cream
- 3/4 cup butter, cubed
- 1-1/3 cups packed brown sugar
- 1/4 cup sugar
- Pinch salt
- 1 cup baking cocoa
- 1/2 cup plus 2 tablespoons light corn syrup
- 2 squares (1 ounce *each*) unsweetened chocolate
- 3 teaspoons vanilla extract
- 1 to 2 teaspoons rum extract

In a heavy saucepan, combine the cream and butter. Cook and stir over medium-low heat until butter is melted. Add the sugars and salt; cook and stir until sugar is dissolved, about 4 minutes. Stir in the cocoa and corn syrup; cook and stir for 3 minutes or until cocoa is blended.

Add chocolate; cook and stir 3-4 minutes longer or until chocolate is melted. Reduce heat to low. Simmer for 12-16 minutes or until desired thickness is reached, stirring constantly. Remove from the heat; stir in extracts. Cool slightly. Serve warm over ice cream. Refrigerate leftovers. **Yield:** about 3-1/2 cups.

Strawberry Puff Pastry Dessert

(Pictured above)

PREP: 30 min. **BAKE:** 15 min. + cooling

My failed attempt to make a triple–layer strawberry malt mousse resulted in this scrumptious dessert. I don't use puff pastry often, but it was simple to work with. My husband declared it one of the best desserts ever. —Anna Ginsberg, Austin, Texas

- 1 package (17.3 ounces) frozen puff pastry
- 5 cups sliced fresh strawberries, *divided*
- 6 squares (1 ounce *each*) white baking chocolate
- 1 package (8 ounces) cream cheese, softened
- 1 teaspoon vanilla extract
- 1 cup confectioners' sugar
- 1/3 cup malted milk powder
- 2 cups heavy whipping cream, whipped
- Strawberry syrup, optional

Thaw one puff pastry sheet (save remaining sheet for another use). Unfold pastry; cut lengthwise into three 3-in.-wide strips. Cut each strip into thirds, making nine squares. Place 1 in. apart on ungreased baking sheets. Bake at 400° for 11-13 minutes or until golden brown. Remove to wire racks to cool.

Place 2-1/2 cups strawberries in a blender; cover and puree. Set aside. In a large microwave-safe bowl, melt the white chocolate; cool slightly. Add cream cheese and vanilla; beat until smooth. Beat in the confectioners' sugar and malted milk powder until smooth. Stir in the puree. Fold in whipped cream.

Split pastry squares in half horizontally. Line an ungreased 13-in. x 9-in. x 2-in. dish with bottom pastry halves, cut side up; spread with 3-1/2 cups strawberry cream. Top with 1 cup of sliced berries. Cover with pastry tops, cut side down.

Spread with remaining strawberry cream. Sprinkle with remaining berries. Drizzle with strawberry syrup if desired. Refrigerate leftovers. **Yield:** 12 servings.

Raisin Pecan Baklava

(Pictured below)

PREP: 30 min. **BAKE:** 20 min. + cooling

This lightened–up version of traditional baklava is to die for, and it looks beautiful on a goody tray. The toasted pecans really stand out, and the Grape–Nuts add wonderful crunch without very many calories. —Liv Vors, Peterborough, Ontario

- 1/3 **cup sugar**
- 1/4 **cup water**
- 3 **tablespoons honey**
- 4-1/2 **teaspoons lemon juice**
- 1/2 **cup chopped pecans, toasted**
- 1/2 **cup Grape-Nuts cereal**
- 1/2 **cup raisins**
- 1/3 **cup packed brown sugar**
- 1/2 **teaspoon ground cinnamon**
- 8 **sheets phyllo dough (14 inches x 9 inches)**

In a small saucepan, combine the sugar, water, honey and lemon juice. Bring to a boil; cook and stir until sugar is dissolved. Remove from the heat.

Combine the pecans, cereal, raisins, brown sugar and the cinnamon. Stir in 3 tablespoons of honey mixture; set aside.

Stack the phyllo sheets on a flat work surface; trim 1 in. from the 9-in. side. Cut in half lengthwise, forming 8-in. x 7-in. rectangles. Overlap two pieces in a greased 8-in. square baking dish; spray with cooking spray. Repeat three times.

Spread nut mixture over top. Overlap two pieces of phyllo to cover nut mixture; spray with cooking spray. Repeat with remaining phyllo. Using a sharp knife, cut into 24 rectangles, about 2-1/2 in. x 1 in.

Bake, uncovered, at 350° for 20-25 minutes or until golden brown. Reheat reserved honey mixture; pour over hot baklava. Cool completely on a wire rack. **Yield:** 2 dozen.

White Chocolate Berry Dessert

(Pictured above and on page 164)

PREP: 35 min. **BAKE:** 40 min. + cooling

After creating this recipe and fine–tuning it a little bit, I knew I had a hit! The sweet flavor of white chocolate combined with strawberries can't be beat. —Sarah Gwyn, Orlando, Florida

- 8 **squares (1 ounce *each*) white baking chocolate**
- 6 **tablespoons butter, cubed**
- 2 **eggs**
- 1/2 **cup sugar**
- 3 **teaspoons vanilla extract**
- 1 **cup all-purpose flour**
- 1/4 **teaspoon salt**

FILLING:
- 1 **package (8 ounces) cream cheese, softened**
- 3 **squares (1 ounce *each*) white baking chocolate, melted and cooled**
- 1 **egg, lightly beaten**
- 1/3 **cup sugar**
- 1/3 **cup sour cream**
- 1 **teaspoon vanilla extract**

TOPPING:
- 1 **carton (8 ounces) frozen whipped topping, thawed**
- 4 **squares (1 ounce *each*) white baking chocolate, melted and cooled**
- 1 **pint fresh strawberries, sliced**

In a microwave-safe bowl, melt white chocolate and butter at 70% power; stir until smooth. Cool.

In a large bowl, beat eggs and sugar until lemon-colored. Beat in melted chocolate mixture and vanilla. Combine flour and salt; beat into egg mixture. Spread into a greased 13-in. x 9-in. x 2-in. baking dish; set aside.

For filling, in a small bowl, beat cream cheese and white chocolate. Beat in the egg, sugar, sour cream and vanilla just until combined. Carefully spread over bottom layer. Cut through filling with a knife to swirl.

Bake at 350° for 40-45 minutes or until a toothpick inserted near the center comes out clean. Cool on a wire rack.

Just before serving, fold whipped topping into white chocolate. Fold in strawberries; spread over dessert. Cut into squares. Refrigerate leftovers. **Yield:** 15 servings.

Cinnamon-Raisin Soft Pretzels

PREP: 40 min. + rising **BAKE:** 15 min.

I came up with this recipe after sampling pretzels at a Pennsylvania Dutch farmers market. They're a nice morning treat—quicker than cinnamon rolls and easy for kids to eat.
—Susie King, Quarrryville, Pennsylvania

> 1 **package (1/4 ounce) active dry yeast**
> 1-1/2 **cups warm water (110° to 115°)**
> 2 **tablespoons brown sugar**
> 1 **teaspoon salt**
> 2 **cups cake flour**
> 2 **to 2-1/4 cups all-purpose flour**
> 3/4 **cup raisins**
> 2 **tablespoons baking soda**
> 2 **cups hot water (120° to 130°)**
> 3/4 **cup sugar**
> 1 **teaspoon ground cinnamon**
> 3 **tablespoons butter, melted**

In a large bowl, dissolve the yeast in warm water. Stir in the brown sugar and salt. Add the cake flour; stir well. Add enough all-purpose flour to form a soft dough. Stir in raisins.

Turn onto a floured surface; knead until smooth and elastic, about 6-8 minutes. Place in a greased bowl, turning once to grease top. Cover and let rise in a warm place until dough has risen slightly, about 30 minutes. Punch dough down; divide into 14 balls. Roll each ball into a 15-in. rope.

In a bowl, dissolve the baking soda in hot water. Dip each rope in the baking soda mixture; drain on paper towels. Form into pretzel shapes and place on greased baking sheets. Bake at 400° for 15 minutes or until golden brown.

Combine sugar and cinnamon in a small bowl. Brush pretzels with butter, then dip in cinnamon-sugar. Serve warm. **Yield:** 14 pretzels.

Cocoa Powder

There are two types of unsweetened cocoa powder: natural and Dutch-processed. Natural cocoa powder tastes bitter and imparts an intense chocolate flavor. Dutch processed is alkalized, which neutralizes the cocoa's acidity; it has a milder flavor and is easier to dissolve in liquids.

Tiramisu Cheesecake Dessert

(Pictured above)

PREP: 20 min. **BAKE:** 40 min. + chilling

I wasn't a big fan of tiramisu until I tried this recipe with its distinctive cheesecake– and coffee–flavored layers. It's one of my favorite desserts to make during the fall.
—Christie Nelson, Taylorville, Illinois

> 1 **package (12 ounces) vanilla wafers**
> 5 **teaspoons instant coffee granules, *divided***
> 3 **tablespoons hot water, *divided***
> 4 **packages (8 ounces *each*) cream cheese, softened**
> 1 **cup sugar**
> 1 **cup (8 ounces) sour cream**
> 4 **eggs, lightly beaten**
> 1 **cup whipped topping**
> 1 **tablespoon baking cocoa**

Layer half of wafers in a greased 13-in. x 9-in. x 2-in. baking dish. In a small bowl, dissolve 2 teaspoons coffee granules in 2 tablespoons hot water. Brush wafers with half of coffee; set remaining mixture aside.

In a large bowl, beat the cream cheese, sugar and sour cream until smooth. Add eggs; beat on low speed just until combined. Divide batter in half. Dissolve remaining coffee granules in remaining hot water; stir into one portion of batter. Spread over wafers. Layer with remaining wafers; brush with reserved coffee. Top with remaining batter.

Bake at 325° for 40-45 minutes or until center is almost set. Cool on a wire rack for 10 minutes. Carefully run a knife around edge of dish to loosen; cool 1 hour longer. Refrigerate overnight.

Spread with whipped topping; dust with cocoa. Refrigerate leftovers. **Yield:** 12 servings.

Cobblers, Crisps & Crumbles

Grand Prize Winner

Apple Crumble

(Pictured above)

PREP: 30 min.
BAKE: 40 min. + cooling

While visiting friends in New Zealand, I was able to watch this dessert being made. Back at home, I came up with my own version. It's great with vanilla ice cream or fresh whipped cream.
—Carol Simpkins, Santa Cruz, California

- **8 sheets phyllo dough (14 inches x 9 inches)**
- **Butter-flavored cooking spray**
- **1/2 cup packed brown sugar**
- **2 tablespoons all-purpose flour**
- **1/2 teaspoon ground ginger**
- **1/2 teaspoon ground cinnamon**
- **4 medium tart apples, peeled and sliced**

TOPPING:

- **1/2 cup all-purpose flour**
- **1/2 cup packed brown sugar**
- **1/2 cup soft whole wheat bread crumbs**
- **1/4 teaspoon ground ginger**
- **1/4 teaspoon ground cinnamon**
- **1/2 cup cold butter**
- **1/4 cup slivered almonds**

Cut phyllo sheets in half; spritz with butter-flavored spray. Layer phyllo, sprayed side up, in a greased 8-in. square baking dish.

In a large bowl, combine the brown sugar, flour, ginger and cinnamon; add apples and toss to coat. Spoon over phyllo dough.

For the topping, combine the flour, brown sugar, bread crumbs, ginger and cinnamon; cut in butter until mixture resembles coarse crumbs. Add almonds; sprinkle over apple mixture.

Bake at 350° for 40-45 minutes or until filling is bubbly and topping is golden. Cool for 10 minutes before serving. **Yield:** 9 servings.

Raspberry Pear Crisp

PREP: 15 min.
BAKE: 25 min. + cooling

We grow our very own luscious red raspberries. The ones we don't feast on are frozen for winter. This hearty recipe combines the berries with fresh pears and a crunchy cereal topping.
—Fancheon Resler, Bluffton, Indiana

- **2 cups sliced peeled fresh pears**
- **2 cups fresh or frozen raspberries**
- **3/4 cup packed brown sugar, divided**
- **1 teaspoon ground cinnamon, divided**
- **1/2 cup all-purpose flour**
- **3 tablespoons cold butter**
- **1 cup cranberry almond whole grain cereal, lightly crushed**
- **Vanilla ice cream, optional**

In a large bowl, combine the pears, raspberries, 1/4 cup brown sugar and 1/2 teaspoon cinnamon. Spoon into a greased 9-in. pie plate.

In a small bowl, combine the flour and remaining brown sugar and cinnamon; cut in butter until mixture resembles coarse crumbs. Stir in cereal. Sprinkle over fruit.

Bake at 375° for 25-30 minutes or until filling is bubbly and topping is golden brown. Cool for 10 minutes. Serve with ice cream if desired. **Yield:** 6 servings.

Editor's Note: If using frozen raspberries, do not thaw before adding to the fruit mixture.

Double-Berry Crisp

(Pictured above)

PREP: 20 min.
BAKE: 25 min. + cooling

This sweet-tart treat has an extra-crispy topping, thanks to the easy addition of cornflakes. Orange juice and orange peel accent the blueberry-raspberry flavor.
—Bernadette Beaton, Goose River, Prince Edward Island

- **1 cup sugar**
- **1/4 cup cornstarch**
- **2 tablespoons orange juice**

1 teaspoon grated orange peel

2 cups fresh *or* frozen raspberries

2 cups fresh *or* frozen blueberries

1 cup old-fashioned oats

1/2 cup cornflakes

1/2 cup packed brown sugar

1/2 teaspoon ground cinnamon

1/4 teaspoon salt

1/4 cup butter, melted

In a large saucepan, combine the sugar, cornstarch, orange juice, orange peel and berries until blended. Bring to a boil; cook and stir for 2 minutes or until thickened and bubbly. Pour into a greased 8-in. square baking dish.

In a bowl, combine the oats, cornflakes, brown sugar, cinnamon and salt; stir in butter. Sprinkle over berry mixture. Bake at 350° for 25-30 minutes or until filling is bubbly. Cool for 10 minutes before serving. **Yield:** 6 servings.

Editor's Note: If using frozen raspberries, do not thaw before adding to the blueberry mixture.

Blueberry Cornmeal Cobbler

(Pictured below)

PREP: 20 min. + standing
BAKE: 35 min.

Cornbread, blueberries and maple syrup butter give this special dessert a taste that's different from any cobbler you've had before. I came across the yummy recipe many years ago.

—*Judy Watson, Tipton, Indiana*

4 cups fresh blueberries

1 cup plus 2 tablespoons sugar

1 tablespoon quick-cooking tapioca

2 teaspoons grated lemon peel

1 teaspoon ground cinnamon

1/4 to 1/2 teaspoon ground nutmeg

TOPPING:

1/2 cup butter, softened, **divided**

1 cup confectioners' sugar

1 egg

1 cup all-purpose flour

1/2 cup cornmeal

2 teaspoons baking powder

1/2 teaspoon baking soda

1/2 teaspoon salt

3/4 cup buttermilk

2 tablespoons maple syrup

In a large bowl, combine the blueberries, sugar, tapioca, lemon peel, ground cinnamon and nutmeg. Let stand for 15 minutes. Pour into a greased 11-in. x 7-in. x 2-in. baking dish.

For topping, in a small bowl, beat 1/4 cup butter and confectioners' sugar. Add the egg; beat well. Combine the flour, cornmeal, baking powder, baking soda and salt; add to creamed mixture alternately with buttermilk, beating just until combined. Pour over berry mixture. Bake at 375° for 35-40 minutes or until a toothpick inserted near the center comes out clean.

In a small saucepan, melt remaining butter over low heat. Remove from the heat; stir in the syrup. Brush over corn bread. Broil 4-6 in. from the heat for 1-2 minutes or until bubbly. Serve warm. **Yield:** 12 servings.

Peach Rhubarb Crisp

(Pictured above right and on page 164)

PREP: 20 min. **BAKE:** 30 min.

When a visit to the local farmers market left me with an abundance of quickly ripening peaches and several stalks of rhubarb, I created this wonderful dessert recipe.

—*Sandy Kimble, Salinas, California*

3/4 cup sugar

3 tablespoons all-purpose flour

1/2 teaspoon ground nutmeg

1/2 teaspoon grated lemon peel

1/8 teaspoon salt

3 cups sliced fresh *or* frozen rhubarb

2-1/2 cups chopped peeled fresh peaches *or* frozen unsweetened peach slices, chopped

TOPPING:

1/2 cup all-purpose flour

1/2 cup old-fashioned oats

1/2 cup packed brown sugar

3/4 teaspoon ground cinnamon

1/8 teaspoon salt

5 tablespoons cold butter

In a large bowl, combine sugar, flour, nutmeg, lemon peel, salt, rhubarb and peaches. Transfer to a greased 11-in. x 7-in. x 2-in. baking dish.

In a bowl, combine the flour, oats, brown sugar, cinnamon and salt. Cut in butter until mixture resembles coarse crumbs; sprinkle over fruit. Bake at 375° for 30-35 minutes or until bubbly and fruit is tender. Serve warm or cold. **Yield:** 6-8 servings.

Editor's Note: If using frozen rhubarb, measure rhubarb while still frozen, then thaw completely. Drain in a colander, but do not press liquid out.

cook and stir the apples in butter over medium heat for 2 minutes. Combine the sugar, flour and cinnamon; stir into skillet. Cook 3 minutes longer. Reduce heat to low; cook, uncovered, for 4-6 minutes or until apples are tender, stirring frequently.

In a small bowl, combine the cheese topping ingredients. For the streusel, in a small bowl, combine flour and sugar; cut in butter until crumbly.

Pat dough onto a greased 14-in. pizza pan, building up edges slightly. Spread with cheese topping, then apple topping. Sprinkle with streusel. Bake at 375° for 20-25 minutes or until crust is golden brown. Serve warm or cold. **Yield:** 10-12 servings.

Apple Pizza

(Pictured above)

PREP: 40 min. **BAKE:** 20 min.

Pizza is a favorite at our house, so when I had some apples to use up, I started searching for an apple–pizza recipe. I tailored this one to fit my family's tastes.
—*Brenda Mowrey, Taylors, South Carolina*

- **2-1/3 to 3 cups all-purpose flour**
- **3 tablespoons sugar**
- **1 package (1/4 ounce) active dry yeast**
- **1/2 teaspoon salt**
- **1/2 cup water**
- **1/4 cup milk**
- **1/4 cup butter, cubed**

APPLE TOPPING:
- **4 cups sliced peeled Granny Smith apples**
- **2 tablespoons butter**
- **1/2 cup sugar**
- **2 tablespoons all-purpose flour**
- **1 teaspoon ground cinnamon**

CHEESE TOPPING:
- **4 ounces cream cheese, softened**
- **1/4 cup packed brown sugar**
- **2 tablespoons caramel ice cream topping**

STREUSEL:
- **2/3 cup all-purpose flour**
- **1/3 cup sugar**
- **1/4 cup cold butter, cubed**

In a large bowl, combine 1-1/2 cups flour, sugar, yeast and salt. In a saucepan, heat water, milk and butter to 120°-130°. Add to dry ingredients; beat for 2 minutes. Stir in enough remaining flour to form a firm dough. Turn onto a floured surface; cover and let rest for 15 minutes.

Meanwhile, for the apple topping, in a large skillet,

Strawberry Tartlets

(Pictured below)

PREP: 25 min. **BAKE:** 10 min. + cooling

This elegant–looking dessert is easy to prepare, and the cute wonton "cups" can be made in advance. They're a different way to present fresh strawberries when entertaining.
—*Joy Van Meter, Thornton, Colorado*

- **12 wonton wrappers**
- **3 tablespoons butter, melted**
- **1/3 cup packed brown sugar**
- **3/4 cup Mascarpone cheese**
- **2 tablespoons honey**
- **2 teaspoons orange juice**
- **3 cups fresh strawberries, sliced**
- **Whipped cream and fresh mint, optional**

Brush one side of each wonton wrapper with butter. Place brown sugar in a shallow bowl; press buttered side of wontons into sugar to coat. Press wontons sugared side up into greased muffin cups. Bake at 325° for 7-9 minutes or until edges are lightly browned. Remove to a wire rack to cool.

In a bowl, combine the cheese, honey and orange juice. Spoon about 1 tablespoon into each wonton cup. Top with strawberries. Garnish with whipped cream and mint if desired. **Yield:** 1 dozen.

Lemon Cheesecake Dessert

(Pictured above)

PREP: 25 min. **BAKE:** 30 min. + chill

Everyone will know spring has arrived when you serve these yummy, yellow cheesecake squares. Cool and refreshing, this dessert cuts easily and keeps for several days in the refrigerator.
—Patty Auxier, Royalton, Kentucky

      2 cups graham cracker crumbs
  1/4 cup sugar
  1/2 cup butter, melted
FILLING:
      4 packages (8 ounces *each*) cream cheese,
        softened
  1-1/4 cups sugar
      1 package (3 ounces) lemon gelatin
      1 teaspoon lemon extract
      5 eggs, lightly beaten
SAUCE:
      1 package (2.9 ounces) cook-and-serve lemon
        pudding mix
  1/4 cup sugar
  2-1/2 cups cold water

In a small bowl, combine cracker crumbs, sugar and butter. Press onto the bottom and 1 in. up the sides of a greased 13-in. x 9-in. x 2-in. baking dish. Refrigerate.

For the filling, in a large bowl, beat cream cheese and sugar until smooth. Add dry gelatin and lemon extract; beat 3 minutes longer. Add eggs; beat on low speed just until combined. Pour into crust.

Bake at 325° for 30-40 minutes or until center is almost set. Cool on a wire rack for 1 hour. Cover and refrigerate overnight.

For the lemon sauce, in a small saucepan, combine the pudding mix and sugar. Gradually stir in water. Cook and stir over medium heat until the mixture comes to a boil. Cook and stir 1-2 minutes longer or until thickened. Transfer to a bowl. Cover the surface with waxed paper; refrigerate until chilled. Serve with dessert. **Yield:** 12 servings (2 cups sauce).

Gingerbread Pudding Cake

(Pictured below and on page 164)

PREP: 20 min. **COOK:** 2 hours + standing

A handful of spices and a half cup of molasses give this delightful dessert a comforting, old-fashioned flavor. It's pretty, too, with a dollop of whipped cream and a mint sprig on top.
—Barbara Cook, Yuma, Arizona

  1/4 cup butter, softened
  1/4 cup sugar
      1 egg white
      1 teaspoon vanilla extract
  1/2 cup molasses
      1 cup water
  1-1/4 cups all-purpose flour
  3/4 teaspoon baking soda
  1/2 teaspoon ground cinnamon
  1/2 teaspoon ground ginger
  1/4 teaspoon salt
  1/4 teaspoon ground allspice
  1/8 teaspoon ground nutmeg
  1/2 cup chopped pecans
TOPPING:
      6 tablespoons brown sugar
  3/4 cup hot water
  2/3 cup butter, melted

In a large bowl, cream butter and sugar until light and fluffy. Beat in egg white and vanilla.

Combine molasses and water until blended. Combine the flour, baking soda, cinnamon, ginger, salt, allspice and nutmeg; add to creamed mixture alternately with molasses mixture, beating well after each addition. Fold in pecans.

Pour into a greased 3-qt. slow cooker. Sprinkle with brown sugar. Combine hot water and butter; pour over batter (do not stir).

Cover and cook on high for 2 to 2-1/2 hours or until a toothpick inserted near the center of cake comes out clean. Turn off heat. Let stand for 15 minutes. Serve warm. **Yield:** 6-8 servings.

Mixed Nut Chocolate Tart

(Pictured below)

PREP: 20 min. **BAKE:** 35 min. + cooling

A buttery shortbread crust holds a delectable filling made with chocolate and a mix of chopped pistachios, almonds and pecans. It's impressive yet easy to prepare. I guarantee it will become one of your most requested desserts.
—Debbie Cross, Sharon, Pennsylvania

    1-1/2 cups all-purpose flour
      1/4 cup sugar
      1/2 cup plus 1 tablespoon cold butter
        6 tablespoons heavy whipping cream
    1-1/2 teaspoons vanilla extract
FILLING:
        1 cup pistachios
        1 cup pecan halves
      3/4 cup unblanched almonds
        3 eggs
      3/4 cup light corn syrup
      1/4 cup packed brown sugar
      1/4 cup butter, melted
    1-1/2 teaspoons almond extract
        1 teaspoon vanilla extract
        1 cup milk chocolate chips
Whipped cream

In a small bowl, combine flour and sugar; cut in butter until mixture resembles fine crumbs. Add cream and vanilla, tossing with a fork until dough forms a ball. Press onto the bottom and up the sides of an ungreased fluted 11-in. tart pan with removable bottom; set aside.

For the filling, place nuts in a food processor; cover and process until chopped. In a large bowl, whisk the eggs, corn syrup, brown sugar, butter and extracts until smooth. Stir in chocolate chips and nut mixture; pour into crust.

Place pan on a baking sheet. Bake at 350° for 35-40 minutes or until center is set. Cool on a wire rack. Store in the refrigerator. Garnish with whipped cream. **Yield:** 12-14 servings.

Banana Split Brownie Pie

(Pictured above and on page 164)

PREP: 30 min. + freezing **BAKE:** 30 min. + freezing

I often use Neapolitan in place of three different ice cream flavors to make this luscious dessert. Days ahead, you can bake the brownie crust, top it with the ice cream and freeze until you need it.
—Tanna Walker, Salina, Kansas

        4 ounces German sweet chocolate, chopped
      1/2 cup butter, cubed
        3 eggs
        1 cup sugar
      1/2 teaspoon vanilla extract
      1/2 cup all-purpose flour
    1-1/3 cups vanilla ice cream
    1-2/3 cups chocolate ice cream
    1-2/3 cups strawberry ice cream
        2 medium firm bananas, sliced
        1 cup fresh strawberries, sliced
      1/2 to 3/4 cup hot fudge ice cream topping, warmed
      1/2 to 3/4 cup strawberry ice cream topping
      1/4 to 1/2 cup toffee bits *or* almond brickle chips
Whipped cream and sliced almonds

In a microwave, melt chocolate and butter; stir until smooth. Cool. In a small bowl, beat the eggs, sugar, vanilla and cooled chocolate mixture. Gradually add flour until well blended. Spread into a greased 9-in. springform pan.

Bake at 350° for 30-35 minutes or until a toothpick inserted near the center comes out clean. Cool on a wire rack. Cover and freeze until firm.

Using 1/3 cup for each scoop, place four scoops of vanilla ice cream, five scoops of chocolate ice cream and five scoops of strawberry ice cream on a waxed paper-lined baking sheet. Freeze until firm. Place vanilla scoops in center of brownie crust; alternate scoops of chocolate and strawberry around edge. Cover and freeze until firm.

Just before serving, remove sides of pan. Arrange bananas and strawberries over ice cream. Drizzle with hot fudge and strawberry toppings. Sprinkle with toffee bits. Garnish with whipped cream and almonds. Cut into wedges. **Yield:** 10 servings.

Fluffy Lemon Squares

(Pictured below and on page 164)

PREP: 25 min. + chilling

These rich bars with a vanilla wafer crust, get their sweet-tart flavor from lemon gelatin, pudding mix and sherbet. They're not only fun to make with my grandchildren, but they're delicious, too. —Joyce Speerbrecher, Grafton, Wisconsin

- 1-1/2 **cups crushed vanilla wafers (about 45 wafers)**
- 1/3 **cup chopped pecans**
- 6 **tablespoons butter, melted**
- 1/2 **cup heavy whipping cream**
- 2 **packages (3 ounces *each*) lemon gelatin**
- 1-1/4 **cups boiling water**
- 1 **package (3.4 ounces) instant lemon pudding mix**
- 1 **pint lemon sherbet, softened**

In a small bowl, combine the wafer crumbs, pecans and butter; set aside 1/4 cup for topping. Press remaining crumb mixture into an ungreased 11-in. x 7-in. x 2-in. dish. Cover and refrigerate for 30 minutes.

Meanwhile, in a small bowl, beat cream until stiff peaks form; set aside. In a large bowl, dissolve gelatin in boiling water. Add pudding mix; beat on low speed for 2 minutes. Add sherbet; beat on low for 1 minute or until soft-set. Gently fold in whipped cream.

Spread over the crust; sprinkle with the reserved crumb mixture. Refrigerate for 1 hour or until set. **Yield:** 12 servings.

Three-Fruit Sundae Sauce

(Pictured above)

PREP: 10 min. **COOK:** 55 min. + chilling

I dreamed up this bright-red sauce that blends rhubarb with strawberries, oranges, cinnamon and lemon peel. It's wonderful over vanilla ice cream. —Sharon Trefren, Grand Bay, Alabama

- 2 **cups sugar**
- 2 **tablespoons cornstarch**
- 6 **cups chopped fresh rhubarb *or* frozen rhubarb**
- 2 **cups fresh *or* frozen sweetened sliced strawberries**
- 2 **medium navel oranges, peeled and sectioned**
- 1 **teaspoon grated lemon peel**
- 3 **cups water**
- 1 **cinnamon stick (3 inches)**

Vanilla ice cream

In a large saucepan, combine the sugar, cornstarch, rhubarb, strawberries, oranges and lemon peel until blended. Stir in the water and cinnamon stick. Bring to a boil; cook and stir for 2 minutes.

Reduce heat; simmer, uncovered, for 50-60 minutes or until thickened. Discard cinnamon stick. Cool. Place in refrigerator until chilled. Serve over ice cream. **Yield:** 7 cups.

Editor's Note: If using frozen rhubarb, measure rhubarb while still frozen, then thaw completely. Drain in a colander, but do not press liquid out.

♪ Oh Nuts!

Nuts can turn rancid over time, so to prevent this, it's best to store them in the freezer. To thaw for a recipe, spread them in a pie plate and place in the oven for a few minutes as the oven preheats. Let cool and chop them to use in baked goods.

Potluck Pleasers

The line at the buffet table is sure to form fast when you contribute any of the large-quantity dishes served up here. Cooking for a crowd has never been easier!

SUPER RECIPES FOR GROUPS. Clockwise from upper left: Mini Chicken Salad Croissants (p. 186), Peanut Butter Chocolate Cupcakes (p. 192), Meaty Pasta Casseroles (p. 194), Festive Rice Salad (p. 194) and Tortellini Spinach Casserole (p. 201).

Forgotten Jambalaya

(Pictured above)

PREP: 35 min. **COOK:** 4-1/4 hours

During the winter, I fix this jambalaya at least once a month. It's so easy…just chop the vegetables, dump everything in the slow cooker and forget it! Even my sons, who are picky about spicy things, like this dish. —Cindi Coss, Coppell, Texas

- 1 can (14-1/2 ounces) diced tomatoes, undrained
- 1 can (14-1/2 ounces) beef *or* chicken broth
- 1 can (6 ounces) tomato paste
- 2 medium green peppers, chopped
- 1 medium onion, chopped
- 3 celery ribs, chopped
- 5 garlic cloves, minced
- 3 teaspoons dried parsley flakes
- 2 teaspoons dried basil
- 1-1/2 teaspoons dried oregano
- 1-1/4 teaspoons salt
- 1/2 teaspoon cayenne pepper
- 1/2 teaspoon hot pepper sauce
- 1 pound boneless skinless chicken breasts, cut into 1-inch cubes
- 1 pound smoked sausage, halved and cut into 1/4-inch slices
- 1/2 pound uncooked medium shrimp, peeled and deveined

Hot cooked rice

In a 5-qt. slow cooker, combine the tomatoes, broth and tomato paste. Stir in the green peppers, onion, celery, garlic and seasonings. Stir in chicken and sausage.

Cover and cook on low for 4 hours or until chicken is tender. Stir in shrimp. Cover and cook 15-30 minutes longer or until shrimp turn pink. Serve with rice. **Yield:** 11 servings.

Grand Prize Winner

Chunky Apple Cake

(Pictured below)

PREP: 20 min. **BAKE:** 40 min. + cooling

This tender, moist cake is full of old-fashioned comfort, and the yummy brown sugar sauce makes it special. For a festive occasion, top individual slices with a dollop of whipped cream and some mint. —Debi Benson, Bakersfield, California

- 1/2 cup butter, softened
- 2 cups sugar
- 1/2 teaspoon vanilla extract
- 2 eggs
- 2 cups all-purpose flour
- 1-1/2 teaspoons ground cinnamon
- 1 teaspoon ground nutmeg
- 1/2 teaspoon salt
- 1/2 teaspoon baking soda
- 6 cups chopped peeled tart apples

BUTTERSCOTCH SAUCE:
- 1/2 cup packed brown sugar
- 1/4 cup butter, cubed
- 1/2 cup heavy whipping cream

In a large bowl, cream the butter, sugar and vanilla. Add eggs, one at a time, beating well after each addition. Combine the flour, cinnamon, nutmeg, salt and baking soda; gradually add to creamed mixture and mix well (batter will be stiff). Stir in apples until well combined.

Spread into a greased 13-in. x 9-in. x 2-in. baking dish. Bake at 350° for 40-45 minutes or until top is lightly browned and springs back when lightly touched. Cool for 30 minutes before serving.

In a large bowl, pour milk over bread crumbs; let stand for 10 minutes. Add the egg, Worcestershire sauce, onion, salt, pepper and cloves. Crumble beef, pork and veal over mixture and mix well (mixture will be soft). Shape into 1-in. balls.

In a large skillet, brown meatballs in oil in batches. Drain on paper towels. Place in a greased 13-in. x 9-in. x 2-in. baking dish.

In a small bowl, dissolve bouillon in water. Stir flour into pan drippings until blended; add the bouillon mixture, jam and chili sauce. Bring to a boil; cook and stir for 1-2 minutes or until thickened. Pour over meatballs.

Cover and bake at 350° for 30-45 minutes or until the meat is no longer pink and the sauce is bubbly. **Yield:** 10-12 servings.

Apple and Carrot Slaw

(Pictured below)

PREP/TOTAL TIME: 30 min.

This crispy, colorful slaw is a true crowd–pleaser at any picnic or church gathering. The apples add color and a touch of sweetness.
—*Julia Livingston, Frostproof, Florida*

- **4 large heads cabbage, shredded**
- **1 pound carrots, shredded**
- **6 medium red apples, finely chopped**
- **3 cups mayonnaise**
- **1/2 cup sugar**
- **1/4 cup white vinegar**
- **3 teaspoons salt**
- **2 teaspoons pepper**

In a very large bowl, combine the cabbage, carrots and apples. In a large bowl, combine the mayonnaise, sugar, vinegar, salt and pepper. Pour over the cabbage mixture and toss to coat. Cover and refrigerate until serving. **Yield:** 42 servings (3/4 cup each).

Meanwhile, for the sauce, in a small saucepan, combine the brown sugar and butter. Cook over medium heat until butter is melted. Gradually add the cream. Bring to a slow boil over medium heat, stirring constantly. Remove from the heat. Serve with cake. **Yield:** 12-14 servings.

Meatballs in Plum Sauce

(Pictured above)

PREP: 1 hour **BAKE:** 30 min.

A tasty sauce made of plum jam and chili sauce coats these moist meatballs beautifully. Make sure the delightful appetizers are on your holiday menus. —*Mary Poninski, Whittington, Illinois*

- **1/2 cup milk**
- **1 cup soft bread crumbs**
- **1 egg, lightly beaten**
- **1 tablespoon Worcestershire sauce**
- **1 medium onion, finely chopped**
- **1/4 teaspoon salt**
- **1/4 teaspoon pepper**
- **1/8 teaspoon ground cloves**
- **1/2 pound lean ground beef**
- **1/2 pound ground pork**
- **1/2 pound ground veal**
- **2 tablespoons canola oil**
- **1/2 teaspoon beef bouillon granules**
- **1/2 cup boiling water**
- **3 tablespoons all-purpose flour**
- **1 cup plum jam**
- **1/2 cup chili sauce**

Mini Chicken Salad Croissants

(Pictured below and on page 182)

PREP: 20 min. + chilling

Fresh-tasting and great for a get-together, this popular chicken salad could also be served on lettuce or alongside a slice of cantaloupe or honeydew melon. For kids, I use halved red seedless grapes instead of the peppers.

—*Patricia Tjugum, Tomahawk, Wisconsin*

- 1/3 cup sour cream
- 1/3 cup mayonnaise
- 4 teaspoons lemon juice
- 1 teaspoon salt
- 1/4 teaspoon pepper
- 3 cups cubed cooked chicken
- 4 celery ribs, thinly sliced
- 1 cup chopped fresh mushrooms
- 1/4 cup chopped green pepper
- 1/4 cup chopped sweet red pepper
- 4 bacon strips, cooked and crumbled
- 1/2 cup chopped pecans, toasted
- 20 lettuce leaves
- 20 miniature croissants, split

In a small bowl, combine the sour cream, mayonnaise, lemon juice, salt and pepper. In a large bowl, combine the chicken, celery, mushrooms and peppers; stir in sour cream mixture until combined. Cover and refrigerate for at least 4 hours.

Just before serving, stir in bacon and pecans. Spoon 1/4 cup chicken salad onto each lettuce-lined croissant. **Yield:** 20 sandwiches.

Coconut Pecan Cupcakes

(Pictured above)

PREP: 50 min. **BAKE:** 20 min. + cooling

Pecan lovers have lots to cheer about with these cupcakes. I created the recipe for my best friend, who loves Italian cream cake but doesn't want a whole cake. They have a wonderful aroma and fabulous flavor.

—*Tina Harrison, Prairieville, Louisiana*

- 5 eggs, *separated*
- 1/2 cup butter, softened
- 1/2 cup shortening
- 2 cups sugar
- 3/4 teaspoon vanilla extract
- 1/4 teaspoon almond extract
- 1-1/2 cups all-purpose flour
- 1/4 cup cornstarch
- 1/2 teaspoon baking soda
- 1/2 teaspoon salt
- 1 cup buttermilk
- 2 cups flaked coconut
- 1 cup finely chopped pecans

FROSTING:

- 1 package (8 ounces) cream cheese, softened
- 1/4 cup butter, softened
- 1/2 teaspoon vanilla extract
- 1/4 teaspoon almond extract
- 3-3/4 cups confectioners' sugar
- 3/4 cup chopped pecans

Let eggs stand at room temperature for 30 minutes, then separate. In a large bowl, cream the butter, shortening and sugar until light and fluffy. Add egg yolks, one at a time, beating well after each addition. Stir in extracts. Combine the flour, cornstarch, baking soda and salt; add to the creamed mixture alternately with buttermilk, beating well after each addition.

In a small bowl, beat the egg whites on high speed until stiff peaks form. Fold into the batter. Stir in the coconut and pecans.

Fill paper-lined muffin cups three-fourths full. Bake at 350° for 20-25 minutes or until a toothpick comes out clean. Cool 10 minutes; remove from pans to wire racks to cool completely.

In a large bowl, combine the frosting ingredients until smooth; frost cupcakes. Store in the refrigerator. **Yield:** 2 dozen.

Cashew-Pear Tossed Salad

(Pictured below)

PREP/TOTAL TIME: 15 min.

A friend who does a lot of catering fixed this salad for our staff Christmas party several years ago, and we all asked for the recipe. The unexpected sweet–salty mix and lovely dressing make it a hit with everyone. —*Arlene Muller, Kingwood, Texas*

- 1 **bunch romaine, torn**
- 1 **cup (4 ounces) shredded Swiss cheese**
- 1 **cup salted cashews**
- 1 **medium pear, thinly sliced**
- 1/2 **cup dried cranberries**

POPPY SEED VINAIGRETTE:

- 2/3 **cup olive oil**
- 1/2 **cup sugar**
- 1/3 **cup lemon juice**
- 2 **to 3 teaspoons poppy seeds**
- 2 **teaspoons finely chopped red onion**
- 1 **teaspoon prepared mustard**
- 1/2 **teaspoon salt**

In a large salad bowl, combine the romaine, Swiss cheese, cashews, pear and cranberries. In a jar with a tight-fitting lid, combine the vinaigrette ingredients; shake well. Drizzle over salad and toss to coat. Serve immediately. **Yield:** 15 servings.

Onions Neptune

(Pictured above)

PREP: 20 min. **BAKE:** 35 min.

I serve this dish as an appetizer and often add whatever ingredients I have handy, such as mushrooms or sun–dried tomatoes. Whether I serve it as is or jazz it up, it's always delicious. —*Todd Noon, Galloway, New Jersey*

- 5 **to 6 medium sweet onions, sliced and separated into rings**
- 1/2 **cup butter, softened, *divided***
- 2 **cans (6 ounces *each*) lump crabmeat, drained, *divided***
- 3 **cups (12 ounces) shredded Swiss cheese**
- 1 **can (10-3/4 ounces) condensed cream of mushroom soup, undiluted**
- 1/2 **cup evaporated milk**
- 1/2 **teaspoon salt**
- 1/4 **teaspoon pepper**
- 12 **to 16 slices French bread (1/4 inch thick)**

In a large skillet, saute onions in 1/4 cup butter until tender. Remove from the heat; gently stir in half of the crab. Spread into a greased 13-in. x 9-in. x 2-in. baking dish. Top with remaining crab. Combine the cheese, soup, milk, salt and pepper; spoon over crab.

Spread remaining butter over one side of each slice of bread; place buttered side up over casserole. Bake, uncovered, at 350° for 35-45 minutes or until golden brown. **Yield:** 12 servings.

chilies. Bring to a boil; cook until liquid is reduced to 4 cups.

For the filling, in a large bowl, combine the cornmeal, baking powder and salt; beat in water, 2 cups pan juices and shortening just until combined (bowl will be full). Refrigerate remaining pan juices.

Drain corn husks and pat dry. (Until ready to use, keep husks covered with plastic wrap and a damp towel to prevent them from drying out.) Spread 3 tablespoons filling over each husk to within 1/4 in. of edges. Top each with 1/4 cup pork and 3 tablespoons filling. Using the husk to lift one long side, roll up filling. Enclose filling with husk; fold bottom end of husk over the top.

In a large steamer basket, position tamales upright with folded bottoms down. Place basket in a Dutch oven over 1 in. of water. Bring to a boil; cover and steam for 25-30 minutes or until cornmeal peels away from husk, adding water to pan as needed. Warm reserved pan juices; serve with tamales. Remove husks before eating. **Yield:** 32 tamales.

Peanut Butter Pudding Dessert

(Pictured below)

PREP: 25 min. **BAKE:** 25 min. + chilling

Here's a fun, layered dessert that will appeal to all ages. If you want it even nuttier, you can use chunky peanut butter, and if you're not a fan of cashews, substitute your favorite nut.
—*Barbara Schindler, Napoleon, Ohio*

  1 cup all-purpose flour
1/2 cup cold butter, cubed
1-1/2 cups chopped cashews, ***divided***

Tamales

(Pictured above)

PREP: 4-1/4 hours **COOK:** 25 min.

Tamales are bundles of corn dough with a savory or sweet filling, typically wrapped in corn husks or banana leaves. Because they take a while to make, they are often served for special occasions and holidays. —*Jacquelynne Stine, Las Vegas, Nevada*

  1 boneless pork shoulder roast (4 pounds)
  4 cups water
  1 cup finely chopped onion
1/3 cup adobo sauce
1/4 cup chili sauce
  2 dried guajillo chilies
1/4 cup lime juice
  4 garlic cloves, peeled
32 corn husks
FILLING:
  7 cups maseca cornmeal
  9 teaspoons baking powder
  3 teaspoons salt
  4 cups warm water (110° to 115°)
1-1/2 cups butter-flavored shortening

Place the first eight ingredients in a Dutch oven. Cover and bake at 325° for 3-4 hours or until meat is very tender.

Meanwhile, place corn husks in a large kettle; cover with cold water and soak for at least 2 hours.

Remove roast and shred meat with two forks; set aside and keep warm. Skim fat from pan juices; discard

    1 package (8 ounces) cream cheese, softened
 1/3 cup creamy peanut butter
    1 cup confectioners' sugar
    1 carton (12 ounces) frozen whipped topping, thawed, *divided*
2-2/3 cups cold milk
    1 package (3.9 ounces) instant chocolate pudding mix
    1 package (3.4 ounces) instant vanilla pudding mix
    1 milk chocolate candy bar (1.55 ounces), coarsely chopped

Place flour and butter in a food processor; cover and process until mixture resembles coarse crumbs. Add 1 cup cashews; pulse a few times until combined.

Press into a greased 13-in. x 9-in. x 2-in. baking dish. Bake at 350° for 25-28 minutes or until golden brown. Cool completely on a wire rack.

In a small bowl, beat the cream cheese, peanut butter and confectioners' sugar until smooth. Fold in 1 cup whipped topping. Spoon over crust.

In another bowl, whisk milk and both pudding mixes for 2 minutes. Let stand for 2 minutes or until soft-set. Spread over cream cheese layer. Top with remaining whipped topping. Sprinkle with chopped candy bar and remaining cashews. Cover and refrigerate for at least 1 hour before serving. **Yield:** 12-16 servings.

Red Potato Salad

PREP: 40 min. + chilling

Red potatoes and hard-cooked eggs add heartiness, and a creamy dressing provides great flavor.
          —Margaret Blomquist, Newfield, New York

    5 pounds medium red potatoes, halved
    5 hard-cooked eggs, chopped
    1 celery rib, finely chopped
 1/2 medium onion, finely chopped
1-1/2 cups mayonnaise
 1/4 cup sweet pickle relish
    3 tablespoons sugar
    2 tablespoons dried parsley flakes
    2 teaspoons prepared mustard
    1 teaspoon salt
    1 teaspoon cider vinegar
 1/8 teaspoon pepper

Place the potatoes in a large kettle; cover with water. Bring to a boil. Reduce heat; cover and cook for 20-25 minutes or until tender. Drain and cool. Cut the potatoes into 3/4-in. cubes.

In a large bowl, combine the potatoes, eggs, celery and onion. In a small bowl, combine the remaining ingredients. Pour over potato mixture and stir gently to coat. Cover and refrigerate for 6 hours or overnight.
Yield: 17 servings (3/4 cup each).

Hint of Mint Fruit Salad

(Pictured above)

PREP: 20 min. + chilling

I love making herbal syrups like the simple dressing for this colorful fruit salad. It definitely adds pizzazz to Easter dinner and other spring gatherings.
          —Sue Gronholz, Beaver Dam, Wisconsin

    1 cup sugar
    1 cup water
    1 cup loosely packed mint sprigs
2-1/2 cups chopped apples
2-1/2 cups chopped ripe pears
    2 cups cubed fresh pineapple
    2 cups sliced fresh strawberries
    1 cup fresh blueberries
    1 cup mayonnaise

In a large saucepan, bring sugar and water to a boil. Reduce heat; simmer, uncovered, for 4 minutes. Remove from the heat. Add mint; cover and steep for 20 minutes. Strain and discard mint. Transfer syrup to a small bowl; refrigerate until chilled.

Just before serving, combine the apples, pears, pineapple, strawberries and blueberries in a large bowl. Stir mayonnaise into mint syrup until blended; pour over fruit and toss to coat. **Yield:** 12 servings.

♪ *Wild about Berries*

Fresh berries should be stored covered in the refrigerator and washed just before using. Use within 10 days of purchase. To wash, place berries a few at a time in a colander in the sink. Gently spray with water and pat dry on paper towels.

Big Yields, Big Flavor

Mac and Cheese For a Bunch

(Pictured above)

PREP: 30 min. **BAKE:** 35 min.

You'll satisfy many taste buds with my comforting dish. This tender macaroni is first covered in a creamy, homemade cheese sauce, and then topped with golden bread crumbs. A true crowd–pleaser!
—Dixie Terry, Goreville, Illinois

3 packages (two 16 ounces, one 7 ounces) elbow macaroni
1-1/4 cups butter, *divided*
3/4 cup all-purpose flour
2 teaspoons salt
3 quarts milk
3 pounds sharp cheddar cheese, shredded
1-1/2 cups dry bread crumbs

Cook macaroni according to package directions until almost tender. Meanwhile, in a large soup kettle, melt 1 cup butter. Stir in flour and salt until smooth. Gradually stir in milk. Bring to a boil; cook and stir for 2 minutes or until thickened. Reduce heat. Add cheese, stirring until melted. Drain macaroni; stir into sauce.

Transfer to three greased 13-in. x 9-in. x 2-in. baking dishes. Melt remaining butter; toss with bread crumbs. Sprinkle over casseroles. Bake, uncovered, at 350° for 35-40 minutes or until golden brown.
Yield: 36 servings (1 cup each).

Rhubarb Cranberry Cookies

(Pictured below)

PREP: 30 min.
BAKE: 10 min./ batch + cooling

I like the hint of sweetness when you bite into the white chocolate in these cookies. It really complements the tart flavor from the rhubarb and cranberries.
—Elaine Scott, Lafayette, Indiana

1 cup butter, softened
1 cup packed brown sugar
1/2 cup sugar
2 eggs
1 teaspoon vanilla extract
1-1/2 cups all-purpose flour
1 teaspoon baking soda
1/2 teaspoon salt
1/2 teaspoon ground cinnamon
2-1/2 cups old-fashioned oats
1-1/2 cups diced frozen rhubarb
1 cup vanilla *or* white chips
1 cup dried cranberries
4 squares (1 ounce *each*) white baking chocolate

In a large bowl, cream the butter and sugars. Beat in eggs and vanilla. Combine the flour, baking soda, salt and cinnamon; gradually add to creamed mixture. Stir in the oats, rhubarb, chips and cranberries.

Drop by tablespoonfuls 2 in. apart onto parchment paper-lined baking sheets. Bake at 350° for 10-12 minutes or until set. Remove to wire racks to cool.

In a microwave-safe bowl, melt white chocolate; stir until smooth. Drizzle over cookies; let stand until set. Store in an airtight container.
Yield: about 5-1/2 dozen.

Tossed Salad with Lemon Vinaigrette

(Pictured above right)

PREP/TOTAL TIME: 25 min.

I often take this dressed–up Caesar salad to church functions or family reunions. Its interesting blend of flavors is a hit with everyone, so I always come home with an empty bowl.
—Teresa Otto, Hartwell, Georgia

1 bunch romaine, torn
1 medium head iceberg lettuce, torn
10 bacon strips, cooked and crumbled
2 cups cherry tomatoes, halved
1 cup slivered almonds

1 cup shredded Parmesan cheese
1 cup salad croutons
VINAIGRETTE:
   3 tablespoons lemon juice
   3 tablespoons grated Parmesan cheese
   2 garlic cloves, minced
1/2 teaspoon salt
1/4 teaspoon pepper
2/3 cup olive oil

In a large salad bowl, combine the first seven ingredients. For the vinaigrette, in a small bowl, combine the lemon juice, grated Parmesan cheese, minced garlic, salt and pepper. Gradually whisk in the olive oil. Drizzle over salad and toss to coat. Serve immediately. **Yield:** 21 servings.

Watermelon Basket

(Pictured at right)

PREP: 30 min. + chilling

I cut a watermelon into a basket shape, then fill it with melon balls to serve with a creamy dip. It makes an attractive centerpiece at parties as well as a delicious fruit salad.
—Christine Johnson, Ricetown, Kentucky

1 large watermelon (10 pounds)
1 medium honeydew, cut into balls
3 cups white cranberry juice

1 cup light corn syrup
2 tablespoons lime juice
FRUIT DIP:
   1 package (8 ounces) cream cheese, softened
1/4 cup milk
   3 tablespoons sugar
   3 tablespoons lemon juice
3/4 teaspoon ground cardamom

Cut a thin slice from the bottom of watermelon with a sharp knife so it sits flat. Mark horizontal cutting line 2 in. above center and around the melon.

For handle, score a 1-1/2-in.-wide strip across the top of melon, connecting both sides to the horizontal line. With a long sharp knife, cut all the way through the rind above the cutting line in a zigzag pattern.

Carefully lift off the side pieces. Remove fruit from both sections and cut into balls. Refrigerate the basket.

In a large bowl, combine watermelon and honeydew balls. In another bowl, whisk cranberry juice, corn syrup and lime juice until blended; pour over melon balls. Cover and chill for 3 hours.

Drain; spoon melon into watermelon basket. For the dip, in a small bowl, beat the cream cheese and milk until smooth. Beat in sugar, lemon juice and cardamom; serve with melon. **Yield:** 32 servings.

Shredded Beef and Slaw Sandwiches

(Pictured above)

PREP: 20 min. **COOK:** 2-3/4 hours

I have often served these tangy, hearty sandwiches for family gatherings and to many work crews. They have always gone over quite well.
—Mary Johnson, Whitehouse, Ohio

4 pounds beef stew meat, cut into 1-inch cubes
2 cups water
2 cups ketchup
1/2 to 3/4 cup Worcestershire sauce
2 tablespoons lemon juice
2 tablespoons prepared horseradish
1 tablespoon prepared mustard
2 teaspoons salt
8 cups shredded cabbage
30 sandwich buns, split

In a Dutch oven, bring the beef and water to a boil. Reduce heat; cover and simmer for 2 hours or until tender.

Remove beef with a slotted spoon; shred with two forks and set aside. Skim fat from cooking liquid. Stir in the ketchup, Worcestershire sauce, lemon juice, horseradish, mustard and salt. Add the shredded beef and cabbage. Bring to a boil. Reduce heat; cover and simmer for 45 minutes or until cabbage is tender.

Spoon 1/3 cup onto each sandwich bun. **Yield:** 30 sandwiches.

Peanut Butter Chocolate Cupcakes

(Pictured above and on page 182)

PREP: 30 min. **BAKE:** 25 min. + cooling

I didn't have any luck finding a peanut butter–filled chocolate cupcake (my two favorite flavors), so I made a chocolate cupcake recipe and experimented with the filling until I found one I liked. —Julie Small, Claremont, New Hampshire

- 1 **package (3 ounces) cream cheese, softened**
- 1/4 **cup creamy peanut butter**
- 2 **tablespoons sugar**
- 1 **tablespoon milk**

BATTER:
- 2 **cups sugar**
- 1-3/4 **cups all-purpose flour**
- 1/2 **cup baking cocoa**
- 1-1/2 **teaspoons baking powder**
- 1 **teaspoon salt**
- 1/4 **teaspoon baking soda**
- 2 **eggs**
- 1 **cup water**
- 1 **cup milk**
- 1/2 **cup canola oil**
- 2 **teaspoons vanilla extract**

FROSTING:
- 1/3 **cup butter, softened**
- 2 **cups confectioners' sugar**
- 6 **tablespoons baking cocoa**
- 3 to 4 **tablespoons milk**

In a small bowl, beat cream cheese, peanut butter, sugar and milk until smooth; set aside.

For the batter, in a large bowl, combine sugar, flour, cocoa, baking powder, salt and baking soda. In another bowl, whisk the eggs, water, milk, oil and vanilla. Stir into dry ingredients just until moistened (batter will be thin).

Fill paper-lined jumbo muffin cups half full with batter. Drop scant tablespoonfuls of peanut butter mixture into center of each; cover with remaining batter.

Bake at 350° for 25-30 minutes or until a toothpick inserted into cake comes out clean. Cool 10 minutes; remove from pans to wire racks. Cool completely.

In a large bowl, combine frosting ingredients until smooth; frost cupcakes. Store in the refrigerator. **Yield:** 1 dozen jumbo cupcakes.

Scalloped Potatoes and Ham

(Pictured below)

PREP: 30 min. **BAKE:** 1 hour 20 min.

A friend of mine served this scrumptious, comforting dish at her wedding. I liked it so much, I asked for the recipe. Covered in a creamy cheese sauce, the potatoes and ham taste delicious. It's perfect when you have a lot of mouths to feed.
—Ruth Ann Stelfox, Raymond, Alberta

- 2 **cans (10-3/4 ounces *each*) condensed cream of mushroom soup, undiluted**
- 2 **cans (10-3/4 ounces *each*) condensed cream of celery soup, undiluted**
- 1 **can (10-3/4 ounces) condensed cheddar cheese soup, undiluted**
- 1 **can (12 ounces) evaporated milk**
- 10 **pounds medium potatoes, peeled and thinly sliced**
- 5 **pounds fully cooked ham, cubed**
- 4 **cups (16 ounces) shredded cheddar cheese**

In two large bowls, combine soups and milk. Add potatoes and ham; toss to coat. Divide among four greased 13-in. x 9-in. x 2-in. baking dishes.

Cover and bake at 325° for 1-1/4 hours or until potatoes are tender. Uncover; sprinkle with cheese. Bake 5-10 minutes longer or until cheese is melted. **Yield:** 4 casseroles (10 servings each).

Spicy Pork Chili

(Pictured above)

PREP: 10 min. **COOK:** 2 hours

This chili, loaded with white beans and cubes of pork, has plenty of bite. But if it's not spicy enough for you, top it with shredded jalapeno jack cheese and finely diced onions.
—Larry Laatsch, Saginaw, Michigan

- **1-1/2 pounds pork tenderloin, cubed**
- **2 large onions, diced**
- **4 celery ribs, diced**
- **2 tablespoons butter**
- **6 cans (15-1/2 ounces *each*) great northern beans, rinsed and drained**
- **4 cans (14-1/2 ounces *each*) chicken broth**
- **2 cups water**
- **2 jalapeno peppers, seeded and chopped**
- **2 teaspoons chili powder**
- **1/2 teaspoon *each* white pepper, cayenne pepper, ground cumin and pepper**
- **2 garlic cloves, minced**
- **1/2 teaspoon salt**
- **1/4 teaspoon dried parsley flakes**
- **1/4 teaspoon hot pepper sauce, optional**
- **1 cup (4 ounces) shredded Monterey Jack cheese**

In a Dutch oven, cook the pork, onions and celery in butter until meat is browned. Stir in the beans, broth, water, jalapenos, spices, garlic, salt, parsley and hot pepper sauce if desired. Bring to a boil. Reduce heat; cover and simmer for 1-1/2 hours.

Uncover; simmer 30-40 minutes longer or until chili reaches desired consistency. Sprinkle with cheese. **Yield:** 15 servings.

Editor's Note: When cutting hot peppers, disposable gloves are recommended. Avoid touching your face.

Layered Summertime Salad

(Pictured below)

PREP/TOTAL TIME: 30 min.

Luscious layers of pasta and veggies make up this super summer salad that can be made ahead for warm-weather picnics and deck parties. It makes enough to feed a crowd.
—Betty Fulks, Onia, Arkansas

- **2 cups uncooked gemelli *or* spiral pasta**
- **1 cup mayonnaise**
- **2 tablespoons lemon juice**
- **1 teaspoon sugar**
- **1/2 teaspoon garlic powder**
- **1/2 cup sliced green onions**
- **4 bacon strips, cooked and crumbled, *divided***
- **4 cups torn romaine**
- **1 cup fresh snow peas, trimmed and halved**
- **1 cup fresh cauliflowerets**
- **1 cup fresh broccoli florets**
- **1 large sweet red pepper, chopped**
- **1/2 cup shredded Swiss cheese**

Cook pasta according to package directions. Meanwhile, in a small bowl, combine the mayonnaise, lemon juice, sugar and garlic powder; set aside. Drain pasta and rinse in cold water; toss with onions and half of the bacon.

In a large salad bowl, layer half of the romaine, pasta mixture, peas, cauliflower, broccoli, red pepper, mayonnaise mixture and cheese. Repeat layers. Sprinkle with remaining bacon. Cover and refrigerate until serving. **Yield:** 16 servings.

Festive Rice Salad

(Pictured below and on page 182)

PREP: 30 min. + cooling

I once had a similar salad at a friend's house and was determined to re-create it at home. After several tries, I came up with this sweet-tart concoction. It's easy to prepare and colorful, too.
—Terri Simpson, Palm Harbor, Florida

- **3/4 cup uncooked long grain rice**
- **1 package (10 ounces) frozen peas, thawed**
- **1 small sweet red pepper, chopped**
- **3/4 cup chopped green onions**
- **1/2 cup dried cranberries**

DRESSING:
- **1/2 cup canola oil**
- **1/3 cup white vinegar**
- **3 tablespoons sugar**
- **1/2 teaspoon dill weed**
- **1/4 teaspoon salt**
- **1/4 teaspoon ground mustard**
- **1/8 teaspoon pepper**

Cook rice according to package directions; cool. In a large bowl, combine the rice, peas, red pepper, onions and cranberries. In a small bowl, whisk the dressing ingredients. Drizzle over salad and toss to coat. Refrigerate until serving. **Yield:** 12 servings.

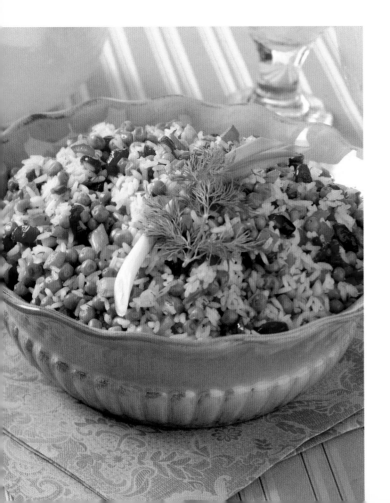

Meaty Pasta Casseroles

(Pictured above and on page 182)

PREP: 45 min. **BAKE:** 35 min.

I love this recipe because it makes two robust casseroles. Every time I fix it, I add something different, such as extra garlic, to give it a flavor boost.   —Debra Butcher, Decatur, Indiana

- **1 package (16 ounces) penne pasta**
- **1 pound ground beef**
- **1 pound bulk Italian pork sausage**
- **1-3/4 cups sliced fresh mushrooms**
- **1 medium onion, chopped**
- **1 medium green pepper, chopped**
- **2 cans (14-1/2 ounces *each*) Italian diced tomatoes**
- **1 jar (25.6 ounces) Italian sausage and garlic spaghetti sauce**
- **1 jar (16 ounces) chunky mild salsa**
- **1 package (8 ounces) sliced pepperoni, chopped**
- **1 cup (4 ounces) shredded Swiss cheese, *divided***
- **4 cups (16 ounces) shredded part-skim mozzarella cheese, *divided***
- **1-1/2 cups shredded Parmesan cheese, *divided***
- **1 jar (26 ounces) three-cheese spaghetti sauce**

Cook pasta according to package directions. Meanwhile, in a Dutch oven, cook the beef, sausage, mushrooms, onion and green pepper over medium heat until meat is no longer pink; drain.

Drain the pasta; add to the meat mixture. Stir in the tomatoes, sausage and garlic spaghetti sauce, salsa and pepperoni.

Divide half of pasta mixture between two greased 13-in. x 9-in. x 2-in. baking dishes. Sprinkle each with 1/4 cup Swiss cheese, 1 cup mozzarella cheese and 1/3 cup Parmesan cheese. Spread 3/4 cup of three-cheese spaghetti sauce over each. Top with remaining pasta mixture and three-cheese spaghetti sauce. Sprinkle with remaining cheeses.

Cover and freeze one casserole for up to 3 months. Cover and bake remaining casserole at 350° for 25 minutes. Uncover; bake 10 minutes longer or until cheese is melted.

To use frozen casserole: Thaw in the refrigerator overnight. Remove from the refrigerator 30 minutes before baking. Cover and bake at 350° for 45 minutes. Uncover; bake 10 minutes longer or until cheese is melted. **Yield:** 2 casseroles (6 servings each).

Slow-Cooked Pork and Beans

PREP: 15 min. **COOK:** 6 hours

I like to get this dish started before leaving for work in the morning. When I get home, my supper's ready! It's a hearty slow-cooker meal that is also good for a potluck.
—*Patricia Hager, Nicholasville, Kentucky*

- 1 **boneless whole pork loin roast (3 pounds)**
- 1 **medium onion, sliced**
- 3 **cans (15 ounces** *each***) pork and beans**
- 1-1/2 **cups barbecue sauce**
- 1/4 **cup packed brown sugar**
- 1 **teaspoon garlic powder**

Cut roast in half; place in a 5-qt. slow cooker. Top with onion. Combine the beans, barbecue sauce, brown sugar and garlic powder; pour over meat. Cover and cook on low for 6 hours or until meat is tender.

Remove roast; shred with two forks. Return meat to slow cooker; heat through. **Yield:** 12 servings.

Peanut Lover's Brownies

(Pictured above right)

PREP: 30 min. + cooling **BAKE:** 30 min. + chilling

Peanut butter lovers won't be able to eat just one of these delectable dessert squares. With a chocolate brownie layer, a graham cracker crust and peanut butter mousse, they're irresistible! —*April Phillips, Lafayette, Indiana*

- 1/2 **cup butter, softened**
- 3/4 **cup all-purpose flour**
- 1/2 **cup graham cracker crumbs**
- 1/4 **cup sugar**
- 1/2 **cup salted peanuts, chopped**

BROWNIE LAYER:
- 3/4 **cup butter, cubed**
- 4 **squares (1 ounce** *each***) unsweetened chocolate, chopped**
- 4 **eggs**
- 2 **cups sugar**
- 2 **teaspoons vanilla extract**
- 1 **cup all-purpose flour**

PEANUT CREAM TOPPING:
- 1 **cup creamy peanut butter**
- 1 **carton (12 ounces) frozen whipped topping, thawed**
- 12 **miniature peanut butter cups, coarsely chopped**

Line a 13-in. x 9-in. x 2-in. baking pan with foil; grease the foil. In a small bowl, combine the butter, flour, cracker crumbs and sugar; press into prepared pan. Bake at 350° for 10-12 minutes or until set. Cool on a wire rack. Sprinkle peanuts over crust.

For the brownie layer, in a microwave, melt butter and chocolate; stir until smooth. In a bowl, combine the eggs, sugar, vanilla and chocolate mixture. Gradually add flour. Spread over crust. Bake for 30-40 minutes or until a toothpick inserted near the center comes out clean. Cool on a wire rack.

For topping, warm peanut butter for 30 seconds in a microwave. Gradually fold in whipped topping; spread over brownies. Refrigerate for 1 hour. Sprinkle with chopped peanut butter cups. Using foil, lift brownies out of pan; remove foil. Cut into bars. Store in the refrigerator. **Yield:** 2 dozen.

♪ *Cup o' Peanut Butter*

Here's a simple and easy way to measure peanut butter: If measuring 1 cup, fill a 2-cup measuring cup with 1 cup of cold water. Add enough peanut butter to raise the water level to the 2-cup mark, making sure the peanut butter is completely immersed. Then pour off all of the water.

Ham Bundles

(Pictured above)

PREP: 55 min. + rising **BAKE:** 20 min.

Whenever I serve ham, I can't wait for the leftovers so I can make these ham buns. My husband often warms them up for breakfast, or you could bring them to your next potluck.
—Chris Sendelbach, Henry, Illinois

    1 **package (1/4 ounce) active dry yeast**
1/4 **cup warm water (110° to 115°)**
3/4 **cup warm milk (110° to 115°)**
1/2 **cup shortening**
    3 **eggs, lightly beaten**
1/2 **cup sugar**
1-1/2 **teaspoons salt**
4-1/2 **to 4-3/4 cups all-purpose flour**
FILLING:
    1 **large onion, finely chopped**
    5 **tablespoons butter,** *divided*
    4 **cups cubed fully cooked ham, coarsely ground**
    4 **bacon strips, cooked and crumbled, optional**
1/4 **to 1/3 cup sliced pimiento-stuffed olives, optional**
1/2 **to 3/4 cup shredded cheddar cheese, optional**

In a large bowl, dissolve yeast in warm water. Add the milk, shortening, eggs, sugar, salt and 2 cups flour; beat until smooth. Add enough remaining flour to form a soft dough.

Turn onto a lightly floured surface; knead until smooth and elastic, about 8 minutes. Place in a greased bowl, turning once to grease top. Cover and let rise in a warm place until doubled, about 1 hour.

Meanwhile, for the filling, in a large skillet, saute onion in 2 tablespoons butter until tender. Add ham and mix well; set aside.

Punch dough down. Turn onto a lightly floured surface; divide into thirds. Roll each portion into a 16-in. x 8-in. rectangle. Cut each rectangle into eight squares. Place a tablespoonful of ham mixture in the center of each square. Add bacon, olives and/or cheese if desired. Fold up corners to center of dough; seal edges.

Place 2 in. apart on greased baking sheets. Cover and let rise in a warm place until doubled, about 45 minutes.

Melt remaining butter; brush over dough. Bake at 350° for 16-20 minutes or until golden brown and filling is heated through. Refrigerate leftovers. **Yield:** 2 dozen.

Dilly Zucchini Dip

(Pictured below)

PREP: 15 min. + chilling

This thick and chunky dip will keep your guests wanting more. When paired with colorful vegetables, it's an appetizer that is pleasing to the eye and the palate.
—Edna Hoffman, Hebron, Indiana

    1 **cup finely shredded zucchini, squeezed dry**
    1 **cup (4 ounces) shredded sharp cheddar cheese**
3/4 **cup mayonnaise**
1/2 **cup chopped walnuts**
    1 **teaspoon lemon juice**
1/2 **teaspoon dill weed**
1/4 **teaspoon pepper**
Assorted fresh vegetables

In a large bowl, combine the first seven ingredients. Cover and refrigerate for 1 hour or until chilled. Serve with vegetables. **Yield:** 2 cups.

Cranberry Gelatin Squares

(Pictured above)

PREP: 30 min. + chilling

This festive gelatin treat is full of cranberries, pineapple and pecans. It's a great recipe to serve on a holiday buffet table.
—*Lucile Cline, Wichita, Kansas*

- 2 **cans (8 ounces *each*) crushed pineapple**
- 2 **packages (3 ounces *each*) strawberry gelatin**
- 3/4 **cup cold water**
- 1 **can (16 ounces) jellied cranberry sauce**
- 1/3 **cup chopped pecans**
- 1 **tablespoon butter**
- 1/2 **cup cold milk**
- 1/2 **cup heavy whipping cream**
- 1 **package (3.4 ounces) instant vanilla pudding mix**
- 1 **package (3 ounces) cream cheese, softened**

Drain the pineapple, reserving juice in a 1-cup measuring cup. Add enough water to measure 1 cup. Set pineapple aside.

In a small saucepan over medium heat, bring pineapple juice mixture to a boil. Remove from the heat; stir in gelatin until dissolved. Stir in cold water; transfer to a bowl. Cover and refrigerate until partially set.

In a small bowl, combine cranberry sauce and reserved pineapple; stir into gelatin mixture. Pour into a 9-in. square dish; cover and refrigerate until firm.

Place pecans and butter in a shallow baking pan. Bake at 350° for 8 minutes or until golden brown, stirring occasionally; cool.

In a small bowl, whisk the milk, cream and pudding mix for 2 minutes. In a small bowl, beat cream cheese until smooth. Add pudding mixture; beat on low speed just until combined. Spread over gelatin. Sprinkle with toasted pecans. Chill until firm. **Yield:** 12 servings.

Corn Tortilla Chicken Lasagna

(Pictured below)

PREP: 40 min. **BAKE:** 35 min. + standing

This Southwest-style lasagna will satisfy a hungry crowd. It can be "stretched" with extra beans, and it's super-easy to put together. People love it! —*Susan Seymar, Valatie, New York*

- 36 **corn tortillas (6 inches)**
- 6 **cups cubed cooked chicken breast**
- 2 **cans (one 28 ounces, one 16 ounces) kidney beans, rinsed and drained**
- 3 **jars (16 ounces *each*) salsa**
- 3 **cups (24 ounces) sour cream**
- 3 **large green peppers, chopped**
- 3 **cans (3.8 ounces *each*) sliced ripe olives, drained**
- 3 **cups (12 ounces) shredded Monterey Jack cheese**
- 3 **cups (12 ounces) shredded cheddar cheese**

In each of two greased 13-in. x 9-in. x 2-in. baking dishes, arrange six tortillas. Top each with 1 cup chicken, 2/3 cup kidney beans, 1 cup salsa, 1/2 cup sour cream, 1/2 cup green pepper, about 1/3 cup olives, 1/2 cup Monterey Jack cheese and 1/2 cup cheddar cheese. Repeat layers twice.

Cover and bake at 350° for 25 minutes. Uncover; bake 10-15 minutes longer or until the cheese is melted. Let stand for 10 minutes before serving. **Yield:** 2 casseroles (12 servings each).

Biscuit-Topped Lemon Chicken

(Pictured below)

PREP: 40 min. **BAKE:** 35 min.

This homey recipe combines two of my favorite things: hot, crusty biscuits and a flavorful lemon–pepper sauce. I've taken it to potlucks and given it as gifts.

—Pattie Ishee, Stringer, Mississippi

2 large onions, finely chopped
4 celery ribs, finely chopped
2 garlic cloves, minced
1 cup butter, cubed
8 green onions, thinly sliced
2/3 cup all-purpose flour
1/2 gallon milk
12 cups cubed cooked chicken
2 cans (10-3/4 ounces *each*) condensed cream of chicken soup, undiluted
1/2 cup lemon juice
2 tablespoons grated lemon peel
2 teaspoons pepper
1 teaspoon salt
CHEDDAR BISCUITS:
5 cups self-rising flour
2 cups milk
2 cups (8 ounces) shredded cheddar cheese
1/4 cup butter, melted

In a Dutch oven, saute the onions, celery and garlic in butter. Add green onions. Stir in flour until blended; gradually add milk. Bring to a boil; cook and stir for 2 minutes or until thickened.

Add the chicken, soup, lemon juice and peel, pepper and salt; heat through. Pour into two greased 13-in. x 9-in. x 2-in. baking dishes; set aside.

For the biscuits, in a large bowl, combine self-rising flour, milk, cheese and butter just until moistened. Turn onto a lightly floured surface; knead 8-10 times. Pat or roll out to 3/4-in. thickness. With a floured 2-1/2-in. biscuit cutter, cut out 30 biscuits.

Place over chicken mixture. Bake, uncovered, at 350° for 35-40 minutes or until golden brown. **Yield:** 15 servings (30 biscuits).

Editor's Note: As a substitute for each cup of self-rising flour, place 1-1/2 teaspoons baking powder and 1/2 teaspoon salt in a measuring cup. Add all-purpose flour to measure 1 cup.

Buffalo Chicken Dip

(Pictured above)

PREP/TOTAL TIME: 30 min.

This is a great, no–fuss dip my family loves for holiday and Super Bowl parties. Everywhere I take it, people ask for the tasty recipe. *—Peggy Foster, Florence, Kentucky*

1 package (8 ounces) cream cheese, softened
1 can (10 ounces) chunk white chicken, drained
1/2 cup buffalo wing sauce
1/2 cup ranch salad dressing
2 cups (8 ounces) shredded Colby-Monterey Jack cheese
Tortilla chips

Spread cream cheese into an ungreased shallow 1-qt. baking dish. Layer with chicken, buffalo wing sauce and ranch dressing. Sprinkle with cheese.

Bake, uncovered, at 350° for 20-25 minutes or until cheese is melted. Serve warm with tortilla chips. **Yield:** about 2 cups.

Cran-Apple Crisp

(Pictured below)

PREP: 30 min. **BAKE:** 35 min. + cooling

An eggnog sauce gives this crunchy oat–topped crisp a distinctive flavor. The apples and cranberries make it a natural for autumn celebrations and holiday get–togethers.
—Mary Lou Timpson, Colorado City, Arizona

- 2 snack-size cups (4 ounces *each*) vanilla pudding
- 1 cup eggnog
- 3/4 cup sugar
- 2 tablespoons all-purpose flour
- 5 cups thinly sliced peeled tart apples
- 2 cups fresh *or* frozen cranberries, thawed

TOPPING:
- 1 cup quick-cooking oats
- 3/4 cup packed brown sugar
- 2/3 cup all-purpose flour
- 1/2 teaspoon ground cinnamon
- 1/2 cup cold butter

In a small bowl, combine the pudding and eggnog until blended; cover and refrigerate until serving. In a large bowl, combine the sugar and flour. Add apples and cranberries; toss to coat. Transfer to an ungreased 13-in. x 9-in. x 2-in. baking dish.

For the topping, in a large bowl, combine the oats, brown sugar, flour and cinnamon; cut in butter until crumbly. Sprinkle over fruit mixture.

Bake at 375° for 35-40 minutes or until filling is bubbly and topping is golden brown. Cool for 10 minutes. Serve with eggnog sauce. **Yield:** 12-14 servings.

Editor's Note: This recipe was tested with commercially prepared eggnog.

Cheddar Ham Strata

(Pictured above)

PREP: 20 min. + chilling **BAKE:** 1 hour + standing

I prepare this ham and egg dish on Christmas Eve and refrigerate it overnight. Then, while we open presents on Christmas morning, I pop it in the oven for breakfast. It's a family tradition.
—Ann Pool, Jerome, Idaho

- 10 slices day-old bread, crusts removed and cubed
- 1 medium onion, finely chopped
- 4 medium fresh mushrooms, finely chopped
- 1/4 cup butter, cubed
- 4 cups (16 ounces) shredded cheddar cheese
- 2 cups cubed fully cooked ham
- 2 tablespoons all-purpose flour
- 8 eggs
- 3 cups milk
- 2 tablespoons prepared mustard
- 1 teaspoon garlic powder
- 1/2 teaspoon salt

Place the bread cubes in a greased 13-in. x 9-in. x 2-in. baking dish. In a small skillet, saute onion and mushrooms in butter; spoon over bread. Sprinkle with cheese, ham and flour. In a large bowl, whisk the eggs, milk, mustard, garlic powder and salt. Pour over ham and cheese. Cover and refrigerate overnight.

Remove from the refrigerator 30 minutes before baking. Bake, uncovered, at 350° for 60-70 minutes or until a knife inserted near the center comes out clean. Let stand for 10 minutes before serving. **Yield:** 12 servings.

greased 13-in. x 9-in. x 2-in. baking dishes. Pour remaining sauce over top.

Bake, uncovered, at 350° for 20 minutes. Sprinkle with remaining cheddar cheese. Bake 4-5 minutes longer or until cheese is melted. Garnish with lettuce, olives and sour cream if desired. **Yield:** 16 enchiladas.

Cinnamon-Sugar Rhubarb Cake

(Pictured below)

PREP: 30 min. **BAKE:** 40 min.

A real crowd-pleaser, this tender snack-like cake is chock-full of rhubarb and sprinkled with a sweet cinnamon-sugar topping. Everyone will be asking either for the recipe or for seconds!
—*Marlys Haber, White, South Dakota*

> 1/2 **cup shortening**
> 1 **cup packed brown sugar**
> 1 **cup sugar,** *divided*
> 1 **egg**
> 1 **teaspoon vanilla extract**
> 2 **cups all-purpose flour**
> 1 **teaspoon baking soda**
> 1/2 **teaspoon salt**
> 1 **cup buttermilk**
> 2 **cups diced fresh** *or* **frozen rhubarb**
> 1 **teaspoon ground cinnamon**

In a large bowl, cream the shortening, brown sugar and 1/2 cup sugar until light and fluffy. Add egg and vanilla; beat for 2 minutes. Combine the flour, baking soda and salt; add to creamed mixture alternately with buttermilk, beating well after each addition. Stir in the rhubarb.

Pour into a greased 13-in. x 9-in. x 2-in. baking dish. Combine the cinnamon and remaining sugar; sprinkle over batter. Bake at 350° for 40-45 minutes or until a toothpick inserted near the center comes out clean.

Cheese Enchiladas

(Pictured above)

PREP: 25 min. **BAKE:** 25 min.

You won't bring home leftovers when you make these easy enchiladas. With a homemade tomato sauce and cheesy filling, they always go fast. You can substitute the cheeses with any variety.
—*Ashley Schackow, Defiance, Ohio*

> 2 **cans (15 ounces** *each***) tomato sauce**
> 1-1/3 **cups water**
> 2 **tablespoons chili powder**
> 2 **garlic cloves, minced**
> 1 **teaspoon dried oregano**
> 1/2 **teaspoon ground cumin**
> 16 **flour tortillas (8 inches), warmed**
> 4 **cups (16 ounces) shredded Monterey Jack cheese**
> 2-1/2 **cups (10 ounces) shredded cheddar cheese,** *divided*
> 2 **medium onions, finely chopped**
> 1 **cup (8 ounces) sour cream**
> 1/4 **cup minced fresh parsley**
> 1/2 **teaspoon salt**
> 1/2 **teaspoon pepper**
> **Shredded lettuce, sliced ripe olives and additional sour cream, optional**

In a large saucepan, combine the first six ingredients. Bring to a boil. Reduce heat; simmer, uncovered, for 4-5 minutes or until thickened, stirring occasionally. Spread 2 tablespoons sauce over each tortilla.

In a large bowl, combine the Monterey Jack, 2 cups cheddar cheese, onions, sour cream, parsley, salt and pepper. Place about 1/3 cup down the center of each tortilla. Roll up and place seam side down in two

Serve warm. **Yield:** 12-16 servings.
   Editor's Note: If using frozen rhubarb, measure rhubarb while still frozen, then thaw completely. Drain in a colander, but do not press liquid out.

Tex-Mex Dip

PREP/TOTAL TIME: 15 min.

Fans of Southwest food will go crazy for this south-of-the-border dip. With refried beans, picante sauce, sour cream and guacamole, what's there not to like?
—*Terri Newton, Marshall, Texas*

   1 **can (16 ounces) refried beans**
1/4 **cup picante sauce**
1-1/2 **cups prepared guacamole**
1/2 **cup sour cream**
1/2 **cup mayonnaise**
4-1/2 **teaspoons taco seasoning**
   1 **cup (4 ounces) shredded cheddar cheese**
   1 **can (2-1/4 ounces) sliced ripe olives, drained**
Chopped green onions, shredded lettuce and chopped tomatoes
Tortilla chips

In a bowl, combine the beans and picante sauce. Spread onto a serving platter. Spread with guacamole. Combine the sour cream, mayonnaise and taco seasoning; spread over guacamole. Sprinkle with cheese, olives, onions, lettuce and tomatoes. Refrigerate until serving. Serve with tortilla chips. **Yield:** 12-14 servings.

Vanilla Pudding Dessert

PREP/TOTAL TIME: 30 min.

So easy to prepare, this eye-catching dessert will go fast, and everyone will want the recipe. Instead of strawberries, you can try peaches, pineapple or even bananas.
—*Betty Clemons, Hartselle, Alabama*

2-3/4 **cups cold milk**
   1 **package (5.1 ounces) instant vanilla pudding mix**
   1 **can (14 ounces) sweetened condensed milk**
   1 **carton (12 ounces) frozen whipped topping, thawed**
   4 **cups crushed vanilla wafers (about 120 wafers)**
   3 **cups sliced fresh strawberries**

In a large bowl, whisk milk and pudding mix for 2 minutes. Let stand for 15 minutes; fold in condensed milk. Set aside 1 tablespoon whipped topping and 2 tablespoons wafer crumbs. Fold remaining whipped topping into pudding.
   In a 3-qt. serving bowl, layer a third of the strawberries, wafer crumbs and pudding mixture. Repeat layers twice. Sprinkle with reserved wafer crumbs; top with reserved whipped topping. Refrigerate until serving. **Yield:** 12-14 servings.

Tortellini Spinach Casserole

(Pictured above and on page 182)

PREP: 20 min. **BAKE:** 20 min.

Spinach gives this popular casserole a fresh taste that will delight even those who say they don't like spinach. In fact, people are often surprised at just how good it is!
—*Barbara Kellen, Antioch, Illinois*

   2 **packages (10 ounces *each*) frozen cheese tortellini**
   1 **pound sliced fresh mushrooms**
   1 **teaspoon garlic powder**
1/4 **teaspoon onion powder**
1/4 **teaspoon pepper**
1/2 **cup butter, *divided***
   1 **can (12 ounces) evaporated milk**
   1 **block (8 ounces) brick cheese, cubed**
   3 **packages (10 ounces *each*) frozen chopped spinach, thawed and squeezed dry**
   2 **cups (8 ounces) shredded part-skim mozzarella cheese**

Cook the tortellini according to package directions. Meanwhile, in a large skillet, saute the mushrooms, garlic powder, onion powder and pepper in 1/4 cup butter until the mushrooms are tender. Remove and keep warm.
   In the same skillet, combine milk and remaining butter. Bring to a gentle boil; stir in brick cheese. Cook and stir until smooth. Drain tortellini; place in a large bowl. Stir in the mushroom mixture and spinach. Add cheese sauce and toss to coat.
   Transfer to a greased 3-qt. baking dish; sprinkle with the mozzarella cheese. Cover and bake at 350° for 15 minutes. Uncover; bake 5-10 minutes longer until heated through and the cheese is melted. **Yield:** 12 servings.

Spiral Pepperoni Pizza Bake

(Pictured below)

PREP: 30 min. **BAKE:** 40 min.

My grandmother used to fix this yummy dish for my Girl Scout troop when I was growing up. Now, I make it for my stepdaughters' scout troop. It's easy to prepare, and the girls always beg me to make it.
—Kimberly Howland, Fremont, Michigan

- 1 package (16 ounces) spiral pasta
- 2 pounds ground beef
- 1 large onion, chopped
- 1 teaspoon salt
- 1/2 teaspoon pepper
- 2 cans (15 ounces *each*) pizza sauce
- 1/2 teaspoon garlic salt
- 1/2 teaspoon Italian seasoning
- 2 eggs
- 2 cups milk
- 1/2 cup shredded Parmesan cheese
- 4 cups (16 ounces) shredded part-skim mozzarella cheese
- 1 package (3-1/2 ounces) sliced pepperoni

Cook pasta according to package directions. Meanwhile, in a Dutch oven, cook the beef, onion, salt and pepper over medium heat until meat is no longer pink; drain. Stir in the pizza sauce, garlic salt and Italian seasoning; remove from the heat and set aside.

In a small bowl, combine the eggs, milk and Parmesan cheese. Drain pasta; toss with egg mixture. Transfer to a greased 3-qt. baking dish. Top with beef mixture, mozzarella cheese and pepperoni.

Cover and bake at 350° for 20 minutes. Uncover; bake 20-25 minutes longer or until golden brown. **Yield:** 12 servings.

Apple Streusel Muffins

(Pictured above)

PREP: 20 min. **BAKE:** 15 min. + cooling

My husband and children enjoy these tender coffee cake–like muffins as a quick breakfast or snack on the run. The drizzle of glaze makes them pretty enough for company.
—Dulcy Grace, Roaring Spring, Pennsylvania

- 2 cups all-purpose flour
- 1 cup sugar
- 1 teaspoon baking powder
- 1/2 teaspoon baking soda
- 1/2 teaspoon salt
- 2 eggs
- 1/2 cup butter, melted
- 1-1/4 teaspoons vanilla extract
- 1-1/2 cups chopped peeled tart apples

STREUSEL TOPPING:
- 1/3 cup packed brown sugar
- 1 tablespoon all-purpose flour
- 1/8 teaspoon ground cinnamon
- 1 tablespoon cold butter

GLAZE:
- 1-1/2 cups confectioners' sugar
- 1 to 2 tablespoons milk
- 1 teaspoon butter, melted
- 1/4 teaspoon vanilla extract
- 1/8 teaspoon salt

In a bowl, combine the flour, sugar, baking powder, baking soda and salt. In another bowl, whisk the eggs, butter and vanilla; stir into dry ingredients just until moistened (batter will be stiff). Fold in apples.

Fill greased or paper-lined muffin cups three-fourths full. For the topping, combine the brown sugar, flour and cinnamon; cut in the butter until crumbly. Sprinkle over the batter.

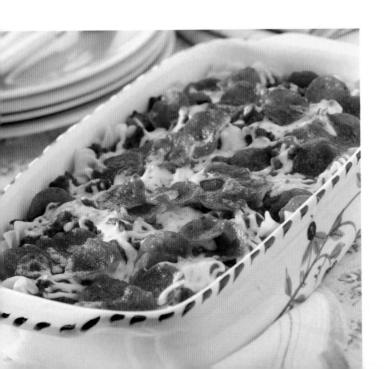

Bake at 375° for 15-20 minutes or until a toothpick comes out clean. Cool for 5 minutes before removing from pan to a wire rack to cool completely. Combine glaze ingredients; drizzle over muffins. **Yield:** 1 dozen.

Blue Cheese Deviled Eggs

PREP: 30 min. + chilling

I hope you'll agree that blue cheese and a hint of hot pepper in the filling puts these deviled eggs a step above the ordinary. They're always well received at a gathering.
—Nina Hall, Spokane, Washington

   24 **hard-cooked eggs**
    1 **cup (4 ounces) crumbled blue cheese**
  2/3 **cup mayonnaise**
    2 **tablespoons minced fresh parsley**
    1 **teaspoon hot pepper sauce**
  1/2 **teaspoon celery seed**
  1/2 **teaspoon pepper**
Diced celery

Cut eggs in half lengthwise. Remove yolks; set whites aside. In a large bowl, mash yolks. Add the blue cheese, mayonnaise, parsley, hot pepper sauce, celery seed and pepper; stir until well blended. Stuff or pipe into egg whites. Refrigerate until serving. Sprinkle with celery. **Yield:** 4 dozen.

Red Cream Soda Punch

(Pictured below)

PREP: 5 min. + chilling

The bright coral color and sweet citrusy flavor of this fizzy punch make it an instant hit with thirsty guests. Don't worry...there'll be plenty to go around! —*Naomi Cross, Millwood, Kentucky*

    4 **quarts cold water**
    2 **cans (12 ounces *each*) frozen orange juice**
      concentrate, thawed

    1 **can (12 ounces) frozen lemonade concentrate,**
      thawed
  1/2 **cup sugar**
    1 **bottle (2 liters) red cream soda, chilled**

In a large punch bowl or several pitchers, combine the water, concentrates and sugar; stir until the sugar is dissolved. Refrigerate for 2 hours or until chilled. Just before serving, stir in the cream soda. **Yield:** about 7 quarts.

Sweet Pea Salad

(Pictured above)

PREP: 30 min. + chilling

This high-yield salad always goes over well at potluck dinners. It combines vegetables with pasta, all in a creamy, sweet-and-sour dressing. —*Betty Otten, Tea, South Dakota*

    5 **pounds uncooked bow tie pasta**
    1 **pound carrots, shredded**
    1 **package (16 ounces) frozen peas, thawed**
   10 **celery ribs, diced**
    1 **small onion, finely chopped**
    5 **cups mayonnaise**
    4 **cups sweetened condensed milk**
2-1/2 **cups sugar**
  3/4 **cup cider vinegar**
  3/4 **cup buttermilk**
    2 **teaspoons salt**
    1 **teaspoon pepper**

Cook pasta according to package directions; drain. In three large bowls, combine the pasta, carrots, peas, celery and onion. In a large bowl, combine the remaining ingredients. Stir a third of the dressing into each bowl of pasta mixture. Cover and refrigerate until chilled. **Yield:** 58 servings.

Cooking for One or Two

Love to cook but don't like the leftovers? You've come to the right spot! Each of the sensational dishes featured here is just perfect for small households.

PAIRED-DOWN DELIGHTS. Clockwise from upper left: An Easy Irish Feast (p. 216), Salisbury Steak Supper (p. 214), Stuffed Pork Dinner for Two (p. 206), Daybreak Favorites (p. 208) and pictured center, Chicken for a Pair (p. 212).

Stuffed Pork Tenderloin

(Pictured at left)

PREP: 20 min. **BAKE:** 50 min.

My grandmother often prepared this dish for Sunday dinner. She loved to cook and eat, especially when she had someone to share her food with.

—Mary Ann Marino, West Pittsburg, Pennsylvania

- **1 pork tenderloin (3/4 to 1 pound)**
- **1/2 cup chopped onion**
- **2 tablespoons butter**
- **1 cup soft bread crumbs**
- **1/4 cup minced fresh parsley**
- **1/4 teaspoon rubbed sage**
- **1/4 teaspoon dried rosemary, crushed**
- **1/4 teaspoon salt**
- **1/8 teaspoon pepper**
- **1 egg, lightly beaten**
- **1 bacon strip**

Make a lengthwise slit about three-fourths of the way through tenderloin; open tenderloin so it lies flat. Flatten to 1/4-in. thickness; set aside.

In a small skillet, saute onion in butter until tender. Add bread crumbs; saute until crumbs are golden brown. Remove from the heat. Stir in the parsley, sage, rosemary, salt, pepper and enough egg to moisten the ingredients.

Spread stuffing on one long side of tenderloin to within 1/4 in. of edges. Close meat and place bacon on top; tie with kitchen string. Place on a rack in a shallow roasting pan.

Bake, uncovered, at 350° for 50-60 minutes or until a meat thermometer reads 160°. Let stand for 5 minutes before slicing. **Yield:** 2 servings.

Baked Garlic Green Beans

(Pictured at left)

PREP/TOTAL TIME: 20 min.

This flavorful dish dresses up frozen green beans with onion, cheese, bread crumbs and garlic. It's easy enough to serve any day of the week, yet special enough for fancy occasions.

—Marilyn Farmer, Centerville, Utah

- **1 tablespoon olive oil**
- **1-1/2 teaspoons cider vinegar**
- **1 teaspoon dried minced onion**
- **1 garlic clove, minced**
- **1/4 teaspoon salt**
- **Dash pepper**
- **1-1/2 cups frozen cut green beans, thawed**
- **1 tablespoon dry bread crumbs**
- **1 tablespoon grated Parmesan cheese**
- **1 teaspoon butter, melted**

In a small bowl, combine the oil, vinegar, onion, garlic, salt and pepper. Add the beans; toss to coat. Transfer to a greased 3-cup baking dish.

Combine the bread crumbs, Parmesan cheese and butter; sprinkle over beans. Bake, uncovered, at 350° for 10-15 minutes or until heated through. **Yield:** 2 servings.

Mixed Fruit Shortcakes

(Pictured below)

PREP/TOTAL TIME: 30 min.

This delightful downsized recipe makes just two biscuit–like shortcakes. Fill them with fresh fruit of your choice and top with whipped cream for an impressive dinner finale.

—Sue Ross, Casa Grande, Arizona

- **1 cup mixed fresh berries**
- **1/2 cup sliced fresh peaches *or* nectarines**
- **4 teaspoons sugar, *divided***
- **1/2 cup all-purpose flour**
- **3/4 teaspoon baking powder**
- **1/8 teaspoon salt**
- **2 tablespoons shortening**
- **3 tablespoons milk**
- **Whipped cream**

In a large bowl, combine the berries, peaches and 2 teaspoons sugar; set aside. In another large bowl, combine the flour, baking powder and salt; cut in shortening until mixture is crumbly. Stir in milk just until moistened. Drop by 1/3 cupfuls 2 in. apart onto an ungreased baking sheet. Flatten into 2-1/2-in. circles. Sprinkle with remaining sugar.

Bake at 425° for 10-12 minutes or until golden brown. Remove to a wire rack to cool. Split shortcakes in half horizontally. Spoon fruit onto bottoms; replace tops. Garnish with whipped cream. **Yield:** 2 servings.

Bacon-Egg English Muffin

(Pictured below)

PREP/TOTAL TIME: 15 min.

I stack cheese, Canadian bacon and poached eggs on an English muffin to make this appealing entree. Perfect for one, this delicious open-face sandwich is special enough for guests, too.
—Terry Kuehn, Waunakee, Wisconsin

- **2 eggs**
- **1 tablespoon cream cheese, softened**
- **1 English muffin, split and toasted**
- **2 slices process American cheese**
- **2 slices Canadian bacon**

In a large skillet, saucepan or omelet pan with high sides, bring 2-3 in. water to a boil. Reduce heat; simmer gently. Break cold eggs, one at a time, into a custard cup or saucer. Holding the dish close to the surface of the water, slip eggs, one at a time, into the water. Cook, uncovered, until whites are completely set and yolks begin to thicken, about 3 minutes.

Meanwhile, spread cream cheese over muffin halves. Top with cheese slices; set aside. In a small skillet, cook Canadian bacon until heated through; place over cheese. Using a slotted spoon, place eggs over bacon. **Yield:** 1-2 servings.

Fruity French Toast

(Pictured at far right)

PREP/TOTAL TIME: 15 min.

My son begged me to try making the stuffed French toast we enjoyed when our family visited Walt Disney World. His encouragement resulted in this easy, delicious breakfast that's a favorite on Saturday morning.
—Nancy Hawthorne, Gettysburg, Pennsylvania

- **1 medium firm banana, sliced**
- **4 slices Texas toast**
- **2 teaspoons confectioners' sugar, divided**
- **2 large strawberries, sliced**
- **1 egg**
- **1/2 cup milk**
- **1/2 teaspoon vanilla extract**
- **1/4 teaspoon ground cinnamon**
- **2 teaspoons butter**
Maple syrup

Place banana slices on two slices of toast. Sprinkle each with 1/2 teaspoon confectioners' sugar. Top with strawberries and remaining toast. In a shallow bowl, whisk the egg, milk, vanilla and cinnamon. Dip toast in egg mixture, coating both sides.

In a large skillet, melt butter over medium heat; cook toast for 2-4 minutes on each side or until golden brown. Sprinkle with remaining confectioners' sugar. Serve with maple syrup. **Yield:** 2 servings.

Berry Banana Smoothies

(Pictured at right)

PREP/TOTAL TIME: 15 min.

My mother gave me this quick-to-fix nutritious smoothie, which is thick, frothy and offers a refreshing fruit flavor. I fix it for breakfast or a bedtime snack.
—Linda Barker, Mohawk, Michigan

- **1-1/2 cups vanilla *or* plain yogurt**
- **2/3 cup orange juice**
- **2 medium ripe bananas, cut into chunks**
- **1 cup halved fresh strawberries**
- **2 teaspoons honey**

In a blender, combine all ingredients; cover and process until smooth. Pour into chilled glasses; serve immediately. **Yield:** 2 servings.

Valentine Cakes

(Pictured below)

PREP: 30 min. **BAKE:** 15 min. + cooling

These individual chocolate layer cakes are a sweet way to say "I love you" even when it's not Valentine's Day.
— Dixie Terry, Goreville, Illinois

- 3/4 **cup all-purpose flour**
- 1/4 **cup sugar**
- 1/4 **cup packed brown sugar**
- 3 **tablespoons baking cocoa**
- 1/2 **teaspoon baking soda**
- 1/8 **teaspoon salt**
- 1/2 **cup water**
- 3 **tablespoons canola oil**
- 1/2 **teaspoon white vinegar**
- 1/2 **teaspoon vanilla extract**

FROSTING:
- 1-1/3 **cups confectioners' sugar**
- 2 **tablespoons baking cocoa**
- 2 to 3 **tablespoons milk**
- 2 **tablespoons butter, melted**
- 1/4 **teaspoon vanilla extract**

Decorating icing and confetti candies

In a large bowl, combine the first six ingredients. Add the water, oil, vinegar and vanilla. Coat an 8-in. square baking dish with cooking spray and dust with flour; add batter.

Bake at 350° for 15-20 minutes or until a toothpick inserted near center comes out clean. Cool for 10 minutes before removing from pan to a wire rack to cool completely.

For the frosting, in a small bowl, beat the confectioners' sugar, cocoa, milk, butter and vanilla until smooth; set aside. Transfer cake to a work surface. Using a 3- to 3-1/2-in. heart-shaped cookie cutter, gently cut out four heart-shaped cakes (set cake scraps aside for another use).

Place one heart on a serving plate; spread with some frosting. Top with a second cake; frost top and sides. Repeat with remaining cakes and frosting. Decorate with icing and candies. **Yield:** 2 servings.

Sweetheart Steaks

(Pictured at right)

PREP: 10 min. **COOK:** 50 min.

I created this recipe when I was planning a steak dinner and wanted a barbecue sauce to go with it. Try the sauce on pork and chicken, too.
— Dolores Jensen, Arnold, Missouri

- 3 **tablespoons Catalina salad dressing**
- 3 **tablespoons honey**
- 3 **tablespoons apricot preserves**
- 3 **tablespoons grape jelly**
- 2 **tablespoons minced chives**
- 2 **tablespoons balsamic vinegar**
- 2 **tablespoons olive oil**
- 2 **tablespoons ketchup**
- 1 **tablespoon soy sauce**
- 3 **garlic cloves, minced**
- 1 **teaspoon ground mustard**
- 1 **teaspoon Worcestershire sauce**
- 1/2 **teaspoon salt**
- 1/2 **teaspoon crushed red pepper flakes**
- 1/4 **teaspoon pepper**
- 2 **beef tenderloin steaks (1-1/2 to 2 inches thick)**

In a small saucepan, combine the first 15 ingredients. Bring to a boil. Reduce heat; simmer, uncovered, for 30 minutes; stirring occasionally. Set aside 1/4 cup sauce for serving and keep warm.

Place steaks on a broiler pan; top with some of the remaining sauce. Broil 4-6 in. from the heat for 10-16 minutes on each side or until meat reaches desired doneness (for medium-rare, a meat thermometer should read 145°; medium, 160°; well-done, 170°), basting occasionally with remaining sauce. Serve with reserved sauce. **Yield:** 2 servings.

Cheese-Stuffed Potatoes

(Pictured above right)

PREP: 15 min. **BAKE:** 1 hour

Cottage cheese is the "secret" ingredient in this creamy side dish. I make myself two potatoes—one for dinner and one for lunch the next day.
— Janet English, Pittsburgh, Pennsylvania

- 2 **medium baking potatoes**
- 1 **small onion, finely chopped**

2 tablespoons water
1/2 cup 4% cottage cheese
1/4 cup buttermilk
    3 tablespoons grated Parmesan cheese
Salt and pepper to taste
    2 tablespoons thinly sliced green onions

Bake potatoes at 400° for 1 hour or until tender. Cut a thin slice off the top of each potato and discard. Scoop out pulp, leaving a thin shell. In a small mixing bowl, mash pulp; set aside.

  In a small skillet, cook and stir the onion in water for 2-3 minutes or until tender. Add the mashed potatoes, cottage cheese, buttermilk, Parmesan cheese, salt and pepper. Stir until blended and heated through. Spoon into potato shells. Sprinkle with green onions. **Yield:** 2 servings.

Simple Substitute

Don't have the buttermilk called for in Cheese-Stuffed Potatoes? Don't worry! You can still serve up their comforting goodness tonight.

  You can always substitute the buttermilk in this recipe with 1/4 cup of plain yogurt, but there are a few different substitutes for buttermilk you can mix up on your own.

  For instance, mix 1 tablespoon of white vinegar or lemon juice with enough milk to measure 1 cup. Stir the mixture, then let it stand for 5 minutes before using. You could also mix 1-3/4 teaspoons cream of tartar into 1 cup of milk.

Honey-Mustard Chicken

(Pictured at far right)

PREP/TOTAL TIME: 30 min.

This entree combines my husband's love for mustard with my love for anything sweet, like honey. The yummy curry taste really sends this dish over the top! We like to enjoy it with rice pilaf.
—Lisa Varner, Greenville, South Carolina

- 1/4 **cup honey**
- 2 **tablespoons butter, melted**
- 2 **tablespoons Dijon mustard**
- 1 **tablespoon orange juice**
- 1/8 **teaspoon curry powder**
- 2 **boneless skinless chicken breast halves**
- 1 **tablespoon canola oil**
- 1/8 **teaspoon salt**
- 1/8 **teaspoon pepper**

Combine the honey, butter, mustard, orange juice and curry powder. Spoon half of the mixture into a greased 8-in. baking dish.

In a skillet, brown chicken in oil. Sprinkle with salt and pepper. Place chicken over sauce in baking dish; turn to coat.

Bake, uncovered, at 350° for 15 minutes. Drizzle with remaining sauce. Bake 5-10 minutes longer or until a meat thermometer reads 170°. **Yield:** 2 servings.

Sweet Herbed Carrots

(Pictured at far right)

PREP/TOTAL TIME: 25 min.

The original recipe, which my mother acquired over 45 years ago, called for two bunches of small carrots so I had to guess how much to use. I eventually got the recipe amounts worked out to my liking. —Beverly Christofferson, Sioux City, Iowa

- 2 **tablespoons butter**
- 1/4 **teaspoon sugar**
- 2 **cups sliced fresh carrots**
- 3 **to 4 lettuce leaves**
- 2 **tablespoons water**
- 2 **tablespoons minced fresh parsley**
- 2 **tablespoons heavy whipping cream**
- 1 **tablespoon minced fresh tarragon** *or*
  1 **teaspoon dried tarragon**
- 1/4 **teaspoon salt**
- 1/8 **teaspoon pepper**

In a large skillet, cook and stir the butter and sugar over medium heat until butter is melted and sugar is dissolved. Stir in carrots; cover with lettuce leaves. Sprinkle with water. Cover and simmer for 15-20 minutes or until carrots are crisp-tender.

Discard lettuce. Stir in the parsley, cream, tarragon, salt and pepper. Bring to a boil. Reduce heat; simmer,

uncovered, for 1-2 minutes or until heated through. Serve with a slotted spoon. **Yield:** 2 servings.

Almond-Lemon Pound Cake

(Pictured at right)

PREP: 20 min. **BAKE:** 40 min. + cooling

This is the first cake I learned to bake more than 30 years ago, and it's still a favorite of mine. You can freeze any leftovers for another time.
—Michaela Rosenthal, Woodland Hills, California

- 1 **teaspoon plus 3/4 cup butter, softened, divided**
- 2 **teaspoons confectioners' sugar**
- 1 **cup slivered almonds**
- 1 **cup sugar**
- 2 **eggs**
- 1/3 **cup sour cream**
- 1 **tablespoon grated lemon peel**
- 1 **cup cake flour**
- 1 **teaspoon baking powder**
- 1/4 **cup lemon juice**

TOPPING:

- 1 **cup** *each* **frozen unsweetened raspberries, strawberries and blueberries**
- 1/4 **cup sugar**
- 2 **tablespoons lemon juice**
- 2 **tablespoons confectioners' sugar**

Grease bottom and sides of 9-in. round baking pan with 1 teaspoon butter. Sprinkle with confectioners' sugar; set aside. Place almonds and sugar in blender or food processor. Cover; process until finely ground.

In a small bowl, cream remaining butter; beat in almond mixture until combined. Add eggs, one at a time, beating well after each addition. Stir in sour cream and lemon peel. Combine the flour and baking powder; add to creamed mixture alternately with lemon juice. Pour into prepared pan.

Bake at 350° for 40-45 minutes or until toothpick inserted near center comes out clean. Cool on wire rack for 10 minutes. Invert onto rack to cool completely.

For topping, in a heavy saucepan, combine the berries, sugar and lemon juice. Cook and stir over medium-low heat for 10 minutes or until mixture begins to thicken. Sprinkle cake with confectioners' sugar. Serve with berry topping. **Yield:** 6 servings.

Perfect Pound Cake

First, bring all of the ingredients to room temperature. Cream butter until fluffy; gradually add sugar. Add eggs one at a time, beating 1 minute after each. Combine dry ingredients; add alternately with liquid in three stages. Do not overbeat.

Salisbury Steak

(Pictured at left)

PREP/TOTAL TIME: 30 min.

Sometimes I forget about this favorite recipe, so my husband will say, "How about Salisbury Steak for dinner?" He really likes it.
—Toni Martin, Byron Center, Michigan

- 1 egg
- 1/4 cup milk
- 1/4 cup dry bread crumbs
- 1 envelope brown gravy mix, *divided*
- 1 teaspoon dried minced onion
- 1/2 pound lean ground beef
- 1/2 cup water
- 1 tablespoon prepared mustard

In a large bowl, whisk egg and milk. Add the bread crumbs, 1 tablespoon gravy mix and onion. Crumble beef over mixture and mix well. Shape into two patties, about 3/4 in. thick.

Broil 3-4 in. from the heat for 6-7 minutes on each side or until meat is no longer pink and a meat thermometer reads 160°.

Place the remaining gravy mix in a small saucepan; stir in the water and mustard. Bring to a boil; cook and stir until thickened. Serve with patties. **Yield:** 2 servings.

Tomato Rice Pilaf

(Pictured at left)

PREP/TOTAL TIME: 25 min.

Parsley, green onion and tomato add festive color to this mild rice dish. I serve the pilaf quite often as a change of pace from potatoes.
—Carole Fraser, North York, Ontario

- 2 teaspoons butter
- 1/2 cup uncooked long grain rice
- 1 small onion, sliced
- 1-1/4 cups chicken broth
- 2 tablespoons chopped green onion
- 2 tablespoons chopped tomato
- 2 tablespoons minced fresh parsley

A Timely Tip

Tomato Rice Pilaf was tested with a 1,100-watt microwave. If your microwave wattage is lower than that, you can still prepare the pilaf using the time-saving device. Simply start with a cook time that is one-third longer than what is called for in the recipe, testing for doneness regularly.

In a 3-cup microwave-safe dish, melt butter. Stir in the rice and onion. Microwave, uncovered, on high for 2-3 minutes or until rice is lightly browned and onion is tender, stirring once. Add broth.

Cover and cook on high for 13-15 minutes or until liquid is absorbed. Stir in the green onion, tomato and parsley. **Yield:** 2 servings.

Editor's Note: This recipe was tested in a 1,100-watt microwave.

Baked Bananas In Orange Sauce

(Pictured above)

PREP/TOTAL TIME: 30 min.

This simply luscious dessert is wonderful served with a scoop of vanilla ice cream. Plus, it looks pretty enough to serve for a special occasion.
—Gusty Crum, Dover, Ohio

- 2 medium firm bananas
- 2 teaspoons butter, melted
- 1/4 cup orange juice
- 2 tablespoons brown sugar
- 2 teaspoons grated orange peel
- Vanilla ice cream

Cut each banana in half lengthwise; place cut side down in a greased 8-in. square baking dish. Brush with butter. Bake, uncovered, at 350° for 10 minutes.

Combine the orange juice, brown sugar and orange peel; pour over bananas. Bake 10 minutes longer. Serve with ice cream. **Yield:** 2 servings.

Corned Beef Supper

(Pictured at left)

PREP: 25 min. **COOK:** 3 hours 50 min.

What better way to celebrate St. Patty's Day than with this one-pot meal? The beef, potatoes and carrots are full-flavored.
—Dawn Fagerstrom, Warren, Minnesota

- **1 small onion, sliced**
- **4 small carrots, cut into chunks**
- **2 medium potatoes, cut into chunks**
- **1 corned beef brisket with spice packet (1 pound)**
- **1/3 cup unsweetened apple juice**
- **2 whole cloves**
- **1 tablespoon brown sugar**
- **1/2 teaspoon grated orange peel**
- **1/2 teaspoon prepared mustard**
- **2 cabbage wedges**

Place onion in a 3-qt. slow cooker. Top with carrots, potatoes and brisket. Combine the apple juice, cloves, brown sugar, orange peel, mustard and contents of spice packet; pour over brisket. Cover and cook on high for 3-1/2 to 4 hours.

Add cabbage; cover and cook 20-30 minutes longer or until meat and vegetables are tender. Strain and discard the cloves; serve the pan juices with the corned beef and vegetables. **Yield:** 2 servings.

Irish Soda Muffins

(Pictured at left)

PREP/TOTAL TIME: 30 min.

Who says muffins have to be boring? These little gems are always a hit. When blueberries are in season, I use them instead of raisins. —Camille Wisniewski, Jackson, New Jersey

- **1 cup plus 2 tablespoons all-purpose flour**
- **1/4 cup plus 1 teaspoon sugar, *divided***
- **1 teaspoon baking powder**
- **1/4 teaspoon baking soda**
- **1/4 teaspoon salt**
- **1/2 cup sour cream**
- **2 tablespoons canola oil**
- **2 tablespoons beaten egg**
- **1/3 cup raisins**

In a small bowl, combine the flour, 1/4 cup sugar, baking powder, baking soda and salt. In another bowl, whisk the sour cream, oil and egg; stir into dry ingredients just until moistened. Fold in raisins.

Fill six greased or paper-lined muffin cups half full. Sprinkle with remaining sugar. Bake at 400° for 15-18 minutes or until a toothpick comes out clean. Cool for 5 minutes before removing to a wire rack. Serve warm. **Yield:** 6 muffins.

Minty Ice Cream Shamrocks

(Pictured above)

PREP: 30 min. + chilling **BAKE:** 10 min. + freezing

With a soft, chewy chocolate cookie and festive mint green ice cream, these fun desserts are a sweet delight. Cut out the cookie wafers in any shape, and use any flavor ice cream you choose.
—Beverly Coyde, Gasport, New York

- **6 tablespoons butter, softened**
- **3/4 cup sugar**
- **1 egg**
- **1-1/2 teaspoons milk**
- **3/4 teaspoon vanilla extract**
- **1-1/3 cups all-purpose flour**
- **1/4 cup baking cocoa**
- **1-1/4 teaspoons baking powder**
- **1/4 teaspoon salt**
- **1-1/2 to 2 cups mint chocolate chip ice cream, softened**

In a small bowl, cream butter and sugar. Add egg, milk and vanilla; mix well. Combine the flour, cocoa, baking powder and salt; gradually add to creamed mixture just until blended. Divide dough into two portions; flatten. Wrap in plastic wrap and refrigerate for 1 hour or until firm.

On a lightly floured surface, roll out dough to 1/8- to 1/4-in. thickness. Cut with a floured 3-in. shamrock cookie cutter. Place 2 in. apart on parchment paper-lined baking sheets. Prick with a fork if desired.

Bake at 350° for 7-10 minutes or until set. Cool for 2 minutes before removing from pans to wire racks to cool completely.

Spread 1/4 to 1/3 cup ice cream over the bottom of six cookies; top with remaining cookies. Wrap individually in plastic wrap; freeze. May be frozen for up to 2 months. **Yield:** 6 servings.

My Mom's Best Meal

Many delicious memories are shared by *Taste of Home* readers who fondly recall their mothers' cooking. Here are eight stories with tempting recipes so you can create these treasured meals, too.

MEMORY-MAKING DINNERS. Clockwise from upper left: Hens with Apricot Rice Stuffing (p. 222), Comforting Broccoli Casserole (p. 246), Mom's Fried Fish (p. 238), Parsnip Pancakes (p. 227) and Ice Cream Cookie Dessert (p. 247).

Her Italian mom's made-from-scratch dinners had mass appeal and left a legacy of love.

By Jodi Grable, Springfield, Missouri

Cooking for a crowd came naturally for my mom, Antoinette DeGear (above). She grew up in an Italian family in Iowa, the youngest of six kids. And she raised eight kids of her own. (I'm the youngest.)

With such a large family, huge gatherings were the norm. Mom loved to entertain, and we often had dinner parties for 30 people or more. Whether she was serving family or guests, she always set a beautiful table with crystal stemware and good china.

When I was a child, Mom always seemed to be cooking. My favorite days were when she was making homemade spaghetti sauce. I'd come home from school and eat a bowl of it like soup!

My mother has always cooked from scratch, and since she was a child of the Depression, she learned to be creative with garden produce and leftovers.

My favorite meal has to be her Hens with Apricot Rice Stuffing, Bacon Squash Saute, Orange and Red Onion Salad and Banana Cream Pie.

We all love apricots, so Mom tried to work them into any recipe she could, including her tender stuffed hens. The sweet apricots and sauteed mushrooms make the wild rice stuffing so moist and flavorful.

Bacon Squash Saute is a delicious way to use up homegrown squash and zucchini. And Mom's pretty onion salad is a pleasing mix of sweet and tangy.

Cream pies are my mom's specialty, and Banana Cream Pie, with sliced almonds on top, is the best. My late husband requested this pie often.

Mom still cooks every day, but now for fewer people (her children, 27 grandchildren and 28 great-grandchildren are scattered across the country). She and my stepfather live near me and my son, Kirsch, and the four of us eat together on weekends.

For Mom's 75th birthday, I compiled a cookbook of her recipes and gave copies to her and my siblings. The cookbook wouldn't have been complete without the recipes I've shared with you. I hope everyone loves them as much as we do.

PICTURED Clockwise from upper left: Hens with Apricot Rice Stuffing, Banana Cream Pie, Bacon Squash Saute and Orange and Red Onion Salad (recipes are on the next page).

Hens with Apricot Rice Stuffing

PREP: 25 min. **BAKE:** 2 hours

　1 cup sliced fresh mushrooms
3/4 cup chopped pecans
1/2 cup chopped onion
　6 tablespoons butter, *divided*
　1 cup cooked wild rice
1/2 cup chopped dried apricots
　1 tablespoon minced fresh parsley
1/2 teaspoon salt
1/4 teaspoon pepper
1/8 teaspoon cayenne pepper
　4 Cornish game hens (20 ounces *each*)
1/2 cup apricot preserves
　1 tablespoon white vinegar

In a large skillet, saute the mushrooms, pecans and onion in 4 tablespoons butter until tender. Stir in the rice, apricots, parsley, salt, pepper and cayenne.

　Spoon about 3/4 cup of the rice mixture into each hen; tie legs together. Place hens, breast side up, on a rack in a shallow roasting pan. Melt the remaining butter; drizzle over hens.

　Bake, uncovered, at 350° for 1-3/4 to 2 hours or until a meat thermometer reads 180° for hens and 165° for stuffing. In a small saucepan, warm preserves and vinegar; spoon over hens. Bake 15 minutes longer.
Yield: 4 servings.

Bacon Squash Saute

PREP/TOTAL TIME: 20 min.

　6 bacon strips, diced
　2 small zucchini, cut into 1/4-inch slices
　2 small yellow summer squash, cut into 1/4-inch slices
　1 medium onion, thinly sliced

In a large skillet, cook the bacon over medium heat until crisp; remove to paper towels. Drain, reserving 2 tablespoons of the drippings. In the drippings, saute the zucchini, yellow summer squash and onion for 6-8 minutes or until crisp-tender. Sprinkle with bacon.
Yield: 4 servings.

Orange and Red Onion Salad

PREP/TOTAL TIME: 15 min.

　4 cups torn romaine
　2 medium navel oranges, peeled and sectioned
　1 small red onion, sliced and separated into rings
1/4 cup olive oil
　3 tablespoons red wine vinegar
　1 teaspoon sugar
1/4 teaspoon salt
1/8 teaspoon pepper

vanilla. Press plastic wrap onto surface of custard; cover and refrigerate for 30 minutes.

Slice the bananas into pastry shell; pour custard over top. Spread with whipped cream; sprinkle with almonds. Chill for 6-8 hours or overnight. Refrigerate leftovers. **Yield:** 6-8 servings.

Banana Basics

The riper a banana becomes, the sweeter it will taste. That's because the starch in bananas turns to sugar as the fruit ripens.

Green-tipped bananas are best for cooking, while yellow are great for salads, cereals or immediate eating. Fully ripe bananas with brown-speckled peels are perfect for baking in breads or mashing into fruit smoothies.

Cooler temperatures slow down the ripening process of bananas, while warmer temperatures speed it up. To make a banana ripen quickly, place it in a brown paper bag with either an apple or tomato and leave it overnight, keeping the bag out of direct sunlight.

On a serving platter, arrange the romaine, oranges and onion. In a jar with a tight-fitting lid, combine the remaining ingredients; shake well. Drizzle over salad; serve immediately. **Yield:** 4 servings.

Banana Cream Pie

PREP: 10 min. COOK: 15 min. + chilling

- 1 cup sugar
- 1/4 cup cornstarch
- 1/2 teaspoon salt
- 3 cups milk
- 2 eggs, lightly beaten
- 3 tablespoons butter
- 1-1/2 teaspoons vanilla extract
- 2 large firm bananas
- 1 pastry shell (9 inches), baked
- 1 cup heavy whipping cream, whipped
- 1 tablespoon sliced almonds, toasted

In a large saucepan, combine the sugar, cornstarch, salt and milk until smooth. Cook and stir over medium-high heat until thickened and bubbly. Reduce heat; cook and stir 2 minutes longer. Remove from the heat. Stir a small amount of hot filling into eggs; return all to the pan. Bring to a gentle boil; cook and stir 2 minutes longer.

Remove from the heat. Gently stir in butter and

Stuffed pork roasts were the centerpiece of her mom's special Sunday noontime meals.

By Lois Frazee, Gardnerville, Nevada

I've spent part of my life teaching college-level nutrition classes and taste-testing for a federal research lab. But my fondest food-related memories center on my mother's kitchen.

My mom, Sarah Catterson (above), taught school for a short time before I was born. From then on, she was devoted, full-time, to taking care of her family—me, brother Donald and our dad, Frehn, who was a chemical engineer.

There weren't a lot of convenience foods back then, so Mom made everything from scratch. I liked to help her, and I learned to cook in the process.

On Sundays, our big meal was at noon, and Mom often served a roast. Her best was Pork Tenderloin with Stuffing, with Zucchini Apple Salad, Parsnip Pancakes and Raspberry Squares.

Pork Tenderloin with Stuffing was so special-looking that Mom served it for company, too. If you like, prepare it with her stuffing or use one of your own favorite recipes.

I think she came up with her refreshing Apple Zucchini Salad because the colors looked so pretty in a glass bowl.

Mom liked parsnips, so she sometimes substituted them in her potato pancake recipe to make Parsnip Pancakes. Parsnips, rutabaga and other root vegetables were plentiful in Winnipeg, Manitoba, where we lived at the time.

A friend gave Mom the recipe for Raspberry Squares. She'd make them when neighbors came to play bridge.

It was the Depression era, so Mom made the most of the food we had. She'd grind up leftover roast from Sunday dinner with gravy for sandwiches.

I inherited Mom's love of cooking and still enjoy preparing meals when my own children visit. I have two daughters, a son and five grandchildren.

I hope you'll share Mom's menu with your family and enjoy it as much as we have.

PICTURED Clockwise from upper left: Pork Tenderloin with Stuffing, Zucchini Apple Salad, Parsnip Pancakes and Raspberry Squares (recipes are on the next page).

2 pork tenderloins (1 pound *each*)
2 tablespoons canola oil

In a small skillet, saute celery and onion in butter until tender. In a bowl, combine the bread cubes, celery mixture, salt and pepper; set aside.

Cut a lengthwise slit down the center of each tenderloin to within 1/2 in. of bottom. Open tenderloins so they lie flat; cover with plastic wrap. Flatten to 1/2-in. thickness. In a large skillet, brown pork in oil on both sides over medium-high heat.

Spoon stuffing onto one tenderloin. Top with the second tenderloin; tie with kitchen string. Place on a rack in a shallow roasting pan.

Bake, uncovered, at 350° for 50-60 minutes or until a meat thermometer inserted into meat reads 160°. Let stand for 5 minutes before slicing. **Yield:** 6 servings.

Zucchini Apple Salad

PREP/TOTAL TIME: 10 min.

2 medium red apples, chopped
2 small zucchini, chopped
1/2 cup coarsely chopped walnuts
2/3 cup Italian salad dressing

In a serving bowl, toss the apples, zucchini, walnuts and salad dressing. **Yield:** 6 servings.

Pork Tenderloin with Stuffing

PREP: 20 min. **BAKE:** 50 min.

4 celery ribs, chopped
1 small onion, chopped
2 tablespoons butter
6 cups cubed day-old bread (1/2-inch cubes)
1/2 teaspoon salt
1/4 teaspoon pepper

Cooking with Pork

Sealed, prepacked fresh cuts of pork can be refrigerated for 2 to 4 days. If you plan to keep it longer than this, wrap it well and store it in the freezer for up to 6 months. Thaw the pork overnight in the refrigerator before cooking.

Fresh pork cooks quickly and needs only to be cooked to an internal temperature of 160° and until the juices run clear. Boneless pork roasts may still be be faint pink in the center.

Unlike beef, cuts of pork have less variation in tenderness. Use dry-heat cooking methods, such as broiling, grilling, pan-broiling, roasting or stir-frying, when a firm texture is desired.

1/4 cup packed brown sugar
1/2 cup butter, melted
 2 packages (8 ounces *each*) cream cheese, softened
3/4 cup sugar
 1 carton (8 ounces) frozen whipped topping, thawed
 2 packages (3 ounces *each*) raspberry gelatin
 2 cups boiling water
 2 cups cold water

In a large bowl, combine the flour, pecans and brown sugar; stir in butter until crumbly. Press into an ungreased 13-in. x 9-in. x 2-in. baking dish. Bake at 350° for 10-13 minutes or until lightly browned. Cool on a wire rack.

In a large bowl, beat cream cheese and sugar until smooth; fold in whipped topping. Spread over crust. Cover and refrigerate for 1 hour.

In a small bowl, dissolve gelatin in boiling water; stir in cold water. Spoon over cream cheese layer. Chill until firm. Cut into squares. **Yield:** 12-16 servings.

Parsnip Pancakes

PREP/TOTAL TIME: 30 min.

 2 pounds parsnips, peeled
 1 teaspoon salt
1/2 cup chopped onion
1/4 cup all-purpose flour
 1 egg, lightly beaten
 1 tablespoon minced chives
 2 to 4 tablespoons canola oil

Place the parsnips in a large saucepan and cover with water; add salt. Bring to a boil over medium-high heat. Reduce heat; cover and cook for 15-20 minutes or until tender.

Drain and place parsnips in a large bowl; mash. Stir in the onion, flour, egg and chives.

Heat 2 tablespoons of oil in a large nonstick skillet over medium heat. Drop the batter by 1/4 cupfuls into oil. Fry in batches until golden brown on both sides, using the remaining oil as needed. Drain on paper towels. **Yield:** 6 servings.

Raspberry Squares

PREP: 20 min. + chilling **BAKE:** 10 min. + cooling

 1 cup all-purpose flour
1/2 cup finely chopped pecans

Her mom's kitchen
was overflowing
with home-cooked,
delicious dishes for
family and friends.

By P. Lauren Fay–Neri, Syracuse, New York

It didn't matter if you were a relative, a neighbor or a friend. When you came to our house, my mother, Madeline Fay (above), would ask, "Did you eat? Sit down and have a bite!"

If you didn't eat at our house, she'd send you home with a container of food. Mom liked to take care of everyone.

When my four brothers and I were growing up, the house was always filled with delicious foods, from soups to desserts. We enjoyed Mom's great home-cooked meals as well as her delicious cookies and cakes. Everything was prepared from scratch; she never used packaged mixes.

One of our favorite meals featured beautiful Holiday Spiral Ham, Candied Carrots, Corn Pudding and Pineapple Sour Cream Pie for dessert.

Mom served the ham, with cranberry-apple relish and pineapple wedges, for holiday dinners. Although I preferred plain carrots to the Candied Carrots, everyone else enjoyed the sweet brown sugar glaze. Her Corn Pudding is delicious served warm. I also like the leftovers served cold.

Pineapple Sour Cream Pie is a refreshing alternative to traditional favorites like apple and pumpkin. Sometimes, instead of preparing meringue, I'll top the pie with fresh whipped cream. I make the pie a day ahead of time and add the whipped cream just before serving.

I'd call my mother a "natural" cook. She'd follow a recipe at first, but then substituted different ingredients. She memorized much of what she did.

I still have my mom's worn, wallpaper-covered cookbook. The envelopes inside are stuffed with recipes she gathered during her lifetime.

Because she didn't write down many of her own recipes, I don't often make a lot of Mom's dishes. But I think of her each night when I put together our meal. I hope you like this special menu.

PICTURED Clockwise from upper left: Holiday Spiral Ham, Pineapple Sour Cream Pie, Candied Carrots and Corn Pudding (recipes are on the next page).

Candied Carrots

PREP/TOTAL TIME: 30 min.

- **2 pounds carrots, cut into sticks**
- **1/4 cup butter**
- **1/4 cup packed brown sugar**
- **1/4 teaspoon salt**
- **1/8 teaspoon white pepper**

Place carrots in a large saucepan; add 1 in. of water. Bring to a boil. Reduce heat; cover and simmer for 8-10 minutes or until crisp-tender. Drain and set aside.

In the same pan, combine the butter, brown sugar, salt and pepper; cook and stir until butter is melted. Return carrots to the pan; cook and stir over medium heat for 5 minutes or until glazed. **Yield:** 8 servings.

Corn Pudding

PREP: 20 min. BAKE: 45 min.

- **1/2 cup butter, softened**
- **1/2 cup sugar**
- **2 eggs**
- **1 cup (8 ounces) sour cream**
- **1 package (8-1/2 ounces) corn bread/muffin mix**
- **1/2 cup milk**
- **1 can (15-1/4 ounces) whole kernel corn, drained**
- **1 can (14-3/4 ounces) cream-style corn**

Holiday Spiral Ham

PREP: 30 min. BAKE: 1-1/2 hours + standing

- **1 fully cooked spiral-sliced ham (8 pounds)**
- **1 fresh pineapple, peeled, cored and cut into four wedges**
- **1 package (12 ounces) fresh *or* frozen cranberries**
- **3 medium apples, peeled and cubed**
- **1-1/4 cups sugar**
- **1 medium navel orange, peeled and cut into chunks**
- **3 tablespoons lemon juice**

Place ham on a rack in a shallow roasting pan. Arrange pineapple wedges around ham. Cover and bake at 325° for 1 to 1-1/2 hours.

Meanwhile, in a large saucepan, combine cranberries and apples. Cook over medium heat until the berries pop, about 15 minutes. Add the sugar, orange chunks and lemon juice. Cook and stir until sugar is dissolved. Remove from the heat.

Spoon half of the cranberry relish over ham. Bake 30 minutes longer or until a meat thermometer reads 140°. Let stand for 10 minutes before serving. Cut pineapple wedges into large chunks; serve with ham and remaining relish. **Yield:** 12-16 servings.

In a large bowl, cream butter and sugar until light and fluffy. Add eggs, one at a time, beating well after each addition. Beat in sour cream. Gradually add muffin mix alternately with milk. Fold in both cans of corn.

Pour into a greased 3-qt. baking dish. Bake, uncovered, at 325° for 45-50 minutes or until set and lightly browned. **Yield:** 8 servings.

Pineapple Sour Cream Pie

PREP: 35 min. **BAKE:** 15 min. + chilling

- 1/2 cup sugar
- 2 tablespoons all-purpose flour
- 1 can (20 ounces) crushed pineapple, undrained
- 1 cup (8 ounces) sour cream
- 3 egg yolks, lightly beaten
- 1 pastry shell (9 inches), baked

MERINGUE:
- 3 egg whites
- 1/2 teaspoon vanilla extract
- 1/4 teaspoon cream of tartar
- 6 tablespoons sugar

In a large saucepan, combine sugar and flour. Stir in pineapple and sour cream until combined. Cook and stir over medium-high heat until thickened and bubbly. Reduce heat; cook and stir 2 minutes longer.

Remove from the heat. Stir a small amount of hot filling into egg yolks; return all to the pan, stirring constantly. Bring to a gentle boil; cook and stir 2

minutes longer. Remove from the heat. Pour into pastry shell.

For the meringue, in a small bowl, beat the egg whites, vanilla and cream of tartar on medium speed until soft peaks form. Gradually beat in sugar, 1 tablespoon at a time, on high until stiff glossy peaks form and sugar is dissolved. Spread evenly over hot filling, sealing edges to crust.

Bake at 350° for 15-18 minutes or until meringue is golden brown. Cool on a wire rack for 1 hour. Refrigerate for at least 3 hours before serving. Refrigerate leftovers. **Yield:** 8 servings.

Quick Ham Hints

- Purchase ham that has a rosy pink color. Also, the meat should feel firm to the touch, not mushy, when pressed with your fingertips.
- Freezing deteriorates ham quality. But if you must freeze, wrap the ham tightly. It can be stored in the freezer for up to 2 months.
- If you're cooking more than one ham, make sure there is uniform space around the hams in the oven so they will cook evenly. They should not be touching.
- Leftover cooked ham should be wrapped tightly and put in the refrigerator within 1 to 2 hours after cooking. Ham may be stored this way for up to 4 days.

A saucy chicken dish takes center stage in her mother's Southern-style supper menu.

By Donna Sasser Hinds, Milwaukie, Oregon

Despite her German heritage and the fact that she raised her family in Oregon, my mother is a Southern belle at heart.

Hazel Bickel Sasser (my mom, above) grew up in Louisville, Kentucky. Her family owned a market, where Mother worked until she married my father, Merlyn, and moved to The Dalles, Oregon.

She took along the recipes she acquired from her German grandmother, her mother and the family's housekeeper, Mattie. Mattie greatly influenced my mother's taste for Southern fare.

So it's no surprise that my mom's best meal features Down-Home Chicken with Poached Corn, Freezer Coleslaw and Gingerbread Boy Cookies.

Down-Home Chicken evolved from a recipe my mother saw on a TV show in the 1950s. We lovingly called it Goopy Chicken because of its thick molasses sauce. Fresh, sweet Poached Corn and crispy Freezer Coleslaw were the perfect complements.

Mother excelled at baking treats, and her Gingerbread Boy Cookies were our favorites. My sister once asked for them instead of birthday cake. (My mom made a round cake and put the cookie boys hand-to-hand around it.)

My dad, who was a railroad conductor, seldom helped in the kitchen, but he was always my mother's biggest fan. He often said he'd put her cooking up against anyone's.

Although my mother doesn't cook much anymore, she made her trademark mashed potatoes for Thanksgiving last year and supervised our family candy-making the day before Christmas.

People always recall Mother's wonderful cooking. My 40-year high school reunion proved it. Former classmates came up to me and asked, "Does your mother still make…?"

I hope you try Mother's menu and that it becomes a favorite with your family.

PICTURED Clockwise from upper right: Gingerbread Boy Cookies, Freezer Coleslaw, Down-Home Chicken and Poached Corn (recipes are on the next page).

Down-Home Chicken

PREP: 30 min. **COOK:** 40 min.

- 1/2 cup all-purpose flour
- 1 teaspoon salt
- 1/2 teaspoon pepper
- 1 broiler/fryer chicken (3 to 4 pounds), cut up
- 1/4 cup canola oil

SAUCE:

- 2/3 cup lemon juice
- 2/3 cup ketchup
- 2/3 cup molasses
- 1/3 cup canola oil
- 1/4 cup Worcestershire sauce
- 1 teaspoon ground cloves
- 1/2 teaspoon salt
- 1/4 teaspoon pepper

Hot cooked rice

In a large resealable plastic bag, combine the flour, salt and pepper. Add chicken, a few pieces at a time, and shake to coat.

In a large skillet, heat oil. Brown chicken in oil on all sides; remove to paper towels. Drain drippings and return chicken to the pan.

For the sauce, combine the lemon juice, ketchup, molasses, oil, Worcestershire sauce, cloves, salt and pepper; pour over chicken. Bring to a boil. Reduce heat; simmer, uncovered, for 35-40 minutes or until chicken juices run clear. Serve with rice. **Yield:** 6 servings.

Poached Corn

PREP/TOTAL TIME: 20 min.

- 5 cups fresh *or* frozen corn
- 2 cups milk
- 4 teaspoons sugar
- 1 tablespoon butter
- 3/4 teaspoon salt
- 1/2 teaspoon pepper

In a large saucepan, combine all the ingredients. Cook over low heat for 10-12 minutes or until the corn is tender, stirring frequently. Serve with a slotted spoon. **Yield:** 6 servings.

Sweet 'n' Spicy Cloves

Through the centuries, cloves have been used to freshen breath, relieve toothaches and even ward off the plague. Nowadays, many people rely on aromatic cloves to spice up ham, pumpkin pie or a hot holiday punch.

Cloves also flavor salad dressings, cookies, baked beans and chili as well as Indian, Chinese and German foods.

Whatever the dish, cloves add a fresh, sweet and spicy taste when used sparingly. Use too much and the pungent flavor can easily overpower a recipe.

Reach for ground cloves to prepare terrific Down-Home Chicken (recipe at left).

1/2 cup molasses
  2 teaspoons white vinegar
  1 egg, lightly beaten
  3 cups all-purpose flour
1/2 teaspoon baking soda
1/2 teaspoon ground ginger
1/2 teaspoon ground cinnamon
1/4 teaspoon salt

In a saucepan, combine the butter, sugar, molasses and vinegar; bring to a boil, stirring constantly. Remove from the heat; cool to lukewarm. Stir in egg. Combine the flour, baking soda, ginger, cinnamon and salt; stir into molasses mixture to form a soft dough.

Divide dough into thirds. Shape each portion into a disk; wrap in plastic wrap. Refrigerate for at least 2 hours or until easy to handle.

On a lightly floured surface, roll dough to 1/4-in. thickness. Cut with a floured 3-in. gingerbread boy cookie cutter. Place on greased baking sheets. Bake at 375° for 7-9 minutes or until edges are firm. Remove to wire racks. **Yield:** 3-4 dozen.

Freezer Coleslaw

PREP: 25 min. + freezing

  1 medium head cabbage (about 2 pounds), shredded
  1 teaspoon salt
  2 cups sugar
  1 cup cider vinegar
1/4 cup water
  1 teaspoon celery seed
  1 teaspoon mustard seed
  1 large carrot, shredded
1/2 cup finely chopped green pepper

In a large bowl, combine cabbage and salt; let stand for 1 hour.

In a large saucepan, combine the sugar, vinegar, water, celery seed and mustard seed. Bring to a boil; boil for 1 minute. Remove from the heat; cool.

Add the carrot, green pepper and vinegar mixture to the cabbage mixture; stir to combine. Transfer to large freezer bags; seal and freeze for up to 2 months.

Remove from the freezer 2 hours before serving. Serve with a slotted spoon. **Yield:** 10 servings.

Gingerbread Boy Cookies

PREP: I hour + chilling **BAKE:** IO min./batch

1/2 cup butter, cubed
1/2 cup sugar

She's hooked on her mom's delicious family fish-fry menu served on Friday evenings at the lake.

By Julie Jahnke, Green Lake, Wisconsin

My mom, Margaret Peterson (above) from Bloomington, Minnesota, never has to fish for compliments when she cooks a meal...especially when we are away on vacation.

Every year, our family spends a week at a lake in northern Minnesota. We've been doing this for 16 years. With my brother and four sisters as well as all our spouses and children, there are now 14 of us.

We all enjoy fishing because my dad taught us when we were young. So the finale of the week is, appropriately, a fish fry. Dad used to say Mom's Fried Fish was the finest he'd ever tried. Sadly, he is no longer with us, but we share fond memories of Dad during our stay at the lake.

Once the fresh fish is cleaned, Mom dips it in an egg wash and rolls it in crushed crackers. My brother, Jim, cooks it outdoors in a deep fryer to a delicious golden brown.

Mom also prepares her tartar sauce and Parsley Red Potatoes. I help her by peeling and slicing the potatoes. The easy-to-prepare spuds cook up tender and buttery on the stove.

She makes Crunchy Floret Salad the night before so the creamy dressing marinates the vegetables. The pretty combination always gets raves.

Mom's Apple Crisp rounds out this satisfying meal. The aroma of baking apples and cinnamon always brings everyone to her cabin. We like this dessert best when served warm, topped with mounded clouds of whipped cream.

Family is so important to my mom. She did her best to have all eight of us at the dinner table every evening when we were growing up.

I'm in awe of how much my mom has done for us over the years. I've told her many times that if I can be half the mother she has been, I'll consider myself a success. I hope her fish-fry menu inspires you to gather your friends around the table as well.

PICTURED Clockwise from upper left: Parsley Red Potatoes, Mom's Apple Crisp, Crunchy Floret Salad and Mom's Fried Fish (recipes are on the next page).

Parsley Red Potatoes

PREP/TOTAL TIME: 25 min.

- 2 **pounds red potatoes**
- 1-1/2 **teaspoons salt**
- 1/3 **cup butter, cubed**
- 2 **tablespoons minced fresh parsley**

Peel off a strip around each potato if desired. Place in a large saucepan; cover with water. Add salt. Bring to a boil; reduce heat. Cover and cook for 15 minutes or until tender; drain. Add butter and parsley; toss until butter is melted. **Yield:** 6 servings.

Crunchy Floret Salad

PREP/TOTAL TIME: 20 min.

- 3 **cups fresh broccoli florets**
- 1-1/2 **cups fresh cauliflowerets**
- 1/2 **pound sliced bacon, cooked and crumbled**
- 1 **cup mayonnaise**
- 2 **to 3 tablespoons sugar**
- 2 **tablespoons cider vinegar**
- 1/4 **teaspoon salt**
- 1-1/2 **cups (6 ounces) shredded cheddar cheese**

Mom's Fried Fish

PREP/TOTAL TIME: 30 min.

- 2 **eggs, beaten**
- 1-1/2 **cups crushed saltines (about 45 crackers)**
- 2 **pounds whitefish fillets, cut in half lengthwise**

Oil for frying

TARTAR SAUCE:

- 1 **cup mayonnaise**
- 2 **tablespoons sweet pickle relish**
- 1 **tablespoon finely chopped onion**

Place eggs and cracker crumbs in separate shallow bowls. Dip fillets into eggs, then coat with crumbs. Let stand for 5 minutes.

In an electric skillet or deep-fat fryer, heat oil to 375°. Fry fillets, a few at a time, for 2 minutes on each side or until fish is golden brown and flakes easily with a fork. Drain on paper towels.

In a small bowl, combine the tartar sauce ingredients. Serve with fish. **Yield:** 6 servings.

salt and remaining sugar; cut in butter until crumbly. Sprinkle over apples, pressing down to smooth top.

Slowly pour the water over the top; sprinkle with the remaining cinnamon. Bake, uncovered, at 400° for 40-45 minutes or until the apples are tender. Serve warm. **Yield:** 8 servings.

Deep Frying

To allow for bubbling up and splattering, the pot in which you deep fry should be filled no more than halfway with oil.

The temperature of the oil is important and can mean the difference between success and disaster. If the oil isn't hot enough, food will absorb it and become greasy; if it's too hot, the food will burn. The most accurate method of testing the temperature is with a deep-frying thermometer.

It's best to fry food in small batches. Large amounts of food will lower the oil temperature, which means it's more likely to soak into the food.

In a large bowl, combine the broccoli, cauliflower and bacon. In a small bowl, whisk the mayonnaise, sugar, vinegar and salt. Pour over salad and mix well. Cover and refrigerate until serving. Stir in the cheese. **Yield:** 6-8 servings.

Mom's Apple Crisp

PREP: 25 min. **BAKE:** 40 min.

- 5 **medium tart apples, peeled and sliced**
- 1-1/4 **cups sugar,** *divided*
- 1-3/4 **teaspoons ground cinnamon,** *divided*
- 1 **cup all-purpose flour**
- 1 **teaspoon baking powder**
- 1/2 **teaspoon salt**
- 1/2 **cup cold butter, cubed**
- 1 **cup water**

In a large bowl, combine the apples, 1/4 cup sugar and 1 teaspoon cinnamon. Transfer to a greased 8-in. square baking dish.

In a small bowl, combine the flour, baking powder,

Turkey with a French accent is the highlight of her mother's best dinner menu...and gets the family reminiscing about the memorable flavors of France.

By Emma Rea, Hermann, Missouri

My mom, Diana Rea (above), never learned to cook while growing up. Her mother wasn't much into cooking, so she didn't pass on a love for it to her daughters. But through many experiments, some flops and hard work, my mom has become a fantastic cook!

After getting married, she and my dad, Tom, moved to France as missionaries. During the 12 years they lived and worked there—and raised a family—my mother developed a real appreciation for good, wholesome food.

She learned to prepare so many mouth-watering dishes from scratch that it was difficult to choose one meal I consider her best. But Turkey with Mushrooms and Cream has to be one of the best authentic French dishes she makes.

The original turkey recipe, Dinde a la Crème et Champignons, uses white wine instead of apple juice, but either way, this main dish is absolutely scrumptious. Mom often serves it for Easter, Christmas and other celebrations.

As an accompaniment, crunchy Hazelnut Vegetable Salad can't be beat. Mom doesn't always add the asparagus spears, but I think the steamed spears make this colorful combination twice as good.

No one passes up Mom's golden brown Yummy Yeast Rolls, served warm with butter. To shape them, we cut them out of the rolled dough with a drinking glass, and they always turn out fine.

Layered Poppy Seed Torte, featuring a sweet, nutty filling and creamy mocha frosting, makes an impressive finale for any occasion. It takes a little time to prepare, but everyone agrees that it's worth the effort!

While living in France, our family entertained almost weekly. Often on Sunday afternoons, we would have friends over for a five-course meal that lasted several hours. In true French style, Mom would serve an appetizer, salad, main dish, cheese and dessert... each as a separate course. Each course was accompanied by crusty baguettes from the bakery.

For birthdays, she'd serve a dish called raclette. It's a special melted cheese poured over potatoes, served with pickled baby onions and tiny dill pickles.

Mom's style hasn't changed much since we moved back to the United States in 2000. She still cooks and bakes from scratch for our family, which now numbers 10. I'm the oldest of eight children; we're home-schooled by Mom and Dad, who's the pastor of a local church.

Every other week, Mom goes to the grocery store, which is 45 minutes away. We grind our own flour, so she buys 50 to 100 pounds of wheat berries at a time. She also buys 25 pounds of pasta and popcorn. (We love popcorn...in France, you sprinkle sugar on it!) We plant a huge garden in the summer with about 60 tomato plants.

My three sisters and I have always helped Mom in the kitchen, so we have a lot of cooking experience. Sometimes we'll make lunch or dinner by ourselves to give her a break. My brothers dry the dishes, take out the garbage and lick the spoons! They leave the cooking to us.

I am about to start college in South Carolina, and one of the first things I plan to do is join the university's kitchen club so I can continue making my mom's fantastic recipes.

I'm sure you'll like them, too. Bon appetit!

Rolls Like Mom Made

It's not difficult to treat your family to a batch of made-from-scratch, golden brown rolls like Yummy Yeast Rolls (recipe on page 243) for dinner. Want to know the keys to making successful yeast rolls? Follow these guidelines the next time you're in the kitchen:

• When mixing dough, always start with a minimum amount of flour until the dough reaches the desired consistency.

• Do not use light or whipped butter, diet spread or tub margarine in place of the butter, stick margarine (with at least 80% oil) or shortening that a recipe calls for.

• Knead dough only until it doesn't tear easily when stretched.

• Let dough rise in a warm (80° to 85°) draft-free area. Proper rising helps in the development of the texture.

PICTURED Clockwise from upper left: Yummy Yeast Rolls, Poppy Seed Torte, Turkey with Mushrooms and Cream and Hazelnut Vegetable Salad (recipes are on the next page).

butter, water and bouillon; cook and stir over medium heat until bouillon is dissolved. Add mushrooms; cook for 10 minutes or until liquid has evaporated. Serve turkey over rice; top with cream sauce and mushrooms. **Yield:** 4 servings.

Hazelnut Vegetable Salad

PREP/TOTAL TIME: 25 min.

- 1/4 **cup olive oil**
- 2 **tablespoons lemon juice**
- 2 **teaspoons cider vinegar**
- 2 **teaspoons honey**
- 1/4 **teaspoon salt**
- 1/4 **teaspoon coarsely ground pepper**
- 1/2 **pound sliced fresh mushrooms**
- 1/2 **medium sweet red pepper, julienned**
- 2 **celery ribs, julienned**
- 3 **tablespoons minced chives**
- 4 **lettuce leaves**
- 8 **asparagus spears, cooked and drained**
- 2 **tablespoons chopped hazelnuts**

For the dressing, in a small bowl, whisk the first six ingredients. In a large bowl, combine the mushrooms, red pepper, celery and chives. Drizzle with dressing and toss to coat. Refrigerate until serving.

 Place the lettuce on salad plates; top with the asparagus and mushroom mixture. Sprinkle with hazelnuts. **Yield:** 4 servings.

Turkey with Mushrooms And Cream

PREP/TOTAL TIME: 30 min.

- 1 **package (17.6 ounces) turkey breast cutlets**
- 1 **tablespoon canola oil**
- 3 **tablespoons butter,** *divided*
- 3/4 **cup water,** *divided*
- 1/4 **cup unsweetened apple juice**
- 2 **teaspoons chicken bouillon granules,** *divided*
- 1/4 **teaspoon pepper**
- 1 **cup (8 ounces) sour cream**
- 1 **pound fresh mushrooms, chopped**

Hot cooked rice

In a large skillet over medium-high heat, cook turkey in oil and 2 tablespoons butter until golden brown and no pink remains; drain. Remove and keep warm.

 In the same skillet, combine 1/2 cup water, apple juice, 1 teaspoon bouillon and pepper; cook and stir over medium heat until bouillon is dissolved. Stir in sour cream; heat through.

 Meanwhile, in another skillet, combine the remaining

Yummy Yeast Rolls

PREP: 25 min. + rising **BAKE:** 15 min.

- 2 to 2-1/2 cups all-purpose flour
- 3 tablespoons sugar
- 1 package (1/4 ounce) quick-rise yeast
- 1/2 teaspoon salt
- 3/4 cup warm water (120° to 130°)
- 2 tablespoons butter, melted

In a large bowl, combine 1-1/2 cups flour, sugar, yeast and salt. Add water and butter; beat on medium speed for 3 minutes or until smooth. Stir in enough remaining flour to form a soft dough.

Turn onto a well floured surface; knead until smooth and elastic, about 4-6 minutes. Cover and let rest for 10 minutes. Roll dough to 3/8-in. thickness; cut with a lightly floured 2-1/2-in. biscuit cutter. Place 2 in. apart on a greased baking sheet. Cover and let rise in a warm place until doubled, about 30 minutes.

Bake at 375° for 11-14 minutes or until lightly browned. Remove to a wire rack. **Yield:** about 1 dozen.

Poppy Seed Torte

PREP: 15 min. + standing **BAKE:** 15 min. + cooling

- 2/3 cup milk
- 1/2 cup poppy seeds
- 1/2 cup butter, softened
- 1 cup sugar
- 2 cups cake flour
- 2 teaspoons baking powder
- 1/4 teaspoon salt
- 3 egg whites

FILLING:
- 1 cup sugar
- 1 cup (8 ounces) sour cream
- 3 egg yolks
- 1 cup chopped walnuts
- 1 teaspoon vanilla extract

MOCHA FROSTING:
- 6 tablespoons butter, softened
- 3 cups confectioners' sugar
- 3 tablespoons baking cocoa
- 3 to 4 tablespoons hot strong brewed coffee

In a bowl, combine milk and poppy seeds; let stand for 1 hour. In a large bowl, cream butter and sugar. Combine the flour, baking powder and salt; add to creamed mixture alternately with poppy seed mixture.

In another bowl with clean beaters, beat egg whites until soft peaks form; fold into batter. Pour into two greased and floured 9-in. round baking pans. Bake at 350° for 15-20 minutes or until a toothpick inserted near the center comes out clean. Cool for 10 minutes before removing from pans to wire racks.

For the filling, in a heavy saucepan, combine the sugar, sour cream and egg yolks. Cook and stir over low heat just until mixture begins to simmer and reaches 160°. Remove from the heat; add nuts and vanilla. Transfer to a bowl; cover with plastic wrap and refrigerate until completely cooled.

For the frosting, in a small bowl, beat butter, confectioners' sugar and cocoa until blended. Add coffee, 1 tablespoon at a time, until mixture achieves spreading consistency.

Place one cake layer on serving plate; spread with filling. Top with second layer; spread with frosting. Store in the refrigerator. **Yield:** 10-12 servings.

Featuring an elegant seafood entree as the main course, this special family-size spread delights everyone at weekly gatherings around her mother's dinner table.

By Kimberly Laabs, Hartford, Wisconsin

It's a tradition at our house to have dinner together each Sunday. Even now that my brother, sister and I are adults, we still gather at my parents' home in Erin, Wisconsin for one of Mom's incredible meals. It's a time that our family makes sure to reserve for each other and we wouldn't have it any other way.

My mom, Sharon Laabs (above), has always made mealtime special...and not just on Sundays. She puts plenty of thought, time and effort into each and every meal she prepares.

She loves to entertain, especially at Christmas. When company is coming, Mom will spend the whole day in the kitchen. She'll serve a four-course meal with appetizers, soup or salad, main course and dessert. Everything has to be perfect...right down to the presentation. My mother's dining room table always looks beautiful with a tablecloth, centerpiece, candles and her good dishes.

When it's a celebration—a birthday, graduation, anniversary, etc.—the person who is special that day can put in a menu request with Mom. If it's someone in the family, he or she also gets to eat off the "red plate," which says "You Are Special Today." Last Christmas, Mom even gave each of us kids a red plate so we can carry on the tradition with our own families.

My mom's very best meal, I think, is the one my sister, Kristin, chose to have as her birthday dinner: Puff Pastry Salmon Bundles, Comforting Broccoli Casserole, Strawberry Spinach Salad and sweet Ice Cream Cookie Dessert.

The Puff Pastry Salmon Bundles make any menu elegant. The crisp pastry and delicious cucumber sauce are a wonderful combination, and the salmon almost melts in your mouth.

Her Comforting Broccoli Casserole is not only flavorful but nutritious, too. And the Strawberry Spinach Salad is a refreshing, colorful toss with a raspberry vinaigrette.

Our entire family loves dessert and can't wait to see what Mom has prepared as a finishing touch to a meal. Her yummy Ice Cream Cookie Dessert is a real favorite...even during cold, winter months.

My mother grew up in Milwaukee and learned to cook from her mom, who was also a wonderful cook. She met my dad, Richard, when they were in the fourth grade! She was a stay-at-home mom when my sister, brother and I were young.

Mom now teaches fourth grade and is assistant principal at an area elementary school. Dad's an executive director of three Lutheran schools.

When Mom cooked for our family of five, she always made too much food—and she still does. Now that our family is larger, though, she can send food home with each of her children.

My sister, Kristin, who's an attorney, is married, as is my brother, Bryan, who's a CPA. He and his wife have a daughter, Calla—my mom's only grandchild. I teach kindergarten at the same school where my mom teaches. It's a privilege to work with her each day and to share her career.

Everyone in our family gets along extremely well. The guys like to golf or attend football games together, while we girls like spending the day at the mall or in the spa. Of course, each week we make a point of joining together for Sunday dinner.

Dinner begins with a prayer and then a big toast to my mom for another wonderful meal.

PICTURED Clockwise from upper left: Strawberry Spinach Salad, Comforting Broccoli Casserole, Ice Cream Cookie Dessert and Puff Pastry Salmon Bundles (recipes are on the next page).

∫ Sweet on Strawberries

Whether you're preparing the Strawberry Spinach Salad (recipe on page 247), a fresh fruit platter or a classic layered shortcake, strawberries will make your dish a winner. Those little red gems have a sweet, refreshing flavor that folks of all ages love.

Peak season for strawberries occurs in April, May and June. When you're purchasing them fresh, look for berries that are shiny, firm and very fragrant. The berry should be almost completely red, although some whiteness near the cap is acceptable.

Refrigerate unwashed strawberries with the cap on until you're ready to use them. Just before using, wash and hull the berries.

Comforting Broccoli Casserole

PREP: 20 min. **BAKE:** 30 min.

- 2 eggs, lightly beaten
- 1 can (10-3/4 ounces) condensed cream of mushroom soup, undiluted
- 1 medium onion, chopped
- 1 cup (4 ounces) shredded cheddar cheese
- 1 cup (4 ounces) shredded Swiss cheese
- 1/2 cup mayonnaise
- 2 tablespoons butter, melted
- 1 package (16 ounces) frozen broccoli cuts, thawed
- 1 package (10 ounces) frozen chopped broccoli (about 3 cups), thawed
- 1/4 cup dry bread crumbs

In a large bowl, combine the first seven ingredients; fold in the broccoli. Transfer to a greased 1-1/2-qt. baking dish. Sprinkle with bread crumbs. Cover and bake at 400° for 30-35 minutes or until heated through. **Yield:** 8 servings.

Editor's Note: Reduced-fat or fat-free mayonnaise is not recommended for this recipe.

Purchasing Fish

When you need fresh fish fillets or steaks from the market, look for firm flesh that has a moist appearance. Don't buy fish that appears dried out. Fresh fish should have a mild, fresh-from-the-ocean smell, not a strong odor.

When purchasing frozen fish, look for packages that are solidly frozen, tightly sealed and free of freezer burn and odor.

Puff Pastry Salmon Bundles

PREP: 20 min. **BAKE:** 25 min.

- 2 packages (17.3 ounces *each*) frozen puff pastry, thawed
- 8 salmon fillets (6 ounces *each*), skin removed
- 1 egg
- 1 tablespoon water
- 2 cups shredded cucumber
- 1 cup (8 ounces) sour cream
- 1 cup mayonnaise
- 1 teaspoon dill weed
- 1/2 teaspoon salt

On a lightly floured surface, roll each puff pastry sheet into a 12-in. x 10-in. rectangle. Cut each into two 10-in. x 6-in. rectangles. Place a salmon fillet in the center of each rectangle.

Beat egg and water; lightly brush over pastry edges. Bring opposite corners of pastry over each fillet; pinch seams to seal tightly. Place seam side down in a greased 15-in. x 10-in. x 1-in. baking pan; brush with remaining egg mixture.

Bake at 400° for 25-30 minutes or until pastry is golden brown. In a small bowl, combine the cucumber, sour cream, mayonnaise, dill and salt. Serve with bundles. **Yield:** 8 servings.

Ice Cream Cookie Dessert

PREP: 15 min. + freezing

- **1 package (18 ounces) cream-filled chocolate sandwich cookies, crushed, *divided***
- **1/4 cup butter, melted**
- **1/2 gallon vanilla ice cream, softened**
- **1 jar (16 ounces) hot fudge ice cream topping, warmed**
- **1 carton (8 ounces) frozen whipped topping, thawed**

In a bowl, combine 3-3/4 cups cookie crumbs and butter. Press into a greased 13-in. x 9-in. x 2-in. dish. Spread with ice cream; cover and freeze until set.

Drizzle fudge topping over ice cream; cover and freeze until set. Spread with whipped topping; sprinkle with remaining cookie crumbs. Cover and freeze for 2 hours or until firm. Remove from the freezer 10 minutes before serving. **Yield:** 12 servings.

Strawberry Spinach Salad

PREP: 20 min. + chilling

- **1/3 cup raspberry vinaigrette**
- **1/2 cup sugar**
- **1 teaspoon salt**
- **1/4 teaspoon prepared mustard**
- **1/2 cup canola oil**
- **4-1/2 teaspoons poppy seeds**
- **1 package (10 ounces) fresh baby spinach**
- **1 pint fresh strawberries, sliced**
- **1/2 cup coarsely chopped pecans, toasted**

In a blender, combine the vinaigrette, sugar, salt and mustard. Cover and process until smooth. While processing, gradually add oil in a steady stream. Stir in poppy seeds. Transfer to a small pitcher or bowl. Refrigerate for 1 hour or until chilled.

Just before serving, toss the spinach, strawberries and pecans in a large salad bowl. Serve with dressing. **Yield:** 8 servings.

Her mom's German heritage flavored many memorable family Christmas dinners over the years.

By Rosemarie Forcum, White Stone, Virginia

SOME of my happiest memories as a child involve holidays spent with family and wonderful foods.

Although my parents, Katherine (above) and Tobias Ress, met in New Jersey, they were both German immigrants. Some of their siblings also came to America and settled nearby...so our Christmas gatherings were large, with all the aunts, uncles and cousins. What feasts we had!

To me, the ultimate Yuletide menu included Roast Christmas Goose, greens with Mixed Herb Salad Dressing, Creamed Fresh Spinach and Apple Plum Streusel Dessert.

I'll never forget the wonderful aroma of my mother's Roast Christmas Goose, stuffed with apple, orange and lemon. She served this dish with greens topped with Mixed Herb Salad Dressing and flavorful Creamed Fresh Spinach.

The festive meal, which also included mashed potatoes and homemade rolls, would end with yummy Apple Plum Streusel Dessert, a coffee cake-like pastry drizzled with icing. Usually, we served it with fresh whipped cream or vanilla ice cream.

My sister and I loved watching our mother in the kitchen and learned how to cook from her. She always fixed wonderful meals for our family.

I inherited my love of cooking from my mom and aunts and still prepare many of Mom's recipes, mostly in winter, since German foods are rich and hearty. Family favorites include goulash, sauerbraten and Wiener schnitzel. At Christmas, Mom's roast goose is often on the menu.

Although it is difficult to get my own children and grandchildren together, when we are, good food like my mom's helps make it a happy and memorable occasion for all.

PICTURED Clockwise from upper left: Roast Christmas Goose, Mixed Herb Salad Dressing, Creamed Fresh Spinach and Apple Plum Streusel Dessert (recipes are on the next page).

Mixed Herb Salad Dressing

PREP/TOTAL TIME: 5 min.

- 6 tablespoons white wine vinegar
- 6 tablespoons canola oil
- 2 tablespoons finely chopped onion
- 1 teaspoon salt
- 1/2 teaspoon *each* dried chives, chervil and tarragon
- 1/2 teaspoon dill weed

Assorted salad greens

In a small bowl, whisk the vinegar, oil, onion and seasonings until blended. Serve with salad greens. **Yield:** 2/3 cup.

Creamed Fresh Spinach

PREP/TOTAL TIME: 20 min.

- 6 packages (6 ounces *each*) baby spinach
- 1/4 cup butter, cubed
- 1/4 cup all-purpose flour
- 1 cup heavy whipping cream
- 1 cup milk
- 2 tablespoons finely chopped onion

Salt and white pepper to taste

Roast Christmas Goose

PREP: 10 min. **BAKE:** 2-1/4 hours + standing

- 1 domestic goose (10 to 12 pounds)

Salt and pepper

- 1 medium apple, peeled and quartered
- 1 medium navel orange, peeled and quartered
- 1 medium lemon, peeled and quartered
- 1 cup hot water

Sprinkle the goose cavity with salt and pepper. Place the apple, orange and lemon in the cavity. Place goose breast side up on a rack in a large shallow roasting pan. Prick skin well with a fork. Pour water into pan.

Bake, uncovered, at 350° for 2-1/4 to 3 hours or until a meat thermometer reads 185°. If necessary, drain fat from pan as it accumulates. Cover goose with foil and let stand for 20 minutes before carving. Discard fruit. **Yield:** 8 servings.

GLAZE:
- **1 cup confectioners' sugar**
- **1 to 2 tablespoons milk**

In a large bowl, cream butter, shortening and sugar. Beat in eggs and extracts until blended. Beat mixture on high speed for 3 minutes. Combine the flour and baking powder; gradually add to creamed mixture. Spread the batter into a greased 15-in. x 10-in. x 1-in. baking pan. Arrange plum and apple slices over batter.

For the streusel, combine the flour and brown sugar. Cut in butter until mixture resembles coarse crumbs; stir in pecans. Sprinkle over fruit.

Bake at 350° for 40-45 minutes or until lightly browned. Cool on a wire rack. For the glaze, whisk confectioners' sugar and milk until smooth. Drizzle over streusel. **Yield:** 16-20 servings.

Duck, Duck, Goose

The demand is not high for ducks or geese at supermarkets, so they are usually kept in the frozen food cases. They are often available during the holiday season.

To store, place the frozen goose in a plastic bag to contain any leakage. At home, refrigerate the goose immediately and use within 1 or 2 days. A whole, completely frozen goose will take up to two days to thaw completely.

Wash and trim spinach, leaving the water that clings to the leaves. Place in a Dutch oven. Bring to a boil. Reduce heat and steam just until wilted, about 4 minutes. Drain and chop; set aside.

Melt butter in a large saucepan over medium heat. Whisk in the flour until smooth. Gradually add cream and milk. Bring to a boil; cook and stir for 2 minutes or until thickened. Stir in the onion, salt and pepper. Fold in spinach; heat through. **Yield:** 8 servings.

Apple Plum Streusel Dessert

PREP: 25 min. **BAKE:** 40 min

- **1/2 cup butter, softened**
- **1/2 cup shortening**
- **1-1/2 cups sugar**
- **4 eggs**
- **1 teaspoon almond extract**
- **1 teaspoon vanilla extract**
- **3 cups all-purpose flour**
- **1/2 teaspoon baking powder**
- **6 to 7 medium unpeeled plums, thinly sliced**
- **5 to 6 medium unpeeled Golden Delicious apples, thinly sliced**

STREUSEL TOPPING:
- **1/3 cup all-purpose flour**
- **1/4 cup packed brown sugar**
- **1/4 cup cold butter**
- **1/4 cup chopped pecans**

Editors' Meals

Taste of Home field editors from across the country are thrilled to share their favorite meals with readers.

FIELD EDITORS' FAVORITES. Clockwise from upper left: Beef Brisket with Mop Sauce Meal (p. 262), Christmas Morning Menu (p. 254), Holiday Crown Roast of Pork Supper (p. 278) and Spring Leg of Lamb Dinner (p. 270).

Christmas Morning Menu

Holiday brunch is a highlight for one field editor and her family.

By Maryellen Hays, Wolcottville, Indiana

WE always enjoy a buffet brunch after our morning church service on Christmas Day. It's so nice to have the family gathered around the table to celebrate this most beautiful of holidays.

Our simple but tasty menu has become an anticipated tradition. It includes Christmas Breakfast Casserole, Triple-Cheese Broccoli Puff, Hot Curried Fruit, Cider Wassail and Apple-Raisin Bundt Cake. This meal works so well for our schedule because much of the food can be prepared ahead of time.

'Twas the Night Before Christmas

Our celebration actually begins on Christmas Eve, when my husband, Ron, and I host a family gathering with a gift exchange and potluck dinner at our home on Big Long Lake, about 45 miles north of Fort Wayne, Indiana. My grandfather built the house we live in, and the property has been in my family since 1927.

During the festivities, we are joined by our daughters, Robin and Heather, and their families, which include grandchildren Anthony, Samantha and Colton and great-granddaughter Gabi. After brunch on Christmas Day, they all move on to celebrate with the other side of their families.

My Christmas Breakfast Casserole is a convenient choice for busy mornings because it's assembled the day before. Light-textured and cheesy, this dish looks and tastes delicious. The bacon in it balances nicely with the other flavors.

Puffy, golden and delicious, Triple-Cheese Broccoli Puff is a lovely side-dish souffle. If you add some diced ham or poultry to the ingredients inside, it easily becomes an entree. Hot Curried Fruit is a comforting, warm accompaniment that's so enjoyable in chilly weather. The recipe came from a cookbook I've had since my days at Indiana State University.

I received the Cider Wassail recipe from a dear friend in Fort Wayne, where we lived for many years. Since it's warm, wonderful and nonalcoholic, we've even served it at church. It's also perfect for a holiday open house, which we host every other year. Ron and I enjoy entertaining, whether it be for a few friends, the family or our congregation after church service. We just love the company of people surrounded by warm, comforting food.

I like to cook just about everything, but baking is my specialty. An old-fashioned holiday treat, Apple-Raisin Bundt Cake is very moist, pleasantly spicy and chock-full of raisins and nuts. If you can wait, this cake truly tastes better baked several days ahead. The extra time allows the flavors to mellow.

A Down-Home Cook

I've often said, "I'm a dump-and-pour cook. If you can't dump and pour it, I can't cook it." What I mean is that I'm not a gourmet cook at all. Plain old home cooking is my style. I use lots of fresh garden produce in season. On almost any road around here, you'll find a fresh-produce stand.

My earliest memories of cooking are from when I was about 4 years old. My wonderful grandmother, Fern Shannon, would lift me onto a kitchen stool that my Grandpa made and then Grandma taught me how to make pancakes.

Ron is the family's expert on the grill. He likes to fire up salmon fillets and steaks as well as hamburgers and hot dogs. Now that we spend two months each winter in Green Valley, Arizona, he enjoys devoting more time to outdoor cooking.

Ron retired from a 34-year teaching career in 1994, and I recently retired from my job working for an insurance company. These days, the two of us spend our spare time volunteering at a local county hospital. We also serve as house managers for the Fort Wayne Civic Theatre and are active in our church.

Sharing my favorite recipes as a *Taste of Home* field editor is a lot of fun. I was also thrilled when another *Taste of Home* cook contacted me after a story I wrote about a Mardi Gras party was published in the February/March 1999 issue.

It was fun to guide her through planning one of her own parties—from ordering the festive beads to planning the menu.

This Christmas, when I'm fixing our brunch, I'll be wondering if some of you readers might be preparing one or more of my recipes for your own celebration. I hope they please your family as much as they do mine.

Triple-Cheese Broccoli Puff

PREP: 15 min. **BAKE:** 50 min. + standing

- 1 cup sliced fresh mushrooms
- 1 tablespoon butter
- 1 package (3 ounces) cream cheese, softened
- 6 eggs
- 1 cup milk
- 3/4 cup biscuit/baking mix
- 3 cups frozen chopped broccoli, thawed
- 2 cups (8 ounces) shredded Monterey Jack cheese
- 1 cup (8 ounces) 4% cottage cheese
- 1/4 teaspoon salt

In a small skillet, saute mushrooms in butter until tender; set aside. In a large bowl, beat the cream cheese, eggs, milk and biscuit mix just until combined. Stir in the broccoli, cheeses, salt and mushrooms.

Pour into a greased round 2-1/2-qt. baking dish. Bake, uncovered, at 350° for 50-60 minutes or until a knife inserted near the center comes out clean. Let stand for 10 minutes before serving. **Yield:** 6-8 servings.

Hot Curried Fruit

PREP: 10 min. **BAKE:** 35 min.

- 1 can (20 ounces) unsweetened pineapple chunks
- 1 can (16 ounces) pitted dark sweet cherries, drained
- 1 can (15-1/4 ounces) pear halves, drained
- 1 can (15-1/4 ounces) peach halves, drained
- 3/4 cup packed brown sugar

Christmas Breakfast Casserole

PREP: 10 min. + chilling **BAKE:** 50 min. + standing

- 7 slices white bread, crusts removed and cubed
- 2 cups (8 ounces) shredded cheddar cheese
- 6 eggs
- 3 cups milk
- 1 teaspoon ground mustard
- 1/2 teaspoon salt
- 1/4 teaspoon pepper
- 6 bacon strips, cooked and crumbled

In a greased 11-in. x 7-in. x 2-in. baking dish, combine the bread cubes and cheese. In a large bowl, whisk the eggs, milk, mustard, salt and pepper; pour over bread and cheese. Top with bacon. Cover and refrigerate overnight.

Remove from the refrigerator 30 minutes before baking. Bake, uncovered, at 350° for 50-55 minutes or until a knife inserted near the center comes out clean. Let stand 10 minutes before serving. **Yield:** 6-8 servings.

1/4 cup butter, melted
1 teaspoon curry powder
1 teaspoon ground cinnamon
1/2 teaspoon ground nutmeg

Drain pineapple, reserving juice. In a greased 2-qt. baking dish, combine the pineapple, cherries, pears and peaches. Combine the brown sugar, butter, curry, cinnamon, nutmeg and reserved juice; pour over fruit.

Cover and bake at 350° for 35-45 minutes or until heated through. **Yield:** 8 servings.

Cider Wassail

(Pictured on page 254)

PREP/TOTAL TIME: 30 min.

2 quarts apple cider
1-1/2 cups orange juice
3/4 cup pineapple juice
1 tablespoon brown sugar
1/2 teaspoon lemon juice
2 cinnamon sticks (3 inches)
Dash ground cinnamon
Dash ground cloves

In a large saucepan, combine all of the ingredients. Bring to a boil. Reduce heat; cover and simmer for 20-30 minutes. Discard cinnamon sticks. Serve hot in mugs. **Yield:** 10-12 servings (2-1/2 quarts).

Apple-Raisin Bundt Cake

PREP: 20 min. **BAKE:** 1 hour + cooling

3/4 cup butter, softened
1-1/2 cups sugar
1 cup plus 2 tablespoons strawberry jam
3-1/3 cups all-purpose flour
1-1/2 teaspoons baking soda
1-1/2 teaspoons ground nutmeg
3/4 teaspoon *each* ground allspice, cloves and cinnamon
1-1/2 cups buttermilk
1-3/4 cups raisins
3/4 cup chopped walnuts
3/4 cup chopped peeled apple
GLAZE:
1 cup confectioners' sugar
4 teaspoons milk

In a large bowl, cream butter and sugar until light and fluffy. Stir in jam. Combine the flour, baking soda and spices; add into creamed mixture alternately with buttermilk, beating well after each addition. Stir in the raisins, walnuts and apple. Pour into a greased and floured 10-in. fluted tube pan.

Bake at 350° for 1 hour or until a toothpick inserted near the center comes out clean. Cool for 10 minutes before removing from pan to a wire rack. Combine glaze ingredients; drizzle over cake. **Yield:** 12-16 servings.

Easy and Cheesy Supper

A few shortcuts don't compromise the rich, satisfying
flavor of this editor's delightful dinner.

By Becky Ruff, Monona, Iowa

A RESIDENT of northeast Iowa for most of my life, I can't imagine living anywhere else. Many people think of Iowa's landscape as being flat, but in this corner of the state, it's very hilly, with scenic bluffs overlooking the mighty Mississippi River.

Although I love to cook, I don't always have the time for long, drawn-out preparations. This lasagna menu is one meal that doesn't tie me up for hours and hours in the kitchen. Plus, it's applauded by everyone in my family.

My Hot Cheddar Mushroom Spread, Golden Squash Soup, Simple Sausage Lasagna, Broccoli with Mustard Sauce and Caramel-Pecan Cheesecake Pie are tasty and satisfying yet easy to fix.

A Delicious Five-Course Meal

Several years ago, I got together with a group of friends from high school for the weekend, and each of us brought our favorite appetizer to snack on. One of the women made Hot Cheddar Mushroom Spread, and we couldn't get enough of it. She happily shared the recipe for this rich and chunky treat, which I've made many times since for various family holiday get-togethers.

Golden Squash Soup made me change my tune about a wonderful autumn vegetable. My early memories of squash include sitting at the table when I was little while my mom tried to coax me into eating it. Even the addition of butter and brown sugar on top wouldn't do the trick.

I had never been a winter squash-eater until I found this recipe in a newspaper a number of years ago. It sounded interesting, so I tried it. The mellow flavor of the squash combined with the zippy taste of the onions and cheddar cheese made me a squash convert. I think this soup is especially good for fall and winter meals. If I'm in a particular hurry, I simply microwave the squash to speed up the cooking time.

Simple Sausage Lasagna is a dish I created after seeing a recipe in a church cookbook that did not call for precooking the noodles. I have loved lasagna since I can remember, but the traditional preparation was too time-consuming after getting home from work.

Now, even when I have enough time, I still don't cook the noodles first for lasagna. My kids, Tony and Katrina, love this convenient version, and it makes a great dish for family get-togethers or anytime. So, my feeling is, why fix anything else?

Easy but not ordinary, my Broccoli with Mustard Sauce has a unique blend of flavors. Tony loves this sauce on a variety of vegetables, and the only "trouble" I've ever had with this recipe was not making enough to please everyone.

An impressive dessert with a pretty layered look, Caramel-Pecan Cheesecake Pie is irresistible and perfect for special meals. I've taken it to potlucks, and I always leave with an empty pie plate. Use your favorite homemade pie crust if you wish. A ready-made frozen crust works well if time is short.

Love for Cooking Started Young

When putting together a yummy dessert like this pie, I think back to when I was about 3 years old. Although just a small child, I would prepare "cakes" for my father to enjoy when he came home from work. They weren't cakes at all, but actually water mixed with every spice I could find in my mom's cupboard! Dad would always smack his lips at this concoction and praise my cooking abilities. To me, it was as if I had made a masterpiece.

As I got older, my parents let me continue experimenting with food and cooking in the kitchen. Ever since, I have retained my love for cooking. And I'm happy to say that my culinary skills have dramatically improved since then!

Besides making wonderful meals for my family, I also work in the dietary department at a residential care facility. I love to cook so much that I look for other food-related opportunities as well. I've helped neighbors and relatives prepare food for large parties. And I've prepared and served food for up to 200 people at a few of my church's social functions.

The fall season brings tourists (leaf-lookers) to this part of the state to take in the spectacular autumn colors. It's also a time of year when a harvest of rich flavors—like those in this favorite meal of mine—are appreciated. Hope you'll give my recipes a try!

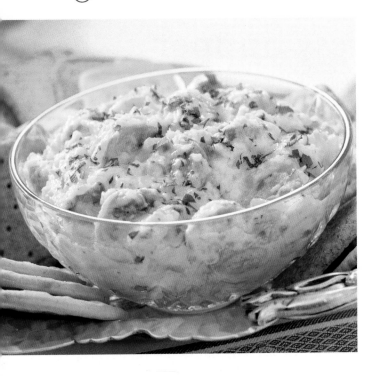

Hot Cheddar-Mushroom Spread

PREP/TOTAL TIME: 25 min.

- **2 cups mayonnaise**
- **2 cups (8 ounces) shredded cheddar cheese**
- **2/3 cup grated Parmesan cheese**
- **4 cans (4-1/2 ounces *each*) sliced mushrooms, drained**
- **1 envelope ranch salad dressing mix**
- **Minced fresh parsley**
- **Assorted crackers**

In a large bowl, combine the mayonnaise, cheeses, mushrooms and dressing mix. Spread into a greased 9-in. pie plate.

Bake, uncovered, at 350° for 20-25 minutes or until cheese is melted. Sprinkle with parsley. Serve with crackers. **Yield:** 3 cups.

Editor's Note: Reduced-fat or fat-free mayonnaise is not recommended for this recipe.

Golden Squash Soup

(Pictured on page 258)

PREP/TOTAL TIME: 30 min.

- **5 medium leeks (white portion only), sliced**
- **2 tablespoons butter**
- **1-1/2 pounds butternut squash, peeled, seeded and cubed (about 4 cups)**
- **4 cups chicken broth**
- **1/4 teaspoon dried thyme**
- **1/4 teaspoon pepper**
- **1-3/4 cups shredded cheddar cheese**
- **1/4 cup sour cream**
- **2 tablespoons thinly sliced green onion**

In a large saucepan, saute leeks in butter until tender. Stir in the squash, broth, thyme and pepper. Bring to a boil. Reduce heat; cover and simmer for 10-15 minutes or until squash is tender. Cool slightly.

In a blender, cover and process squash mixture in small batches until smooth; return to the pan. Bring to a boil. Reduce heat to low. Add cheese; stir until soup is heated through and cheese is melted. Garnish with sour cream and onion. **Yield:** 6 servings (about 2 quarts).

Simple Sausage Lasagna

PREP: 20 min. **BAKE:** 55 min. + standing

- **1 pound bulk pork sausage**
- **1 jar (26 ounces) spaghetti sauce**
- **1/2 cup water**
- **2 eggs, beaten**
- **3 cups (24 ounces) 4% cottage cheese**
- **1/3 cup grated Parmesan cheese**
- **1 to 2 tablespoons dried parsley flakes**
- **1/2 teaspoon *each* garlic powder, pepper, dried basil and oregano**
- **9 uncooked lasagna noodles**
- **3 cups (12 ounces) shredded part-skim mozzarella cheese**

In a large skillet, cook sausage over medium heat until no longer pink; drain. Stir in the spaghetti sauce and water. Simmer, uncovered, for 10 minutes. Meanwhile, in a large bowl, combine the eggs, cottage cheese,

Caramel-Pecan Cheesecake Pie

PREP: 15 min. **BAKE:** 35 min. + chilling

- 1 package (8 ounces) cream cheese, softened
- 1/2 cup sugar
- 4 eggs
- 1 teaspoon vanilla extract
- 1 unbaked pastry shell (9 inches)
- 1-1/4 cups chopped pecans
- 1 cup caramel ice cream topping

In a small bowl, beat the cream cheese, sugar, 1 egg and vanilla until smooth. Spread into pastry shell; sprinkle with pecans.

In a small bowl, whisk the remaining eggs; gradually whisk in the caramel topping until blended. Pour over the pecans.

Bake at 375° for 35-40 minutes or until lightly browned (loosely cover with foil after 20 minutes if pie browns too quickly). Cool on a wire rack for 1 hour.

Refrigerate for 4 hours or overnight before slicing. Refrigerate leftovers. **Yield:** 6-8 servings.

Parmesan cheese, parsley and seasonings.

Spread 1/2 cup meat sauce into a greased 13-in. x 9-in. x 2-in. baking dish. Layer with three noodles and a third of the cheese mixture, meat sauce and mozzarella cheese. Repeat layers twice.

Cover and bake at 375° for 45 minutes. Uncover; bake 10 minutes longer or until noodles are tender. Let stand for 15 minutes before serving. **Yield:** 12 servings.

Broccoli with Mustard Sauce

PREP/TOTAL TIME: 25 min.

- 2 pounds fresh broccoli florets, cauliflowerets *or* sliced carrots
- 1/2 cup mayonnaise
- 1/3 cup milk
- 1/4 cup grated Parmesan cheese
- 1/4 cup shredded Swiss cheese
- 2 teaspoons lemon juice
- 2 teaspoons prepared mustard

Salt and pepper to taste

Place broccoli in a steamer basket; place in a large saucepan over 1 in. of water. Bring to a boil; cover and steam for 5-8 minutes or until crisp-tender.

Meanwhile, in a small microwave-safe bowl, combine the remaining ingredients. Cover and microwave at 50% power for 2 minutes or until heated through, stirring every 30 seconds. Drain broccoli. Serve with sauce. **Yield:** 4 servings.

Editor's Note: This recipe was tested in a 1,100-watt microwave.

Meat-and-Potato Lovers' Menu

North meets South in this field editor's dinner of tender brisket, tasty sides and a delightful dessert.

By Darlis Wilfer, West Bend, Wisconsin

FOR THOSE who love to cook—and those who love to eat—I'm sharing a hearty meal that's great for a family gathering or a casual dinner party.

My popular menu features Beef Brisket with Mop Sauce, Comforting Potato Casserole, Tossed Salad with Carrot Dressing, Grandma's Honey Muffins and Poppy Seed Cake. As you will see, I'm not a gourmet cook...I just like to put a different twist on food that people enjoy.

There's No Place Like Home

My husband, Chuck, and I have been married for over 50 years. He's a "meat-and-potatoes" guy, and I am fond of desserts. Three of our five children and their families live nearby, and we get together often for holidays and special occasions. I'm in my glory with a houseful of hungry folks to feed!

Before settling in Georgia, our son Mike and daughter-in-law Sharon lived in Texas. There, we discovered mop sauce. This delicious concoction is traditionally prepared in batches for Texas ranch-style barbecue. The slabs of beef are so large that the sauce is brushed on the meat with a mop!

Beef Brisket with Mop Sauce was quick to gain everyone's approval. "You can make this again, Mom!" they agreed. We just love the zesty flavor of the sauce and think you will, too.

Tossed Salad with Carrot Dressing always draws favorable comments. It tastes so fresh and is easy to mix up. We love going to the farmer's market on Saturdays in summer and fall to buy fresh produce. I like to dress up homegrown lettuce with cut veggies, chow mein noodles, dried cranberries and shredded cabbage.

Comforting Potato Casserole was a dish I first tasted at a wedding reception, and I asked the caterer for the recipe. I make these snazzy potatoes often, as do our daughters, who appreciate that the recipe can be made ahead.

I fondly remember my Grandma Wheeler making her honey muffins. We'd eat them fresh from the oven...nice and warm. Getting the correct measurements for her recipe was quite a challenge because she didn't have them written down. She used "a pinch of this" and "a handful of that," and knew when there was enough flour because it "felt right."

Deciding which dessert recipe to add to my menu was difficult. I asked the family, and each person had a different suggestion. I chose old-fashioned Poppy Seed Cake. Tender and chock-full of poppy seeds, it has a yummy cream cheese frosting. I got the cake recipe from my longtime friend Mabel, who is of Finnish descent and bakes up a storm.

Generations of Great Cooks

I'm from a German family in which the grandmothers and mothers took care to pass along cooking lore to their children. My mom, Lorraine, still remembers learning from her mom and grandmother. I'm now passing on those skills and heritage recipes to my children and grandchildren. I especially love to take an old recipe, tweak it to my liking and mix new with old. Usually, they're surprisingly compatible.

Browsing through cookbooks and *Taste of Home* magazines gives me plenty of new ideas. What a privilege to have been asked to be one of the magazine's first field editors, in 1993.

I often think of the *Taste of Home* "family" of cooks and the many smiles they have brought to our table. When my family and friends enjoy my cooking, they are also complimenting the many fellow subscribers who have shared their recipes.

My wish is that this meal brings smiles and good eating to you!

From-Scratch Frosting

It's a good idea to sift confectioners' sugar before using it to make homemade frosting. If there are any lumps in the sugar, there will likely be lumps in the frosting. In addition, if you will be piping frosting onto the cake, lumps in the frosting may clog your decorating tips.

Comforting Potato Casserole

PREP: 10 min. **BAKE:** 1-1/2 hours

- 2 cans (10-3/4 ounces *each*) condensed cream of mushroom soup, undiluted
- 2 cups (16 ounces) sour cream
- 2 cups (8 ounces) shredded part-skim mozzarella cheese
- 5 green onions, sliced
- 1 package (32 ounces) frozen Southern-style hash brown potatoes, thawed

In a large bowl, combine the soup, sour cream, cheese and onions; add in potatoes; toss to coat.

Transfer to a greased 2-1/2-qt. baking dish. Bake, uncovered, at 350° for 1-1/2 hours or until potatoes are tender. **Yield:** 10-12 servings.

Tossed Salad with Carrot Dressing

PREP/TOTAL TIME: 25 min.

- 3/4 cup red wine vinegar
- 1 cup sugar
- 2 celery ribs, cut into chunks
- 1 small onion, cut into chunks
- 1 small carrot, cut into chunks
- 1/2 teaspoon salt
- 3/4 cup canola oil

SALAD:
- 8 cups spring mix salad greens
- 2 medium tomatoes, cut into wedges
- 1 medium cucumber, sliced

Beef Brisket with Mop Sauce

PREP: 20 min. **BAKE:** 2 hours

- 1/2 cup water
- 1/4 cup cider vinegar
- 1/4 cup Worcestershire sauce
- 1/4 cup ketchup
- 1/4 cup dark corn syrup
- 2 tablespoons canola oil
- 2 tablespoons prepared mustard
- 1 fresh beef brisket (3 pounds)

In a large saucepan, combine the first seven ingredients. Bring to a boil, stirring constantly. Reduce heat; simmer for 5 minutes, stirring occasionally. Remove from the heat.

Place the brisket in a shallow roasting pan; pour sauce over the top. Cover and bake at 350° for 2 to 2-1/2 hours or until meat is tender. Let stand for 5 minutes. Thinly slice meat across the grain. **Yield:** 10-12 servings.

Editor's Note: This is a fresh beef brisket, not corned beef.

2 green onions, sliced
1/2 cup chow mein noodles
1/2 cup shredded cheddar cheese
1/2 cup dried cranberries

In a blender, combine the first six ingredients; cover and process until smooth. While processing, gradually add oil in a steady stream. Transfer to a bowl or small pitcher; cover and refrigerate until serving.

For the salad, in a large bowl, combine the salad ingredients. Stir dressing and serve with salad. Refrigerate leftover dressing. **Yield:** 10 servings (3 cups dressing).

Grandma's Honey Muffins

PREP/TOTAL TIME: 30 min.

2 cups all-purpose flour
1/2 cup sugar
3 teaspoons baking powder
1/2 teaspoon salt
1 egg
1 cup milk
1/4 cup butter, melted
1/4 cup honey

In a bowl, combine the flour, sugar, baking powder and salt. In another bowl, whisk the egg, milk, butter and honey; stir into dry ingredients just until moistened.

Fill greased or paper-lined muffin cups three-fourths full. Bake at 400° for 15-18 minutes or until a toothpick comes out clean. Remove from pan to a wire rack. Serve warm. **Yield:** 1 dozen.

Poppy Seed Cake

PREP: 20 min. + standing **BAKE:** 25 min. + cooling

1/3 cup poppy seeds
1 cup milk
4 egg whites
3/4 cup shortening
1-1/2 cups sugar
1 teaspoon vanilla extract
2 cups all-purpose flour
2 teaspoons baking powder
FROSTING:
1 package (8 ounces) cream cheese, softened
1/2 cup butter, softened
1 teaspoon vanilla extract
2 cups confectioners' sugar

In a small bowl, soak poppy seeds in milk for 30 minutes. Place egg whites in a large bowl; let stand at room temperature for 30 minutes.

In another large bowl, cream the shortening, sugar and vanilla. Combine flour and baking powder; add to creamed mixture alternately with poppy seed mixture. Beat egg whites until soft peaks form; fold into batter.

Pour into a greased 13-in. x 9-in. x 2-in. baking dish. Bake at 375° for 25-30 minutes or until a toothpick inserted near the center comes out clean. Cool on a wire rack.

For frosting, in a small bowl, beat the cream cheese, butter and vanilla until smooth. Gradually beat in confectioners' sugar. Spread over cake. Store in the refrigerator. **Yield:** 12-15 servings.

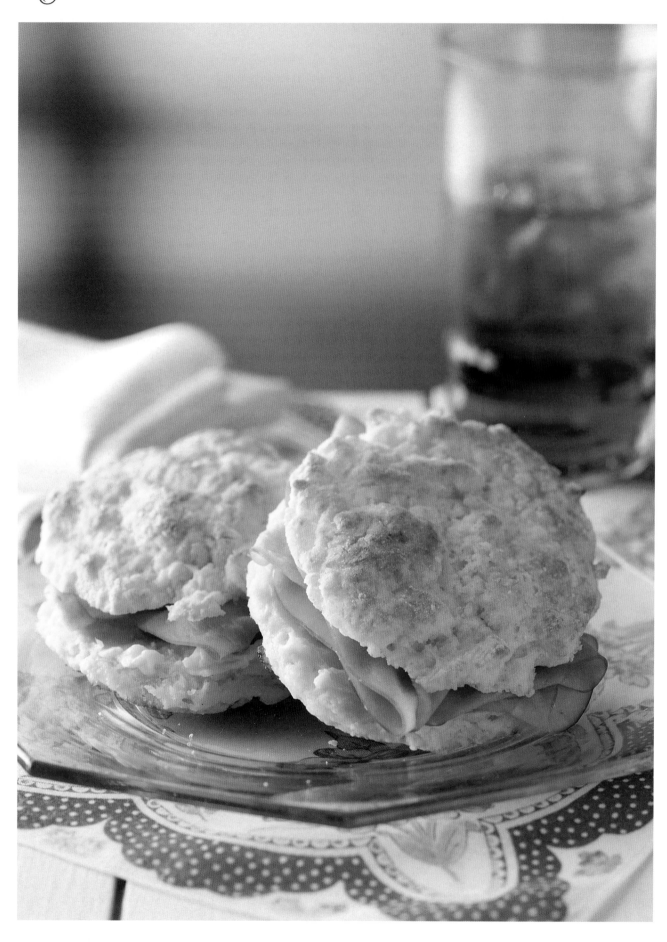

Sunny Lunch in Bloom

Midday meals blossom thanks to a flowery, refreshing menu from this entertaining field editor.

By Betsy Hedeman, Timonium, Maryland

ON A BEAUTIFUL spring or summer afternoon, I love to host a luncheon on my screened porch. Good food and a casual fresh-air atmosphere are always a treat—whether my group includes my husband, Bill, and me with friends or is a "just us girls" get-together.

On the menu are Curried Carrot Soup, hearty Ham on Biscuits, Chow Mein Chicken Salad and Creamy Lime Sherbet garnished with attractive Candied Flowers.

Curried Carrot Soup is full of flavor and has such a pretty color. The curry is pleasant but not overpowering, and thyme adds another dimension. It's a wonderful starter for our lunch.

"Remarkably good" is typical of what guests say about Chow Mein Chicken Salad. Crisp lettuce, chow mein noodles and toasted almonds and sesame seeds make it nice and crunchy.

To save time the day of the meal, I prep the ingredients for the chicken salad the night before. A glass pint jar works great for shaking up the dressing.

Bringing Home Blue Ribbons

I've always had plenty of glass jars around the house. For many years, we had a large garden, and I canned pickles, preserves and more. With my creations, I've been fortunate enough to bring home many blue ribbons from the Maryland State Fair.

When State Fair officials asked me to be a food judge, I was delighted. I was still allowed to enter any category that I would not judge.

Other than fair prizes, I've won about 15 food contests—for candy, vegetables, salads and recipes that incorporate Maryland crabmeat. I've also won the Pillsbury Pie Contest twice—with my damson plum and cherry pie recipes.

For my luncheon, I like to serve Ham on Biscuits instead of the typical sandwiches. I use Smithfield Southern cured ham, but whatever kind you like will taste great on the tender homemade biscuits.

Creamy Lime Sherbet is wonderfully smooth and refreshing. While it's a winner all by itself, dressing up the servings with Candied Flowers makes a lovely and elegant finale for a luncheon menu.

My daughters and granddaughters were delighted by and eager to know more about the flowers. To coat the petals with the meringue powder mixture, I use a kid's new paintbrush.

And yes, if you follow the recipe (making sure to use edible flowers that have not been chemically treated), Candied Flowers are edible—delicate and delicious!

Not "Retired" from Cooking

I've recently retired from judging and competing at fairs. And Bill and I have moved from our home of 30 years into a retirement community. But I say, once a cook, always a cook!

I quickly broke in the kitchen in our smaller quarters and got involved in soup parties, appetizer challenges and other food events here.

Whenever an issue of *Taste of Home* magazine arrives in the mailbox, I sit right down to read and digest the recipes. I'm still adding new ones to my bread box-size Plexiglas recipe file. I've always said, "If the house ever catches on fire, my recipe box is the first thing I would grab."

I've compiled some of my favorite recipes into a "Granny's Grub" cookbook for my granddaughters. I pulled this popular luncheon menu from my big box as well.

Candied Flowers

PREP: 30 min. + standing

- **2 teaspoons meringue powder**
- **2 tablespoons water**
- **40 to 50 edible blossoms *or flower petals of your choice, such as pansies, edible orchids or rose petals***
- **1-1/4 cups superfine sugar**

In a small bowl, dissolve the meringue powder in the water. Lightly brush over all sides of the flowers to coat completely. Sprinkle with the sugar. Let dry on a waxed paper-lined baking sheet for 1-2 days. Use as a garnish for dessert. **Yield:** 40-50 candied flowers.

Editor's Note: Meringue powder is available from Wilton Industries, Inc. Call 1-800/794-5866 or visit *www.tasteofhome.com* for a Web site link. Make sure to properly identify flowers before picking. Double-check that the flowers are edible and have not been treated with chemicals.

with a floured 2-1/2-in. biscuit cutter.

Place the biscuits 1 in. apart on an ungreased baking sheet. Bake at 450° for 8-12 minutes or until golden brown. Split biscuits in half; spread with the softened butter. Place the ham on biscuit bottoms; replace tops. **Yield:** 8 sandwiches.

Curried Carrot Soup

PREP: 15 min. **COOK:** 30 min.

- 1 large onion, chopped
- 2 teaspoons sesame oil
- 5 cups vegetable broth
- 4 medium carrots, grated (about 1-3/4 cups)
- 1-1/2 teaspoons curry powder
- 1 teaspoon dried thyme
- 1 bay leaf
- 1 package (3 ounces) cream cheese, cubed
- 5 tablespoons minced fresh parsley
- 1/4 teaspoon salt

Dash cayenne pepper, optional

In a large saucepan, saute onion in oil. Stir in the broth, carrots, curry, thyme and bay leaf. Bring to a boil. Reduce heat; simmer, uncovered, for 25-30 minutes or until carrots are tender.

Discard the bay leaf. Cool slightly. Transfer half of the soup to a blender; add half of the cream cheese. Cover and process until smooth; return to the pan. Repeat with remaining soup and cream cheese. Heat through. Stir in the parsley, salt and cayenne pepper if desired. **Yield:** 4 servings.

Ham on Biscuits

PREP/TOTAL TIME: 30 min.

- 1 cup all-purpose flour
- 2 teaspoons sugar
- 1-1/8 teaspoons baking powder
- 1/4 teaspoon baking soda
- 1/8 teaspoon salt
- 2 tablespoons cold butter
- 1/2 cup 4% cottage cheese
- 1 egg
- 3 tablespoons milk
- 8 teaspoons butter, softened
- 1/2 pound sliced deli ham

In a small bowl, combine the flour, sugar, baking powder, baking soda and salt; cut in the cold butter until the mixture resembles coarse crumbs. In a small bowl, beat the cottage cheese for 2 minutes. Beat in egg and milk until blended. Stir into the crumb mixture just until moistened.

Turn onto a lightly floured surface; knead 8-10 times. Pat or roll out to 1/2-in. thickness; cut out eight biscuits

In a large salad bowl, combine the lettuce, chow mein noodles, chicken, onions, almonds and sesame seeds.

In a jar with a tight-fitting lid, combine the vinaigrette ingredients; shake well. Drizzle over salad; toss to coat. Serve immediately. **Yield:** 4 servings.

Creamy Lime Sherbet

PREP: 20 min. + freezing

- 2 cups milk
- 1-1/4 cups sugar
- 1/3 cup lime juice
- 1-1/2 teaspoons grated lime peel
- 2 to 3 drops green food coloring, optional
- 1 carton (8 ounces) frozen whipped topping, thawed

In a large saucepan, combine the milk and sugar. Cook and stir over medium heat until the sugar is dissolved and mixture reaches 175°. Refrigerate until chilled.

Stir in the lime juice, lime peel and food coloring if desired. Freeze in an ice cream freezer according to manufacturer's directions.

Transfer the sherbet to a 2-1/2-qt. freezer container. Allow to soften slightly; fold in the whipped topping. Freeze for at least 4 hours before serving. If desired, garnish sherbet with Candied Flowers (recipe on page 279). **Yield:** 1-1/2 quarts.

Chow Mein Chicken Salad

PREP/TOTAL TIME: 20 min.

- 4 cups shredded lettuce
- 1 cup chow mein noodles
- 2/3 cup cubed cooked chicken breast
- 2 green onions, chopped
- 4 teaspoons sliced almonds, toasted
- 4 teaspoons sesame seeds, toasted

VINAIGRETTE:

- 1/4 cup canola oil
- 4-1/2 teaspoons white wine vinegar
- 1 tablespoon sugar
- 1/4 teaspoon pepper
- 1/8 teaspoon salt

Toasting Tips

You can toast sesame seeds in a dry skillet over medium heat for 10-15 minutes until they are lightly browned, stirring occasionally. Or bake them on an ungreased baking sheet at 350° for 10-15 minutes or until lightly browned. Be sure to watch them carefully to avoid scorching.

To toast almonds, spread them on a baking sheet and bake at 350° for 5 to 10 minutes or until they are lightly toasted. Remember to watch them carefully so they don't burn.

Lovely Spring Feast of Lamb

This creative editor loves to write about food—and to share the secrets of her best-loved recipes.

By Millie Vickery, Lena, Illinois

WITH all the treasured recipes I've collected over the years, it's impossible to narrow them down to one favorite meal. But this dinner of Crusty Roast Leg of Lamb, Springtime Asparagus Medley, Cracked Pepper Salad Dressing, Banana Citrus Sorbet and Strawberry-Banana Angel Torte is a wonderful way to celebrate the spring season.

These five recipes are among hundreds I've included in my "Cooking with Millie" newspaper column over the years and put together in a cookbook with that same title. I love to try new recipes and adjust them to my taste…to share good recipes with friends…and to entertain.

A Feast for Special Occasions

Crusty Roast Leg of Lamb is a delightful entree for Easter. It would also be perfect for St. Patrick's Day, since lamb is a traditional favorite of the Irish. With its golden herb crust, this roast makes a beautiful presentation surrounded by apple slices and potatoes on the serving platter.

I grow lots and lots of mint in my little garden and like to serve lamb with mint jelly or mint sauce on the side. Fresh mint also makes a great garnish for any lamb dish, along with pear or apricot halves and red grapes.

For over 50 years, I cooked with joy for my late husband, Eugene "Vic." Now I live alone, but I still love to have family and guests for dinner. I like to be creative and have fun with food.

My mom, a wonderful cook, was always adding something for extra color and appeal. Her influence is evident in my eye-catching tossed salad, served with flavorful Cracked Pepper Salad Dressing. It is creamy, delicious and simple to mix up.

Often, I'll start a meal with a salad, then surprise guests with a sorbet refresher before the main course. Banana Citrus Sorbet is a recipe from my friend Adrianne St. George, who gave elegant parties.

A zippy sauce brings out the flavor of the vegetables in Springtime Asparagus Medley. Accented by blue cheese and crunchy almonds, this dish is delicious hot or cold.

When a recipe is easy but it looks like you fussed, it's

definitely a keeper. Strawberry-Banana Angel Torte, with its luscious creamy filling and fresh fruit, is one of these desserts.

Of course, you can make the angel food cake from scratch if you have the time and the egg whites. But buying the cake or baking it from a mix gets you off to a quick start.

Never Too Busy to Cook

Over the years, I've won many awards in cooking contests and have given programs on garnishing techniques. I've won many writing awards, too. Currently, I'm typing my husband's last book on the computer. He wrote 10 books after retiring from his practice, including *House Calls: Life of a Country Doctor*. Vic also wrote poetry, including some fun poems about me and my cooking.

My life changed dramatically after I lost him. Despite the fact I am often alone, I keep very busy. Recently, I sold the big Victorian home where we lived for decades and moved to an apartment. I still spend much of my time at our vacation home on nearby Apple Canyon Lake.

Whether here or there, you'll often find me in the kitchen, trying a new recipe or making an old favorite. I'm sure you and your family will enjoy the mouthwatering menu here!

Roasting Lamb

The leg of lamb you buy may have a thin, papery white membrane (the fell) covering it, which should be removed before roasting. Do this by cutting and creating a tab of fell to hold onto near the narrow end of the leg. Grab with a paper towel and pull, making sure to pull across, not up. Then trim the fat, which carries a strong flavor that can overpower the meat's delicate flavor. Leave just a few streaks of fat to provide moisture as the lamb cooks.

Place the lamb fat side up on the rack in a shallow roasting pan. Insert a meat thermometer into the thickest muscle, being careful not to let the thermometer rest on a bone or in fat.

Springtime Asparagus Medley

PREP/TOTAL TIME: 25 min.

- 1 cup water
- 1-1/2 pounds fresh asparagus, trimmed and cut into 2-inch pieces
- 2 small tomatoes, cut into wedges
- 3 tablespoons cider vinegar
- 3/4 teaspoon Worcestershire sauce
- 1/3 cup sugar
- 1 tablespoon grated onion
- 1/2 teaspoon salt
- 1/2 teaspoon paprika
- 1/3 cup canola oil
- 1/3 cup sliced almonds, toasted
- 1/3 cup crumbled blue cheese, optional

In a large saucepan, bring water to a boil. Add asparagus; cover and cook for 3-5 minutes or until crisp-tender. Drain. Add tomatoes; cover and keep warm.

In a blender, combine vinegar, Worcestershire sauce, sugar, onion, salt and paprika; cover and process until smooth. While processing, gradually add oil in a steady stream. Pour over asparagus mixture; toss to coat.

Transfer to a serving bowl; sprinkle with almonds and blue cheese if desired. Serve warm. **Yield:** 8-10 servings.

Crusty Roast Leg of Lamb

PREP: 20 min. BAKE: 2 hours + standing

- 1 large onion, finely chopped
- 1 can (14-1/2 ounces) chicken broth
- 1 boneless leg of lamb (4 to 5 pounds)
- 1 cup soft bread crumbs (about 2 slices)
- 2 tablespoons butter, melted
- 1/2 teaspoon herbes de Provence

Dash salt and pepper

- 2-1/2 pounds medium potatoes, peeled and cut into wedges
- 1 large tart apple, sliced

Place onion in the bottom of a roasting pan; pour broth over onion. Place leg of lamb on a rack in the roasting pan. Combine the bread crumbs, butter and seasonings; spread over meat. Bake, uncovered, at 325° for 1 hour.

Add the potatoes to the pan; bake 30 minutes longer. Add apple; bake 30 minutes longer or until potatoes are tender and meat reaches desired doneness (for medium-rare, a meat thermometer should read 145°; medium, 160°; well-done, 170°).

Remove the vegetables and apple slices and keep warm. Let roast stand for 10-15 minutes before slicing. **Yield:** 10 servings.

Editor's Note: Look for herbes de Provence in the spice aisle. It is also available from Penzeys Spices. Call 1-800/741-7787 or visit www.penzeys.com.

until blended. Transfer to a large bowl; stir in water and orange juice.

Fill cylinder of ice cream maker two-thirds full; freeze according to manufacturer's directions. Refrigerate remaining mixture until ready to use. Transfer to a freezer container; freeze for 2-4 hours before serving. May be frozen for up to 1 month. **Yield:** 2-1/2 quarts.

Strawberry-Banana Angel Torte

PREP/TOTAL TIME: 20 min.

- 1 prepared angel food cake (8 inches)
- 1/2 cup sour cream
- 1/4 cup sugar
- 1/4 cup pureed fresh strawberries
- 3/4 cup sliced ripe bananas
- 1/2 cup sliced fresh strawberries
- 1 cup heavy whipping cream, whipped

Halved fresh strawberries

Split cake horizontally into three layers; place bottom layer on a serving plate. In a large bowl, combine sour cream, sugar and pureed strawberries; fold in bananas and sliced strawberries. Fold in whipped cream.

Spread a third of the filling between each layer; spread the remaining filling over top. Cover and refrigerate until serving. Garnish with halved strawberries. **Yield:** 8-10 servings.

Cracked Pepper Salad Dressing

PREP: 15 min. + chilling

- 2 cups mayonnaise
- 1/4 cup water
- 1/4 cup milk
- 1/4 cup buttermilk
- 2 tablespoons grated Parmesan cheese
- 1 tablespoon coarsely ground pepper
- 2 teaspoons finely chopped green onion
- 1 teaspoon lemon juice
- 1/2 teaspoon garlic salt
- 1/2 teaspoon garlic powder

In a small bowl, whisk all ingredients until blended. Cover and chill for at least 1 hour. May be stored in the refrigerator for up to 2 weeks. **Yield:** 2-1/2 cups.

Banana Citrus Sorbet

PREP: 10 min. + freezing

- 1/2 cup lemon juice
- 3 medium ripe bananas, cut into chunks
- 1-1/2 cups sugar
- 2 cups cold water
- 1-1/2 cups orange juice

Place lemon juice and bananas in blender; cover and process until smooth. Add sugar; cover and process

Savory Seafood Supper

One of our field editors cooks up a fresh menu that's
everyday-simple but company-special.

By Sundra Hauck, Bogalusa, Louisiana

WHEN Thanksgiving, Christmas and New Year's are behind us for yet another year, my husband, Ron, and I are happy for the change of pace. Although we truly enjoy the rich, traditional food during the holidays, we welcome the basic, simple foods that are the signature "taste of our home."

We've entertained and been entertained plenty, and now we really enjoy just sitting down together for a simple but delicious meal. One of our favorites is this one, featuring Chunky Crawfish Spread, Citrus Quencher, Sunday Shrimp Pasta Bake, Olive-Cucumber Tossed Salad and No-Bake Chocolate Pie.

A Simple Meal from the Bayou

Crawfish are my favorite, and Chunky Crawfish Spread (pictured on page 276) is just the right touch for conversation and snacking while the main course is finishing up in the oven.

Complementing the rest of the meal with its sweet-tart taste, my sparkling Citrus Quencher is truly refreshing. It's so easy to mix up that I serve this sunny beverage year-round.

The Sunday Shrimp Pasta Bake isn't just for Sunday, but it is that good. This delicious dish also serves us well on a Saturday night before a big football game or even during the week, if time allows.

Seafood is plentiful here, so we enjoy it often. Shrimp (or "shrimps," as my 101-year-old mother-in-law, Bertha, calls them) are Ron's favorite.

We often enjoy shrimp and crawfish at the same meal. But if not, I make sure to rotate the two.

The Olive-Cucumber Tossed Salad can be prepped ahead of time and plated up at the last minute. I combine the dressing with the olives and sliced cucumbers in advance.

Sometimes dessert has to be served a bit later, as this is a filling meal. But when you bring out the No-Bake Chocolate Pie, no one will turn it down. It's a winner on any occasion.

Leftovers are not a problem when I prepare this meal for just the two of us. We appreciate these dishes just as much the second time around. If it's too much

food for us, I take the leftovers to my workplace the next day and share with co-workers. There's always plenty to go around because I cook "big." It's the way I learned how to cook.

There's Always Time for a Hearty Meal

I work full-time in a medical office, but I still look forward to preparing a nice supper for us. I go into the kitchen, turn on my favorite radio station and cook. It's very relaxing to me.

Since I work away from home full-time, friends have asked how I manage to find time to cook. I tell them…lists. That's my secret. Lists. It's actually a bit of a joke with those who know me well.

I organize a meal—the menu, the shopping list, even the seating arrangement for special occasions.

The bonus for me is that Ron cleans up. Isn't that just the most wonderful thing of all? I think so!

We were married several years ago. Ron was born in New Orleans and spent most of his life there. He's retired from the U.S. Postal Service.

I'm a Bogalusa native and have a son, a daughter and son-in-law, and two young grandsons. My family loves Ron as if he has been with us always.

My personal cooking pleasures didn't begin until I was an adult. I have come a long way and now am even asked to prepare foods for weddings and showers on occasion. I must admit, however, that I much prefer the simple pleasures of cooking for my husband, family, friends and co-workers.

Ron enjoys his retirement by staying active and spending plenty of time outdoors. He has worked as a nature guide at a local boys' and girls' summer camp and is active in the Knights of Columbus.

I'm a member of the Secular Franciscans (a Roman Catholic fraternity), play in a Po-Ke-No group and enjoy "Eight Is Enough"—a group of ladies who get together several times a year.

Together, Ron and I like what we call "day-tripping." We take jaunts around Louisiana and nearby Mississippi. Often, our destination is Baton Rouge to visit our grandchildren. "The grands" are our hearts, so we visit for any occasion that comes up—from soccer games to birthday party celebrations.

I hope you enjoy my recipes as much as we do.

Sunday Shrimp Pasta Bake

PREP: 30 min. **BAKE:** 25 min.

- 12 **ounces uncooked vermicelli**
- 1 **medium green pepper, chopped**
- 5 **green onions, chopped**
- 6 **garlic cloves, minced**
- 6 **tablespoons butter, cubed**
- 2 **tablespoons all-purpose flour**
- 2 **pounds deveined peeled cooked medium shrimp**
- 1 **teaspoon celery salt**
- 1/8 **teaspoon pepper**
- 1 **pound process cheese (Velveeta), cubed**
- 1 **can (10 ounces) diced tomatoes and green chilies, drained**
- 1 **can (4 ounces) mushroom stems and pieces, drained**
- 1 **tablespoon grated Parmesan cheese**

Cook vermicelli according to package directions. Meanwhile, in a large skillet, saute the green pepper, onions and garlic in butter until tender. Gradually stir in the flour until blended. Stir in the shrimp, celery salt and pepper; cook, uncovered, over medium heat for 5-6 minutes or until heated through.

In a microwave-safe bowl, combine the process cheese, tomatoes and mushrooms. Microwave, uncovered, on high for 3-4 minutes or until cheese is melted, stirring occasionally. Add to shrimp mixture.

Chunky Crawfish Spread

PREP: 20 min. + chilling

- 1 **package (16 ounces) frozen cooked crawfish tails, thawed**
- 1 **package (8 ounces) cream cheese, softened**
- 1 **medium green pepper, finely chopped**
- 1 **medium sweet red pepper, finely chopped**
- 1 **small onion, finely chopped**
- 6 **garlic cloves, minced**
- 1/2 **to 1 teaspoon Creole seasoning**
- 1/2 **teaspoon salt**
- 6 **to 12 drops hot pepper sauce**

Assorted crackers

Chop the crawfish; pat dry. In a small bowl, beat the cream cheese. Add the peppers, onion, garlic, Creole seasoning, salt and hot pepper sauce; stir in the crawfish. Cover and refrigerate for at least 2 hours. Serve with crackers. **Yield:** 3 cups.

Crawfish Facts

Also known as crayfish or crawdads, crawfish are freshwater crustaceans that are common in France, Scandinavia and also the United States. They are harvested from the waters of the Mississippi Basin and are popular in Louisiana-style cooking. Like lobster, crawfish turn bright red when cooked.

Citrus Quencher

(Pictured on page 274)

PREP/TOTAL TIME: 5 min.

> 2 **liters lemon-lime soda, chilled**
> 3/4 **cup limeade concentrate**
> 1/2 **cup orange juice**

In a large pitcher, combine all ingredients. Serve over ice. **Yield:** 8 servings (2-1/2 quarts).

No-Bake Chocolate Pie

PREP: 15 min. + chilling

> 7 **milk chocolate candy bars (1.55 ounces *each*), chopped**
> 20 **large marshmallows**
> 1/2 **cup milk**
> 2 **cups whipped topping**
> 1 **graham cracker crust (9 inches)**
> **Additional whipped topping, optional**

In a large heavy saucepan, combine the candy bars, marshmallows and milk. Cook and stir over low heat until smooth. Remove from the heat; cool. Fold in whipped topping; pour into crust.

Cover and refrigerate for 4 hours or overnight. Garnish with additional whipped topping if desired. **Yield:** 8 servings.

Drain vermicelli; stir into skillet.

Pour into a greased 13-in. x 9-in. x 2-in. baking dish. Sprinkle with Parmesan cheese. Bake, uncovered, at 350° for 25-30 minutes or until heated through. **Yield:** 8 servings.

Editor's Note: This recipe was tested in a 1,100-watt microwave.

Olive-Cucumber Tossed Salad

PREP: 15 min. + marinating

> 1 **cup Italian salad dressing**
> 2 **medium cucumbers, peeled, halved, seeded and sliced**
> 1 **cup pimiento-stuffed olives, halved**
> 1 **teaspoon Creole seasoning**
> 2 **packages (10 ounces *each*) ready-to-serve salad greens**

In a large bowl, combine the salad dressing, cucumbers, olives and Creole seasoning. Cover and refrigerate for at least 30 minutes. Just before serving, place the salad greens in a large bowl; add cucumber mixture and toss to coat. **Yield:** 8 servings.

Editor's Note: The following spices may be substituted for 1 teaspoon of Creole seasoning: 1/4 teaspoon *each* salt, garlic powder and paprika; and a pinch each of dried thyme, ground cumin and cayenne pepper.

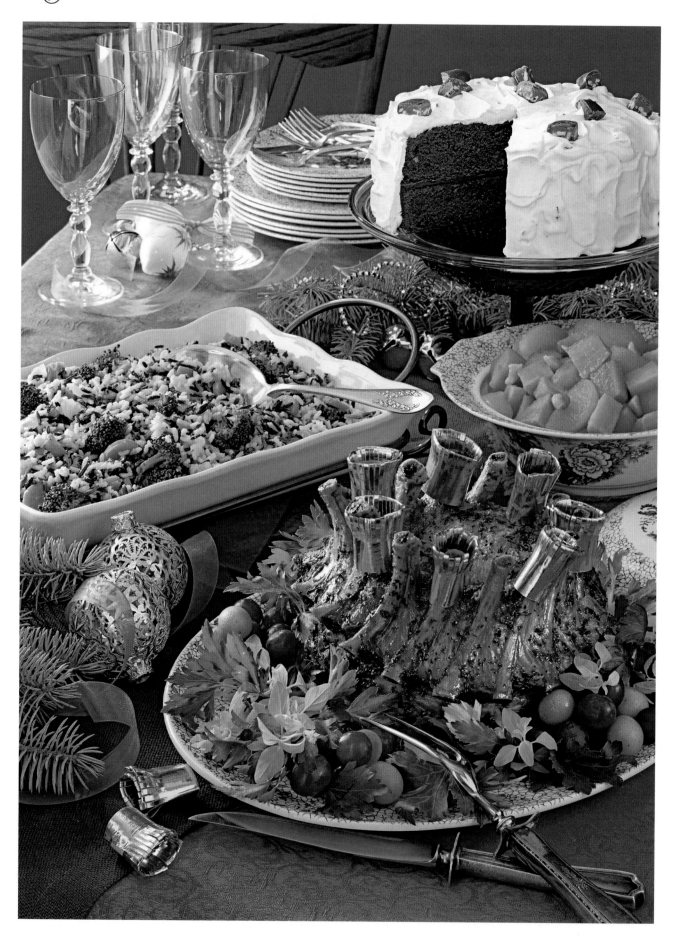

Crown Roast for Christmas

Elegant pork entree forms the centerpiece of this
Taste of Home field editor's holiday meal.

By Dianne Bettin, Truman, Minnesota

I LOVE to feed people. And, even though our family has an extremely busy lifestyle, I don't mind taking time out to cook for family, friends and sometimes even strangers!

My husband, Doug, and I have a 350-sow hog operation and grain farm. I have been volunteering with pork producers' organizations for almost 20 years.

So it's no surprise that pork stars on many of my menus. During the holidays and on other special occasions, I enjoy showcasing an elegant yet easy-to-prepare Crown Roast of Pork. Two of my favorite side dishes to serve with the roast are Wild Rice Pilaf and Cashew-Peach Sweet Potatoes. Devil's Food Caramel Torte is a great finish!

A Center Stage Roast

A crown roast makes Christmas dinner extra special. I order the roast by how many ribs I want—figure on one per person. Just talk to your butcher or grocery store meat manager a few days ahead. An herb rub accents the pork's flavor. Be sure to use a meat thermometer to guarantee that your roast is done to perfection (see tip at right).

I like to make the Wild Rice Pilaf a day ahead, which allows the rosemary and other flavors time to blend. This make-ahead approach also makes mealtime preparations go smoother the day of the dinner. The rice pilaf reheats well in the microwave. I frequently take it to potlucks—the only bad thing about that is I rarely have any leftovers to bring home!

I ran across the Cashew-Peach Sweet Potatoes recipe while hunting for variations on the old standby sweet potato bake. I have a vegetable garden and found the recipe one particularly prolific year.

When I cook, I tend to focus on the main meal. The dessert oftentimes is an afterthought. That's why I was thrilled when my sister-in-law, Nicki, showed up at a gathering with scrumptious Devil's Food Caramel Torte. It was definitely one of those recipes I had to add to my collection.

I love food and confess that while most people travel to sightsee, I travel to eat! Even when I go to our famous Mall of America here in Minnesota, I spend more time eating than shopping. My favorite stop is a wonderful sushi bar.

Not Just A Family Affair

As a member of the National Pork Board—an industry-nominated, government-appointed position—I help promote pork across the country and even overseas. I enjoy cooking new foods that I find on my travels, especially if they involve pork! Doug and our children—Tyler and Marisa—are good sports about trying everything I put in front of them.

Doug and I enjoy traveling and camping. Although the farm doesn't give him much free time, he manages to accompany me to some of my out-of-state meetings. We also enjoy time at the lake and around the campfire.

With our youngest off to college, our life will be very different now! I plan to fill some of the void with trying new recipes, especially tried-and-true ones from *Taste of Home*.

I hope you'll "pick pork" and consider this menu for your own Christmas dinner!

Dianne's Pork Pointers

◆ The old practice of overcooking pork is no longer necessary for food safety. The deliciously improved pork cuts of today are best when left slightly pink in the center, cooked to an internal temperature of 160°.

◆ I remove my crown roast (and other cuts, too!) from the oven when the meat reaches 150° and let it rest for about 10 minutes before carving. This allows the temperature to continue to rise to 160° while sealing in the juices.

◆ New research from the USDA reveals that pork tenderloin contains only 2.98 grams of fat per 3-ounce cooked serving. A 3-ounce cooked skinless chicken breast has 3.03 grams of fat. So when you want to stick to healthy cooking, keep pork in mind!

Wild Rice Pilaf

PREP: 1 hour **BAKE:** 25 min.

- 2 cans (14-1/2 ounces *each*) chicken broth
- 3/4 cup uncooked wild rice
- 1 cup uncooked long grain rice
- 1 large onion, chopped
- 2 medium carrots, halved lengthwise and sliced
- 1 garlic clove, minced
- 1/2 teaspoon dried rosemary, crushed
- 1/2 cup butter, cubed
- 3 cups fresh broccoli florets
- 1/4 teaspoon pepper

In a large saucepan, bring broth to a boil. Add wild rice; reduce heat. Cover and cook for 30 minutes. Add long grain rice; cook 20-25 minutes longer or until liquid is absorbed and rice is tender.

Meanwhile, in a large skillet, saute the onion, carrots, garlic and rosemary in butter until vegetables are tender. Stir in the rice, broccoli and pepper.

Transfer to a greased shallow 2-qt. baking dish. Cover and bake at 350° for 25-30 minutes or until the broccoli is crisp-tender. Fluff with a fork before serving.
Yield: 10 servings.

Crown Roast of Pork

PREP: 15 min. **BAKE:** 3 hours + standing

- 1 tablespoon dried parsley flakes
- 1 tablespoon canola oil
- 1 teaspoon salt
- 1/2 teaspoon pepper
- 1 pork crown roast (14 ribs and about 8 pounds)
Foil *or* paper frills for rib ends

Combine the parsley, oil, salt and pepper; rub over roast. Place on a rack in a large shallow roasting pan. Cover rib ends with pieces of foil. Bake at 350° for 3 to 3-1/2 hours or until a meat thermometer reads 160°.

Transfer the roast to a serving platter. Let stand for 10-15 minutes. Remove foil pieces. Garnish rib ends with foil or paper frills. Cut between ribs to serve.
Yield: 14 servings.

**1 package (7 ounces) milk chocolate turtle
  candies, chopped, *divided***
1 tablespoon baking cocoa
1-1/2 cups heavy whipping cream
1/3 cup caramel ice cream topping
1 can (16 ounces) chocolate frosting
**Additional milk chocolate turtle candies, broken,
  optional**

Line two 9-in. round baking pans with waxed paper;
grease the paper and set aside. In a large bowl, combine
the cake mix, buttermilk, oil and eggs. Beat on low
speed for 30 seconds. Beat on medium for 2 minutes.
Combine 1 cup candies and cocoa; fold into batter.

Pour into prepared pans. Bake at 350° for 25-30
minutes or until a toothpick inserted near the center
comes out clean. Cool for 10 minutes before removing
from pans to wire racks to cool completely. Remove
waxed paper.

In a small bowl, beat the cream until it begins to
thicken. Add caramel topping; beat until stiff peaks
form. Fold in remaining candies.

Place one cake layer on a serving plate; spread with
chocolate frosting. Top with remaining cake layer; frost
top and sides of torte with cream mixture. Garnish with
additional candies if desired. Refrigerate until serving.
Yield: 12 servings.

Cashew-Peach Sweet Potatoes

PREP: 45 min. **BAKE:** 40 min.

6 medium sweet potatoes
1/2 cup packed brown sugar
1/3 cup coarsely chopped cashews
1/2 teaspoon salt
1/4 teaspoon ground ginger
1 can (15-1/4 ounces) sliced peaches, drained
3 tablespoons butter

Place sweet potatoes in a large saucepan or Dutch
oven; cover with water. Bring to a boil. Reduce heat;
cover and cook for 30-45 minutes or just until tender.
Drain and cool slightly; peel and cut into cubes.

Combine the brown sugar, cashews, salt and ginger.
Place half of the sweet potatoes in an ungreased 11-in. x
7-in. x 2-in. baking dish; top with half of the peaches and
brown sugar mixture. Repeat layers; dot with butter.

Cover and bake at 350° for 30 minutes. Uncover; bake
10 minutes longer or until bubbly and heated through.
Yield: 10 servings.

Devil's Food Caramel Torte

PREP: 40 min. **BAKE:** 25 min. + cooling

1 package (18-1/4 ounces) devil's food cake mix
1 cup buttermilk
1/2 cup canola oil
3 eggs

Meals in Minutes

The next time you need a meal on the table in a snap, turn to this effortless chapter. Here you'll find several menus that are completely table ready in just 30 minutes...or less!

FAST FIXES. Clockwise from upper left: Chicken with Paprika Cream (p. 295), Shrimp Scampi (p. 285), Chicken Florentine Panini (p. 287), Pepper-Rubbed Red Snapper (p. 291) and pictured center, Apricot Honey Chicken (p. 289).

Treat Your Gang to an Italian-Style Supper

ON EVENINGS when your family's ready for dinner but you're not, a quick solution is often frozen pizza or carry-out chicken.

This fast-to-fix meal, made up of three reader favorites, delivers from-scratch flavor in just 30 minutes. Try it out tonight!

Shrimp Scampi, from Lori Packer of Omaha, Nebraska, looks like you fussed but is a snap to prepare. Lemon and herbs enhance the shrimp, and the bread crumbs lend a pleasing crunch. Served over angel hair pasta, this main dish is pretty enough for company.

"Garlic-Almond Green Beans is my family's favorite way to eat this popular vegetable," Genny Monchamp says from Redding, California. "The beans stay so tender and crisp. To speed things up even more, you could use frozen green beans instead of fresh."

Short and sweet, the recipe for yummy Granola Fudge Clusters uses only four ingredients. "I have overheard people say, 'You have to try one of these,' when I serve them at get-togethers," shares Loraine Meyer of Bend, Oregon. "I always double the batch because no one can eat just one."

Shrimp Scampi

PREP/TOTAL TIME: 20 min.

- 3 to 4 garlic cloves, minced
- 1/4 cup butter, cubed
- 1/4 cup olive oil
- 1 pound uncooked medium shrimp, peeled and deveined
- 1/4 cup lemon juice
- 1/2 teaspoon pepper
- 1/4 teaspoon dried oregano
- 1/2 cup grated Parmesan cheese
- 1/4 cup dry bread crumbs
- 1/4 cup minced fresh parsley

Hot cooked angel hair pasta

In a 10-in. ovenproof skillet, saute garlic in butter and oil until tender. Stir in the shrimp, lemon juice, pepper and oregano; cook and stir for 2-3 minutes or until shrimp turn pink. Sprinkle with Parmesan cheese, bread crumbs and parsley.

Broil 6 inches from the heat for 2-3 minutes or until the topping is golden brown. Serve over the pasta.
Yield: 4 servings.

Garlic-Almond Green Beans

PREP/TOTAL TIME: 20 min.

- 1 pound fresh green beans
- 2 garlic cloves, minced
- 1 tablespoon olive oil
- 1/4 cup slivered almonds, toasted

Pepper to taste

Place the beans in a large saucepan and cover with water. Bring to a boil; cook, uncovered, for 8-10 minutes or until crisp-tender.

Meanwhile, in a large skillet, cook the minced garlic in oil for 2-3 minutes. Drain the beans. Add the beans, slivered almonds and pepper to the skillet; toss to coat.
Yield: 4 servings.

Granola Fudge Clusters

PREP/TOTAL TIME: 25 min.

- 1 cup (6 ounces) semisweet chocolate chips
- 1 cup butterscotch chips
- 1-1/4 cups granola cereal without raisins
- 1 cup chopped walnuts

In a microwave-safe bowl, melt the chocolate and butterscotch chips; stir until smooth. Stir in granola cereal and walnuts.

Drop by tablespoonfuls onto waxed paper-lined baking sheets. Refrigerate for 15 minutes or until firm.
Yield: about 2-1/2 dozen.

Have a Meltdown?

To melt chocolate in the microwave, place it in a microwave-safe bowl. Melt semisweet chocolate at 50% power and milk chocolate at 30% power. Stir frequently until the chocolate is melted; do not overheat. If there are large chunks of chocolate, chop them up so the chocolate melts evenly.

You can also melt chocolate in a heavy saucepan over low heat; stir until smooth. Even small amounts of water in the mixture can make the chocolate unusable, so be sure all bowls and pots are completely dry.

Combine Three Favorites For a Fast Lunch

WHAT goes together better than a hearty sandwich, hot soup and a salad? Your family will enjoy relaxing with this laid-back, 30-minute menu that works as a satisfying lunch or a light supper.

Chicken Florentine Panini, from Lee Bremson of Kansas City, Missouri, brings an Italian flair to this speedy meal. The grilled sandwich combines chicken with provolone cheese, spinach and red onion.

Why buy bottled dressing when you can make delicious, homemade Thousand Island Salad Dressing in a jiffy? This tangy version comes from Elizabeth Montgomery of Taylorville, Illinois.

"Ramen Corn Chowder tastes as good as if it simmered for hours, but it's ready in 15 minutes," writes Darlene Brenden of Salem, Oregon. "I thought the original recipe was lacking in flavor, so I jazzed it up with extra corn and bacon bits."

Chicken Florentine Panini

PREP/TOTAL TIME: 25 min.

- 1 **package (6 ounces) fresh baby spinach**
- 2 **teaspoons olive oil**
- 1/4 **cup butter, softened**
- 8 **slices sourdough bread**
- 1/4 **cup creamy Italian salad dressing**
- 8 **slices provolone cheese**
- 1/2 **pound shaved deli chicken**
- 2 **slices red onion, separated into rings**

In a large skillet, saute the spinach in olive oil for 2 minutes or until wilted. Butter one side of each slice of bread. Spread the unbuttered side of four slices with the salad dressing; layer with a cheese slice, chicken, spinach, onion and another cheese slice. Top with the remaining bread, buttered side up. Cook in a panini maker or on a griddle until golden brown on both sides. **Yield:** 4 servings.

Ramen Corn Chowder

PREP/TOTAL TIME: 15 min.

- 2 **cups water**
- 1 **package (3 ounces) chicken ramen noodles**
- 1 **can (15-1/4 ounces) whole kernel corn, drained**
- 1 **can (14-3/4 ounces) cream-style corn**
- 1 **cup milk**
- 1 **teaspoon dried minced onion**
- 1/4 **teaspoon curry powder**
- 3/4 **cup shredded cheddar cheese**
- 1 **tablespoon crumbled cooked bacon**
- 1 **tablespoon minced fresh parsley**

In a small saucepan, bring water to a boil. Break the noodles into large pieces. Add noodles and contents of seasoning packet to water. Reduce heat to medium. Cook, uncovered, for 2-3 minutes or until the noodles are tender.

Stir in the corn, cream-style corn, milk, onion and curry; heat through. Stir in the cheese, bacon and parsley until blended. **Yield:** 4 servings.

Thousand Island Salad Dressing

PREP/TOTAL TIME: 15 min.

- 1-1/2 **cups mayonnaise**
- 1/2 **cup chili sauce**
- 1 **hard-cooked egg, chopped**
- 2 **tablespoons finely chopped celery**
- 2 **tablespoons finely chopped green pepper**
- 2 **tablespoons chopped pimiento-stuffed olives**
- 1 **tablespoon grated onion**

In a small bowl, combine all ingredients. Cover and refrigerate until serving. **Yield:** 2 cups.

All Dressed Up

Sour cream- and mayonnaise-based salad dressings, like Thousand Island Salad Dressing (recipe above), go well with sturdy greens such as iceberg and romaine lettuce. Delicate greens such as Bibb or Boston lettuce are best with vinegar and oil dressings.

Toss greens with your dressing immediately before serving the salad or place the greens in a salad bowl and pass the dressing at the table. Keep in mind that putting too much dressing on the salad will make it soggy.

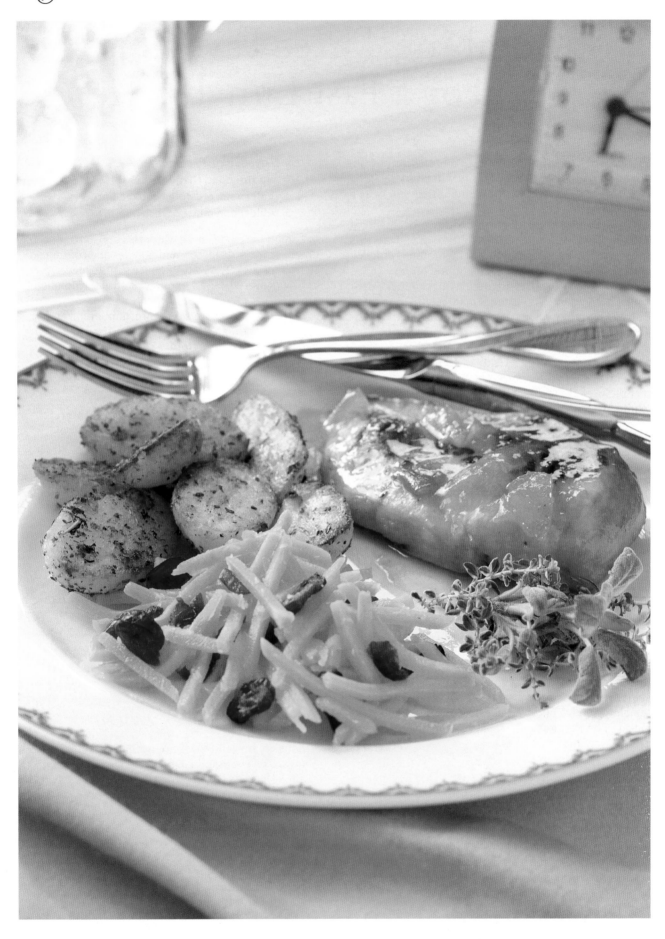

Chicken and Veggies Please Families

YOU JUST returned home, the clock's ticking and the rest of your family will be walking through the front door any moment now. Don't worry! You won't disappoint them when this appealing, nutritious and quick menu is sizzling to perfection on the stovetop.

Apricot Honey Chicken from Kathy Hawkins of Gurnee, Illinois boasts a sweet, fruity sauce. There's no need to heat up the oven for this flavorful entree, so you can even enjoy it during the summer. Try the sauce with ham slices as well.

"I saw something similar to Favorite Herbed Potatoes prepared on television and decided to make my own version using the herbs I had on hand," says Naomi Olson of Hamilton, Michigan. "To cut preparation time, I even substituted canned potatoes for fresh ones, and we liked it just as much."

Gingered Cranberry-Carrot Slaw gives this meal a nice tang with cranberries and a sweet-tart pineapple dressing. Genise Krause of Sturgeon Bay, Wisconsin shared the refreshing recipe.

Apricot Honey Chicken

PREP/TOTAL TIME: 25 min.

- 4 **boneless skinless chicken breast halves (5 ounces *each*)**
- 1 **tablespoon canola oil**
- 3 **tablespoons apricot preserves**
- 2 **tablespoons orange juice**
- 4 **teaspoons honey**

In a large skillet, cook chicken in oil over medium heat for 7-9 minutes on each side or until juices run clear. Combine the preserves, orange juice and honey; pour over chicken. Cook for 2 minutes or until heated through. **Yield:** 4 servings.

Gingered Cranberry-Carrot Slaw

PREP/TOTAL TIME: 10 min.

- 1/2 **cup unsweetened pineapple juice**
- 2 **tablespoons honey**
- 1 **tablespoon lemon juice**
- 1 **teaspoon cider vinegar**
- 3 **cups shredded carrots**
- 1/2 **cup dried cranberries**
- 1 **to 2 tablespoons minced fresh gingerroot**

In a large bowl, whisk the pineapple juice, honey, lemon juice and vinegar until smooth. Add the carrots, cranberries and ginger; toss to coat. Cover and refrigerate until serving. **Yield:** 4 servings.

Favorite Herbed Potatoes

PREP/TOTAL TIME: 20 min.

- 2 **cans (15 ounces *each*) whole potatoes, drained and halved lengthwise**
- 1 **tablespoon butter**
- 1 **tablespoon olive oil**
- 1-1/2 **teaspoons dried parsley flakes**
- 1/2 **teaspoon dried basil**
- 1/2 **teaspoon dried thyme**
- 1/2 **teaspoon rubbed sage**
- 1/2 **teaspoon dried rosemary, crushed**
- 1/2 **teaspoon garlic powder**
- 1/4 **teaspoon paprika**
- 1/4 **teaspoon pepper**

In a large skillet over medium heat, cook potatoes in butter and oil for 6-8 minutes or until browned. Add the remaining ingredients; cook and stir for 2-3 minutes or until well coated. **Yield:** 4 servings.

Surefire Success

For a no-fuss supper with loads of tasty appeal, you can't go wrong with this finger-licking combination of recipes. To make sure you beat the clock, start by assembling Gingered Cranberry-Carrot Slaw. When done, set the dish in the refrigerator to chill while you prepare the rest of the meal.

As the chicken cooks in the oil, brown the potatoes in butter and oil in another skillet. When it's time to flip the chicken over, the potatoes should be just about ready for the seasonings.

Once the potatoes are ready, turn off the heat and cover the skillet to keep them warm. Complete the main course by mixing up the sauce and adding to the chicken, and dinner is served. For extra flair, add a loaf of bread from the bakery and pick up some ice cream for dessert!

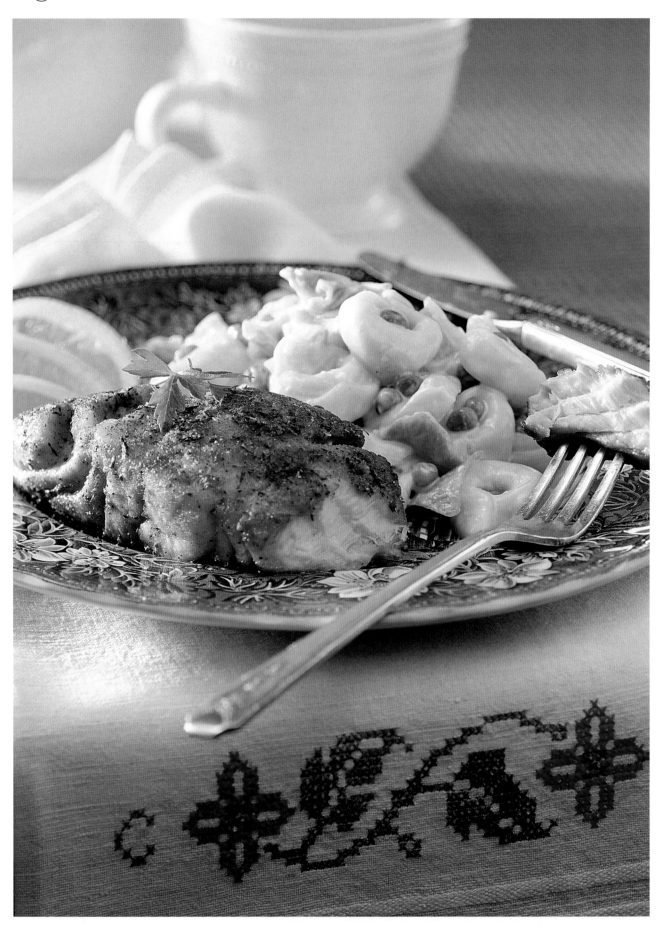

Skillet Seafood Menu Is Easy and Elegant

RUNNING ERRANDS, attending after-school events, working late…it all adds up to less time in the kitchen. But you'll need no more than half an hour to put this extra-special meal on the table.

"I can prepare Pepper-Rubbed Red Snapper in a flash on a weeknight or when guests visit for dinner," relates Windy Byrd of Freeport, Texas. "And the recipe really comes in handy whenever family members bring home a great catch."

Scott Jones of Tulsa, Oklahoma likes to whip up Prosciutto Tortellini as a hearty side dish. "I just spruce up frozen store-bought pasta with peas, prosciutto and a smooth, cheesy sauce," he explains.

For the finale, add five-ingredient Frosty Almond Dessert from Phyllis Schmalz of Kansas City, Kansas. "It's a quick and easy dessert without a lot of fuss," she notes. "Best of all, it's yummy!"

Pepper-Rubbed Red Snapper

PREP/TOTAL TIME: 15 min.

1/2 teaspoon onion powder
1/2 teaspoon garlic powder
1/2 teaspoon dried thyme
1/2 teaspoon white pepper
1/2 teaspoon cayenne pepper
1/2 teaspoon pepper
1/8 teaspoon salt
4 red snapper fillets (8 ounces *each*)
3 tablespoons butter, melted

In a small bowl, combine the first seven ingredients. Dip the fish fillets in butter, then rub with spice mixture.

In a large nonstick skillet, cook the fish fillets over medium-high heat for 2-4 minutes on each side or until fish flakes easily with a fork. **Yield:** 4 servings.

Prosciutto Tortellini

PREP/TOTAL TIME: 20 min.

1 package (19 ounces) frozen cheese tortellini
1 tablespoon all-purpose flour
1 cup half-and-half cream
1/2 cup shredded part-skim mozzarella cheese
1/2 cup shredded Parmesan cheese
10 thin slices prosciutto, chopped
1 package (10 ounces) frozen peas
1/4 teaspoon white pepper

Cook the tortellini according to the package directions. Meanwhile, in a large skillet, combine flour and cream until smooth; stir in the cheeses. Bring to a boil; cook and stir for 2 minutes or until thickened. Reduce heat.

Drain tortellini; add to the cheese sauce. Stir in the prosciutto, peas and pepper. Cook for 5 minutes or until heated through. **Yield:** 4 servings.

Frosty Almond Dessert

(*Not pictured*)

PREP/TOTAL TIME: 10 min.

4 cups vanilla frozen yogurt
1 cup ice cubes
1/2 cup hot fudge ice cream topping
1/4 teaspoon almond extract
Whipped topping and baking cocoa, optional

In a blender, place half of the yogurt, ice cubes, fudge topping and extract; cover and process for 1-2 minutes or until smooth. Stir if necessary. Pour into chilled dessert glasses.

Repeat with remaining yogurt, ice, fudge topping and extract. Garnish with whipped topping and baking cocoa if desired. **Yield:** 4 servings.

Defrosting Do's

The thicker the package of fish or shellfish, the longer it will take to defrost. Here are two food-safe methods of defrosting:

• **Refrigeration defrosting.** When defrosting fish or shellfish in the refrigerator, place a tray under the package to catch any liquid or juices and keep the refrigerator clean. Allow 12 or more hours to thaw a 1-pound package.

• **Cold-water thawing.** This is an option that takes less time than refrigeration defrosting but requires more attention. The fish or shellfish must be in a leakproof bag such as its original tightly sealed wrapper. If its package is not leakproof, then place it in a heavy-duty plastic bag.

Next, submerge the wrapped seafood in cold tap water. Change the water every 30 minutes until the seafood is thawed. For this method of defrosting, allow 1 to 2 hours for every pound.

Quick and Colorful Cuisine Ideal For Summer Cookouts

WHEN warm summer breezes beckon, even folks who love to cook want to spend less time in the kitchen and more time on the patio or porch. When fresh air builds appetites, a filling fast-to-fix meal is the order of the day.

The complete-meal menu here consists of favorites from three great cooks and was combined by the *Taste of Home* Test Kitchen staff. Not only is the menu ideal for July Fourth celebrations and weeknight meals alike, but you can have everything ready to serve in just half an hour!

"I created French Onion Burgers one day when I needed to stretch a pound of hamburger," recalls Beth Johnson of Dalton, Ohio. "When we have high school boys help with baling hay, this is one of their favorite foods to enjoy after the work is done."

With its pretty pink blush and tart refreshing flavor, Cranberry Lemonade is sure to satisfy, glass after glass after glass. Darlene Brenden of Salem, Oregon shared this summer thirst-quencher.

Old Glory Angel Food makes a colorful dessert for your Fourth of July celebration. It's easy to assemble, but the triple layers and stars-and-stripes topping look like you fussed.

"One July, we invited a couple over for a backyard barbecue," relates Anne Nabbefeld from Greenville, Wisconsin. "The woman had recently become a United States citizen, so I created this cake specifically for her. It was a big hit."

French Onion Burgers

PREP/TOTAL TIME: 20 min.

- 1 can (4 ounces) mushroom stems and pieces, drained and diced
- 1 can (2.8 ounces) french-fried onions
- 1 tablespoon Worcestershire sauce
- 1/2 teaspoon salt
- 1 pound ground beef
- 4 hamburger buns, split

Lettuce leaves and tomato slices

In a large bowl, combine the mushrooms, onions, Worcestershire sauce and salt. Crumble beef over mixture and mix well. Shape into four patties.

Grill, uncovered, over medium heat or broil 4 in. from the heat for 6-9 minutes on each side or until no longer pink. Serve on hamburger buns with lettuce and tomato. **Yield:** 4 servings.

Old Glory Angel Food

PREP/TOTAL TIME: 20 min.

- 1 loaf (10-1/2 ounces) angel food cake
- 1 carton (8 ounces) frozen whipped topping, thawed, *divided*
- 1 cup quartered fresh strawberries
- 1 cup fresh blueberries

Additional blueberries and strawberries

Split cake horizontally into thirds. Place bottom layer on a serving platter. Combine 1 cup whipped topping and strawberries; spread over bottom layer. Top with second cake layer.

Combine 1 cup topping and blueberries; spread over second layer. Top with remaining cake layer. Spread with remaining topping. Arrange additional berries over top of cake to form a flag. **Yield:** 8 servings.

Cranberry Lemonade

PREP: 5 min. **COOK:** 15 min. + chilling

- 3/4 cup sugar
- 2/3 cup lemon juice
- 3 cups cold water
- 1 cup cranberry juice

In a small saucepan, combine sugar and lemon juice. Cook and stir over medium heat until sugar is dissolved. Stir in the cold water and cranberry juice. Cool; pour into a pitcher. Refrigerate until chilled. Serve over ice. **Yield:** 4 servings.

Patriotic Party Pizzazz

It's a snap to give July picnics festive flair with these fun (and fast!) ideas:

Turn strawberry shortcake into a red, white and blue dessert by adding blueberries and topping with whipped cream.

Enhance a bowl of fruit punch with strawberries and blueberries. Or freeze the berries in ice cubes and add the cubes to the punch.

Poke American flag picks into cupcakes spread with red, white or blue frosting or top sugar cookies with red and blue sprinkles.

Spice Up Dinnertime with These Well-Seasoned Dishes

SPENDING TIME preparing an elaborate meal is no big deal for those who like to cook. But some days, speed is the key ingredient in what you whip up for your hungry clan.

The complete menu here is comprised of family favorites from three super cooks. You can have it ready to serve in just 30 minutes.

"Chicken with Paprika Cream is quick to make when you buy boned and skinned chicken breasts," notes Marilou Robinson of Portland, Oregon. "Serving it over rice lets you get every last bit of the tasty paprika-flavored cream."

Steamed Broccoli Florets, with a tart mustard vinaigrette, is a delightful fast-to-fix recipe from Peggy Van Arsdale of Crosswicks, New Jersey. "My Aunt Marion was a wonderful cook. I have many recipes from her, including this one," Peggy says.

Tender sliced mushrooms and a sprinkling of Parmesan cheese dot crisp Mushroom Bread Wedges, made with convenient refrigerated crescent rolls. You can also serve them with soup, chili or a salad. After one bite they're sure to become staples in your kitchen. Patricia Mele of Apollo, Pennsylvania contributed the recipe.

Chicken with Paprika Cream

PREP/TOTAL TIME: 25 min.

- 6 boneless skinless chicken breast halves
- 6 tablespoons butter, *divided*
- 1 tablespoon canola oil
- 6 green onions, chopped
- 1 to 2 tablespoons paprika
- 2 cups heavy whipping cream
- 1 teaspoon salt
- 1/4 teaspoon pepper

Hot cooked rice
Additional chopped green onions, optional

In a large skillet, brown chicken in 1 tablespoon butter and oil over medium heat. Cover and cook for 5-7 minutes or until juices run clear. Remove chicken; keep warm.

In same skillet, saute onions until tender. Reduce heat to medium. Add paprika and remaining butter; heat until butter is melted. Stir in cream, salt and pepper; cook and stir until sauce is thickened, about 4 minutes. Serve with chicken over rice. Garnish with chopped green onions if desired. **Yield:** 6 servings.

Steamed Broccoli Florets

PREP/TOTAL TIME: 15 min.

- 1/4 cup sugar
- 3 tablespoons cider vinegar
- 2 tablespoons canola oil
- 2 tablespoons water
- 1/2 teaspoon prepared mustard

Dash *each* **salt, pepper and ground mustard**
- 1 pound fresh broccoli florets

In a jar with a tight-fitting lid, combine the sugar, vinegar, oil, water, prepared mustard, salt, pepper and ground mustard; shake well. Set aside. Place broccoli in a steamer basket. Place in a saucepan over 1 in. of water; bring to a boil.

Cover and steam for 5-8 minutes or until crisp-tender. Place in a serving bowl. Shake dressing; drizzle over broccoli and toss to coat. **Yield:** 6 servings.

Mushroom Bread Wedges

PREP/TOTAL TIME: 25 min.

- 1 tube (8 ounces) refrigerated crescent rolls
- 1/2 pound fresh mushrooms, sliced
- 3 tablespoons butter, melted
- 1/4 cup grated Parmesan cheese
- 1/4 teaspoon Italian seasoning

Separate crescent dough into eight triangles and place on a greased 12-in. round pizza pan with points toward the center; seal perforations.

In a small bowl, combine the mushrooms and butter; toss to coat. Spoon mushroom mixture over dough. Sprinkle with Parmesan cheese and Italian seasoning.

Bake at 375° for 15-20 minutes or until crust is golden brown and mushrooms are tender. **Yield:** 8 servings.

Paprika Particulars

Paprika is a powder made by grinding dried sweet red peppers. Its flavor can range from mild to hot. Hot paprika is always labeled such; sweet paprika is often just labeled "paprika." Hot paprika is indeed hot—if it's all you have, use sparingly.

Fix a Pork Chop Supper in a Snap

TIME isn't always on your side when it comes to getting a decent dinner on the table for a hungry family. What you need is a meal that's fast, filling and tasty, too.

Our Test Kitchen home economists came up with the quick-to-fix meal here using favorite recipes from three great cooks. It's not only delicious...it's also ready to serve in just 30 minutes.

Janette Hutchings of Festus, Missouri covers her succulent Raspberry Pork Chops with a glaze made with mustard, vinegar and jam. Fixed fast in a skillet, these tender chops are simply the best. They're fancy enough for company or perfect for a casual family meal.

Corn Zucchini Saute makes a colorful accompaniment to the pork chops or to any Mexican-style meal. "I've loved this dish since I was a child," says Sylvia Sonnenburg of Ogden, Utah.

"I've found a fun way to serve cheesecake," Janice Greenhalgh from Florence, Kentucky says about her Cheesecake Waffle Cups. The crunchy store-bought "bowls" hold a smooth cream cheese filling that's layered with cherry pie filling. They're a snap to prepare and attractive, too. Blueberry pie filling would be a wonderful alternative.

Raspberry Pork Chops

PREP/TOTAL TIME: 25 min.

- **4** boneless pork loin chops (5 ounces *each*)
- **1** tablespoon canola oil
- **1/4** cup cider vinegar
- **1/4** cup seedless raspberry jam
- **1** tablespoon prepared mustard

In a large skillet, brown pork chops on both sides over medium heat in oil. Stir in the vinegar, jam and mustard. Reduce heat; cover and simmer for 10-15 minutes or until juices run clear.

Remove chops and keep warm. Bring sauce to a boil; cook until liquid is reduced by half, stirring occasionally. Serve with pork chops. **Yield:** 4 servings.

Corn Zucchini Saute

PREP/TOTAL TIME: 30 min.

- **3/4** cup chopped sweet onion
- **3** tablespoons olive oil
- **2** garlic cloves, minced
- **3** medium zucchini, quartered lengthwise and sliced
- **1** plum tomato, seeded and chopped
- **1** can (15-1/4 ounces) whole kernel corn, drained
- **1/4** cup water
- **1** tablespoon dried parsley flakes
- **1/4** teaspoon salt
- **1/4** teaspoon pepper
- **1/2** cup shredded cheddar cheese

In a large skillet, saute onion in oil until tender. Add garlic; saute for 1 minute. Add the zucchini and tomato. Cook for 5 minutes, stirring occasionally.

Stir in the corn, water, parsley, salt and pepper. Bring to a boil. Reduce heat; simmer, uncovered, for 10 minutes. Sprinkle with cheese. Cover and cook 2 minutes longer or until cheese is melted. **Yield:** 4 servings.

Cheesecake Waffle Cups

PREP/TOTAL TIME: 10 min.

- **1** package (8 ounces) cream cheese, softened
- **1** can (14 ounces) sweetened condensed milk
- **1/3** cup lemon juice
- **1** teaspoon vanilla extract
- **4** waffle bowls
- **1** cup cherry pie filling

In a small bowl, beat the cream cheese until smooth. Gradually beat in the milk until smooth. Stir in lemon juice and vanilla. Spoon about 1/3 cup into each waffle bowl; top with 2 tablespoons pie filling. Repeat layers. **Yield:** 4 servings.

Crazy for Zucchini

Handle zucchini carefully because they're thin-skinned and easily damaged. To pick the freshest zucchini, look for a firm heavy squash with a moist stem end and a shiny skin. Smaller squash are generally sweeter and more tender than larger ones.

One medium (1/3 pound) zucchini yields about 2 cups sliced or 1-1/2 cups shredded zucchini. Store in a plastic bag in the refrigerator crisper for 4 to 5 days. Zucchini is full of beta carotene, B vitamins, folic acid, vitamin C and calcium.

Meals on a Budget

SMART SAVINGS FOR SUPPER. Clockwise from upper left: Tuna Cheese Melts (p. 314), Traditional Meat Loaf (p. 301), Family-Pleasing Sloppy Joes (p. 303), Sausage with Apple Sauerkraut (p. 313) and center, Chinese New Year Skillet (p. 305).

Feed Your Family For $1.50 a Plate!

YOU CAN'T BEAT meat loaf when you want to serve your family a satisfying, homey meal any time of the year. You'll take comfort in knowing this flavorful meat loaf menu won't break your grocery budget.

Topped with a sweet sauce, Traditional Meat Loaf tastes so good that you might want to double the recipe so everyone can have seconds. "This meat loaf also freezes well," adds Gail Graham of Maple Ridge, British Columbia.

Mildred Sherrer of Fort Worth, Texas likes the combination of tomato, beans and hard-cooked egg in her Green Bean Salad. And the savory, delicious Parmesan Potato Balls from Pat Habiger of Spearville, Kansas round out this economical menu.

Traditional Meat Loaf

PREP: 15 min. **BAKE:** 1 hour + standing

- 1 egg, lightly beaten
- 2/3 cup milk
- 3 slices bread, crumbled
- 1 cup (4 ounces) shredded cheddar cheese
- 1 medium onion, chopped
- 1/2 cup finely shredded carrot
- 1 teaspoon salt
- 1/4 teaspoon pepper
- 1-1/2 pounds ground beef
- 1/4 cup packed brown sugar
- 1/4 cup ketchup
- 1 tablespoon prepared mustard

In a large bowl, combine the first eight ingredients. Crumble beef over mixture and mix well. Shape into a loaf. Place in a greased 9-in. x 5-in. x 3-in. loaf pan.

In a small bowl, combine the brown sugar, ketchup and mustard; spread over loaf. Bake at 350° for 60-75 minutes or until no pink remains and a meat thermometer reads 160°. Drain. Let stand for 10 minutes before slicing. **Yield:** 6 servings.

Parmesan Potato Balls

PREP: 45 min. **BAKE:** 15 min.

- 2-1/2 pounds potatoes, peeled and cubed (about 3 large potatoes)
- 2 ounces cream cheese, softened
- 2 tablespoons milk
- 1 tablespoon butter, softened
- 1/4 cup grated Parmesan cheese
- 1 tablespoon chopped green onion
- 2-1/2 teaspoons onion soup mix
- 1/2 teaspoon salt
- 1/8 teaspoon hot pepper sauce
- Dash pepper
- 1 egg, lightly beaten
- 1-1/2 cups crushed cornflakes

Place potatoes in a large saucepan and cover with water. Bring to a boil. Reduce heat; cover and cook for 15-20 minutes or until tender. Drain.

In a large bowl, mash the potatoes. Beat in the cream cheese, milk and butter until smooth. Stir in the Parmesan cheese, onion, soup mix, salt, hot pepper sauce and pepper. Shape into 1-1/2-in. balls.

Place the egg and cornflakes in separate shallow bowls. Dip potato balls in egg, then roll in crumbs. Place on ungreased baking sheets.

Bake at 400° for 15-18 minutes or until crisp and golden brown. **Yield:** 4-1/2 dozen.

Green Bean Salad

PREP: 25 min. + chilling

- 1 pound fresh green beans
- 3 tablespoons olive oil
- 2 tablespoons balsamic vinegar
- 1/2 teaspoon Dijon mustard
- 1/4 teaspoon salt
- 1/8 teaspoon pepper
- 1 medium tomato, seeded and chopped
- 1 small onion, chopped
- 2 tablespoons minced fresh parsley
- 2 teaspoons capers, drained
- 1 hard-cooked egg, chopped

Place beans in a large saucepan and cover with water. Bring to a boil; cook, uncovered, for 8-10 minutes or until crisp-tender. Drain and immediately place beans in ice water. Drain and pat dry. Place in a large bowl.

In a small bowl, whisk the oil, vinegar, mustard, salt and pepper. Pour over beans and toss to coat. Add the tomato, onion, parsley and capers; gently toss. Cover and refrigerate for at least 2 hours. Just before serving, sprinkle with egg. **Yield:** 6 servings.

Feed Your Family For $1.75 a Plate!

IN summertime, the livin' is easy. Here's a great way to simplify meals during that laid-back season. Just prepare these all-time-favorite sloppy joes. They're sure to be popular with the entire family.

You'll find that casual dining can be cost-effective as well as satisfying. You can feed your family these saucy beef sandwiches, along with a garden-fresh veggie side dish and spicy spuds, for about $1.75 a plate. Now that's good eating!

"My grandchildren love my Family-Pleasing Sloppy Joes," Patricia Ringle writes from Edgar, Wisconsin. "I like this recipe because it can be made ahead of time and can also be put in the slow cooker. I've found it freezes well, too."

"German Cukes and Tomatoes really sparks up a meal and goes fairly well with everything from grilled steak to tuna salad," says Karen Ann Bland of Gove, Kansas. "I like to serve it in individual, lettuce-lined glass bowls with a sour cream star piped on top and a sprinkling of dill."

All the way from Keego Harbor, Michigan, Autumn McNamara writes, "When my husband and I barbecue with friends, we always bring Spicy Potato Wedges, and everyone loves them. They're a favorite accompaniment to almost anything we cook on the grill."

With this affordable and tasty menu, everyone will be satisfied and happy. It's a meal that can't be beat!

Family-Pleasing Sloppy Joes

PREP: 10 min. **COOK:** 45 min.

  2 pounds ground beef
  1 large onion, chopped
1-1/4 cups ketchup
1/2 cup water
  1 tablespoon brown sugar
  1 tablespoon white vinegar
1/2 teaspoon salt
1/2 teaspoon ground mustard
1/2 teaspoon chili powder
1/4 teaspoon ground allspice
  8 sandwich buns, split

In a Dutch oven, cook the ground beef and chopped onion over medium heat until the meat is completely cooked and no longer pink; drain. Stir in the ketchup, water, brown sugar, white vinegar, salt, ground mustard, chili powder and ground allspice. Bring to a boil. Reduce the heat; simmer, uncovered, for 35-40 minutes or until heated through.

Spoon about 1/2 cup meat mixture onto each bun.
Yield: 8 servings.

German Cukes and Tomatoes

PREP/TOTAL TIME: 20 min.

  2 medium cucumbers, thinly sliced
  4 green onions, thinly sliced
  2 tablespoons minced fresh parsley
1/4 cup sour cream
  2 tablespoons snipped fresh dill
  1 tablespoon cider vinegar
1/2 teaspoon salt
1/4 teaspoon prepared mustard
1/8 teaspoon pepper
  1 tablespoon milk, optional
  3 small tomatoes, sliced

In a large bowl, combine the cucumbers, onions and parsley. In a small bowl, combine the sour cream, fresh dill, vinegar, salt, mustard and pepper. Stir in the milk if dressing with a thinner consistency is desired. Pour the dressing over the cucumber mixture and toss to coat. Divide among eight salad plates; top with tomatoes.
Yield: 8 servings.

Spicy Potato Wedges

PREP: 15 min. **BAKE:** 30 min.

1/4 cup canola oil
  1 tablespoon chili powder
  2 teaspoons onion powder
  2 teaspoons garlic salt
  1 teaspoon sugar
  1 teaspoon paprika
3/4 teaspoon salt
1/4 to 1/2 teaspoon cayenne pepper
3-1/2 pounds large red potatoes, cut into wedges

In a large bowl, combine the first eight ingredients; add potatoes and toss to coat. Arrange in a single layer on greased baking sheets.

Bake at 400° for 30-35 minutes or until the potato wedges are tender and golden brown, turning once.
Yield: 8 servings.

Feed Your Family For $1.55 a Plate!

CELEBRATE the Chinese New Year with gusto—or enjoy easy-to-make Asian food any time of the year—with this budget menu that lets you feed the whole gang for roughly $1.55 a plate.

Our Test Kitchen put the menu together using tried-and-true recipes from three *Taste of Home* readers, so you know it's delicious!

Chinese New Year Skillet was inspired by a recipe on the back of a rice package in 1957, notes Sherilyn West of Lubbock, Texas. "If you like pork, I guarantee you'll love this recipe," she says. "It satisfies even the heartiest appetites."

Egg Drop Soup is the perfect way to start an Asian meal and requires just five ingredients. "If you want, you can add two minced water chestnuts," says Jenny Haen of Red Wing, Minnesota. "They add a wonderfully crunchy texture to the soup."

Beverly Preston of Fond du Lac, Wisconsin started making Almond Cookies after enjoying similar ones at her favorite Chinese restaurant. "These crisp cookies have wonderful almond flavor," she says. "They're a fitting end to a 'Far East' feast."

Chinese New Year Skillet

PREP: 15 min.   COOK: 25 min.

- 1 pound boneless pork butt roast, cut into 1/2-inch cubes
- 1 tablespoon canola oil
- 1 can (20 ounces) unsweetened pineapple tidbits
- 2 tablespoons white wine vinegar
- 1 tablespoon sugar
- 3/4 teaspoon salt
- 1/4 teaspoon garlic powder
- 1 cup uncooked long grain rice
- 1 tablespoon cornstarch
- 2 tablespoons water
- 1/2 cup coarsely chopped green pepper
- 1 medium tomato, cut into wedges
- 2 tablespoons Worcestershire sauce

In a large skillet, cook pork in oil over medium heat on all sides until pork is lightly browned; drain. Drain pineapple, reserving juice in a 2-cup measuring cup; set pineapple aside.

Add enough water to the juice to measure 1-1/4 cups; then stir into the pork. Add the vinegar, sugar, salt and garlic powder. Bring to a boil, stirring constantly.

Reduce heat; cover and simmer for 20 minutes or until the meat is tender. Meanwhile, cook the rice according to package directions.

In a small bowl, combine the cornstarch and water until smooth; stir into the pork mixture. Bring to a boil; cook and stir for 2 minutes or until thickened. Stir in the green pepper, tomato, Worcestershire sauce and reserved pineapple; heat through. Serve with rice. **Yield:** 4 servings.

Egg Drop Soup

PREP/TOTAL TIME: 10 min.

- 5 cups chicken broth
- 1/2 teaspoon sugar
- 1 egg, lightly beaten
- 1/3 cup sliced fresh spinach
- 2 green onions, sliced

In a large saucepan, bring the broth and sugar to a boil over medium heat. Reduce heat to low. Drizzle beaten egg into hot broth. Remove from the heat; stir in spinach and onions. **Yield:** 4 servings.

Almond Cookies

PREP: 10 min.   BAKE: 10 min./batch + cooling

- 1 cup shortening
- 1/2 cup plus 3 tablespoons sugar, *divided*
- 1/4 cup packed brown sugar
- 1 egg
- 1 teaspoon almond extract
- 2 cups all-purpose flour
- 1-1/2 teaspoons baking powder
- 1/8 teaspoon salt
- 3 tablespoons sliced almonds

In a small bowl, cream the shortening, 1/2 cup sugar and brown sugar. Beat in egg and extract.

Combine the flour, baking powder and salt; gradually add to creamed mixture and mix well. Shape into 1-in. balls. Roll in remaining sugar.

Place 2 in. apart on ungreased baking sheets. Flatten with the bottom of a glass. Press three almond slices into the center of each.

Bake at 350° for 9-11 minutes or until edges are lightly browned. Cool for 2 minutes on pan before removing to wire racks. **Yield:** 3 dozen.

Feed Your Family For $1.60 a Plate!

FOR LOW-COST comfort food, try a menu of Caraway Pot Roast from Violet Beard of Marshall, Illinois. You'll also enjoy the delicious accompaniments of Mashed Potato Casserole from Margaret Lindberg of Richland, Washington and Fluffy Pineapple Dessert from Donna Gaston, Coplay, Pennsylvania.

Caraway Pot Roast

PREP: 10 min. COOK: 2-3/4 hours

- 1 boneless beef chuck roast (3 pounds)
- 2 tablespoons canola oil
- 2 medium onions, sliced
- 2 medium carrots, cut into large chunks
- 1 cup apple cider *or* apple juice
- 1 tablespoon caraway seeds
- 2 garlic cloves, minced
- 3/4 teaspoon salt, *divided*
- 1/2 teaspoon pepper, *divided*
- 2 tablespoons cornstarch
- 1/4 cup cold water
- 1/2 cup sour cream

In Dutch oven, brown roast in oil on all sides over medium-high heat; drain. Combine onions, carrots, cider, caraway, garlic, 1/2 teaspoon salt and 1/4 teaspoon pepper; pour over roast. Bring to boil; reduce heat. Cover; simmer 2 to 2-1/2 hours or until meat is tender.

Remove roast and vegetables; keep warm. Strain pan juices into 2-cup measuring cup. Skim fat; add enough water to measure 2 cups. Return to pot. Combine cornstarch and cold water until smooth; gradually stir into pan juices. Bring to a boil; cook and stir for 2 minutes or until thickened. Remove from the heat; stir in the sour cream and remaining salt and pepper. Serve with roast and vegetables. **Yield:** 8 servings.

Mashed Potato Casserole

PREP: 30 min. BAKE: 30 min.

- 3 pounds potatoes, peeled and cubed
- 1 package (8 ounces) cream cheese, cubed
- 1 cup (8 ounces) sour cream
- 1/4 cup milk
- 1 small onion, chopped
- 1 teaspoon garlic salt
- 1/2 teaspoon salt

- 2 tablespoons butter, melted
- 1/4 teaspoon paprika

Place the potatoes in a large saucepan and cover with water. Bring to a boil. Reduce heat; cover and simmer until tender. Drain; place potatoes in a large bowl. Add the cream cheese, sour cream, milk, onion, garlic salt and salt; beat until blended.

Transfer to a greased 2-qt. baking dish. Drizzle with butter; sprinkle with paprika. Cover and bake at 350° for 30-35 minutes or until heated through. **Yield:** 8 servings.

Fluffy Pineapple Dessert

PREP: 25 min. BAKE: 45 min. + cooling

- 1 cup butter, softened
- 1 cup sugar, *divided*
- 7 egg yolks, *divided*
- 1/2 cup sour cream
- 2-1/2 cups plus 3 tablespoons all-purpose flour, *divided*
- 1 teaspoon baking powder
- 1/2 teaspoon salt
- 2 cans (20 ounces *each*) crushed unsweetened pineapple, undrained
- 2 teaspoons vanilla extract

TOPPING:
- 5 egg whites
- 10 tablespoons sugar
- 1 teaspoon vanilla extract
- 1/2 cup finely chopped walnuts

In a large bowl, cream butter and 1/2 cup sugar. Add 3 egg yolks and sour cream; mix well. Combine 2-1/2 cups flour, baking powder and salt; gradually add to yolk mixture. Press into a greased 13-in. x 9-in. x 2-in. baking dish. Bake at 350° for 12-15 minutes or until set and edges are lightly browned.

Meanwhile, in a small saucepan, combine remaining each of sugar, yolks and flour; stir in pineapple. Cook and stir over medium heat until mixture reaches 160° and coats back of a metal spoon. Remove from heat; stir in vanilla. Pour over crust. Bake at 350° for 15 minutes.

For the topping, beat egg whites until soft peaks form. Gradually add sugar and vanilla, beating until stiff peaks form. Spread over hot filling, sealing edges to the pan. Sprinkle with walnuts. Bake 15 minutes longer or until golden brown. Cool on a wire rack for 1 hour. Store in the refrigerator. **Yield:** 16 servings.

Feed Your Family
For $2.00 a Plate!

DON'T SAVE HAM for a special Sunday dinner. At this price, you can ham it up any night of the week! In Chilliwack, British Columbia, Cornelia Whiteway serves Barbecued Ham and Peaches for a main dish that's both economical and irresistible. It is easy enough for a convenient weeknight meal, but elegant enough for a fancy dinner.

To complete the meal, add the pretty Three-Fruit Salad from Sue Gronholz of Beaver Dam, Wisconsin. Delight everyone at the table with Pear-Filled Bundt Cake from Barbara Sievert of Yorktown, Virginia.

Barbecued Ham and Peaches

PREP/TOTAL TIME: 20 min.

- 1/4 **cup ketchup**
- 1 **tablespoon brown sugar**
- 1 **tablespoon cider vinegar**
- 2 **teaspoons Worcestershire sauce**
- 1 **teaspoon canola oil**
- 1/4 **teaspoon pepper**
- 4 **boneless fully cooked ham slices (4 ounces *each*)**
- 1 **can (8-1/2 ounces) sliced peaches, drained**

In a small bowl, combine the ketchup, brown sugar, vinegar, Worcestershire sauce, oil and pepper; brush some of the mixture over ham slices. Place each slice on a greased 12-in. square of heavy-duty foil. Top with peaches; drizzle with remaining ketchup mixture.

Fold foil over ham and peaches and seal tightly. Grill, covered, over medium heat for 5-6 minutes in each side or until heated through. **Yield:** 4 servings.

Three-Fruit Salad

PREP: 10 min. **COOK:** 15 min. + cooling

- 1 **can (20 ounces) pineapple chunks**
- 1/3 **cup sugar**
- 1 **tablespoon cornstarch**
- 1 **tablespoon lemon juice**
- 1/8 **teaspoon salt**
- 2 **eggs, lightly beaten**
- 1 to 2 **small ripe bananas, sliced**
- 1 **cup halved seedless red grapes**
- 1 **cup miniature marshmallows**
- 6 **cups torn lettuce**

Drain pineapple, reserving juice; set pineapple aside. In a small saucepan, combine the sugar, cornstarch, lemon juice, salt and reserved juice until smooth. Bring to a boil over medium heat, stirring until sugar is dissolved.

Remove from the heat. Stir a small amount of hot juice mixture into eggs; return all to the pan, stirring constantly. Bring to a gentle boil; cook and stir for 2 minutes. Transfer to a small bowl; cool.

Just before serving, in a bowl, combine the bananas, grapes, marshmallows, pineapple and cooled dressing. Serve over lettuce. **Yield:** 4 servings.

Pear-Filled Bundt Cake

PREP: 25 min. **BAKE:** 35 min. + cooling

- 1/2 **cup butter, softened**
- 1/2 **cup sugar**
- 3 **eggs**
- 1/2 **teaspoon vanilla extract**
- 2 **cups all-purpose flour**
- 1 **teaspoon baking powder**
- 1 **teaspoon baking soda**
- 1/3 **cup orange juice**

FILLING:
- 1/2 **cup packed brown sugar**
- 1/2 **cup diced peeled ripe pear**
- 1/2 **cup sliced almonds**
- 2 **tablespoons all-purpose flour**
- 4-1/2 **teaspoons butter, melted**
- 1/2 **teaspoon ground cinnamon**

GLAZE:
- 1/2 **cup confectioners' sugar**
- 2-1/4 **teaspoons orange juice**

In a large bowl, cream the butter and sugar. Add eggs, one at a time, beating well after each addition. Beat in the vanilla. Combine the flour, baking powder and baking soda; add to creamed mixture alternately with the orange juice.

Pour half of the batter into a greased 10-in. fluted tube pan. Combine the filling ingredients; sprinkle over batter. Top with remaining batter. Smooth top with a spatula.

Bake at 350° for 35-40 minutes or until a toothpick inserted near the center comes out clean. Cool for 10 minutes before removing from pan to a wire rack. Combine glaze ingredients; drizzle over cake. **Yield:** 16-20 servings.

Feed Your Family For $2.00 a Plate!

IF REAL spareribs don't always fit in your budget, try this lip-smacking, economical substitute. Janice Porterfield of Atlanta, Texas turns chicken thighs into Chicken Spareribs with a zippy barbecue-style sauce. You might have to make extras!

You'll also enjoy the two satisfying sides. "I always take my nice and light Cottage Cheese Yeast Rolls to potlucks, where they disappear quickly," writes Angie Merriam of Springfield, Ohio.

Using fresh spinach instead of frozen really enhances the flavor of classic Creamed Spinach, shared by Ann Van Dyk of Wrightstown, Wisconsin.

Chicken Spareribs

PREP: 5 min. **COOK:** 30 min.

- 8 bone-in chicken thighs
- 2 tablespoons canola oil
- 1 cup water
- 2/3 cup packed brown sugar
- 2/3 cup soy sauce
- 1/2 cup apple juice
- 1/4 cup ketchup
- 2 tablespoons cider vinegar
- 2 garlic cloves, minced
- 1 teaspoon crushed red pepper flakes
- 1/2 teaspoon ground ginger
- 2 tablespoons cornstarch
- 2 tablespoons cold water

In a Dutch oven, brown the chicken over medium heat in oil in batches on both sides; drain. Return all of the chicken to the pan.

In a large bowl, combine the water, brown sugar, soy sauce, apple juice, ketchup, vinegar, garlic, pepper flakes and ginger; pour over chicken. Bring to a boil. Reduce heat; cover and simmer for 20 minutes or until chicken juices run clear.

Remove the chicken to a platter and keep warm. Combine the cornstarch and water until smooth; stir into cooking juices. Bring to a boil; cook and stir for 2 minutes or until thickened. Serve with the chicken. **Yield:** 4 servings.

Cottage Cheese Yeast Rolls

PREP: 30 min. + rising **BAKE:** 10 min./batch

- 2 packages (1/4 ounce *each*) active dry yeast
- 1/2 cup warm water (110° to 115°)
- 2 cups (16 ounces) 4% cottage cheese
- 2 eggs
- 1/4 cup sugar
- 2 teaspoons salt
- 1/2 teaspoon baking soda
- 4-1/2 cups all-purpose flour

In a large bowl, dissolve the yeast in warm water. In a small saucepan, heat the cottage cheese to 110°-115°. Add the cottage cheese, eggs, sugar, salt, baking soda and 2 cups of flour to the yeast mixture; beat until smooth. Stir in enough remaining flour to form a firm dough (dough will be sticky).

Turn onto a floured surface; knead until smooth and elastic, about 6-8 minutes. Place in a greased bowl, turning once to grease top. Cover and let rise in a warm place until doubled, about 1 hour.

Punch the dough down. Turn onto a lightly floured surface; divide into 30 pieces. Shape each piece of dough into a roll by gently rolling the pieces between the palms of your hands. Place 2 in. apart on greased baking sheets. Cover and let the rolls rise until doubled, about 30 minutes.

Bake at 350° for 10-12 minutes or until golden brown. Remove to wire racks. **Yield:** 2-1/2 dozen.

Creamed Spinach

PREP/TOTAL TIME: 25 min.

- 3/4 pound fresh spinach, torn
- 2 tablespoons olive oil
- 6 tablespoons butter, cubed
- 1/4 cup chopped onion
- 1/4 cup all-purpose flour
- 1/2 teaspoon salt
- 1/8 teaspoon ground nutmeg
- 1-1/2 cups milk

In a Dutch oven, cook the fresh spinach in olive oil for 3 minutes or until wilted. Transfer to a cutting board; chop. Melt the cubed butter in the Dutch oven. Add the chopped onion; saute in the butter for 2 minutes or until crisp-tender.

Stir in the flour, salt and ground nutmeg until combined. Gradually whisk in the milk until blended. Bring to a boil; cook and stir for 2 minutes or until thickened. Add the chopped spinach. Reduce the heat to low; cook, uncovered, for 5 minutes or until heated through. **Yield:** 4 servings.

Feed Your Family For $2.10 a Plate!

THERE'S NO NEED to scrimp on flavor thanks to this scrumptious (and inexpensive) supper that features Sausage with Apple Sauerkraut. It was created by Carolyn Schmeling of Brookfield, Wisconsin, who based her recipe variation on a traditional sausage and sauerkraut dish. With just the right touch of caraway and fennel seeds, the sauerkraut is wonderfully sweet. For some extra tang, drizzle on some mustard.

"My mother used to serve Crispy Potato Cubes when I was growing up, and she included the recipe in a cookbook she made for me when I got married," writes Jenelle Piepmeier of Severna Park, Maryland. "They fill the kitchen with a heavenly aroma."

Barbara Carlucci of Orange Park, Florida developed Green Beans with Walnuts in her kitchen and has prepared it many times. "It requires just 15 minutes," she says. "The sauce is yummy not only on green beans but also on fresh or frozen broccoli."

Sausage with Apple Sauerkraut

PREP: 10 min. **COOK:** 35 min.

- 1 medium sweet onion, sliced
- 3 tablespoons butter
- 2 medium apples, peeled and shredded
- 1 tablespoon lemon juice
- 1 can (8 ounces) sauerkraut, rinsed and well drained
- 1/2 cup unsweetened apple juice
- 1 teaspoon caraway seeds
- 1/2 teaspoon fennel seeds, crushed
- 1 package (16 ounces) smoked Polish sausage

In a large skillet, saute onion in butter for 15 minutes or until lightly browned.

In a large bowl, toss the apples with lemon juice. Add the apples, sauerkraut, apple juice, caraway and fennel seeds to the onion. Bring to a boil. Reduce heat; cover and simmer for 15 minutes. Meanwhile, heat the sausage according to package directions; cut into slices. Serve with sauerkraut. **Yield:** 4 servings.

Crispy Potato Cubes

PREP: 10 min. **BAKE:** 35 min.

- 1/3 cup all-purpose flour
- 3/4 teaspoon salt
- 1/2 teaspoon dried thyme
- 1/2 teaspoon dried marjoram
- 1/8 teaspoon pepper
- 5 medium potatoes, peeled and cut into 1-inch cubes
- 1/4 cup butter, melted
- 1 garlic clove, minced
- 1 bay leaf

In a large resealable plastic bag, combine the flour, salt, thyme, marjoram and pepper. Add the potatoes; seal bag and shake to coat. Pour the butter into a 13-in. x 9-in. x 2-in. baking dish; stir in the garlic. Add the potatoes and bay leaf.

Cover and bake at 450° for 20 minutes. Uncover and stir; bake 15-20 minutes longer or until the potatoes are lightly browned and tender. Discard bay leaf. **Yield:** 4 servings.

Green Beans with Walnuts

PREP/TOTAL TIME: 15 min.

- 1 package (16 ounces) frozen cut green beans
- 1/4 cup chopped walnuts, *divided*
- 1/4 cup teriyaki sauce
- 2 tablespoons butter, cubed

In 1-1/2-qt. microwave-safe dish, combine the beans, 2 tablespoons walnuts, teriyaki sauce and butter. Cover and microwave on high for 3 minutes; stir. Cook 5-6 minutes longer or until beans are tender. Sprinkle with remaining walnuts. **Yield:** 4 servings.

Editor's Note: This recipe was tested in a 1,100-watt microwave.

Apple a Day

Everyone knows that "an apple a day keeps the doctor away." That's because apples are rich in vitamins A, B1, B2 and C. They also contain numerous minerals, such as calcium, phosphorous, magnesium and potassium.

Although apples are available year-round, they each have their own peak season. Select apples that are firm and have a smooth, unblemished skin that is free from bruises.

Store unwashed apples in the refrigerator away from other vegetables with strong aromas. Apples can be refrigerated for up to 6 weeks.

Feed Your Family for $1.10 a Plate!

LOOKING for ways to save on your grocery bill while still serving your family delicious and nutritious meals? Leave it to our readers to come up with some taste-tempting solutions!

Our Test Kitchen home economists have put together this satisfying meal with recipes from three great cooks. It makes a filling lunch or a light summer supper...at just $1.10 per person.

For her Tuna Cheese Melts, Bernadine Dirmeyer of Harpster, Ohio dresses up a typical tuna sandwich with American cheese and rye bread spread with a mixture of sour cream and garlic salt. Cooked in a skillet, this sandwich oozes with flavor.

Radish Potato Salad from Lydia Garcia of Hanover, Pennsylvania is well coated with a delicious and creamy dill dressing. This summery salad, made with radish slices and chopped eggs, is not only pretty but easy to prepare, too.

"Cinnamon-Sugar Crisps are a favorite with children...and adults, too," says Kim Marie Van Rheenen of Mendota, Illinois. These sweet and spicy refrigerator cookies go great with a cup of coffee or a glass of milk. You won't be able to eat just one!

Tuna Cheese Melts

PREP/TOTAL TIME: 25 min.

- **1/2 cup sour cream**
- **1/2 teaspoon garlic salt**
- **8 slices rye *or* white bread**
- **1 can (6 ounces) tuna, drained and flaked**
- **2 tablespoons mayonnaise**
- **4 slices process American cheese**
- **4 tablespoons butter, *divided***

In a small bowl, combine sour cream and garlic salt; spread on one side of each slice of bread. In another small bowl, combine tuna and mayonnaise; spread on four slices of bread. Top with cheese and remaining bread; gently press together.

Melt 2 tablespoons butter in a large skillet over medium heat. Add two sandwiches; toast sandwiches until bread is lightly browned on both sides and cheese is melted. Repeat with remaining butter and sandwiches. **Yield:** 4 servings.

Radish Potato Salad

PREP: 30 min. + chilling

- **5 medium red potatoes (about 1-1/2 pounds)**
- **1 cup sliced radishes**
- **2 hard-cooked eggs, chopped**
- **3/4 cup mayonnaise**
- **3 tablespoons minced fresh dill**
- **2 tablespoons cider vinegar**
- **1 tablespoon sugar**
- **1/4 teaspoon salt**
- **Dash pepper**

Place potatoes in a saucepan and cover with water. Bring to a boil. Reduce heat; cover and cook for 15-20 minutes or until tender. Drain and cool.

Peel and cube potatoes; place in a large bowl. Add radishes and eggs. In a small bowl, combine the mayonnaise, dill, vinegar, sugar, salt and pepper. Pour over potato mixture; gently toss to coat. Cover and refrigerate for at least 1 hour. **Yield:** 4 servings.

Cinnamon-Sugar Crisps

PREP: 30 min. + chilling **BAKE:** 15 min.

3/4 cup butter, softened
1/3 cup sugar
1/3 cup packed brown sugar
** 1 egg**
** 1 teaspoon vanilla extract**
1-3/4 cups all-purpose flour
** 1 teaspoon ground cinnamon**
1/4 teaspoon salt
** 2 tablespoons colored sprinkles**

In a large bowl, cream the butter, sugar and brown sugar together until light and fluffy. Beat in the egg and vanilla. Combine the flour, cinnamon and salt; gradually add to the creamed mixture and mix well. Shape into a 12-in. roll; wrap in plastic wrap. Refrigerate for 2 hours or until firm.

Unwrap and cut into 1/2-in. slices. Place 2 in. apart on ungreased baking sheets. Decorate with sprinkles.

Bake at 350° for 10-12 minutes or until lightly browned. Remove to wire racks to cool. **Yield:** 3-1/2 dozen.

Feed Your Family for $1.85 a Plate!

GROCERY BUDGET a little tight? Don't worry! You can still enjoy foods that are satisfying and full of flavor.

Three frugal cooks prove it with this mouth-watering meal that's perfect for a springtime luncheon or a light supper. Our Test Kitchen home economists estimate the total cost of this meal at about $1.85 per setting.

Canned salmon and frozen peas streamline the preparation of hearty Salmon Chowder from Pat Waymire of Yellow Springs, Ohio. Shredded Swiss and cheddar cheeses, along with cauliflower and dill weed, add flavor to this appealing dish.

"I love my bread machine and am always trying new recipes in it," says Joy McMillan from The Woodlands, Texas. "Cracked Pepper Bread is one of my successes. When it's baking, the whole kitchen smells wonderful." Basil, garlic, chives and Parmesan cheese give this tall tender loaf a real Italian flavor.

Bernice Morris from Marshfield, Missouri dresses up her Garden Lettuce Salad with tomatoes, radishes, green onions, crisp bacon, hard-cooked eggs and a creamy homemade dressing. "It's a nice change from our usual wilted lettuce salad," she says. "This salad's also good with fried chicken and mashed potatoes or with a barbecue dinner."

Salmon Chowder

PREP/TOTAL TIME: 20 min.

- **1 cup thinly sliced green onions**
- **2 celery ribs, thinly sliced**
- **2 tablespoons butter**
- **2 tablespoons all-purpose flour**
- **1/2 teaspoon salt**
- **1/2 teaspoon dill weed**
- **4 cups milk**
- **2 cups cauliflowerets, cooked**
- **1 can (14-3/4 ounces) salmon, drained, skin and bones removed**
- **1 package (10 ounces) frozen peas, thawed**
- **1/2 cup shredded Swiss cheese**
- **1/2 cup shredded cheddar cheese**

In a large saucepan, saute onions and celery in butter until tender. Stir in the flour, salt and dill until blended. Gradually add milk. Bring to a boil; cook and stir for 2 minutes or until thickened. Add the cauliflower, salmon and peas; heat through. Stir in the cheeses until melted. Serve immediately. **Yield:** 8 servings.

Cracked Pepper Bread

PREP: 10 min. **BAKE:** 3 hours

- **1-1/2 cups water (70° to 80°)**
- **3 tablespoons olive oil**
- **3 tablespoons sugar**
- **2 teaspoons salt**
- **3 tablespoons minced chives**
- **2 garlic cloves, minced**
- **1 teaspoon garlic powder**
- **1 teaspoon dried basil**
- **1 teaspoon cracked black pepper**

1/4 cup grated Parmesan cheese
4 cups bread flour
2-1/2 teaspoons active dry yeast

In bread machine pan, place all ingredients in order suggested by manufacturer. Select basic bread setting. Choose crust color and loaf size if available. Bake according to bread machine directions (check dough after 5 minutes of mixing; add 1 to 2 tablespoons of water or flour if needed). **Yield:** 1 loaf (2 pounds, 16 slices).

Garden Lettuce Salad

PREP/TOTAL TIME: 15 min.

5 **cups torn leaf lettuce**
2 **medium tomatoes, chopped**
3 **hard-cooked eggs, sliced**
3/4 **cup sliced radishes**
4 **bacon strips, cooked and crumbled**
3 **green onions, sliced**

DRESSING:
3/4 **cup mayonnaise**
1 **tablespoon red wine vinegar**
1 **teaspoon lemon-lime soda**
1/2 **teaspoon salt**
1/2 **teaspoon sugar**

In a salad bowl, toss the lettuce, tomatoes, hard-cooked eggs, radishes, bacon and onions. In a small bowl, whisk together the dressing ingredients. Serve with salad. **Yield:** 6 servings.

Feed Your Family for $1.65 a Plate!

EATING WELL at today's prices isn't impossible. The frugal yet flavorful meal here combines recipes from three creative cooks. Our Test Kitchen staff estimates the total cost at about $1.65 per serving.

Traditional lasagna fixin's (minus the meat) make up the ingredient list for Vegetable Noodle Bake, a satisfying casserole shared by Dixie Terry of Goreville, Illinois. The egg noodles are a great substitute for the usual lasagna noodles. "If you're out of hamburger, serve this dish and no one will even notice it's meatless because it's so tasty," Dixie assures.

Potato, tomato and onion complement the fresh green beans in colorful Green Bean Salad. A subtle oil-and-vinegar dressing lends fresh herb flavor to the mix. The recipe comes from the kitchen of Sarah Maranto of Bakersfield, California.

No one will be able to eat just one of Gail Wiese's yummy Chocolate Ribbon Bars, full of butterscotch, peanut butter and chocolate flavor. "Over the years I've accumulated quite a few recipes from my co-workers, and this one is so easy to prepare," says Gail from her home in Athens, Wisconsin.

Vegetable Noodle Bake

PREP: 15 min. **BAKE:** 20 min.

- **1 can (14-1/2 ounces) diced tomatoes, drained**
- **3/4 cup canned tomato puree**
- **1/3 cup chopped onion**
- **1-1/4 teaspoons dried oregano**
- **1/4 teaspoon garlic powder**
- **1/4 teaspoon salt**
- **1/8 teaspoon pepper**
- **2-1/2 cups uncooked medium egg noodles**
- **1/2 cup 4% cottage cheese**
- **1 package (10 ounces) frozen chopped spinach, thawed and squeezed dry**
- **1/3 cup shredded American cheese**

In a large saucepan, combine the diced tomatoes, tomato puree, onion, dried oregano, garlic powder, salt and pepper. Bring to a boil. Reduce heat; simmer, uncovered, for 15 minutes.

Meanwhile, cook noodles according to package directions; drain.

Spread 1/3 cup tomato mixture in a greased, shallow 2-qt. baking dish. Top with half of the noodles. Spread with cottage cheese; top with spinach. Drizzle with 1/2 cup tomato mixture; top with remaining noodles and tomato mixture. Sprinkle with American cheese. Cover and bake at 350° for 20-25 minutes or until cheese is melted. **Yield:** 4 servings.

Green Bean and Tomato Salad

PREP: 15 min. **COOK:** 15 min.

- **1 medium potato, peeled**
- **1/2 pound fresh green beans, cut into 2-inch pieces**
- **1 medium tomato, cubed**
- **1/2 small red onion, sliced and separated into rings**
- **2 tablespoons red wine vinegar**
- **2 tablespoons canola oil**
- **2 tablespoons minced fresh oregano**
- **2 tablespoons minced fresh parsley**
- **1/8 teaspoon salt**

Place potato in a saucepan and cover with water. Bring to a boil; reduce heat; cover and simmer for 15-20 minutes or until tender. Drain and cool; cut into cubes.

Meanwhile, place the green beans in a saucepan and cover with water. Bring to a boil; reduce heat. Cook, uncovered, for 6-8 minutes or until crisp-tender. Drain and then cool.

In a large serving bowl, combine the beans, potato, tomato and onion. In a jar with a tight-fitting lid, combine the remaining ingredients; shake well. Pour over the bean mixture; toss to coat. **Yield:** 4 servings.

Chocolate Ribbon Bars

PREP: 20 min. + chilling

1 package (10 to 11 ounces) butterscotch chips
1 cup peanut butter
8 cups crisp rice cereal
2 cups (12 ounces) semisweet chocolate chips
1/4 cup butter, cubed
2 tablespoons water
3/4 cup confectioners' sugar

In a large microwave-safe bowl, combine the butterscotch chips and peanut butter and melt; stir together until smooth. Gradually stir in the crisp rice cereal until it is well coated. Press half of the mixture into a greased 13-in. x 9-in. x 2-in. pan; set the remaining mixture aside.

In another large microwave-safe bowl, melt semisweet chocolate chips and butter. Stir in water until blended. Gradually add the confectioners' sugar, stirring until smooth.

Spread over cereal layer. Cover and refrigerate for 10 minutes or until chocolate layer is set. Spread remaining cereal mixture over the top. Chill before cutting. **Yield:** 2 dozen.

Editor's Note: Reduced-fat or generic brands of peanut butter are not recommended for this recipe.

Seasons of Good Taste

From breezy spring days to chilly winter evenings, there are countless ways to celebrate throughout the year.

DELICIOUS CELEBRATIONS. Clockwise from upper left: Turkey with Sausage-Corn Bread Stuffing (p. 332), Rustic Roasted Vegetable Tart (p. 327), Ultimate Caramel Apples (p. 331), Russian Cream (p. 330) and center, Pickled Baby Carrots (p. 323).

Spring Has Sprung

Strawberry Pretzel Dessert

(Pictured below)

PREP: 15 min. + chilling

I love the sweet–salty flavor of this pretty layered dessert. Sliced strawberries and gelatin top a smooth cream cheese filling and crispy pretzel crust. —Wendy Weaver, Leetonia, Ohio

- 1/3 **cup crushed pretzels**
- 2 **tablespoons butter, softened**
- 2 **ounces cream cheese, softened**
- 1/4 **cup sugar**
- 3/4 **cup whipped topping**
- 2 **tablespoons plus 1-1/2 teaspoons strawberry gelatin powder**
- 1/2 **cup boiling water**
- 1 **cup sliced fresh strawberries**

In a bowl, combine pretzels and butter. Press onto the bottom of two 10-oz. greased custard cups. Bake at 375° for 6-8 minutes or until set. Cool on a wire rack.

In a small bowl, combine the cream cheese and sugar. Fold in the whipped topping. Spoon over crust. Refrigerate for 30 minutes.

Meanwhile, in a bowl, dissolve gelatin in boiling water. Cover and refrigerate for 20 minutes or until slightly thickened. Fold in strawberries. Carefully spoon over filling. Cover and refrigerate for at least 3 hours. **Yield:** 2 servings.

Peeps Sunflower Cake

(Pictured above)

PREP: 15 min. **BAKE:** 30 min. + cooling

The inspiration for this cake came from one of my favorite flowers, the sunflower. The yellow Peeps make for eye–catching flower petals, and the chocolate chips resemble the seeds in the center. It's really easy to make but looks impressive.
—Bethany Eledge, Cleveland, Tennessee

- 1 **package (18-1/4 ounces) yellow cake mix**
- 2 **cans (16 ounces *each*) chocolate frosting**
- 19 **yellow chick Peeps candies**
- 1-1/2 **cups semisweet chocolate chips**

Prepare and bake cake according to package directions, using two greased and waxed paper-lined 9-in. round baking pans. Cool for 10 minutes before removing from pans to wire racks to cool completely; carefully remove waxed paper.

Level tops of cakes. Spread frosting between layers and over the top and sides of cake.

Without separating Peeps and curving slightly to fit, arrange chicks around edge of cake for sunflower petals. For sunflower seeds, arrange chocolate chips in center of cake. **Yield:** 12 servings.

Pickled Baby Carrots

(Pictured above and on page 320)

PREP: 20 min. + chilling

With mild herb flavor and crunchy texture, these baby carrots make a delightful addition to an appetizer tray or a casual meal. Plan ahead because they need to chill for several hours.
—Audrey Cremer, Harmony, Minnesota

- **2 pounds fresh baby carrots**
- **2/3 cup white wine vinegar**
- **1/2 cup honey**
- **2 tablespoons mustard seed**
- **2 tablespoons dill weed**
- **1 teaspoon salt**

Place 1 in. of water in a large saucepan; add carrots. Bring to a boil. Reduce heat; cover and simmer for 5-6 minutes or until crisp-tender. Drain.

In a large bowl, combine the remaining ingredients. Stir in carrots. Cover and refrigerate for 8 hours or overnight, stirring several times. Serve with a slotted spoon. **Yield:** 8-10 servings.

Grand Prize Winner

Stuffed Ham with Raisin Sauce

(Pictured at right)

PREP: 30 min. **BAKE:** 1-3/4 hours

This impressive ham makes a great centerpiece for a holiday dinner, but I've served it most often for brunch. It always draws rave reviews.
—Jeanne Miller, Big Sky, Montana

- **1 boneless fully cooked ham (6 to 7 pounds)**
- **1 large onion, chopped**
- **1/4 cup butter, cubed**
- **2 cups corn bread stuffing mix**
- **1-1/2 cups chopped pecans, toasted**
- **1/2 cup minced fresh parsley**
- **1/4 cup egg substitute**
- **2 tablespoons prepared mustard**
- **1/2 cup honey**
- **2 tablespoons orange juice concentrate**
- **RAISIN SAUCE:**
  - **1/2 cup packed brown sugar**
  - **2 tablespoons all-purpose flour**
  - **1/2 teaspoon ground mustard**
  - **1/2 cup raisins**
  - **1-1/2 cups water**
  - **1/4 cup cider vinegar**

Using a sharp thin-bladed knife and beginning at one end of the ham, carefully cut a 2-1/2-in. circle about 6 in. deep; remove cutout. Cut a 1-1/2-in. slice from the end of removed piece; set aside. Continue cutting a 2-1/2-in. tunnel halfway through ham, using a spoon to remove pieces of ham (save for another use). Repeat from opposite end of ham, cutting and removing ham until a tunnel has been cut through entire length of ham.

In a skillet, saute onion in butter until tender. In a large bowl, combine stuffing mix, pecans, parsley, egg substitute and mustard. Stir in onion. Stuff ham; cover end openings with reserved ham slices. Place in a shallow roasting pan.

Bake, uncovered, at 325° for 1-1/4 hours. In a small saucepan, combine honey and orange juice concentrate; cook and stir for 1-2 minutes or until blended. Brush over ham. Bake 30 minutes longer or until a meat thermometer reads 140°.

For sauce, combine the brown sugar, flour, mustard and raisins in a saucepan. Gradually add water and vinegar. Bring to a boil; cook and stir for 1-2 minutes or until thickened. Serve with ham. **Yield:** 12-14 servings.

Overnight Asparagus Strata

(Pictured above)

PREP: 15 min. + chilling **BAKE:** 40 min. + standing

I've made this tasty egg dish for breakfast and brunch. With its English muffin crust, this is not your run-of-the-mill strata. Friends always ask for the recipe.—Lynn Licata, Sylvania, Ohio

- 1 **pound fresh asparagus, trimmed and cut into 1-inch pieces**
- 4 **English muffins, split and toasted**
- 2 **cups (8 ounces) shredded Colby-Monterey Jack cheese, *divided***
- 1 **cup diced fully cooked ham**
- 1/2 **cup chopped sweet red pepper**
- 8 **eggs**
- 2 **cups milk**
- 1 **teaspoon salt**
- 1 **teaspoon ground mustard**
- 1/4 **teaspoon pepper**

In a large saucepan, bring 8 cups of water to a boil. Add the asparagus; cover and cook for 3 minutes. Drain and immediately place the asparagus in ice water. Drain and pat dry.

Arrange six English muffin halves, cut side up, in a greased 13-in. x 9-in. x 2-in. baking dish. Fill in spaces with remaining muffin halves. Sprinkle with 1 cup cheese, asparagus, ham and red pepper. In a bowl, whisk the eggs, milk, salt, mustard and pepper; pour over muffins. Cover and refrigerate overnight.

Remove from the refrigerator 30 minutes before baking. Sprinkle with remaining cheese. Bake, uncovered, at 375° for 40-45 minutes or until a knife inserted near the edge comes out clean. Let stand for 5 minutes before cutting. **Yield:** 6-8 servings.

Almond-Butter Cookie Bouquet

(Pictured below)

PREP: 2 hours + chilling **BAKE:** 10 min./batch + cooling

I insert these cookie pops into a block of foam fitted into a basket or bowl and cover the foam with cellophane to make a great centerpiece or hostess gift. —Krissy Fossmeyer, Huntley, Illinois

- 1-1/4 **cups butter, softened**
- 1-3/4 **cups confectioners' sugar**
- 2 **ounces almond paste**
- 1 **egg**
- 1/4 **cup milk**
- 1 **teaspoon vanilla extract**
- 4 **cups all-purpose flour**
- 1/2 **teaspoon salt**
Wooden skewers *or* lollipop sticks
ICING:
- 1 **cup confectioners' sugar**
- 4 **teaspoons evaporated milk**
Food coloring of your choice

In a large bowl, cream butter and confectioners' sugar until light and fluffy; add almond paste. Beat in the egg, milk and vanilla. Combine flour and salt; gradually add to creamed mixture. Cover and refrigerate for 1 hour.

On a lightly floured surface, roll out dough to 1/4-in. thickness. Cut out with floured 3-in. cookie cutters. Place 1 in. apart on ungreased baking sheets. Insert sticks. Bake at 375° for 7-8 minutes or until firm. Let stand 2 minutes before removing to wire racks to cool.

In a bowl, whisk confectioners' sugar and milk. Divide into small bowls; tint with food coloring. Gently spread icing over cookies. Decorate with other colors of icing if desired. **Yield:** about 2-1/2 dozen.

Minted Lamb and Veggie Kabobs

(Pictured above)

PREP: 30 min. + marinating **GRILL:** 10 min.

Mint leaves give these lamb kabobs an enticing flavor and aroma. Served with brown rice, the eye-catching meat and vegetable skewers look and taste special enough to dish up for company. —*Michael Rose, Grand Prairie, Texas*

- 3 tablespoons olive oil
- 2 tablespoons lemon juice
- 4 garlic cloves, minced
- 2 teaspoons dried basil
- 1 teaspoon dried oregano
- 1 teaspoon pepper
- 1/2 teaspoon salt
- 1/2 teaspoon dried thyme
- 1 pound boneless leg of lamb, cut into 1-inch cubes
- 1 medium sweet red pepper, cut into 1-inch pieces
- 1 medium sweet yellow pepper, cut into 1-inch pieces
- 1 medium zucchini, cut into 1/4-inch slices
- 1 small red onion, cut into chunks
- 16 medium fresh mushrooms
- 1 cup fresh mint leaves

Hot cooked brown rice

In a large resealable plastic bag, combine the oil, lemon juice, garlic, basil, oregano, pepper, salt and thyme; add lamb. Seal bag and turn to coat; refrigerate for 30 minutes.

On eight metal or soaked wooden skewers, alternately thread the lamb and vegetables with mint leaves.

Grill, covered, over medium heat for 4-5 minutes on each side or until meat reaches desired doneness and vegetables are tender. Serve with rice. **Yield:** 4 servings.

Spring Breeze Cheesecake Pie

(Pictured below)

PREP: 30 min. + chilling **COOK:** 15 min. + cooling

I combined two of my favorite foods, cheesecake and rhubarb, to come up with this mouth-watering dessert. It's so creamy and colorful, everyone who tries it loves it. —*Deanna Taylor, Ainsworth, Nebraska*

- 1 package (8 ounces) cream cheese, softened
- 1/3 cup sugar
- 1 cup (8 ounces) sour cream
- 2 teaspoons vanilla extract
- 1 carton (8 ounces) frozen whipped topping, thawed
- 1 graham cracker crust (9 inches)

TOPPING:
- 3 cups chopped fresh *or* frozen rhubarb
- 1/3 cup sugar
- 1/8 teaspoon ground cinnamon
- 1 tablespoon cornstarch
- 2 tablespoons cold water

In a small bowl, beat cream cheese until smooth. Gradually beat in sugar. Add sour cream and vanilla; mix well. Set aside 1/2 cup whipped topping for garnish; cover and refrigerate. Beat 1/2 cup whipped topping into cream cheese mixture; fold in remaining whipped topping. Spoon into the crust. Cover and refrigerate for at least 2 hours.

For topping, in a large saucepan, bring the rhubarb, sugar and cinnamon to a boil. Reduce heat; simmer, uncovered, for 5-8 minutes or until rhubarb is tender. In a small bowl, combine cornstarch and cold water until smooth. Gradually stir into rhubarb mixture. Return to a boil; cook and stir for 1-2 minutes or until thickened. Cool to room temperature.

Cut pie into slices; top with rhubarb sauce and reserved whipped topping. **Yield:** 6-8 servings.

Summer Livin' is Easy

cheese slice. Cut out each sandwich with a butterfly-shaped cookie cutter.

Cut 12 olives in half lengthwise; place two halves, cut side down, in the center of each sandwich for butterfly body. Cut remaining whole olives into slices; place two on each wing. Set olive ends aside.

Cut a small hole in the corner of a pastry or plastic bag; insert a small start tip. Fill bag with reserved cream cheese mixture. Pipe star on each olive slice; pipe two stars on front of each butterfly body for eyes. Cut olive ends into small pieces; place on eyes. **Yield:** 1 dozen.

Ladybug Cake

(Pictured at left)

PREP: 15 min. **BAKE:** 1 hour + cooling

This cute chocolate dessert stole the show at my son's bug-themed birthday party. It was really easy to make. I baked the batter in a bowl, tinted the frosting a vivid red with paste food coloring and decorated the cake with licorice and gumdrops.
—Lenore Walters, Oklahoma City, Oklahoma

　　1　**package (18-1/4 ounces) chocolate cake mix**
　1-1/4　**cups water**
　　1/3　**cup canola oil**
　　3　**eggs**
　　1　**tablespoon mayonnaise**
　1-1/3　**cups vanilla frosting**
Red paste food coloring
　　2　**large white gumdrops**
　　3　**large black gumdrops**
　　1　**rope black licorice**
　　1　**shoestring black licorice**

In a large bowl, beat the cake mix, water, oil, eggs and mayonnaise on low speed for 30 seconds. Beat on medium for 2 minutes. Pour into a greased and floured 2-qt. ovenproof bowl.

Bake at 350° for 60-70 minutes or until a toothpick inserted near the center comes out clean. Cool for 10 minutes before removing from bowl to a wire rack to cool completely. Place on a serving plate.

In a small bowl, combine the frosting and food coloring. Spread over cake. For eyes, flatten the white gumdrops and shape into ovals; place on ladybug. Cut the black gumdrops horizontally into three slices; discard tops. Slightly flatten slices; place two on white gumdrops for pupils, securing with a toothpick if necessary. Arrange the remaining slices on body for spots, pressing down gently.

Cut rope licorice into six pieces; insert into cake for legs. Cut a small piece from the shoestring licorice; add for mouth. **Yield:** 12-16 servings.

Butterfly Cheese Sandwiches

(Pictured above)

PREP/TOTAL TIME: 30 min.

These adorable little sandwiches are easy to make and are perfect for a child's birthday party.
—Lenore Walters, Oklahoma City, Oklahoma

　　1　**package (8 ounces) cream cheese, softened**
　　2　**tablespoons milk**
　　1/2　**teaspoon garlic powder**
　　1/2　**teaspoon onion powder**
　　12　**slices white bread**
　　12　**slices American cheese**
　　22　**pitted ripe olives**

In a small bowl, beat the cream cheese, milk, garlic powder and onion powder until smooth; set side 1/4 cup. Spread 1 tablespoon of the remaining cream cheese mixture over each slice of bread. Top each with a

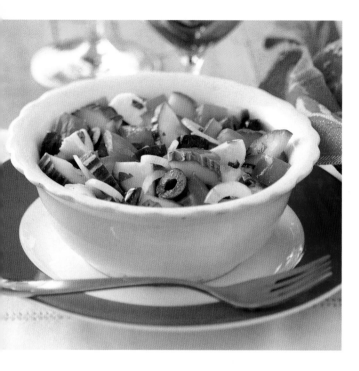

Tomato-Cucumber Mozzarella Salad

(Pictured above)

PREP: 20 min. + chilling

I used fresh mozzarella for the first time some years ago and loved it. I wanted to incorporate it into as many dishes as possible and came up with this salad. It has quickly become a mainstay at my house. —*Jennifer Klann, Corbett, Oregon*

- 1/3 cup olive oil
- 2 tablespoons red wine vinegar
- 2 tablespoons balsamic vinegar
- 1 teaspoon sugar
- 1/2 teaspoon salt
- 1/2 teaspoon dried oregano
- 1/4 teaspoon pepper
- 3 medium tomatoes, chopped
- 1 English cucumber, quartered and cut into 1/4-inch slices
- 1 small green pepper, chopped
- 1/4 cup thinly sliced onions
- 12 pitted Greek olives, sliced
- 2 tablespoons minced fresh parsley
- 1 tablespoon minced fresh basil
- 4 ounces fresh mozzarella cheese, cubed

In a jar with a tight-fitting lid, combine the first seven ingredients; shake well.

In a large bowl, combine the tomatoes, cucumber, green pepper, onions, olives, parsley and basil. Drizzle with dressing; toss to coat. Cover and refrigerate for at least 15 minutes. Just before serving, stir in cheese. Serve with a slotted spoon. **Yield:** 8 servings.

Rustic Roasted Vegetable Tart

(Pictured below and on page 321)

PREP: 45 min. **BAKE:** 20 min.

No one will miss the meat in this appealing tart. The flaky, rustic–style crust holds an assortment of flavorful veggies simply seasoned with garlic and olive oil. It's guaranteed to make an impression. —*Marie Rizzio, Interlochen, Michigan*

- 1 small eggplant, cut into 1-inch pieces
- 1 large zucchini, cut into 1/4-inch slices
- 4 plum tomatoes, chopped
- 1 medium sweet red pepper, cut into 1-inch pieces
- 4 tablespoons olive oil, *divided*
- 4 garlic cloves, minced
- 1/2 teaspoon salt
- 1/8 teaspoon pepper
- 1 sheet refrigerated pie pastry
- 1 tablespoon cornmeal
- 2 tablespoons shredded Parmesan cheese

Minced fresh basil, optional

In a large bowl, combine the vegetables, 3 tablespoons olive oil, garlic, salt and pepper. Transfer to an ungreased 15-in. x 10-in. x 1-in. baking pan. Bake at 450° for 25-30 minutes or until the vegetables are tender and the moisture has evaporated, stirring every 10 minutes.

On a lightly floured surface, roll pastry into a 13-in. circle. Sprinkle cornmeal over a greased 14-in. pizza pan; place pastry on prepared pan. Spoon the vegetable mixture over pastry to within 1-1/2 in. of edges. Fold up the edges of the pastry over filling, leaving center uncovered. Brush the pastry with remaining oil.

Bake at 450° for 20-25 minutes or until crust is golden brown. Sprinkle with Parmesan cheese. Cut into wedges. Garnish with basil if desired. **Yield:** 8 servings.

In a deep-fat fryer or electric skillet, heat oil to 375°. Drop batter by heaping tablespoonfuls into hot oil; fry for 1-1/2 minutes on each side or until golden brown. Drain on paper towels. Serve warm with jam. **Yield:** 2 dozen fritters (3/4 cup jam).

Corn Fritters with Caramelized Onion Jam

(Pictured above)

PREP: 30 min. **COOK:** 15 min.

A friend's husband, who's a chef, made light and fluffy corn fritters, accompanied by a perfect sweet–tart jam. This recipe is my own version. I serve them with soups and barbecued chicken or pork. —Kim Cupo, Albany, Georgia

- 1 **large sweet onion, halved and thinly sliced**
- 1 **tablespoon olive oil**
- 2 **teaspoons balsamic vinegar**
- 1/3 **cup apple jelly**
- 1/3 **cup canned diced tomatoes**
- 1 **tablespoon tomato paste**
- 1/8 **teaspoon curry powder**
- 1/8 **teaspoon ground cinnamon**

Dash salt and pepper

FRITTERS:

- 2 **cups biscuit/baking mix**
- 1 **can (11 ounces) gold and white corn, drained**
- 2 **eggs, lightly beaten**
- 1/2 **cup milk**
- 1/2 **cup sour cream**
- 1/2 **teaspoon salt**

Oil for frying

In a small skillet, saute onion in oil until golden brown. Add vinegar; cook and stir for 2-3 minutes. Set aside.

In a small saucepan, combine the jelly, tomatoes, tomato paste, curry, cinnamon, salt and pepper. Cook over medium heat for 5-7 minutes or until heated through. Add onion mixture. Cook and stir for 3 minutes; set aside and keep warm.

For the fritters, combine the baking mix, corn, eggs, milk, sour cream and salt just until combined.

Spicy Zucchini Quesadillas

(Pictured below)

PREP/TOTAL TIME: 15 min.

My family loves Mexican food, so I created this easy recipe one summer when our garden was bursting with zucchini. For milder quesadillas, use Monterey Jack instead of pepper Jack cheese. If you want them spicier, add some red pepper flakes or chopped jalapenos. —Linda Taylor, Lenexa, Kansas

- 1 **large onion, chopped**
- 1/2 **cup chopped sweet red pepper**
- 1 **teaspoon plus 2 tablespoons butter, softened, divided**
- 2 **cups shredded zucchini**
- 2 **tablespoons taco seasoning**
- 8 **flour tortillas (7 inches)**
- 8 **ounces pepper Jack cheese, shredded**

Salsa, sour cream and pickled jalapeno pepper slices

In a large skillet, saute the onion and red pepper in 1 teaspoon butter for 3 minutes. Stir in zucchini and taco seasoning; saute 3-4 minutes longer or until vegetables are tender. Remove from the heat.

Spread remaining butter over one side of each tortilla. Place tortillas butter side down on a griddle. Sprinkle about 1/4 cup cheese and 1/4 cup zucchini mixture over half of each tortilla; fold over.

Cook over low heat for 1-2 minutes on each side or until cheese is melted. Serve with salsa, sour cream and jalapenos. **Yield:** 4 servings.

Blackberry Crisp

(Pictured above)

PREP: 15 min. **BAKE:** 20 min.

I adapted this comforting dessert from a recipe given to me by my mother-in-law. When I make this for my kids, there are never any leftovers! —Marliss Lee, Independence, Missouri

- 2 **cups fresh *or* frozen blackberries**
- 2 **tablespoons sugar**
- 1 **teaspoon cornstarch**
- 1-1/2 **teaspoons water**
- 1/2 **teaspoon lemon juice**
- 1/2 **cup quick-cooking oats**
- 1/4 **cup all-purpose flour**
- 1/4 **cup packed brown sugar**
- 1/2 **teaspoon ground cinnamon**
- 1/4 **cup cold butter**

Vanilla ice cream

Place blackberries in a greased 1-qt. baking dish. In a small bowl, combine the sugar, cornstarch, water and lemon juice until smooth. Pour over berries. Combine the oats, flour, brown sugar and cinnamon; cut in butter until crumbly. Sprinkle over berries.

Bake, uncovered, at 375° for 20-25 minutes or until filling is bubbly. Serve warm with ice cream. **Yield:** 2 servings.

Peaches & Cream Tart

(Pictured at right)

PREP: 30 min. **BAKE:** 15 min. + cooling

Fresh peach slices and big, juicy raspberries crown this beautiful tart, and are complemented by an almond-flavored cream filling and macaroon crust. It's the perfect dessert to serve to guests during peach season.
—Brenda Harmon, Hastings, Minnesota

- 2 **cups crumbled soft macaroon cookies**
- 1 **cup ground pecans**
- 3 **tablespoons butter, melted**
- 1/2 **cup heavy whipping cream**
- 1 **package (8 ounces) cream cheese, softened**
- 1/3 **cup sugar**
- 2 **teaspoons orange juice**
- 1 **teaspoon vanilla extract**
- 1/4 **teaspoon almond extract**
- 4 **medium peaches, peeled and sliced *or* 3 cups frozen unsweetened sliced peaches, thawed**
- 2 **tablespoons lemon juice**
- 1/2 **cup fresh raspberries**
- 1/4 **cup apricot preserves**
- 2 **teaspoons honey**

In a food processor, combine the crumbled cookies, pecans and butter; cover and process until blended. Press onto the bottom and up the sides of an ungreased 11-in. fluted tart pan with removable bottom.

Place pan on a baking sheet. Bake at 350° for 12-14 minutes or until golden brown. Cool completely on a wire rack.

In a small bowl, beat cream until soft peaks form; set aside. In another small bowl, beat cream cheese and sugar until smooth. Beat in orange juice and extracts. Fold in whipped cream. Spread over crust.

In a small bowl, combine peaches and lemon juice. Arrange peaches and raspberries over filling.

In a small saucepan, combine preserves and honey. Cook and stir over low heat until melted; strain. Brush over fruit. Store in the refrigerator. **Yield:** 10 servings.

Cover and refrigerate for 3 hours or until set. Just before serving, garnish with fresh raspberries and mint if desired. **Yield:** 4 servings.

Golden Corn Quiche

(Pictured below)

PREP: 20 min. **BAKE:** 35 min. + standing

I serve cut–up fresh fruit with this comforting quiche, which my vegetarian son really enjoys. You could also pair it with a slice or two of ham. Try it for brunch or dinner.
—*Donna Gonda, North Canton, Ohio*

- 1 **unbaked pastry shell (9 inches)**
- 1-1/3 **cups half-and-half cream**
- 3 **eggs**
- 3 **tablespoons butter, melted**
- 1/2 **small onion, cut into wedges**
- 1 **tablespoon all-purpose flour**
- 1 **tablespoon sugar**
- 1 **teaspoon salt**
- 2 **cups frozen corn, thawed**

Line unpricked pastry shell with a double thickness of heavy-duty foil. Bake at 375° for 5 minutes. Remove foil; bake 5 minutes longer.

In a blender, combine the cream, eggs, butter, onion, flour, sugar and salt; cover and process until blended. Stir in corn; pour into crust.

Bake for 35-40 minutes or until a knife inserted near the center comes out clean. Let stand for 10 minutes before cutting. **Yield:** 8 servings.

Russian Cream

(Pictured above and on page 320)

PREP: 20 min. + chilling

What a pretty parfait! Layered with fresh raspberries, it's a summertime treat. Because I'm a busy veterinarian, I like making this sweet treat for my family because it comes together quickly.   —*Barbara Ulrich, Newark Valley, New York*

- 1 **envelope unflavored gelatin**
- 1/2 **cup cold water**
- 1 **cup heavy whipping cream**
- 3/4 **cup sugar**
- 1 **cup (8 ounces) sour cream**
- 1/2 **teaspoon vanilla extract**
- 1 **package (10 ounces) frozen sweetened raspberries, thawed**

Fresh raspberries and mint sprigs, optional

In a small saucepan, sprinkle gelatin over cold water; let stand for 1 minute. Bring to a boil; cook and stir until gelatin is dissolved. Remove from the heat; set aside.

In another saucepan, heat whipping cream and sugar over medium heat until sugar is dissolved and mixture is lukewarm. Remove from the heat; stir in gelatin mixture until completely dissolved. Cover and refrigerate for 30 minutes or until slightly thickened.

Stir in the sour cream and vanilla. In each of four parfait glasses, place a scant 1/4 cupful of cream mixture; top each with a rounded tablespoonful of raspberries. Repeat layers. Top each with a scant 1/4 cup of the cream mixture.

Fall Is Flavorful

In a small microwave-safe bowl, microwave white chocolate at 50% power for 1-2 minutes or until melted; stir until smooth. Transfer to a small heavy-duty resealable plastic bag; cut a small hole in a corner of bag. Drizzle over apples. Repeat with semisweet chocolate. Sprinkle tops with remaining pistachios if desired. Chill until set. **Yield:** 6 servings.

Apple-Cherry Pork Chops

(Pictured below)

PREP/TOTAL TIME: 30 min.

You'll never want pork chops any other way once you try this recipe. I season the juicy chops with a fragrant herb rub and serve them with a scrumptious apple and cherry sauce.
—*Doris Heath, Franklin, North Carolina*

- 2 **boneless pork loin chops (1/2 inch thick and 5 ounces** *each***)**
- 1/4 **teaspoon dried thyme**
- 1/8 **teaspoon salt**
- 1 **tablespoon olive oil**
- 2/3 **cup apple juice**
- 1 **small apple, sliced**
- 2 **tablespoons dried cherries** *or* **cranberries**
- 2 **tablespoons chopped onion**
- 1 **teaspoon cornstarch**
- 1 **tablespoon cold water**

Rub pork chops with thyme and salt. In a skillet, cook pork in oil for 3-4 minutes on each side or until juices run clear. Remove and keep warm.

In the same skillet, combine the apple juice, apple, cherries and onion. Bring to a boil.

In a small bowl, combine cornstarch and water until smooth; stir into skillet. Bring to a boil; cook and stir for 1-2 minutes or until thickened. Spoon over pork chops. **Yield:** 2 servings.

Ultimate Caramel Apples

(Pictured above and on page 321)

PREP: 45 min. **COOK:** 25 min. + chilling

I have such a sweet tooth that I've been known to make a dessert just to satisfy my craving. One day when I was in the mood for caramel, I came up with these fun treats.
—*Clarissa Loyd, Mineral Wells, Texas*

- 6 **medium Red Delicious apples**
- 6 **Popsicle sticks**
- 1 **cup sugar**
- 1 **cup light corn syrup**
- 1/4 **cup water**
- **Pinch baking soda**
- 1/4 **cup butter, cubed**
- 1/4 **cup heavy whipping cream**
- 1/2 **cup shelled pistachios, chopped,** *divided*
- 3 **squares (1 ounce** *each***) white baking chocolate, chopped**
- 3 **squares (1 ounce** *each***) semisweet chocolate, chopped**

Line a baking sheet with waxed paper and grease the paper; set aside. Wash and thoroughly dry apples. Insert a Popsicle stick into each; place on prepared pan. Chill.

In a large heavy saucepan, combine the sugar, corn syrup and water; bring to a boil over medium heat, stirring occasionally. Stir in baking soda. Stir in butter until melted; gradually add cream, stirring constantly. Cook and stir until a candy thermometer reads 242° (firm-ball stage). Remove from heat and cool to 200°.

Place 1/4 cup pistachios in a shallow dish. Dip apples into caramel mixture until completely coated, then dip the bottom of each in pistachios. Return to baking sheet; chill.

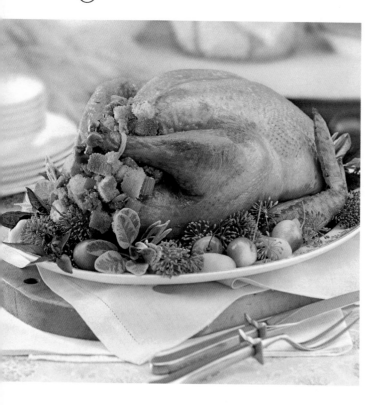

In a large bowl, combine the first five ingredients. Combine eggs, milk and oil; stir into dry ingredients just until moistened. Pour into a greased 13-in. x 9-in. x 2-in. baking pan. Bake at 425° for 18-20 minutes or until a toothpick comes out clean. Cool on a wire rack.

In a Dutch oven, cook sausage over medium heat until no longer pink; drain and set aside. In the same pan, saute celery, onions, mushrooms and red pepper in butter until tender. Stir in the broth, seasonings and sausage. Bring to a boil. Reduce heat; simmer, uncovered, for 10 minutes. Remove from the heat. Cut corn bread into 1/2-in. cubes; fold into sausage mixture.

Just before baking, loosely stuff the turkey. Place remaining stuffing in a greased 13-in. x 9-in. x 2-in. baking dish; cover and refrigerate. Remove from the refrigerator 30 minutes before baking.

Skewer turkey openings; tie drumsticks together with kitchen string. Place breast side up on a rack in a roasting pan. Brush with melted butter. Bake, uncovered, at 325° for 3-3/4 to 4-1/2 hours or until a meat thermometer reads 180° for the turkey and 165° for the stuffing, basting occasionally with pan drippings (cover loosely with foil if turkey browns too quickly).

Bake additional stuffing, covered, for 45-50 minutes. Uncover; bake 10 minutes longer or until lightly browned. Cover turkey with foil and let stand for 20 minutes before removing stuffing and carving. **Yield:** 12 servings (16 cups stuffing).

Turkey with Sausage-Corn Bread Stuffing

(Pictured above and on page 320)

PREP: 1 hour + cooling   **BAKE:** 3-3/4 hours + standing

Complement your bird with this savory stuffing. I've made this recipe for many potlucks and church suppers, and everyone raves about it...even those who usually don't like stuffing.
—June Kathrein, Delta, Colorado

- 2-1/2 **cups yellow cornmeal**
- 1-1/2 **cups all-purpose flour**
- 1/4 **cup sugar**
- 6 **teaspoons baking powder**
- 1-1/2 **teaspoons salt**
- 2 **eggs**
- 2 **cups milk**
- 6 **tablespoons canola oil**

STUFFING:
- 1 **pound bulk sage pork sausage**
- 1 **bunch celery, chopped**
- 2 **medium onions, chopped**
- 1 **cup chopped fresh mushrooms**
- 1/2 **cup chopped sweet red pepper**
- 1/2 **cup butter, cubed**
- 1 **can (49-1/2 ounces) chicken broth**
- 2 to 3 **tablespoons rubbed sage**
- 1 **tablespoon poultry seasoning**
- 1/2 **teaspoon pepper**
- 1 **turkey (14 to 16 pounds)**

Additional butter, melted

Rice-Stuffed Acorn Squash

(Pictured above right)

PREP: 45 min.   **BAKE:** 20 min.

We often make this side dish in the fall, after harvesting fresh squash from our garden. A hint of Asian flavor offers a different, unexpected accent. I especially enjoy the pleasant flavor combination of mozzarella and ginger.
—Lydia Garcia, Gettysburg, Pennsylvania

- 2 **large acorn squash**
- 3/4 **cup uncooked long grain rice**
- 1-1/2 **cups water**
- 2 **tablespoons soy sauce**
- 1 **medium onion, chopped**
- 1/4 **cup butter, cubed**
- 2 **medium tart apples, peeled and chopped**
- 1 **cup (4 ounces) shredded part-skim mozzarella cheese**
- 1/2 **cup chopped walnuts**
- 1/2 **cup half-and-half cream**
- 1/4 **cup balsamic vinegar**
- 3 **tablespoons honey**
- 3 **teaspoons minced fresh gingerroot**
- 1 **teaspoon curry powder**

Cut squash in half; remove seeds. Place cut side down in a greased 13-in. x 9-in. x 2-in. baking dish. Cover and bake at 350° for 40-45 minutes or until tender.

Meanwhile, in a large saucepan, bring the rice, water and soy sauce to a boil. Reduce the heat; cover and simmer for 15-18 minutes or until the liquid is absorbed and rice is tender.

In a large skillet, saute onion in butter until almost tender. Add apples; saute for 3 minutes. Remove from the heat; stir in the cooked rice, cheese, walnuts, cream, vinegar, honey, ginger and curry.

Turn squash over; stuff with rice mixture. Bake, uncovered, for 20-25 minutes or until heated through. **Yield:** 4 servings.

Wicked Witch Cupcakes

(Pictured at right)

PREP: 1-1/4 hours **BAKE:** 20 min. + cooling

More fun than frightening, these whimsical witches cast their spell on every sweet tooth. Everyone will be delighted with these pointy-hat cupcake characters.
—Joan Antonen, Arlington, South Dakota

- 1/2 cup butter, softened
- 1 cup sugar
- 2 eggs
- 1-1/2 cups all-purpose flour
- 1/2 cup baking cocoa
- 1 teaspoon baking soda
- 1/2 teaspoon baking powder
- 1/2 teaspoon salt
- 1-1/4 cups milk
- 1 can (16 ounces) vanilla frosting
- Green food coloring
- **WITCH HATS:**
    - 1 can (16 ounces) vanilla frosting
    - 2 teaspoons milk
- Assorted food coloring of your choice
    - 12 to 16 ice cream sugar cones
- Fruit Roll-Ups, licorice and assorted candies of choice

In a large bowl, cream butter and sugar until light and fluffy. Add eggs, one at a time, beating well after each addition. Combine the flour, cocoa, baking soda, baking powder and salt; add to creamed mixture alternately with milk. Beat just until combined.

Fill paper- or foil-lined muffin cups two-thirds full. Bake at 350° for 18-22 minutes or until a toothpick comes out clean. Cool for 10 minutes before removing from pan to a wire rack to cool completely. Tint frosting green; frost cupcakes. For hats, combine frosting and milk; tint with food coloring. Frost ice cream cones. Using small cookie cutters, cut out shapes from Fruit Roll-Ups; arrange on hats. Add licorice for hair and candies for faces. Place a hat on each witch. **Yield:** about 1 dozen.

Editor's Note: Chocolate frosting and jimmies may also be used to decorate witch hats.

wrap in plastic wrap. Refrigerate for 1 hour or until firm.

For the filling, in a small saucepan, bring the sugar, butter and water to a boil; cook and stir for 1 minute. Cook, without stirring, until mixture turns a golden amber color, about 7 minutes.

Remove from the heat; gradually stir in cream. Return to heat; stir in honey and salt until smooth. Stir in walnuts and cranberries. Bring to a boil. Reduce heat; simmer, uncovered, for 5 minutes. Remove from the heat; cool to room temperature.

On a lightly floured surface, roll out one portion of the dough into an 11-in. circle. Transfer to an ungreased 9-in. fluted tart pan with a removable bottom; trim pastry even with edge. Add the filling. Roll out remaining dough to fit top of tart; place over filling. Trim and seal edges. Cut slits in pastry.

Brush with egg white; sprinkle with coarse sugar. Bake at 400° for 20-25 minutes or until filling is bubbly. Cool on a wire rack. **Yield:** 10-12 servings.

Spiced Squash Muffins

PREP: 20 min. **BAKE:** 15 min.

When I created these moist muffins one day with our garden-fresh squash, my three year-old son kept asking for more. That batch disappeared quickly...and so did the second one!
—TaeRee Glover, Nelson, Nebraska

- 2 cups all-purpose flour
- 1/3 cup packed brown sugar
- 2 teaspoons baking powder
- 1 teaspoon ground cinnamon
- 1/2 teaspoon salt
- 1/4 teaspoon ground ginger
- 1/4 teaspoon ground nutmeg
- 2 eggs, beaten
- 3/4 cup mashed cooked butternut squash
- 3/4 cup light corn syrup
- 1/4 cup butter, melted
- 1/4 cup canola oil
- 1 teaspoon vanilla extract

TOPPING:
- 1/2 cup packed brown sugar
- 1 teaspoon ground cinnamon
- 4 teaspoons cold butter

In a large bowl, combine the first seven ingredients. In another bowl, combine the eggs, squash, corn syrup, butter, oil and vanilla; stir into the dry ingredients just until moistened.

Fill greased or paper-lined muffin cups three-fourths full. In a small bowl, combine brown sugar and cinnamon; cut in butter until crumbly. Sprinkle over batter.

Bake at 400° for 15-20 minutes or until a toothpick comes out clean. Cool for 5 minutes before removing from pan to a wire rack. Serve warm. **Yield:** 1 dozen.

Cranberry Walnut Tart

(Pictured above)

PREP: 30 min. + chilling **BAKE:** 20 min. + cooling

Both attractive and delicious, this flaky tart combines a tender golden brown crust with a sweet filling that might remind you of baklava. It's a holiday favorite at our house.
—Patricia Harmon, Baden, Pennsylvania

- 2-1/2 cups all-purpose flour
- 1 cup cold butter, cubed
- 1/4 cup sugar
- 2 egg yolks
- 3 tablespoons cold water
- 1 tablespoon lemon juice
- 1/2 teaspoon grated lemon peel

FILLING:
- 1 cup sugar
- 1/4 cup butter, cubed
- 1/4 cup water
- 2/3 cup heavy whipping cream
- 3 tablespoons honey
- 1/2 teaspoon salt
- 2 cups chopped walnuts
- 1/2 cup dried cranberries
- 1 egg white, beaten
- 1 teaspoon coarse sugar

Place flour, butter and sugar in a food processor; cover and process until mixture resembles coarse crumbs. Add egg yolks, water, lemon juice and peel; cover and process until dough forms a ball. Divide dough in half;

Winter Celebrations

Beef Rib Roast

(Pictured above)

PREP: 15 min. **BAKE:** 2 hours + standing

My mom, Elizabeth, topped beef roast with bacon and onion. Whenever I prepare it, I can't help but reminisce about the wonderful things she did for her children.
—Betty Abel Jellencich, Utica, New York

- **1 bone-in beef rib roast (4 to 5 pounds)**
- **1 garlic clove, minced**
- **1 teaspoon salt**
- **1/2 teaspoon pepper**
- **1 small onion, sliced**
- **6 to 8 bacon strips**

Place roast, fat side up, on a rack in a shallow roasting pan. Rub with garlic, salt and pepper; top with onion and bacon.

Bake, uncovered, at 325° for 2-3 hours or until meat reaches desired doneness (for medium-rare, a meat thermometer should read 145°; medium, 160°; well-done, 170°).

Transfer to warm serving platter. Let stand for 10-15 minutes before slicing. **Yield:** 10-12 servings.

Coconut Snowmen

(Pictured at right)

PREP: 4 hours + chilling

My mom made her basic coconut candy recipe for years, but I took it a step further and created jolly snowman heads. These cute little characters are worth the extra effort because they're always a big hit!   *—Donell Mayfield, Rio Rancho, Minnesota*

- **4 cups flaked coconut, coarsely chopped**
- **3-3/4 cups confectioners' sugar**
- **2/3 cup sweetened condensed milk**
- **1/4 cup butter, softened**
- **1-1/2 cups vanilla *or* white chips**
- **2 packages (11-1/2 ounces *each*) milk chocolate chips**
- **1 package (10-1/2 ounces) large marshmallows**
- **Black, orange and red decorator icing**
- **Green leaf-shaped decorator candies**

In a large bowl, combine coconut, confectioners' sugar, milk and butter. Shape into 1-1/4-in. balls; place on waxed paper-lined baking sheets. Loosely cover and chill for 1-1/4 hours or until firm.

In a microwave-safe bowl, melt vanilla chips; stir until smooth. Dip balls in melted chips; place on waxed paper-lined baking sheets. Chill until firm, about 15 minutes. Set aside remaining melted vanilla chips.

Melt the chocolate chips; stir until smooth. For hats, dip each marshmallow in chocolate; place on a waxed paper-lined baking sheet, allowing excess to drip down. Swirl the marshmallows in chocolate on waxed paper to create hat brims. Chill until firm, about 15 minutes.

Level the top of coated coconut balls. Attach marshmallows hats, using reserved melted vanilla chips. With black icing, add eyes and a mouth to each face; with orange icing, add a nose. Use red icing and leaf candies for holly on hats. Store in an airtight container. **Yield:** 4 dozen.

Spinach and Sausage Pork Loin

(Pictured above)

PREP: 20 min. **BAKE:** 2 hours + standing

Two of our children live relatively close, and we invite them frequently for an evening meal. They seem to enjoy the fact that Dad has done the cooking. This special roast is one of our favorites. —*Ed Leland, Van Wert, Ohio*

- 1 package (10 ounces) frozen chopped spinach, thawed and squeezed dry
- 1 egg, beaten
- 1/2 cup slivered almonds, toasted
- 1/4 cup dry bread crumbs
- 2 tablespoons minced fresh parsley
- 1 tablespoon onion soup mix
- 4 garlic cloves, minced
- 1 teaspoon dried thyme, *divided*
- 1 teaspoon pepper
- 1/2 pound bulk Italian sausage
- 1 boneless pork loin roast (about 3 pounds)
- 1 tablespoon olive oil

In a large bowl, combine 1/2 cup spinach, egg, almonds, bread crumbs, parsley, soup mix, garlic, 1/2 teaspoon thyme and pepper. Crumble sausage over mixture and mix well. (Save the remaining spinach for another use.)

Make a lengthwise slit down the center of the roast to within 1/2 in. of bottom. Open roast so it lies flat; cover with plastic wrap. Flatten slightly. Spread sausage mixture over meat. Close and tie several times with kitchen string; secure ends with toothpicks. Place fat side up on a rack in a shallow roasting pan. Brush with oil; sprinkle with remaining thyme.

Bake, uncovered, at 350° for 2 to 2-1/2 hours or until a meat thermometer inserted into roast and sausage mixture reads 160°. Let stand for 10-15 minutes. Remove string and toothpicks before slicing. **Yield:** 10 servings.

Italian Herb Muffins

(Pictured below)

PREP: 20 min. **BAKE:** 15 min.

While preparing spaghetti for dinner one day, I realized I was out of bread as an accompaniment and thought, "Why not make an herb muffin instead?" I created this recipe, and it was a hit. —*Cyndee Page, Reno, Nevada*

- 2 cups all-purpose flour
- 2 tablespoons grated Parmesan cheese
- 1 tablespoon sugar
- 1 tablespoon Italian seasoning
- 3 teaspoons baking powder
- 1 teaspoon salt
- 1 egg
- 3/4 cup milk
- 1/2 cup canola oil
- 1/4 cup butter, softened
- 1/2 teaspoon garlic powder

In a bowl, combine the flour, Parmesan cheese, sugar, Italian seasoning, baking powder and salt. In another bowl, whisk the egg, milk and oil; stir into dry ingredients just until moistened.

Fill greased or paper-lined muffin cups three-fourths full. Bake at 400° for 15-20 minutes or until a toothpick comes out clean. Cool for 5 minutes before removing from pan to a wire rack.

In a small bowl, combine the butter and garlic powder. Serve with warm muffins. **Yield:** 10 muffins.

Brussels Sprouts with Water Chestnuts

(Pictured above)

PREP/TOTAL TIME: 30 min.

This reliable recipe dates back to the 1970s. A dash of nutmeg adds interest to the fast-to-fix combination of buttery brussel sprouts and crunchy water chestnuts.
—*Ruth Peterson, Jenison, Michigan*

  1 **pound fresh brussels sprouts**
  3 **tablespoons butter**
  1/2 **cup sliced water chestnuts**
  1/4 **teaspoon salt**
Dash pepper and ground nutmeg

Remove any loose leaves and trim the stem ends of the brussels sprouts. Cut an "x" in the core end of each with a sharp knife.

  Place sprouts in a steamer basket; place in a large saucepan over 1 in. of water. Bring to a boil; cover and steam for 8-10 minutes or until crisp-tender.

  In a large skillet, melt butter. Add the water chestnuts, salt, pepper and nutmeg; heat through. Stir in brussels sprouts. **Yield:** 6 servings.

Festive White Chocolate Cheesecake

(Pictured at right)

PREP: 30 min. **BAKE:** 35 min. + chilling

A buttery shortbread crust, creamy white chocolate filling and tangy cranberry-raspberry sauce add up to one mouth-watering dessert. Top with whipped cream and berries, you have a real showstopper.   —*Mary Alice Graves, Kempton, Indiana*

  2 **cups crushed shortbread cookies**
  1/4 **cup butter, melted**

FILLING:
  2 **packages (8 ounces *each*) cream cheese, softened**
  1 **cup vanilla *or* white chips, melted and cooled**
  2/3 **cup sour cream**
  3/4 **cup sugar**
  1 **tablespoon grated orange peel**
  1 **teaspoon vanilla extract**
  3 **eggs, lightly beaten**
SAUCE:
  1 **cup whole-berry cranberry sauce**
  1/2 **cup seedless raspberry jam**
  1/2 **teaspoon grated orange peel**
TOPPING:
  2 **cups heavy whipping cream**
  1/4 **cup confectioners' sugar**

In a small bowl, combine cookie crumbs and butter. Press onto the bottom of a greased 9-in. springform pan; set aside.

  For the filling in a large bowl, beat cream cheese, chips, sour cream, sugar, orange peel and vanilla until smooth. Add eggs; beat on low speed just until combined. Pour over crust. Place pan on a baking sheet.

  Bake at 350° for 35-40 minutes or until center is almost set. Cool on a wire rack for 10 minutes. Carefully run a knife around edge of pan to loosen; cool 1 hour longer. Refrigerate overnight.

  In a small saucepan, combine sauce ingredients. Cook and stir over medium heat until blended. Cool.

  Just before serving, remove sides of springform pan. Spoon sauce over cheesecake to within 1 in. of edges. In a small bowl, beat cream and confectioners' sugar until stiff peaks form. Pipe over sauce. Refrigerate leftovers.
Yield: 12 servings.

Peanut Butter Christmas Mice

(Pictured above)

PREP: 30 min. **BAKE:** 10 min./batch + cooling

With their red licorice tails, candy noses and peanut ears, these chewy "mice" were always a hit at classroom parties. My children are in their teens now, but they still ask me to make these cookies for the holidays.
—*Nancy Rowse, Bella Vista, Arkansas*

- 1 cup creamy peanut butter
- 1/2 cup butter, softened
- 1/2 cup sugar
- 1/2 cup packed brown sugar
- 1 egg
- 1 teaspoon vanilla extract
- 1-1/2 cups all-purpose flour
- 1/2 teaspoon baking soda
- 1/2 cup peanut halves
- 2 tablespoons green and red M&M's miniature baking bits
- 4 teaspoons miniature semisweet chocolate chips

Cake decorator holly leaf and berry candies
- 60 to 66 pieces red shoestring licorice (2 inches *each*)

In a large bowl, cream the peanut butter, butter, sugar and brown sugar. Beat in the egg and vanilla. Combine the flour and baking soda; gradually add to the creamed mixture. (Dough will be soft.) Refrigerate for 1 hour or until easy to handle.

Roll into 1-in. balls. Place 2 in. apart on ungreased baking sheets. Pinch each ball at one end to taper. Insert two peanut halves in center of each ball for ears. Add one M&M baking bit for nose and two chocolate chips for eyes. Arrange holly and berry candies in front of one ear.

Bake at 350° for 8-10 minutes or until set. Gently insert one licorice piece into each warm cookie for tail. Remove to wire racks to cool completely. **Yield:** about 5 dozen.

Editor's Note: Reduced-fat or generic brands of peanut butter are not recommended for this recipe.

Spicy Seafood Bisque

PREP/TOTAL TIME: 30 min.

This spicy soup, featuring shrimp, crabmeat and tomatoes, gets its zip from hot pepper sauce and cayenne pepper. It's easy to prepare and dresses up any meal.
—*Kevin Weeks, North Palm Beach, Florida*

- 1/2 cup chopped onion
- 1/2 cup chopped celery
- 2 tablespoons butter
- 4 cups chicken broth
- 3 cups tomato juice
- 1 can (14-1/2 ounces) diced tomatoes, undrained
- 1 tablespoon Worcestershire sauce
- 1 teaspoon seafood seasoning
- 1 teaspoon dried oregano
- 1/2 teaspoon garlic powder
- 1/2 teaspoon hot pepper sauce
- 1/4 teaspoon cayenne pepper
- 1 bay leaf
- 1/2 cup uncooked small shell pasta *or* elbow macaroni
- 1 pound uncooked medium shrimp, peeled and deveined
- 1 can (6 ounces) crabmeat, drained, flaked and cartilage removed

In a large saucepan, saute onion and celery in butter until tender. Add the broth, tomato juice, tomatoes, Worcestershire sauce and seasonings; bring to a boil. Reduce heat; cover and simmer for 20 minutes.

Discard bay leaf. Add pasta to the soup; cook, uncovered, until tender. Add shrimp and crab; simmer 5 minutes longer or until the shrimp turn pink. **Yield:** 10-12 servings (about 3 quarts).

Crab and Brie Strudel Slices

(Pictured above)

PREP: 45 min. **BAKE:** 20 min.

Mouth-watering brie, succulent crab and a hint of pear make this wintry appetizer a favorite.
—Jennifer Pfaff, Indianapolis, Indiana

- 1/2 **pound fresh crabmeat**
- 6 **ounces Brie *or* Camembert cheese, rind removed and cut into 1/4-inch cubes**
- 2-1/2 **cups finely chopped peeled ripe pears**
- 1/2 **cup thinly sliced green onions**
- 1/2 **cup diced fully cooked ham**
- 2 **teaspoons lemon juice**
- 1 **garlic clove, minced**

Dash pepper

- 14 **sheets phyllo dough (14 inches x 9 inches)**
- 3/4 **cup butter, melted**

In a large bowl, combine the first eight ingredients; set aside.

Place a piece of plastic wrap larger than a sheet of phyllo on a work surface. Place one phyllo sheet on plastic wrap; brush with butter. (Keep remaining phyllo covered until ready to use.) Repeat six times. Spread half of crab filling to within 1 in. of edges. Fold the two short sides over filling. Using the plastic wrap to lift one long side, roll up jelly-roll style.

Transfer to a greased 15-in. x 10-in. x 1-in. baking pan; discard plastic wrap. Brush top with butter; score top lightly at 1-in. intervals. Repeat with remaining phyllo, butter and filling.

Bake at 375° for 20-25 minutes or until golden brown. Let stand for 5 minutes. Cut into slices along scored lines. **Yield:** 2 dozen.

Lemon Cream Puffs

(Pictured below)

PREP: 20 min. + cooling **BAKE:** 30 min.

The fluffy filling for these light crisp shells has a delectable citrus flavor. They are a special treat for holiday get-togethers.
—Doreen Martin, Kitimat, British Columbia

- 1/2 **cup water**
- 1/4 **cup butter, cubed**
- 1/2 **cup all-purpose flour**
- 2 **eggs**

LEMON FILLING:

- 1 **egg, beaten**
- 1/3 **cup sugar**
- 3 **tablespoons lemon juice**
- 2 **tablespoons butter, cubed**
- 1 **cup heavy whipping cream**
- 2 **teaspoons sugar**

Confectioners' sugar

In a saucepan, bring water and butter to a boil. Add flour all at once, stirring until a smooth ball forms. Remove from the heat; let stand for 5 minutes. Add eggs, one at a time, beating well after each addition. Continue beating until mixture is smooth.

Drop by rounded tablespoonfuls 3 in. apart onto greased baking sheets. Bake at 400° for 30-35 minutes or until golden brown. Remove to wire racks. Immediately split puffs and remove tops; discard soft dough from inside. Set puffs and tops aside to cool. For filling, in a small heavy saucepan, combine the egg, sugar, lemon juice and butter. Bring to a boil over medium heat; cook and stir for 5-7 minutes or until mixture is thick enough to coat a metal spoon.

Remove from the heat. Cool quickly by placing pan in a bowl of ice water; stir for 2 minutes. Transfer to a bowl; press plastic wrap onto surface of filling. Chill for 1 hour or until partially set.

In a bowl, beat cream and sugar until stiff peaks form; fold into lemon mixture. Fill cream puffs; replace tops. Dust with confectioners' sugar. **Yield:** 10 servings.

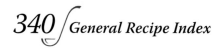

General Recipe Index

This handy index lists every recipe by food category, major ingredient and/or cooking method, so you can easily locate recipes to suit your needs.

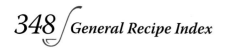

Alphabetical Recipe Index

This handy index lists every recipe in alphabetical order so you can easily find your favorite recipes.